Racial Formation in the United States

Racial Formation in the United States is appearing here in an entirely new edition, 20 years since its last publication. Authors Michael Omi and Howard Winant have maintained the structure and vision of their classic work, but have completely revised and rewritten every chapter. The ambitious purpose of the book remains the same: to develop a theory of race and racism adequate to their complexity, historical depth, and ongoing political importance. *Racial Formation* explains how concepts of race are created and transformed, how race shapes U.S. society, and how it permeates both identities and institutions. Some of the contemporary themes that Omi and Winant discuss are: the steady journey of the U.S. toward a majority nonwhite population, the creativity and political legacy of post-World War II anti-racism, the linkage between colorblind racial ideology and neoliberalism, the new racial genomics, the emergence of "implicit bias" accounts of race, the rise of a mass immigrants rights movement, the achievement of race/class/gender intersectionality theories, and the election and reelection of a black president of the United States.

In Part I the authors review and critique the main theories of race—the ethnicity-, class-, and nation-based paradigms—examining the main contemporary trends and limits in racial theory. In Part II they offer their own advanced theory of racial formation, placing the racialized body much more front and center in the analysis, without diminishing in any way their commitment to a social constructionist account of race. Omi and Winant argue that throughout U.S. history race has provided a "template" for patterns of inequality, marginalization, and difference; this is a new claim for their book. In their view no other social conflict—not class, not sex/gender, not colonialism or imperialism—can ever be understood without taking race into account.

The new Part III treats U.S. racial history up to 2013. Omi and Winant look anew at the radical challenge presented by the black movement in the post-World War II years. They stress the movement's alliances (and sometimes conflicts) with other racial justice, gender justice, and anti-imperialist movements. They argue that because it virtually reinvented U.S. politics and greatly expanded the horizons of democracy and equality, its containment became the top priority of the U.S. power structure. Part III therefore treats the dynamics of racial reaction at greater length than did earlier editions of *Racial Formation*, exploring not only the Nixon, Reagan, and Bushes' years in power, but also the accommodations of Clinton and Obama to colorblind racial ideology and to the regime of neoliberalism.

Omi and Winant continue to see race as a fundamental organizing principle of social life, one that deeply structures politics, economics, and culture in the United States. They rethink race as intersectional, ubiquitous, and unstable, continually operating at the crossroads of social structure and identity. Because race is socially constructed and historically conflictual, it is continually being made and remade in everyday life. Race is constantly in formation.

Test questions and a range of additional instructor support materials, prepared by Cameron Lippard, Associate Professor of Sociology at Appalachian State University, are available on a password-protected website, www.routledge.com/cw/omi *to faculty and administrative staff who have been approved to request Review Copies by Routledge.*

Titles of Related Interest from Routledge

Middle Class Meltdown in America: Causes, Consequences, and Remedies
Kevin T. Leicht and Scott T. Fitzgerald

Black Sexual Politics: African Americans, Gender, and the New Racism
Patricia Hill Collins

Black Feminist Thought: Knowledge, Consciousness, and the Politics of Empowerment
Patricia Hill Collins

Race, Law, and American Society: 1607–Present, Second Edition
Gloria J. Browne-Marshall

The Nation and Its Peoples: Citizens, Denizens, Migrants
Edited by John S.W. Park and Shannon Gleeson

Racist America: Roots, Current Realities, and Future Reparations, Third Edition
Joe Feagin

The Enduring Color Line in U.S. Athletics
Krystal Beamon and Chris Messer

The Pains of Mass Imprisonment
Benjamin Fleury-Steiner and Jamie Longazel

Racial Formation in the United States

Third Edition

MICHAEL OMI AND HOWARD WINANT

NEW YORK AND LONDON

Test questions and a range of additional instructor support materials, prepared by Cameron Lippard, Associate Professor of Sociology at Appalachian State University, are available on a password-protected website, www.routledge.com/cw/omi *to faculty and administrative staff who have been approved to request Review Copies by Routledge.*

Third edition published 2015
by Routledge
711 Third Avenue, New York, NY 10017

and by Routledge
2 Park Square, Milton Park, Abingdon, Oxon, OX14 4RN

Routledge is an imprint of the Taylor & Francis Group, an informa business

First edition published by Routledge 1986
Second edition published by Routledge 1994

Library of Congress Cataloging-in-Publication Data
Omi, Michael.
Racial formation in the United States / by Michael Omi & Howard Winant. — Third edition.
pages cm
Includes bibliographical references and index.
1. United States--Race relations. 2. United States—Social conditions—1960–1980. 3. United States—Social conditions—1980– I. Winant, Howard. II. Title.
E184.A1O46 2014
305.800973—dc23
2014002651

ISBN: 978-0-415-52098-0 (hbk)
ISBN: 978-0-415-52031-7 (pbk)
ISBN: 978-0-203-07680-4 (ebk)

Typeset in Ehrhardt MT
by Apex CoVantage, LLC

Printed and bound in the United States of America by Sheridan Books, Inc. (a Sheridan Group Company).

Contents

Author Biographies

Michael Omi is Associate Professor of Ethnic Studies and Associate Director of the Haas Institute for a Fair and Inclusive Society at the University of California, Berkeley.

Howard Winant is Professor of Sociology at the University of California, Santa Barbara. Winant is the founding director of the University of California Center for New Racial Studies (UCCNRS), a MultiCampus Research Program Initiative.

Preface and Acknowledgments

This book has been a long time coming. It has been nearly 30 years since the initial publication of *Racial Formation in the United States* (1986), and 20 years since the appearance of the second edition (1994). Over the years, much has changed and much has remained the same in the overall patterns, structures, discourses, and individual/collective experiences of race and racism in the United States. Legally sanctioned forms of racial discrimination may have receded, but racial inequality and racial injustice have stubbornly persisted. In many ways racism has proliferated, adopted new guises, and deepened. Continuity and change are also apparent in racial theory: how race and racism are recognized, defined, and narrated keeps changing too. Racial politics, both state-based and experiential, have shifted as new understandings of race and racism are applied in the public sphere and in everyday life. Given the continuing instability of the concept of race and the uncertainty and anxiety about its meaning, a reworking and restatement of the racial formation perspective was long overdue.

But what should be retained from the earlier editions of *Racial Formation*? What ideas required further elaboration, what should be revised, and what updating was needed in order to account for new and emergent issues of racial theory and politics? We deliberated deeply, read widely, and argued passionately with one another about these questions as we prepared this third edition of the book.

Racial Formation has been our intellectual "home" for decades. So we initially saw this revision as a "home remodeling" project. Our visions of what we wanted to do initially clashed. Scale was a big issue. One of us saw the project as a modest renovation. Imagining the chapters as rooms, he wanted simply to update each room, freshen the paint, rearrange the furniture, and bring in some new pieces to complement the revised décor. The other author wanted to knock down the walls, change the plumbing and electrical work, install new windows and insulation, and perhaps shore up the foundation.

The final product represents a synthesis of both our desires and plans. Because so much had changed over the two decades since the second edition of *Racial Formation*, a lot more than remodeling was required. The steady journey of the United States towards a majority nonwhite population, the ongoing evisceration of the political legacy of the early post-World War II civil rights movement, the initiation of the "war on terror" with its attendant Islamophobia, the rise of a mass immigrants rights movement, the formulation of race/class/gender "intersectionality" theories, and the election and reelection of a black president of the United States were some of the many new racial conditions we had to address. While the house of *Racial Formation* was still standing, while its theoretical foundation was still intact, the home was very out-of-date and old-fashioned. The book needed reconstruction, although its basic design remained quite elegant.

In this new edition we have kept the book's structure intact: It begins with a critique of existing racial theories, proceeds to offer our own new theory, and then applies our theory to recent political developments and prevailing U.S. racial dynamics. While we have maintained the original design of our home, we have radically revised and rewritten each chapter.

We believe that the original book's core formulations have stood up quite well over the years. But much of its early content has not aged like fine wine. Many of the empirical materials and examples of racial politics referenced in the previous editions are now dated and have been removed. We have tried to provide current empirical reference points as far as possible, knowing full well that these too will be superseded. Race is unstable, flexible, and subject to constant conflict and reinvention. Rather than seeing the present moment—whatever moment that is—as distilling the *longue durée* of racial politics, we in the United States should recognize that we live in history. Especially in this country there is a desire for instant solutions for problems, even for deep-seated conflicts: Just add boiling water, just heat and serve. If the bad news is that there are no quick fixes for structural racism, the good news is that we live in history. We built this society over historical time; we can rebuild it as well.

While our theory has been highly generative, it has drawn a good deal of criticism too. We are grateful for that; we have learned from our critics that parts of our analysis were cryptic and opaque, and that there were significant gaps in our coverage. Our discussion of the prevailing paradigms of racial theory in Part I required a substantial makeover to engage more recent literature and to sharpen analytic distinctions both within and among different paradigms.

The core theory of racial formation in Part II has elicited both praise and criticism. In this version of *Racial Formation*, we place the racial body—the phenomic/corporeal/"ocular" dimensions of racialization—much more front and center, without diminishing in any way our commitment to the social construction of race. The body was largely undertheorized in our earlier accounts.

We argue that race has been a master category, a kind of template for patterns of inequality, marginalization, and difference throughout U.S. history. This is a new claim for us. We are not suggesting that race has been primordial or primary, or that it has operated as some sort of "fundamental contradiction." Rather we are emphasizing its ubiquity: its presence and importance. We are noting that no other social conflict—not class, not sex/gender, not colonialism or imperialism—can ever be understood independently of it.

Speaking of racial history, in the previous edition of our book, Part III ended at the dawn of the Clinton era. Obviously, much has transpired since the early 1990s.

The new Part III treats U.S. racial history up to 2013, extending into the Obama period. We have expanded our account of The Great Transformation, the rising phase of the political trajectory of race. We look anew at the civil rights movement and the black power movement (brown power, red power, and yellow power movements too). We focus greater attention on the radical threat these movements posed to the despotic regime of the United States, notably as they combined with "second-wave" feminism, the anti-imperialist movement that began with opposition to the Vietnam war, and the dawning LGBT movement.

We have argued that the U.S. racial regime is fundamentally despotic; radical challenges to it occur only rarely. The post-World War II political trajectory of race that preoccupies this book was only the second such challenge in U.S. history; the first full-scale confrontation with racial despotism, of course, came a century earlier with the Civil War and Reconstruction. From the vantage point of the 21st century we can see that the political trajectory of race that we study in this book consists of a vital and radical democratic interruption of U.S. racial despotism, followed by an extended racial reaction. The all-too-brief Great Transformation, we argue, set in motion permanent political and cultural shifts that 40 years of racial reaction have been required to control. And those radical challenges have still not been controlled. They remain disruptive, transformative, explosive.

The black movement inspired a tremendous democratic upsurge, not only in the United States but all around the world. Part III has been extended to treat at greater length the racial reaction that returned to power in about 1970. To make sense of these immense political effects, we focus intensively in Part III—and throughout the book—on the racial ideology of colorblindness: on its genealogy and ascendance to hegemonic status in the United States. Colorblindness is today the prevailing mode of racial "common sense." We make a number of key claims about it; one of our main arguments is that colorblindness is a component, an enabler so to speak, of neoliberalism, the hegemonic economic project of our time. But we do not disparage colorblindness in every way. While we roundly criticize colorblind racial ideology, we also note its aspirational qualities and potential for rearticulation.

We made a lot of changes in this edition, but our overall purpose and vision remain the same. We want to provide an account of how concepts of race are created and transformed, how they become the focus of political conflict, and how they come to shape and permeate both identities and institutions. Without some notion of the socially constructed meaning of race, it is hard to grasp the way racial identity is assigned and assumed, or to perceive the deeply embedded racial dimensions of everyday experience. Similarly, without an awareness that the concept of race is subject to permanent political contestation, it is difficult to recognize the enduring role race plays in shaping social structure—in establishing and reproducing social inequalities, and in organizing political initiatives and state action across the entire U.S. body politic.

The concept of racial formation that we first advanced in the 1980s was a reaction to the dominant modes of theorizing about race in both mainstream social science and left anti-racist politics. In many ways the post-World War II social science disciplines still reproduced white supremacist assumptions. This led them to conceptualize race and racism as aberrant and anomalous in U.S. society, rather than as constitutive elements of the nation-state, foundational ideas about the nature of the American people, and lineaments of the limited democracy that operated in every U.S. institution, public and private. In prevailing social science research, race was conceptualized and operationalized in a fixed and static manner that failed to recognize the changing meaning of race over historical time and in varied social settings. Race was understood much too simply: as an independent variable that was correlated with other variables to assess the scope and degree of economic inequality, health disparities, residential segregation, or incarceration rates. Could one effectively analyze patterns of residential segregation, to take one example, without considering the racial categories that were utilized and encoded in research, in public documents, in legal decisions and how they changed over time and place? Didn't one have to ask not only how race shaped segregation, but how segregation reciprocally shaped race? Didn't one have to examine how segregation invested racial categories with content and meaning? Asking these questions led us to interrogate the race concept itself and to think about its socially constructed nature.

On the political left, we were critical of the assumptions that guided Marxist analyses of race in the 1970s and 1980s—both social-democratic and Marxist-Leninist, both sectarian and humanist. In Marxist approaches race was seen as epiphenomenal to class and class relations. Racism was understood as a form of "false consciousness," an ideology and practice utilized by the capitalist class to sow discontent among workers, to create artificial divisions within the working class, and prevent the emergence of unified class-consciousness and organization. In such arguments, the independent role of race was never considered. Also on the left, we were critical of nationalist positions of various types: notably pan-/diasporic accounts and internal colonialism theories. Such approaches tended to ignore or homogenize variations within racially identified groups and categories, to disparage the racial hybridity that is so widespread in the United States, and to import their political programs (many Marxists did this too) from elsewhere, notably the anti-imperial movements of the global South and East.

Parting with both mainstream social science and left political theorizing about race, we tried to imagine it as a fundamental principle of social organization—one that deeply structured polity, economy, culture, and society in the United States. Central to this was to see race as a legitimate and autonomous social concept that needed to be critically engaged in its own right. Then and now, we emphasize the fundamental instability of the race concept. Race, we claim, operates in the space of intersections, at the crossroads where social structure and experience meet. It is socially constructed and historically fluid. It is continuingly being made and remade in everyday life. Race is continually in formation.

Our concept of racial formation also developed in relationship to political struggles. Both of us were engaged and transformed by struggles of the new social movements of the 1960s and 1970s: the black power movement and other movements of color, the "second-wave" feminist movement and queer movement, the anti-war movement, the insurgent labor movement, the student movement, and the struggles for ethnic studies on university campuses. These new social movements expanded and deepened the very meaning of politics in the United States. What we term "the politicization of the social" was articulated in these political spaces and times. Though it is sometimes disparaged as "identity politics," we affirm that designation and support that current. We recognize that, messy and processual as this politicization of the social is, it goes much deeper than the mainstream definition of politics as who gets what, when, and how. It is not outside the social structures of violence, injustice, inequality, and stigmatization; indeed it is deeply and more self-consciously embedded within those structures. The politicization of the social, developed and led by the black movement in the post-World War II United States, is the application to current conditions of the radical pragmatism developed by John Dewey, W.E.B. Du Bois, and C.L.R. James, and in our time by Cornel West, Judith Butler, Kimberlé Crenshaw, and others. Drawing upon categories of difference and marginalization, this emergent politics represents a shift toward the radical democracy we so desperately need today.

Our concept of racial formation has also been forged in struggle with each other. We wouldn't have it any other way. The work before you is the product of the intense discussion and argument, endless rewriting, and compromise that a deep and loving collaboration requires. After more than 30 years of working together, we are so aware of each other's idiosyncrasies that we can often complete each other's sentences. Ours is an enduring, productive, and at times challenging relationship. We continue to enjoy the rare privilege of working together, of questioning each other and ourselves as deeply as we know how to do in the process of arduous intellectual labor. Over the years, we have more and more learned to respect, trust, depend on, and love one another. We are very grateful for our friendship, and appreciate the chance to acknowledge it here.

There are, of course, others whom we want to thank. The substantive changes made in this revised edition have been motivated not only by contemporary events and crises that have profoundly shaped the meaning of race, but by the work of race scholars and activists seeking to understand the protean nature of race and racism. We have learned a great deal from their ideas and political practice and have incorporated their insights, and their vision of social justice, throughout this revised edition. We are particularly indebted to those whose work has deepened, extended, and at times critically challenged our concept of racial formation. They have creatively engaged the theory and, in so doing, advanced new ways of thinking about race and opposing racism in all their multiple manifestations and dimensions. While no list of all those who have helped us can ever be complete, we would like to offer our thanks to:

Bob Blauner
Eduardo Bonilla-Silva
Devon Carbado
Gary Delgado
Mitch Duneier
Troy Duster
Hardy Frye
Evelyn Nakano Glenn
Ramón Gutiérrez
Michael Hanchard
Cheryl Harris
Lane Ryo Hirabayashi
Daniel Martinez HoSang
Moon-Kie Jung
Terence Keel
Oneka LaBennett
Marc Mauer
Jonathan Okamura
Gary Y. Okihiro
John S.W. Park
Andrew Penner
john a. powell
Laura Pulido

David Montejano
David Roediger
Debbie Rogow
Steve Rutter
Aliya Saperstein
Nikhil Pal Singh
Dana Y. Takagi
Yasuko Takezawa
France Winddance Twine
Geoff Ward
Gabriel Winant
Dianne Yamashiro-Omi

We'd particularly like to thank Cameron Lippard at Appalachian State University for producing a broad range of instructor support materials for this third edition, available to instructors on our book's password protected website. We also wish to thank the following, who provided many thoughtful comments and suggestions to Routledge, based on their use of our second edition in their teaching:

Eric Ishiwata	Colorado State University
Rhacel Parreñas	University of Southern California
Daryl Maeda	University of Colorado
Tony Roshan Samara	George Mason University
Lisa Brush	University of Pittsburgh
Crystal Parikh	New York University
Nina Banks	Bucknell University
Rudy Busto	University of California, Santa Barbara
Ruby Mendenhall	University of Illinois at Urbana-Champaign
Lisa Tessman	Binghamton University
Jennifer Ho	University of North Carolina, Chapel Hill
Emily S. Lee	California State University, Fullerton
Laura Barraclough	Kalamazoo College

Miguel Ceballos	University of Nebraska, Lincoln
Eric Boehme	Dension University
Matthew Hughey	University of Connecticut
Nancy López	University of New Mexico
Darrel Allan Wanzer	University of North Texas
Clement Lai	Cornell University
Johnson Cheu	Michigan State University
Karthick Ramakrishnan	University of California, Riverside
Michael Jerryson	Eckerd College
Joyce Bell	University of Pittsburgh
Niambi M. Carter	Purdue University
Christopher James Perez	University of Maryland
Gniesha Y. Dinwiddie	University of Maryland
Jessica Vasquez	University of Oregon
Eric Love	Dickinson College
Derrick M. Bryan	University of Alabama
Phoebe Godfrey	University of Connecticut
Sujani K. Reddy	Amherst College
David Embrick	Loyola University, Chicago
Amy Sueyoshi	San Francisco State University
Tanya Golash-Boza	University of California, Merced
Derek Martin	Southern Illinois University, Carbondale
Jeffrey Langstraat	University of North Dakota
Ronald Nerio	City University of New York, Graduate Center
Arthur Scarritt	Boise State University
Sophia Wallace	Rutgers
Eric Fure-Slocum	St. Olaf College

Michael Omi
Howard Winant

Introduction: Racial Formation in the United States

Mic Check! Mic Check!

Can we talk about race and racism? They are just as prevalent as ever, though awareness of their presence is often suppressed. The racial present always needs to be studied and explained anew. Race and racism remain central in our lives, but they are changing too.

Let us introduce this book with the call-out "Mic Check!" a request to speak that is commonly associated with the Occupy movement, but is actually a couple of decades older than that.[1] This Introduction frames our major concerns in the book. We adopt the term "Mic Check," because we see our work as a call-out, a demand that new attention be paid to the deepening crisis of race and racism in the contemporary United States.

Way back in 1993, funkmaster George Clinton (our favorite Clinton), urged folks to "Paint the White House Black" (Clinton 1993; see also Lusane 2011; Jeffries 2013). A mere 15 years later in 2008, what was a once a hip-hop racial fantasy became a reality with the election of Barack Obama.

In the immediate wake of the Obama victory, the claim that the United States was now a "post-racial" society enjoyed popular dissemination and acceptance. The "fact of blackness" in the White House was interpreted as resounding proof that the nation was moving "beyond race." That a black man[2] could be elected to the highest post in the land was cited as a stunning testament to how far the nation had come in moving beyond the discriminatory racial attitudes and exclusions of the past.

But lest we lapse into a comforting scenario of advancing progress towards the eventual eclipse of racism, a bit of perspective is warranted. A reporter once told Malcolm X that the passage of key pieces of civil right legislation was clear proof that things were getting better for blacks. In response, Malcolm countered that it did not show improvement to stick a knife nine inches into someone, pull it out six inches, and call it progress. "But some people," Malcolm observed, "don't even want to admit the knife is there" (Malcolm X, quoted in Lipsitz 1998, 46).

The "knife," the weapon and wound of racial disadvantage and dispossession, continues to be ignored today. Structural forms of racial inequality persist and in many cases have deepened. Empirical studies on health care access, educational opportunity, and incarceration rates demonstrate continuing inequalities along racial lines. The Great Recession that began in 2008 and was rooted in the subprime home mortgage crisis had extensive racial dimensions. People of color were more than three times as likely as whites to have subprime and high-cost loans. Such loans accounted at one point for more than 55 percent of all black and Latin@ mortgages (Rogers 2008). The distribution of economic resources, the patterns of cultural consumption, and the organization of residential space are all social processes in which race operates as a fundamental organizing principle of inequality and difference. Americans may have "painted the White House black," but race remains a fundamental category of (dis)empowerment in the United States. As a nation, we appear deeply unable to challenge or even address the significance of race in our own lives, as well as the enduring forms of racism and the attitudes, policies, and practices that sustain them.

Persistent racial inequality and difference are rendered illegible in U.S. popular political discourse. Many people in the United States believe that the goals of the civil rights movement have been substantially achieved, that racial discrimination is a thing of past, and that we are rapidly evolving into a truly colorblind society. "Race thinking," it is argued, no longer significantly informs our perceptions, shapes our attitudes, and influences our individual, collective, and institutional practices. Indeed, it is said that the most effective anti-racist consciousness, policy, and practice is simply to ignore race. We are urged to see people as individuals only, not as persons or groups whose identities or social positions have been shaped and organized by race.

After Obama's January 27, 2010 State of the Union speech, MSNBC host Chris Matthews said of the President, "He is post-racial, by all appearances. I forgot he was black tonight for an hour" (Matthews 2010). But can anyone in the contemporary United States really ever "forget" race? Can we actually suspend how we immediately "see" and "read" people with whom we come into contact? Can we avoid categorizing people into existing racial categories? In short, can we actually transcend racial distinctions and meanings as we navigate our institutional and everyday lives? As Martha and the Vandellas once put it, "Got nowhere to run to, baby, nowhere to hide" (1965). The ubiquity of race is inescapable across nearly every social domain.

But race and racial meanings are neither stable nor consistent. Contradictions abound today, as they have in the past. Most overt forms of racial discrimination have been outlawed, but racial inequalities pervade every institutional setting. A professed desire to be colorblind bumps up against the ubiquity of race consciousness, both in political life and everyday life. Consider the problematic nature of racial identity itself. The U.S. Census employs a system of racial classification, but many individuals and groups cannot locate themselves within it. They cannot conveniently fit into any of the designated racial categories. A person's own sense of racial identity may differ significantly from how other people see and categorize her/him. Some individuals actively resist imposed categories by "performing" race in a subversive manner. A white person, for example, might take on the linguistic patois and stylistic gait we commonly associate with contemporary blackness. Over a person's life course, they may "switch" racial identities—or be transferred to a new racially defined group, as a result of changes in state-based racial classification, the emergence of new group definitions, or even a longing to claim a suppressed or long-abandoned identity, real or imagined. For example, since the 1960 Census, there has been a dramatic increase in the American Indian population in the United States. (Passel 1996, 79). Such an increase is not driven by actual growth, but by increased numbers of Americans claiming Native identity.

Racial identity is a slippery thing. Given these many contradictions, how might we begin to grasp the overall meaning of race in the United States? In this book we discuss *the centrality of race in the organization of political life in the United States.* We attempt to develop an overarching perspective on both race and racism in this country. Our hope is to provide a coherent conceptual framework by which we can grasp the importance of race as a key category: of inequality, of difference/identity, and of agency, both individual and collective. Such a framework also seeks to understand racial change—how concepts and ideologies of race and racism evolve, transform, and shift over historical time. We engage in a deep interrogation of racial theory, both past and present. We try to understand and contextualize the race concept. We explore how race has both informed and been informed by prevailing political conflicts.

Racial Theory

Race and racism in the United States have been shaped by a centuries-long conflict between white domination and resistance by people of color. Theories of race and racism have necessarily been molded by the same relationships. Informed to a large extent by the needs of dominant groups who required the nation-state they were building to be both organized and intelligible for the purposes of rule,[3] racial theory for years served mainly the interests of the powerful—white settlers, slave owners, colonial and later national elites. Entire systems of rule—labor and political regimes among others—had to be organized, structured, regulated, and explained. The concept of race, developing unevenly in the Americas from the arrival of Europeans in the Western Hemisphere down to the present, has served as a fundamental organizing principle of the social system. Practices of distinguishing among human beings according to their corporeal characteristics became linked to systems of control exploitation, and resistance.

Since race and racism involve violence, oppression, exploitation, and indignity, they also generate movements of resistance and theories of resistance. The necessity to comprehend and explain the modern world extended beyond the oppressors to the oppressed, who sought to understand the calamities that had befallen them through conquest, kidnapping, mass murder, enslavement, exclusion, and genocide. While early resistance-based theories of race have largely been suppressed and hidden, the past is being excavated and examined in new and greater detail. We now have a large number of slave narratives to draw upon, for example. Recent work in African and Spanish colonial history, as well as work on indigenous and Arabic texts produced in the Americas, has increased our awareness of early resistance-based accounts of what we would now call race and racism.[4]

Despite the enormous legacy and volume of racial theory, the concept of race remains poorly understood and inadequately explained. This is true not only in everyday life but also in the social sciences, the humanities, law, medicine, and the biological sciences. Because race operates as a "common-sense" concept, a basic component of social cognition, identity, and socialization, everyone considers herself/himself an expert on the subject. Race seems obvious and in some ways superficial. What is there to explain? Race appears to be a given attribute, an ordinary "social fact." That one has a racial identity is thus no more problematic, no more worthy of interpretation, than that one has a head upon one's shoulders. That's just the way it is.

But when asked what race *means*, what the significance is of being black, white, brown, red, or yellow, difficulties rapidly set in. Over the ages these categories' meanings have varied a great deal: They have carried religious, scientific, political, and cultural weight. Race has been understood as a sign of God's pleasure or displeasure, as an indicator of evolutionary development, as a key to intelligence, and as a signifier in human geography, among many other things. Concepts of race have conformed to the exigencies of time and place. In rising empires, the imperatives of conquest have shaped ideas about racial hierarchy, with portrayals of the strong and superior occupiers contrasted with the weak and inferior natives. In periods of social dislocation and economic decline, race has come to mark those groups who signify corruption and dilution of the national spirit and purpose. When secularism and scientism have contended against religious dogma, efforts to classify, categorize, and rank humanity along racial lines have come to the fore. Today, we reject many (though not all) of the earlier incarnations, understandings, and uses of the race concept. Indeed, in the contemporary United States it is frequently claimed that race has become meaningless, that it is an outdated idea, a throwback to earlier, benighted times, an empty signifier at best. No wonder confusion reigns.

Race and the Social Sciences

Attention to race has risen and fallen in the social sciences, driven once again by racial "common sense." The great social theorists of the 19th-century, towering figures such as Karl Marx and Frederick Engels, Emile Durkheim, and Max Weber, were all consumed with analyzing the transition from feudalism to capitalism, and interpreting the dynamic forces shaping modern (i.e., 19th-century European) society. Although they shared this central intellectual concern, these thinkers could not agree on which structural relationships were the most important factors explaining the rise of that modern, capitalist society, with its "rational-legal" form of authority and complex division of labor. What they could agree upon, though, was the belief that racial and ethnic social bonds, divisions, and conflicts were remnants of a pre-industrial order that would decline in significance in the modern period.[5] Marx and Engels, for example, predicted that as society split up into two great, antagonistic classes, social distinctions such as race and ethnicity would decrease in importance.

In fairness to Marx and Engels, they did consider race in their discussion of "primitive accumulation," the launching-phase of modern capitalism. Marx writes:

> The discovery of gold and silver in America, the extirpation, enslavement, and entombment in mines of the aboriginal population, the beginning of the conquest and looting of the East Indies, the turning of Africa into a warren for the commercial hunting of blackskins, signalized the rosy dawn of the era of capitalist production. These idyllic proceedings are the chief momenta of primitive accumulation. On their heels treads the commercial war of the European nations with the globe for a theater. It begins with the revolt of the Netherlands from Spain, assumes giant dimensions in England's Anti-Jacobin War, and is still going on in the opium wars with China.
>
> (1967, 351)

Furthermore, in their support of the abolitionist cause they linked race to the working-class movement, both in Britain and the United States; Marx famously asserted in *Capital* that "labor cannot emancipate itself in a white skin where in a black skin it is branded" (1967, 329). Writing somewhat later, Weber and Durkheim were much less cognizant of the complexities of race.[6]

The "founding fathers" of American sociology (men such as Albion Small, William Graham Sumner, and Edward A. Ross) were explicitly concerned with racial hierarchy and racial classification, which they saw in terms of evolutionary theory.[7] Social science was shaped, not only by the European founding fathers, but also by the Social Darwinist currents of the period. As did virtually all the early figures, these men adhered to the unquestioned white supremacy of their time. Their work contributed, sometimes inadvertently but often by intention, to the racist hysteria of the late 19th and early 20th centuries. The epoch of the emergence of modern social science in the United States coincided with a sustained period of racial reaction, marked by the institutionalization of Jim Crow in the South, the success of the movement for Asian exclusion, and the rise of eugenics. Especially in this atmosphere, adherence to biologistic perspectives on race severely limited innovation and social scientific interest in this field.[8]

As nearly every race-oriented U.S. social scientist pursued the chimera of "natural" racial hierarchy, a small number of scholars, almost all of them black, challenged mainstream (i.e., white) conceptions of race, and implicitly racism as well, although that term did not yet exist. Led by the protean intellectual and activist W.E.B. Du Bois, such scholars as Alain Locke, Kelly Miller, William Monroe Trotter, Anna Julia Cooper, and others created a social science of race and racism, refusing and refuting the biologistic racism of their white contemporaries. These writers and activists were largely denied entrance to the whites-only universities of the time. Based in historically black colleges and universities like Howard, Atlanta (now Clark-Atlanta), and Fisk and active in community-based institutions and organizations, these people were the true intellectual leaders of their time, at least in respect to racial theory. Although there were some minor lapses here and there, their work was premised on then radical understandings of the meaning of equality, political and social rights, and on a commitment to a fully democratic and racially inclusive U.S. society.[9] Besides breaking new ground in racial theory, Du Bois's *The Philadelphia Negro: A Social Study* virtually invented modern, empirically grounded sociology in the United States as well (Du Bois 1998 [1899]).

Only in the 1920s did mainstream sociology even begin to catch up to these pioneering black efforts. Led by Robert E. Park, the "Chicago School of Sociology" began after World War I to rework social scientific approaches to race, and eventually reinvented much of the wheel that Du Bois had created two decades earlier. Park had earlier been a publicist and ghost-writer for Booker T. Washington; in his later years he taught at Fisk, having been invited there by Charles S. Johnson, a former student and major sociologist of race in his own right (Johnson 1996 [1934]), who had become the university's president.

Park and other progressive white thinkers largely succeeded in mainstreaming a socially grounded, if not political, concept of race, and countering the racial biologism that had dominated racial theory in an unbroken fashion throughout U.S. history. Chicago sociology would shape the dominant theoretical and methodological assumptions about race for the greater part of the 20th century and beyond. That black scholars could not have achieved this result is a bitter but obvious truth that speaks directly to their marginalization in the field. Just as black popular music—blues and jazz—could only gain popular currency when white musicians played it, black racial theory could only begin to make headway in the "mainstream" social sciences when reframed and advanced by white scholars.[10]

Chicago School racial theory still left a lot to be desired. It was deterministic and resolutely apolitical. Park's "race-relations cycle," for example, still widely regarded as one of the most important contributions to the field, understood its subject as moving through four stages—contact, conflict, accommodation, and assimilation—leaving such matters as collective action and political agency out of the picture, and postulating assimilation (presumably into whiteness) as the positive end-state of "race relations." Park proposed the cycle as a theoretical law of historical development, a way of analyzing group relations and assessing a "minority" group's progress along a fixed continuum.[11]

Beginning with Park's concepts, a set of assumptions have gradually come to characterize the field and serve as guides for social scientists investigating the nature of race in the United States. Blauner discusses these assumptions as follows:

> First, the view that racial and ethnic groups are neither central nor persistent elements of modern societies. Second, the idea that racism and racial oppression are not independent dynamic forces but are ultimately reducible to other causal determinants, usually economic or psychological. Third, the position that the most important aspects of racism are the attitudes and prejudices

> of Americans. And, finally, the so-called *immigrant analogy*, the assumption, critical in contemporary thought, that there are no essential long-term differences—in relation to the larger society—between the *third world* or racial minorities and the European ethnic groups.
>
> (2001 [1972], 2; emphasis original)

These assumptions are as much political as they are theoretical. They neglect both the institutional and ideological nature of race in America, and the systematic entrenchment of racial dynamics in such spheres as education, art, social policy, law, religion, and science. They focus attention on race as an irrational construct, a product of individual "attitudes and prejudices" rather than a social structure deeply rooted, not only in ideas and beliefs, but also in institutions, fundamental patterns of inequality, social geography, and the exercise of political power.[12] Such assumptions make it impossible to grasp the specificity of racism and racial conflict in the United States. They lead the analyst toward evolutionary models that optimistically predict the gradual absorption of racially identified groups into the (implicitly white) mainstream of American political, economic, and cultural life.[13] Racial theories based on these assumptions—launched in the 1920s and reaching down to the present—reveal as much about the prevailing state of racial politics and racial ideology when they were produced as they do about the nature of race relations.

The Trajectory of Racial Politics

At any given moment, we are in a particular phase of the *trajectory* of racial politics. Our idea of trajectory refers to a political process, in which rising phases of mobilization are followed by declining phases. From the long-run standpoint, the trajectory of racial politics is a process of "cumulative and cyclical development"[14] taking place over centuries: the *longue durée*. To consider seriously the depth and variety of racial rule and of resistance to it is to contemplate the genealogy of race and racism (Martinot 2002) in the United States and on a global scale. Over the centuries, we see North America as a terrain both for populating (with settlers) and depopulating (the removal and genocide of the original inhabitants). Over the centuries, we see the United States as both a key part of the slavery system and as a locus for abolitionism and "abolition democracy" (Du Bois). Over the centuries, we see the United States as—always and simultaneously—an anticolonial and colonial nation-state.

While past racial atrocities are now commonly acknowledged, optimistic observers of our nation's recent history offer a vision of a society trying to live up to democratic and egalitarian principles by slowly extending and applying them to the gnawing issues of race. We are in the midst, so it is claimed, of a period of enlightened progress—an unfolding drama of racial incorporation that will not be thwarted or reversed. A truly colorblind society, it is argued, will eventually emerge. How did we get to this point and where might we be headed?

A cursory glance at American history reveals that far from being colorblind, the United States has always been an extremely race-conscious nation. From the very inception of the republic to the present moment, race has been a profound determinant of one's political rights, one's location in the labor market, and indeed one's sense of identity. The hallmark of this history has been racism. While groups of color have been treated differently, all can bear witness to the tragic consequences of racial oppression. The United States has confronted each group with a unique form of despotism and degradation. The examples are familiar: Native Americans faced removal and genocide, blacks were subjected to racial slavery and Jim Crow, Latin@s were invaded and colonized, and Asians faced exclusion.[15] While the ethos of equality has been invoked quite frequently, this has usually served merely to justify blatant inequality and mistreatment.

Recent U.S. racial history has followed a more complex and contradictory path. The country has experienced successive waves of racial turbulence and quiescence. Political challenges to the U.S. racial regime have been followed by containment of such challenges, sometimes through reform and sometimes through repression. Reforms that were supposed to diminish the depth and extent of racism have undoubtedly had some positive effects, but overall they have produced contradictory, even ironic results. Racial injustice and racial inequality, exclusion, violence, and neglect, are all so deeply rooted in the nation that just reducing them "moderately"—while presumably preferable to exacerbating them or treating them with "benign neglect"—may *itself* have baleful consequences. Inadequate and vulnerable civil rights measures, after all, have also served to ratify and reinvigorate the underlying racial regime.[16]

By the 1960s, because of the upheavals and challenges that developed during and after World War II, race occupied the center stage of American politics in a manner unprecedented since the Civil War era a century earlier. Civil rights struggles and ghetto revolts, as well as controversies over state policies of reform and repression, highlighted a period of intense conflict in which the meaning of race was fiercely politically contested. Civil rights laws and the Voting Rights Act of 1965 enfranchised millions whose democratic rights had long been denied. Congress also sought to curtail discrimination in the labor and housing markets. A long-overdue reform in U.S. immigration law (the Immigration and Nationality Act of 1965) laid the foundation for the massive demographic shifts that were to follow over the next decades. However limited some of these legislative and judicial reforms would turn out to be, the decade saw the greatest expansion of democratic rights in the nation's history. As virtually all observers agree, the political and policy-oriented transformations of the 1960s were driven by massive popular mobilization, notably for civil rights and racial equality.

There was a moment, a spark of recognition before the assassinations and upheavals of 1968, when it was recognized that the accomplishments of the black movement had opened up a broader prospect for radical democratic transformation in the United States. The black movement at that moment was deeply torn between radical and centrist currents; black power politics were particularly under attack: by the state, the right-wing, and the "moderates" as well. The "long hot summers," the restive ghettos across the country, were a particular target for attack. But at that point the movement was still active and growing; the Black Panther Party was galvanizing the ghetto and its example was influencing Native American, Latin@, and Asian American organizing as well. The Poor People's Movement was being built by SCLC and its allies, so a transracial movement of the poor was at least imaginable. Even at the state level, adjustments to the new domestic balance of forces were underway: The War on Poverty and the Great Society were promising redistribution as J. Edgar Hoover was killing Panthers (Haas 2011). In the streets, the anti-war movement and the developing "second-wave" feminist movement were coming into their own.

The spark of radical democratic hope was brief indeed. It was murdered with Martin Luther King, Jr. in Memphis on April 4, 1968, with Robert F. Kennedy in Los Angeles on the night of June 5, 1968, in Chicago at the Democratic Party convention in late August of 1968, and in hundreds of other setbacks as well. Indeed, after King was killed more than 100 cities went up in flames.

It seems reasonable to argue that the containment of the movement began with those killings and riots and burnings. Still it required an extended process, a comprehensive reordering of U.S. political life, to block the advance of the black movement and its allies toward greater equality and "participatory democracy." We have experienced nearly half a century of reactionary racial politics since that peak moment in the late 1960s.

Yet the movement has not been destroyed. Its accomplishments live on as a gift from earlier generations of activists and thinkers to later ones. Yes, the reforms it achieved have been largely neutralized by state-based reaction, by authoritarian populist movements, and by colorblind racial hegemony as well. But racial reaction could not destroy the increased awareness, the enhanced race consciousness, and the profoundly politicized identities that sprang from the black movement and its feminist, working-class, anti-imperialist, and queer allies. The epochal confrontation between the post-World War II anti-racist movement—what we call the Great Transformation—and the racial reaction that succeeded it, has generated a new type of crisis in U.S. society.

"[C]risis," Gramsci famously wrote, "consists precisely in the fact that the old is dying and the new cannot be born: in this interregnum, morbid phenomena of the most varied kind come to pass" (1971, 276). Using the Gramscian formula, we suggest that in the U.S. there has developed, during the extended declining phase of the political trajectory of race, an enormous and chronic crisis. "Chronic" is not a word usually associated with the term "crisis," which usually signifies an acute problem, not an extended one. But, as Dr. Dre reminds us, we have not yet emerged from this ongoing pattern of racial contradiction, the chronic racial dilemma we are still in. It is quite mind-boggling, when looked at as a whole: On the one hand, the old verities of established racism and white supremacy have been officially discredited, not only in the United States but fairly comprehensively around the world. On the other hand, racially informed action and social organization, racial identity and race consciousness, continue unchecked in nearly every aspect of social life! On the one hand, the state (many states around the world) now claims to be colorblind, non-racialist, racially democratic; while, on the other hand, in almost every case, those same states need race to rule. Consider in the United States alone: race and electoral politics, race and social control, race and legal order...

Why don't our heads *explode* under the pressures of such cognitive dissonance?

Looking Forward in this Book

Despite all the upheaval we have experienced in recent years, the outcome of contemporary racial conflict remains uncertain and unresolved. The continuing ebb and flow of racial politics, and the intense contradictions it evokes, beg for a new interpretation. This book developed from our desire to comprehend the centrality of race in U.S. life and to understand how ideologies of race have changed over the past 50 years. Our discussion is divided into three parts. First, we survey how the concept of race has been interpreted in the main currents of social scientific thought. Then, we propose our own account of the race concept and racial politics. Finally, we trace how ideologies of race have shifted over the past 50 years in order to discern the overall political trajectory of race and racism in the present-day United States.

Now that we have introduced our approach and theoretical premises, we turn to a brief chapter outline in the remaining part of this Introduction.

In Part I, *Paradigms of Race: Ethnicity, Class, and Nation*, we examine recent racial theory in the United States. We argue that this theory is encompassed by three paradigmatic approaches to race and racism—approaches based on the categories of ethnicity, class, and nation. These approaches are *paradigms*,[17] in the sense that they have particular core assumptions and highlight particular key issues and research variables. Racial paradigms have implicit and explicit policy and political action orientations; they also serve as guides for research and education about race and racism.

There are, of course, limitations to this approach. We do not suggest that these three paradigms encompass all the racial theories generated during the period under consideration, but we do think that they embrace the vast bulk of them and demarcate the major lines of debate. Specific theories, and the paradigms themselves, are treated as *ideal types*: That is, our concept of paradigms is a distillation for the purpose of analysis of complex and variegated theoretical arguments. A qualification to our approach, therefore, is the recognition that often a specific viewpoint, concept, or study cannot be neatly classified in one or the other paradigm. In many cases particular analyses of race—political, jurisprudential, or academic, say—which we locate in one paradigm, contain arguments that resemble those suggested within another paradigm. We discuss each of these main currents in racial theory, devoting a chapter to each. While these theoretical approaches all contributed to our understanding race in the United States, each was flawed in its own way, limited by its particular need to *reduce* race to a manifestation of some other, supposedly more fundamental, sociopolitical concept. To overcome this reductionism is a key objective of our racial formation approach.

Chapter 1 examines *ethnicity* theory—a perspective that arose in the post-World War I years as an insurgent challenge to the religious doctrines and biologistic accounts of race that prevailed at that time. From its initial efforts to explain the social upheavals brought about by vast waves of immigration to the United States around the turn of the 20th century, ethnicity theory focused on U.S. processes of incorporation such as assimilation and cultural pluralism. The early concerns of ethnicity theory involved inclusion and its obstacles in respect to different European immigrant groups. At this time, the acceptance and integration of Europeans was still in doubt, while that of immigrants of color was highly restricted, and groups of color were subject to overt discrimination.

From the end of World War II through the 1960s, however, racial conditions changed. The emphasis on incorporation was extended to the situation of blacks and other groups of color who continued to be marginalized and excluded. Drawing analogies to the assimilation and integration of European immigrant groups, ethnicity scholars were initially optimistic regarding the integration of blacks and other groups of color. The rise in the late-1960s and early-1970s of radical social movements based in communities of color caught ethnicity theorists by surprise. Movements rejected the assimilationist and pluralist visions that were central to ethnicity theory by demanding group recognition and political rights, resource redistribution, and broad cultural transformation. In response to the perceived radical threat, ethnicity theorists moved rightward, gravitating to neoconservative positions that emphasized individualism, not "groupism," and embracing colorblind racial policies and practices.

Chapter 2 considers *class* theories of race, accounts that afford primacy to economic structures and processes. Class theories render race legible by examining economic inequalities along racial lines. Within the broader class paradigm, we examine three general analytic orientations to race. We designate these as the market-, stratification-, and class conflict-based approaches. These three currents of the class paradigm are grounded in different economic spheres: exchange relationships (markets), systems of distribution (stratification), and conflict over labor exploitation (in Marxist terms, conflict over the "social relations of production").

Efforts to interpret racial inequality as a consequence of economic relationships obviously have an important role to play in understanding race as an overall phenomenon. Yet these efforts uniformly fail to account for the role of race as a *cause* of existing economic relationship. Both market-based and stratification-approaches tend to detach economic life from social and political life. Class conflict theories (generally Marxist) admirably recognize race–class interaction more comprehensively, but they still reduce race to a subset of labor-based conflict in which class trumps race. While inequality is certainly an important dimension of race and racism, we argue that race cannot simply be reduced to an economic matter. Politics, culture, and many other other social factors shape economic life as much as they are shaped by it; these are all eminently racial matters.

Chapter 3 considers *nation*-based theories of race. These have their origins in the imperial seizures of territory and the settler colonialism of the modern era. Since the imperial dawn, the ideas of race and nation have been deeply connected through concepts of *peoplehood*. Both as North American colonies of European empires, and then as a nation-state of its own, the United States identified as white. This identification as a white nation remains visible in the associations with whiteness that are visible across extensive historical time in such concepts as "the American people" and in U.S. nationalism more generally.

The concept of peoplehood, however, did not operate only among the ruling whites. It was present from the start among the racialized "others" as well. Africans and their descendants, Native Americans, Latin@s and Caribeñ@s subject to conquest and settlement, and immigrants who were not white (or not yet white) understood their identity collectively in terms of peoplehood: For them, the concept was born out of resistance. Many were drawn toward insurgent nationalisms, as the possibilities of inclusion and full citizenship were consistently denied them. Thus nation-based concepts of race became rooted, not only in the dominant group, but also in subordinate ones. The production of racial otherness generated not only the mark of oppression but also the mark of resistance. While the nation-based paradigm supplies a valuable concept—peoplehood—to the overall corpus of racial theory, it is still reductionist vis-à-vis race. Nation-based theories treat race as a mere manifestation of the presumptively deeper concept of "the nation," and project "internal" colonial relations of domination and resistance forward into the present.

In Part II, *Racial Formation*, we advance our own theory of racial formation, departing from ethnicity-, class-, and nation-based understandings. We do not repudiate these paradigms across the board, but criticize their limitations and seek to incorporate them in a larger, more realistic, and in our view more practically radical account, based in our theory of racial formation.

In Chapter 4, *The Theory of Racial Formation*, we stress that race is a social construction and not a fixed, static category rooted in some notion of innate biological differences. The construction of race and racial meanings can be understood as part of a universal phenomenon of classifying people on the basis of real or imagined attributes. We all engage in "making up people" (Hacking 2006, 1999) as a way to navigate in the social world—to situate ourselves and others in the context of social hierarchies, to discern friend from foe, and to provide a guide to social interactions with different individuals and groups. Race is not unique as a category of difference. Gender, class, age, nationality, and culture have all been invoked to capture, and in many cases explain, difference. This process is not benign. It involves "othering," which is used to justify subordinate status, unequal treatment, to structure oppression and exploitation in numerous ways. It is important to note, on the flip side, that resistance to such oppressive practices also involves the creation of social categories of difference.

To say that race is socially constructed is to argue that it varies according to time and place. Concepts and ideologies of race have shifted over historical time and differ according to the sociohistorical conditions in which race is embedded. There are many examples. Consider the Irish and the Jews, groups who were not considered racially "white" earlier in the U.S. history, yet eventually became white (Ignatiev 1995; Brodkin 1998).[18] Consider Asian Americans, who have been popularly regarded as either a "yellow peril" or a "model minority" depending on the historical period in question, the configuration of racial hierarchy in the United States, and the prevailing tenor of United States–Asia relations (Okihiro 1994; Jun 2011). Widening the scope beyond the United States, it is apparent that what race means in different regional and national settings is highly variable. What race means in Brazil, Japan, or in South Africa is dramatically different from what it means in the United States. This underscores the fact that race is a fluid and flexible social concept (Fredrickson 1997).

While acknowledging the inherent instability and socially constructed characteristics of race, we argue that there is a crucial *corporeal* dimension to the race-concept. Race is *ocular* in an irreducible way. Human bodies are visually read, understood, and narrated by means of symbolic meanings and associations. Phenotypic differences are not necessarily seen or understood in the same consistent manner across time and place, but they are nevertheless operating in specific social settings. Not because of any biologically based or essential difference among human beings across such phonemic variables as "color" or "hair texture," but because such sociohistorical practices as conquest and enslavement classified human bodies for purposes of domination—and because these same distinctions therefore became important for resistance to domination as well—racial phenotypes such as black and white have been constructed and encoded through the language of race.[19] We define this process as *racialization*—the extension of racial meaning to a previously racially unclassified relationship, social practice, or group.

We also advance the concept of *racial projects* to capture how racial formation processes occur through a linkage between structure and representation. Racial projects are efforts to shape the ways in which human identities and social structures are racially signified, and the reciprocal ways that racial meaning becomes embedded in social structures. We see racial projects as building blocks in the racial formation process; these projects are taking place all the time, whenever race is being invoked or signified, wherever social structures are being organized along racial lines. Racial formation is thus a vast summation of signifying actions and social structures, past and present, that have combined and clashed in the creation of the enormous complex of relationships and identities that is labeled race.

Chapter 5, *Racial Politics and the Racial State*, focuses on the political sociology of race, the social organization of power along racial lines. A central concern here is the historical development and contemporary orientation of the U.S. racial state. We stress the porous boundary between state and civil society, especially where race is concerned. The racial state inhabits us, so to speak; it is within our minds, our psyches, our hearts. At the same time we shape and reshape the state, identifying with it or aganist it, carrying out the signifying action that is the essence of political life, both collectively and individually. In this chapter, we stress the shift *from racial domination to racial hegemony* that has taken place in the post-World War II period. We highlight the trajectory of racial politics, the first rising and then declining path of the anti-racist movement that has taken shape up to now (we are writing this in 2013). We argue that the anti-racist movements that arose in the 1960s dramatically expanded the political space available for challenging racism by ushering in the *politicization of the social.* The chief achievement of the black movement and its allied new social movements was the enlargement and deepening of U.S. politics. Issues previously regarded as private and therefore outside the realm of formally defined politics were now embraced by an expansive politics of identity. Such an expansion of the terrain of politics by race-based social movements, and then by gender-, anti-imperialist, queer-, and other movements as well, represents a radical and permanent shift. It is a shift, however, that cannot be regarded as an exclusively progressive transformation. In the wake of the left-wing politicization of the social at the hands of the black movement, feminist movement, and gay movement, a racial reaction took shape. Right-wing movements proved themselves capable of rearticulation as well, reframing the emancipatory politics of the black movement and its allies, first as threats to whites, then as "reverse racism," and finally seeking an erasure of race itself through colorblind racial ideology.

In Part III, *Racial Politics Since World War II*, we apply our racial formation approach to recent racial history. The post-World War II period, up to the present historical moment, is our central concern: The transformation of U.S. racial despotism in the period up to about 1970, and then the containment of those democratic and transformational movements during subsequent decades, is the overarching theme of these chapters.

Movements rise and fall, both on the political left and the right. The civil rights era can be seen in terms of rising and declining phases of a political trajectory or cycle: proceeding from the relative abeyance of racial justice movements before World War II, and then moving through a phase characterized by the dramatic rise and impact of the civil rights, black power, and allied movements in the 1960s. This "rising phase" of the cycle culminated in the achievement of partial movement victories during the 1960s. It was quickly followed by incorporation and containment of the movement challenge, starting in about 1970. In Chapter 6—*The Great Transformation*—we consider the development of the anti-racist movement, focusing particular attention on the 1960s. We trace the transformation of the black movement from an inclusion-oriented reform movement seeking to end segregation and achieve full political citizenship for blacks, to a broader radical democratic movement allied with the other social movements that collectively sought the redistribution of resources, an end to U.S. imperialism, and social citizenship not only for blacks but for other excluded and oppressed groups as well. It was this expansive radical potential, combined with these allied movements' inability to attract majority (mainly white) support, that led to their containment and prolonged decline.

The postwar racial trajectory, then, entered its declining phase in about 1970; Chapter 7—*Racial Reaction: Containment and Rearticulation*—discusses the development over time of a center-right power bloc capable of counterattacking and curtailing the influence of the radical democratic movements that had developed through the 1960s. The racial reaction moved on various fronts simultaneously, using violent tactics of repression and assassination as well as seeking to *rearticulate* movement demands and the emancipatory politics of identity in individualistic, repressive, and reactionary ways.

The declining phase of the movement, brought about largely by racial reaction, has continued until today, achieving a new racial hegemony based upon the concept of *colorblindness.* In Chapter 8—*Colorblindness, Neoliberalism, and Obama*, we argue that colorblind racial ideology underwrites the neoliberal accumulation project in the United States, and that neither colorblindness nor neoliberalism would be politically feasible without the other. We also consider the deep contradictions between colorblindness and race-consciousness as both ideology and practice. "Painting the White House Black" under Obama, it turns out, deeply heightened the tensions of colorblind hegemony, even though Obama tried hard to minimize the anti-racist commitments that were always at least implicit in his presidency.

In sum, after World War II a system of racial *hegemony* was substituted for the earlier system of racial *domination.* It took a great amount of blood, sweat, and tears to accomplish these limited reforms, this "Second Reconstruction." To do away with official Jim Crow, to end the 1924 McCarran–Walter immigration restrictions, as well as ending the Vietnam War and legalizing abortion, were enormous triumphs, but they were not definitive. They were generally vulnerable, not so much to "backlash" and rollback, as to erosion and subversion, what we have termed rearticulation. To outlaw *de jure* segregation did not prevent the preservation of segregation *de facto* by other means. To overturn the highly restrictive immigration policies that had lasted from the 1920s to the 1960s did not prevent the continuity, and indeed the increase, of a draconian system of immigrant deportation and imprisonment that continues to this day.

The success of racial reform policies—the various civil rights acts and court decisions of the 1960s—worked to incorporate and thus defuse movement opposition. This incorporation required that tangible concessions be made without altering the underlying *structural racism* that was characteristic of the United States. It also required the marginalization and, in some cases, destruction of those sectors of anti-racist opposition that were more recalcitrant about accepting limited (aka moderate) reforms. Once reforms had been enacted and legislated, once some movement demands and movement activists had been incorporated, a subsequent stage of the hegemonic racial project was the rearticulation of racial meanings in a series of steps that culminated in colorblind racial hegemony. Unsteady, limited, and contradictory, the colorblind concept of race will retain its hegemonic perch until it can be challenged or rearticulated yet again.

We live in racial history. The racial instability that has characterized the whole of American history continues unabated. The unsettled meaning of race, and the continuing elusiveness of a genuine, substantive racial democracy in the United States, presents the country with both countless problems and limitless opportunities. In this book's conclusion—*The Contrarieties of Race*—we highlight some of the dilemmas that the country, and perforce the reader, face today. We pose such questions as: What do you want *your* race-consciousness to be? What do *you* consider a democratic and just racial policy in the United States?

To recognize that race is historically and politically constructed is not only to see it as a "moving image," as something we make and remake over time; it is also to acknowledge our power, both collective and individual, to transform the meaning of race. We created this meaning-system and the social order it supports. We can change it as well.

Notes

1. The earliest use of this term that we can find is a track with that title located on a 1999 Rage Against the Machine record, *The Battle of Los Angeles*.
2. The depth and degree of Obama's blackness was widely debated. On the far right, he was branded an African revolutionary, enacting his father's anticolonial revenge fantasies (D'Souza 2012). In the black community, Debra Dickerson and Cornel West, among others, cast Obama's blackness—his authenticity—into serious doubt (Dickerson 2007; on West see Thompson 2011; see also Lowndes 2013). Others worried that electing a black president would defuse whatever reform-oriented demands the black movement could muster (Bobo 2008). In various statements, Obama somewhat inconsistently wrestled with his blackness: discussing his growing recognition and acceptance of it in his youth, his own encounters with prejudice and discrimination, and in his most comprehensive political analysis of racism ("A More Perfect Union"—3/18/2008), the contradictions and limitations of U.S. democracy in respect to race.
3. On "intelligibility" and domination, see Scott 1998.
4. Some key slave narratives are collected in Gates, ed. 2002. On Spanish colonialism in the North American Southwest, see Gutiérrez 1991. Enslaved Africans included many Muslims, some of whom were literate in Arabic. On Muslims and Arabic-language accounts of slavery and the slave trade, see Opoku-Agyemang et al., eds., 2008; see also Thornton 1998. On indigenous views, see Thornton 1987.
5. Blauner writes: "[T]he general conceptual frame of European theory implicitly assumed the decline and disappearance of ethnicity in the modern would; it offered no hints in the other direction. Without significant alteration, American sociology synthesized this framework into its models of social structure and change" (Blauner 2001 [1972], 4). See also Schwendinger and Schwendinger 1974, 39.
6. Weber's treatment of the concept of *ethnie* under the rubric of "status" (a relational category based on "honor") is in some ways a social constructionist approach; but in Weber's voluminous output there is no intensive consideration of the modern imperial phenomenon, and there are numerous instances of European chauvinism (especially during the World War I years, when Weber was somewhat afflicted with German nationalism—see Weber 1994, 131;

Weber 1996, 255). In fairness, Weber also recognized racism, notably anti-black racism in the United States. See his remarks on U.S. racial attitudes in Gerth and Mills, eds., 1958, 405–406. Weber's sensitivity to U.S. racial matters may be attributed, at least in part, to the orientation provided him by Du Bois. See Lewis 1993, 225, 277.

Durkheim too ranks the world eurocentrically, distinguishing rather absolutely between "primitive" and "civilized" peoples based on the limited ethnology available to him; he also muses in abstractly racial ways: Racial categories are employed as "social types" in *Suicide*, for example.

7. They were also "liberal Anglo-Saxonists," as John H. Stanfield (1982, 189–190) has termed them. See also Winant 2007.
8. "After a promising start in the early period, the study of race and ethnic relations suffered.... With little room for ethnic and racial phenomena in the macroscopic models of social structure and process, the field was isolated from general sociological theory and particularly from those leading conceptual themes that might have provided coherence and useful lines of inquiry: stratification, culture, community. The study of race relations developed in a kind of vacuum; no overall theoretical framework guided its research and development" (Blauner 2001 [1972], 5).
9. In a series of five lectures given at Howard University in 1915, Alain Leroy Locke, who had been the first African American Rhodes Scholar and had attended the London Race Congress in 1911, presented a very worked-out and extremely "modern" theory of race, an account fully compatible with social constructionist views, and one deeply politically engaged as well. Locke had been greatly influenced by Du Bois, as were all the leading resistance scholars of the time (Locke 1992). The remarkable Anna Julia Cooper, writer, educator, and activist, more or less founded black feminism. Born a slave in 1858, Cooper was the principal of the M Street High School, a prestigious, segregated black institution in Washington D.C., at the time of the publication of her still-influential book *A Voice from the South: By A Woman from the South* in 1892 (Cooper 1998; Guy-Sheftall 2009). William Monroe Trotter, a black journalist and activist, was a Harvard graduate and one of the founders of both the Niagara Movement and the NAACP. Supposedly a descendant of Jefferson through Sally Hemings, Trotter challenged Woodrow Wilson in a White House meeting, and defied Booker T. Washington's accommodationist racial politics when the latter gave a speech in Boston (Fox 1971). Kelly Miller, Professor of Mathematics at Howard University, founded the Sociology Department there in 1895 and taught at Howard until 1935 when he retired as Dean of Arts and Sciences. A prolific author, Miller's book *Race Adjustment* (1908) sought to reframe the dispute between Booker T. Washington and W.E.B. Du Bois. In a review of economist Frederick L. Hoffman's *Race Traits and Tendencies of the American Negro*, one of the leading eugenics-based works to argue for the innate inferiority of African Americans, Miller used census data to argue that Hoffman's claims were statistically flawed (Miller 1897; see also Stepan and Gilman 1993).
10. On the Chicago sociology of race, see Bulmer 1986; Steinberg 2007.
11. Lyman notes: "It [the race-relations cycle] was ideology too, for Park believed that once the racial cycle was completed, the social arena would be cleared of those racial impediments interfering with the inevitable class struggle" (1972, 27).
12. The concept of "institutional racism," often conflated with that of "structural racism," was first floated in Ture/Carmichael and Hamilton 1992 (1967); see also Knowles and Prewitt, eds. 1969.

13. As early as 1967 Pierre van den Berghe wrote that

    in spite of the claim of many social scientists that detachment and objectivity are possible and that they can dissociate their roles as scientists and as private citizens, much of the work done by North Americans in the area of race has, until the last three or four years, been strongly flavored with a great deal of optimism and complacency about the basic "goodness" of American society and with the cautious, slightly left-of-center, reformist, meliorative, gradualist approach of "liberal" intellectuals.... The field has been dominated by a functionalist view of society and a definition of the race problem as one of integration and assimilation of minorities into the mainstream of a consensus-based society. (1967, 7)

14. This concept is taken from Myrdal (1963, 1962 [1944]). See also Winant 2001.
15. This is an introductory formulation. We shall have more to say later about the numerous variations (ethnic, national, class-based) possible within racial identity. Among Latin@s, for example, the Puerto Rican, Central American, and Cuban cases all retain distinct aspects; among Asians, Vietnamese and other Southeast Asians, South Asians and Filipinos all have particular histories in the United States. There are those whose racial category is ambiguous at present (e.g., Middle Eastern and South Asian Americans-MEASA, Sami, Persians, Uighur). Further still, racial classification, as we shall argue below, is always flexible, a process without an end point or finality of any kind.
16. *Bush v. Gore* (U.S. Supreme Court 2000), let it be remembered, was decided as a voting rights case. Many Supreme Court decisions favoring corporate elites have also been grounded in civil rights laws. The best-known example of this is *Santa Clara County v. Southern Pacific Railroad* (U.S. Supreme Court 1886), which afforded "personhood" status to corporations, anticipating a host of later decisions including *Citizens United v. Federal Election Commission* (U.S. Supreme Court 2010). See also Beatty 2007, 172.
17. The concept of a *paradigm* in scientific or scholarly investigation gained currency after the appearance of Kuhn 1970. Our usage of the term is slightly at variance with Kuhn's. A racial paradigm, in our view, is an assumed theoretical category that classifies racial phenomena. Today, there is a strong reluctance in social scientific circles to indulge in "race-thinking" (undoubtedly due to the legacy of biologism with which pre-World War II scholarship encountered issues of race). This is yet another incentive to understand race in terms of other, supposedly more fundamental or objective, social scientific categories.
18. Not entirely, of course. There are black Irish and black Jews in the United States today, Latin@s who consider themselves Irish or Jewish, and numerous other variations on these identities as well.
19. Walter Johnson writes of the buyers in the New Orleans slave market:

    As the experienced guided the inexperienced [in the slave marketplace], slaves' bodies were made racially legible. The buyers' inspections, the parts they fingered, the details they fetishized, and the homosocial connections they made with one another gave material substance to antebellum notions of "blackness" and "whiteness" and outlined for observers the lineaments of a racial gaze. Out of the daily practice of slavery, they reproduced the notions of race that underwrote the system as a whole. (2001, 161)

PART I

Paradigms of Race: Ethnicity, Class, and Nation

CHAPTER 1

Ethnicity

Introduction

In this chapter we examine the historical and theoretical trajectory of ethnicity-based theories of race from their *early years* as an insurgent and occasionally politically engaged set of arguments for assimilation, cultural pluralism, inclusion, and democracy, through their *ascent to dominance* in the mid-20th century, to their ongoing *decline and fall* in the late 20th and early 21st centuries. Throughout, we frame ethnicity theory as a paradigm: It is an approach to race that affords primacy to cultural variables. Ethnicity theory was in fact the first mainstream social scientific account of race to understand it as a socially constructed phenomenon.

Theoretically, the ethnicity paradigm represents the mainstream of the modern sociology of race. The paradigm has passed through three major stages: a pre-1940s stage in which the emergent paradigm challenged the biologistic (and at least implicitly racist) view of race which was dominant at that time; a 1940s to late 1960s stage during which the paradigm operated as the left/liberal "common sense" approach to race, and during which two recurrent themes—assimilationism and cultural pluralism—were prominent; and a post-1960s stage, in which ethnicity-oriented accounts of race focused on defending conservative (or "neoconservative") individualism against what was perceived as the radical assault of group rights.

Ethnicity theories arose in the early years of the 20th century, in anthropology and sociology most centrally, but elsewhere as well.[1] In the United States, the development of the ethnicity concept was largely driven by massive European immigration around the turn of the 20th century. The millions of new European immigrants were whites "of a different color" (Jacobson 1999). Their identity and social status needed to be assigned. Their relationships to their new country and to their "mother country" needed to be understood (Thomas and Znaniecki 1984 [1918–1920]).

Yet ethnicity theory has also been losing its grip. In response to the racial conflicts of the 1960s, ethnicity-based approaches to race abandoned their earlier progressivism, opting for neoconservatism, a center-right racial ideology that key ethnicity theorists helped to found (Glazer and Moynihan 1970 [1963]; Murray 1994 [1984]; Thernstrom and Thernstrom, 1999; Wilson and Herrnstein 1985). Since the early 1970s, neoconservative approaches to race have fueled the racial reaction in the United States, operating in an effective although at times uneasy alliance with the new right. Under the banner of "colorblindness" this alliance has attempted to forge a new "post-racial" hegemony, a new "common sense." The contemporary United States is not only "post-racial" in this account, but also "post-civil rights." In a colorblind society, it is claimed, racial inequality, racial politics, and race-consciousness itself would be greatly diminished in importance, and indeed relegated to the benighted past when discrimination and prejudice ruled.

To treat race as a matter of ethnicity is to understand it in terms of *culture*. It is to undermine the significance of corporeal markers of identity and difference, and even to downplay questions of descent, kinship, and ancestry—the most fundamental demarcations in anthropology. Because cultural orientations are somewhat flexible—one can speak a different language, repudiate a previous religious adherence or convert to another, adopt a new "lifestyle," switch cuisine, learn new dances—ethnicity theories of race tend to regard racial status as more voluntary and consequently less imposed, less "ascribed."

There are immense and obvious problems with this approach, too many for us adequately to address here. Just to pick one item: The assignment of group identity on the basis of physical appearance—the corporeal—has served for half a millennium as a practical tool in the organization of human hierarchy and domination, and as a tool of resistance as well. Who is a native, and who a settler? Who is a slave, and who a citizen? These and other distinctions, while sometimes made inaccurately on the basis of "ocular" criteria, have nevertheless generally facilitated imperial rule, "primitive accumulation," mass labor recruitment, and all the main practices of human subjection on view throughout the modern world. It is not so easy to be "colorblind," after all.

Guided by ethnicity theory, Americans have come to view race as a cultural phenomenon. Racial identity is often seen as parallel to other forms of status-based group identity, such as that of "hyphenated American" groups (Italian-Americans), gendered groups (women), groups identified by sexual orientation (LGBTQ), and religiously identified groups (Catholics, Muslims). In this account race is understood as a fundamentally ethnic (i.e., cultural) matter. It is conceptualized in terms of attitudes and beliefs, religion, language, "lifestyle," and group identification. In ethnicity-based approaches, the race-concept is thus reduced to something like a preference, something variable and chosen, in the way one's religion or language is chosen. Racism too is reduced in importance: It is seen as a mere matter of attitudes and beliefs, involving such issues as prejudice, beliefs about others, and individual practices: "I'm not racist; I treat everyone equally."

There is an undeniable affinity between the concept of race as a cultural phenomenon and such ideas as assimilation, cultural pluralism, diversity, and multiculturalism. The connection is commonly made between ethnicity theories of race and the democratic ideals with which the United States has always identified itself, however much these ideals were (dis)honored in reality. You see, "we" may not be a perfect democracy, we may not be a fully equal society, but at least we believe in the full inclusion of all, "without regard for race, creed, or color." Sometimes in U.S. history such professions of inclusiveness have appeared quite radical, quite subversive. At other moments, they seem to liquidate racial difference and thus freedom and democracy, to deny deep historical injustice, and to insist on universalizing the dominant—white—culture. Indeed, sometimes these concepts are doing both simultaneously: The offer of inclusion may be a Faustian bargain, in which one (or even a group) achieves acceptance at the price of deracination. In other words, it may sometimes be an offer you can't refuse, to quote Mario Puzo. Du Bois wrote in 1960, at age 92, when the civil rights movement was on the rise in the United States:

> [W]hat we must now ask ourselves is when we become equal American citizens what will be our aims and ideals and what we will have to do with selecting these aims and ideals. Are we to assume that we will simply adopt the ideals of Americans and become what they are or want to be and that we will have in this process no ideals of our own?
>
> That would mean that we would cease to be Negroes as such and become white in action if not completely in color. We would take on the culture of white Americans doing as they do and thinking as they think.
>
> Manifestly this would not be satisfactory. Physically it would mean that we would be integrated with Americans losing first of all, the physical evidence of color and hair and racial type. We would lose our memory of Negro history and of those racial peculiarities which have long been associated with the Negro. We would cease to acknowledge any greater tie with Africa than with England or Germany. We would not try to develop Negro music and Art and Literature as distinctive and different, but allow them to be further degraded as is the case now. We would always, if possible, marry lighter-hued people so as to have children who are not identified with the Negro race, and thus solve our racial problem in America by committing race suicide....
>
> (Du Bois 1973 [1960], 149–150)

Ethnicity theories of race grew out of reaction and accommodation to two fundamental features of U.S. racial dynamics: *biologistic understandings of race*, and *Puritanism*, the founding religious/political orientation of the White Anglo-Saxon Protestant (and actually Calvinist) settlers of North America.

The ethnicity-based paradigm arose in the early 20th century as an explicit challenge to the prevailing racial views of the period. The then-prevalent biologistic paradigm continued to explain racial inferiority as part of a natural order of humankind. Whites were considered the superior race; white skin was the norm, the most advanced form of the human body. Other nonwhite corporeal features, such as dark skin color, nappy hair, or variations in eye shape, had to be explained in respect to the white norm. Religious doctrine had long been employed for this purpose. Since the early days of slavery and colonization the "curse of Ham" had been invoked to connect the phenotype of dark skin with God's displeasure, espcially with black people, but also with others deemed nonwhite (Haynes 2002).

With the development of evolutionary theory—and especially after the 1859 appearance of Darwin's *The Origin of Species*, scientific accounts of racial difference became prevalent. Race was equated with distinct hereditary characteristics and linked to the degree of "development" of a group:[2] not only its physicality (the "beauty" and even the supposed smell of its members, for example),[3] but also its attributed mental and social level (the group's level of "civilization"), were identified with race.[4] Differences in intelligence, temperament, and sexuality (among other traits) were deemed to be racial in character. Racial intermixture was seen as a sin against nature that would lead to the creation of "biological throwbacks." These were some of the assumptions in Social Darwinist, Spencerist, and eugenicist thinking about race.[5]

But by the early decades of the 20th century, biologistic accounts of race were losing coherence. Already in the late 19th century racial biology had come in for significant criticism by black scholars, notably Martin Delaney, W.E.B. Du Bois, and Kelly Miller. But the white "mainstream" was quite oblivious to black voices.[6] Biological theories of race eventually were attacked by adherents of Progressivism and were also called into question by the work of the Chicago School of sociology. The Progressive attack was led by Horace Kallen, who introduced the concept of *cultural pluralism*, which was to become a key current of ethnicity theory (Kallen 1915, 1924). The Chicago sociologists were led by Robert E. Park, who had been secretary and publicist for Booker T. Washington, and whose approach embodied the other major current of the ethnicity paradigm, *assimilationism*.

The Puritan legacy was imparted by the primordial U.S. ethnic group: White Anglo-Saxon Protestants. This group is not often seen through the ethnicity lens, but that is certainly a worthwhile angle on them. Puritanism's history has been exhaustively examined: It was an orthodox Protestant sect, Calvinist in its orientation, that was in flight from the conformist and repressive pressures of early Reformation England. Quite repressive itself, ferociously patriarchal (Salem anyone?),[7] archetypically Protestant-ethic practitioners (Max Weber, can you dig?), and slave-owning as well (Condé 1994), the broad cultural orientation of this early settler community has steadily and continuously organized and influenced North American ideas of identity and belonging in ways that are deeply intertwined with concepts of race. The tendency to apply to racially defined groups key beliefs and values whose origins lie in the settlement of North America by English immigrants—and later European ones—has been discussed extensively (Miller 1956; Dewey 1984 [1930]; Rogin 1996; White 2010).

This militant, authoritarian, Calvinist sect, quite closely related to the Dutch Reformed Church (NHK) of the Afrikaaners, set the basic ethnic pattern in North America. That pattern, insistent upon strict doctrinal adherence, individualism, repression (especially sexual repression), and a sort of primitive communitarianism of the elect, generated many of the components of what we now call "American exceptionalism."

Baptism was grafted onto this pattern; especially Southern Baptism, a white denomination that split from other Baptist currents in the 1840s over issues of slavery[8] and was abandoned by most of its remaining black congregants after the Civil War. The resulting synthesis (or syncresis) was Southern white Protestantism, now a national religious movement.[9]

The ending of Reconstruction in 1877 signaled the rise of a new southern racial regime. The post-Civil War United States, now a traumatized "republic of suffering" (Faust 2009), shaken by emancipation and threatened by Reconstruction, reconstituted itself by recurring, as far as possible, to its white nationalist fundamentals. In the South, this meant coercive debt peonage, denial of political rights, segregation, and negrophobic terrorism. A major economic downturn in 1873 had deeply depressed wages and heightened unemployment. A national railroad strike in 1877 was defeated after 45 days of armed attacks on workers by national guards, federal troops, and marines. In the West, 1877 also marked the onset of white working-class assaults on communities of Asian descent and the start of a comprehensive program of expulsion, exclusion, and expropriation of Chinese and Japanese (Pfaelzer 2008). That same year, Crazy Horse surrendered (and was promptly murdered) in the Black Hills of South Dakota, marking the approaching end of Indian resistance (with the Nez Perce Long March in 1890) and the "closing of the frontier."

After 1877 the U.S. colorline started to be inscribed around Europe, rather than through it, chiefly because of the sheer demographic weight of the new immigrants, and also because other racial conflicts drew attention away. These Atlantic immigrants were not WASPs and not considered white: While not black or Asian either, they did possess an intermediate racial status. In the nation's industrial heartland, immigrant workers were induced to refashion themselves as white and to compete with each other for that coveted status (Roediger 2005). The cultivation of European workers' desires for inclusion became a political and corporate priority in the turn-of-the-20th-century United States: It was a powerful antidote to the radicalism and syndicalism that were brewing among these same workers. Ensuring that European immigrants would not be racialized as blacks and Asians had been, guaranteeing that they would not be equated with the (barely) emancipated ex-slaves or the "coolies" who had built the western railroads and cleared the California heartland for agriculture (Saxton 1971; Almaguer 2008 [1994]), effectively renewed the "psychological wage" dynamic that Du Bois had analyzed as a crucial means for cementing the loyalties of working-class whites in the antebellum South (Du Bois 2007 [1935]; see also Morgan 2003 [1975]).

Beginning in the early 20th century, ethnicity theory challenged this politico-religious bloc, basing itself largely on the incorporation of tremendous waves of non-English, and indeed non-Protestant, European immigrants who had inundated the eastern seaboard and Midwest by that time. Joining their millions of Irish immigrant predecessors, Italians, Slavs, Jews, Greeks, and Middle Easterners entered the mix and required that over time they be admitted to whiteness (Brodkin 1998; Jacobson 1999; Guglielmo 2004).

These demographic shifts generated pressing needs for social scientific theory and analysis at the turn of the 20th century. The ethnicity paradigm became the core of that framework: modern, urban, social scientific, progressive and reform-oriented, but decidedly not radical.[10]

Ethnicity theory's main empirical reference point in the United States was the study of immigration and the social patterns resulting from it. Two distinct currents emerged: assimilationism and cultural pluralism. Both largely emphasized European, white immigrants, what Horace Kallen called "the Atlantic migration." While recognizing the presence of blacks and to a lesser degree, that of Asians, writers on ethnicity sought to incorporate those groups' experiences into the broad ethnic framework: The arrival of "strangers in the land" (Higham 2002 [1955]), the resettlment of "the uprooted" (Handlin 2002 [1951]), and the subsequent management and eventual overcoming of the consequent cultural differences.

Chicago sociologists Robert E. Park and his student Louis Wirth saw the development of ethnic enclaves and what Park called a "mosaic of segregated peoples" as stages in a cycle leading to assimilation. Kallen's perspective, by contrast, focused on the eventual democratic acceptance of different immigrant-based cultures (Kallen 1915, 1924). The origins of the concepts of "ethnicity" and "ethnic group," then, lay outside the experience of those identified (not only today, but already in Park's and Kallen's time), as racial minorities: Afro-Americans, Latin Americans, Native Americans, and Asian Americans.

In its early days, ethnicity-based theory concentrated on problems of migration and what Park called "culture contact."[11] The approach was largely ethnographic and tended to downplay conflict, not to mention racial politics. This limited the early work in numerous ways and reflected a large-scale neglect of black scholarship, notably that of W.E.B. Du Bois but also work by Alain Locke, William Monroe Trotter, Kelly Miller, Anna Julia Cooper, Monroe Work, and numerous others. Park's aversion to political sociology and insistence on value-free methodology—always a chimera in social scientific research—inhibited the effectiveness of Chicago sociology as racial critique. Racial inequality and injustice were not seen as outcomes or objects of state policy, but as phenomena of civil society. Lacking a focus on the racial state, Park (and to varied extents the Chicago researchers he mentored) argued that racial conflict itself would generate egalitarian and inclusive pressures; this was the essence of the "race relations cycle" (Park 1950; Lyman 1972, 27–51). Political alliances with progressives, immigrant groups, feminists, the labor movement, or among people of color themselves, were not considered viable; this view may have descended from Park's previous association with Booker T. Washington.[12] Park's sociology of race also tended to analogize U.S. racial struggles with the European ethnic conflicts he had observed during his graduate school days in Heidelberg. In his view, the European model of "ethnocracy" (Persons 1987, 79–83) paralleled U.S. racial stratification, explaining both prejudice and discrimination (whites' defense of their dominant status) and the ineluctable pressures of assimilation (blacks and other minorities overcoming the cultural disadvantages imposed by slavery and exclusion).

Chicago School sociology owed a lot to pragmatism, the progressive and democratic philosophical orientation whose influence in Chicago was linked to John Dewey's tenure at the university.[13] Pragmatism shaped Thomas and Znaniecki's work, helped to generate the social psychology of George Herbert Mead and his student Herbert Blumer, and oriented the urbanism of the Sociology department, which maintained cautious relationships with reform-oriented currents in the city. For example, Jane Addams, social activist and founder of Hull House, had an adjunct relationship with the Sociology department (Bulmer 1986; Deegan 2002). Pragmatism brought an empirical richness and a modicum of respect to Chicago School studies of immigrants, blacks, working-class neighborhoods, and urbanism. It afforded a certain recognition of the independent agency and interpretive capacity of these social actors, something that was routinely denied at the time. Pragmatist social scientific premises, then, opened a window to racial democracy, since blacks were acknowledged to have the ability to understand and act upon their own experience. Like Du Bois before them (Katz and Sugrue, eds. 1998), Park and his students approached black and other nonwhite communities with a degree of interest and respect not previously shown to them by white scholars. In an additional important departure, Park trained black students: Such illustrious scholars as E. Franklin Frazier, Charles S. Johnson,[14] and Oliver C. Cox received their degrees under Park (Steinberg 2007).

For all these reasons—most centrally because of its pragmatist orientation—Chicago sociology could acknowledge black experience to a greater extent than any mainstream (that is, white) social science discipline had ever done. Park and his students also studied racial conflict: in Chicago's anti-black racism, in European anti-semitism, in California's and Hawai'i's hostility towards Asians, and elsewhere. They understood this conflict as but an early stage of the deterministic "race relations cycle" that constituted the core of Park's approach. The "cycle" not only ended in assimilation: the eventual liquidation of difference that was later to play such a crucial role in the ethnicity paradigm of race. It also reduced all race conflict to cultural terms—denying or at least downplaying the political-economic dimensions (super-exploitation, slavery, exclusion, violence), the national dimensions (empire, sovereignty over a given territory, political self-determination), and indeed the corporeal markers (the role of the racialized body) that occupy such crucial positions in the social construction of race.

Despite these significant limits, Park and his students recognized the agency of the racially subordinated and oppressed, and so departed from the biologistic and Social Darwinist concept of race that had dominated the early sociology of race in the United States. This constituted a real innovation, an important reform in the field. The combination of all these developments (and many more factors we cannot examine here, such as the centrality of micro-level work at Chicago later developed by Mead and extended and modified by Blumer)—revitalized the sociology of race in numerous ways. In particular, the Chicago School's emphasis on an empirically driven approach to race brought new attention to issues of variability, agency, and conflict among racially defined groups. Work at Chicago at long last incorporated at least some of the insurgent insights pioneered by Du Bois—previously relegated to sociology's margins because of his radicalism as well as his race—into the disciplinary mainstream.

Horace Kallen's alternative approach to ethnicity theory—"cultural pluralism"—was less influential that the assimilation-oriented position of Park, although in recent decades something very close to this current has been reincarnated as "multiculturalism." An immigrant himself, Kallen challenged the assimilationist and ethnocentric dimensions of the progressive—and implicitly WASP—elite, which was expressed in both Theodore Roosevelt and Woodrow Wilson's Anglophilia.[15] A former student of William James at Harvard, Kallen experienced the intense anti-semitism and nativism of the campus (and the country) in his early years.[16]

Another important source of the immigrant analogy was the monumental study produced over 1918–1920 by Chicago sociologists W.I. Thomas and Florian Znaniecki, which significantly reconceptualized the sociology of migration (Thomas and Znaniecki 1984 [1918–1920]). This enormous project combined a great deal of primary data with a humanistic account of migration that was largely unprecedented, especially in scope and scale. Although they weren't primarily concerned with race, Thomas and Znaniecki's work broke new ground by dispensing with the racism common in then-existing work on immigration. They theorized their subjects as world-aware agents who comparatively assessed their situations in Central Europe and Chicago, using political, economic, and cultural criteria. Basing their research on primary data—employment records, ship manifests, Polish village records, and letters back and forth—Thomas and Znaniecki's five-volume work was essentially a transcontinental community study that dealt with labor, religion, gender and sexuality, and numerous other quotidian topics, all in the context of the economic and political sociology of migration. This was a quite different perspective on the "huddled masses"; Thomas and Znaniecki should be seen as the founders of today's sophisticated sociology of migration.

A generally parallel path was taken by anthropology over roughly the same period. Although we are primarily concerned with sociology's role in framing ethnicity theory in its early years, we would be remiss if we did not mention Franz Boas's influential role here. Boas virtually founded cultural anthropology in the United States. The Boasian legacy meshed nicely with ethnicity theory. His fundamental claim was that cultural variation among distinct peoples could neither be ranked hierarchically nor classified along a scale that ran from savagery to civilization. He sought both to counter nativist and eugenicist positions in the public sphere, and to rethink social science fundamentally, so as to surpass such positions. He bequeathed a remarkable anti-racist, though somewhat uneven, legacy. His contributions were based upon decades of work at Columbia and at the American Museum of Natural History, where in his early career he had to coexist (and contend) with various eugenicist stalwarts, politicians, and trustees. In the anti-racist annals of American social science, Boas's contribution is exceeded only by that of Du Bois, with whom he was associated at various points (Baker 1998). He trained dozens of influential anthropologists (among them Zora Neale Hurston, Gilberto Freyre, Ruth Benedict, and Melville Herskovitz), and deeply reoriented the field in the United States and beyond.[17]

The combination of these political influences and theoretical/analytical currents shaped the sociology of race (as well as other social scientific disciplines such as anthropology and psychology), especially as the ethnicity paradigm climbed to theoretical dominance. The adoption of the immigrant analogy and the emphasis on immigrant incorporation and assimilation were the two most central examples of this. These themes continue to exert tremendous influence even today. Notably, the immigrant analogy involves a "default to whiteness," especially visible in its treatment of assimilation, inclusion, and integration. This "default" is sometimes explicit, but more often it is what Moon-Kie Jung calls an "unconscious"[18] feature of social scientific concepts of race.

With the advent of the somewhat egalitarian vision of the New Deal[19] and of the anti-fascism of World War II,[20] the ethnicity paradigm definitively dislodged the biologistic view in what appeared to be a triumph of liberalism. Yet this victory was a hollow one where racial minorities were concerned, for the new paradigm was solidly based in the framework of European (white) ethnicity, and could not appreciate the extent to which racial dynamics differed from ethnic ones. In particular, it could not transcend the culturally determined framework that lies at the core of ethnicity theory. What was the relationship between ethnicity and political economy: not just inequality/stratification, but also exploitation and coercion? What was the relationship between ethnicity and the corporeal: We know what a racialized body is, but what is an ethnicized body? Were the historical experiences that people of color encountered similar to those of white Europeans? Were the trajectories for their perceived eventual incorporation and assimilation the same? To these questions ethnicity theorists generally answered yes. Many anti-racist activists and movement groups, though, begged to differ.

Ascent to Dominance

Ethnicity theory began as a liberal[21] challenge to religious and biologistic accounts of race. It operated on cultural territory, between the parameters of assimilationism and pluralism. Ethnic groups were implicitly white (or becoming white), and religious differences were minimized. Thus the ethnicity paradigm challenged bedrock U.S. racial ideology only to a limited extent: It was more concerned with "whiteness of a different color" (Jacobson 1999) than with racialized "others," notably black people. Only after World War II was the immigrant analogy stretched at all; only then did social scientists move from a focus on the U.S. "racial frontier"—a phrase of Park's that incorporated imperial and nativist assumptions and was pregnant with problematic meanings—toward more comprehensive attention to the idea of racial "otherness" within the American nation (Park 1950 [1926]; see also Ross 1914).

To apply the immigrant analogy to non-Europeans was a large social scientific project. Like most racial theory, it was driven by ineluctable political events, most of them linked to the social upheavals that rocked the United States during and after World War II.

Black "Immigrants": The vast majority of U.S. black folk were not immigrants; the black presence in the United States predates that of most white-identified groups. But the great preponderance of U.S. blacks remained in the South. The South moved north, as Robert Coles (1971) famously wrote, because labor shortages in defense industries and an effective unemployment rate of near-zero percent (by 1944 or so) impelled their internal migration. This was actually the second "great migration" of blacks to the North; a similar wave of black souls had flowed north during World War I (Griffin 1996; Marks 1989). Northern black votes, combined with the return of more than one million black veterans who were less likely to accept segregation and racism, both "down South" and "up South" (i.e., in the North) brought renewed pressures for civil rights. Many civil rights movement leaders were veterans (Parker 2009). With a renewed political force behind it, and with an obvious set of urban precedents close at hand, the immigration model began to be applied to blacks. This was not illogical, given the vastly augmented presence of black folk in the urban North, and to some extent the urban West. Irving Kristol's famous (1966) declaration, "The Negro today is like the immigrant of yesterday," was not the first attempt to locate black history within the immigration framework. Already in the late 1940s the immigrant analogy was being invoked, sometimes by blacks themselves (Reid 1947; Denby 1989 [1952]; see also Taueber and Taueber 1964; Tolnay 1997; Sugrue 1996).

Asian American "Immigrants": Ethnicity theory also re-encountered the Asian American experience during and after the war. In 1943 FDR signed the Magnuson Act, repealing the Chinese Exclusion Act that had prevented Chinese from naturalizing since 1882.[22] After the war, the incarceration of Japanese Americans under the infamous 1942 Executive Order 9066 also received social scientific attention. Notable in this regard was the Japanese American Evacuation and Resettlement Study (JERS), which was directed at the University of California, Berkeley by Dorothy Swaine Thomas, widow of William I. Thomas and a formidable social scientific methodologist in her own right. (Thomas and Nishimoto 1946; Thomas, Kikuchi, and Sakoda 1952). Collaborators on the JERS study included Nisei (second generation Japanese American) such as Charles Kikuchi, Togo Tanaka, and Tamotsu Shibutani who had themselves experienced wartime incarceration under the infamous Executive Order 9066.[23] Important research was also conducted clandestinely by incarcerated Japanese American scholars, notably Tamie Tsuchiyama and Richard Nishimoto.[24] Japanese naturalization only became possible in 1953; the United States did not apologize or undertake redress and reparations for this immense injustice until 1988, when many of its victims had already died.[25]

Latin@ Immigrants: Mexicans—the largest Latin@ group in the United States—also began their journey toward immigrant status during and after World

War II. Having become U.S. citizens as a result of conquest in the mid-19th century, Mexican Americans had been subject to sustained efforts at exclusion and marginalization, especially in Texas and in California (Foley 1999). The U.S.–Mexican border had undergone successive stages of fortification and militarization, especially in consequence of the Mexican revolution of 1910–1924 (Romo 2005). After the Johnson–Reed Act of 1924, legal Mexican immigration was problematic, although in practice travel across the border has been continuous. The 1930s saw extensive mass deportations of Mexican@s from the Southwest, particularly from Southern California, as a consequence of prevalent anti-Mexican race-baiting and intense job competition in the Depression years (Balderrama and Rodriguez 2006 [1995]). These oppressive circumstances did not permit recognition of Mexican@s as "immigrants," much less as the citizens many already were. Many Mexican American U.S. citizens were summarily deported. When labor-demand rose during World War II, the U.S. government initiated the "bracero" program for temporary contract laborers, with the strong support of agribusiness and the acquiescence of the Mexican government. But braceros were not permitted immigrant status (Ngai 2005). So the appearance after the war of Mexican American advocacy organizations like the GI Forum, and the initiation of anti-discrimination lawsuits like the *Méndez* and *Hernandez* cases, represented some early steps in the Latin@ struggle for civil rights (Lopez 2003).

As long as race could be subsumed under the ethnicity label, in short, the immigrant analogy could be applied. Thus when the civil rights movement began to gain traction in the 1940s and 1950s, ethnicity-based accounts were initially sympathetic. Kristol's declaration that "The Negro today is like the immigrant of yesterday" was continuous with a long line of northern, left-liberal, and often Jewish efforts to ally with and harness the black struggle to a revamped, post-Dixiecrat, Democratic Party. Jewish writers had been the key theorists of ethnicity since the 1920s: Among these were Horace Kallen, Walter Lippman, Max Lerner, Milton Gordon, and Nathan Glazer. Jews were very active in the civil rights movement, had longstanding associations with liberalism and the left, and were clearly unhappy with the tendency—evident in both the Puritan roots and Southern Baptist currents in mainstream American Protestantism—to see the United States as a "Christian nation." They properly linked biologistic racism with Nazism and the Holocaust.

So ethnicity theory's repudiation of religious and biologistic forms of discrimination and exclusion, and its claim that ethnicity (including race) was but a cultural distinction, overlapped with anti-racist political movements. Culture, after all, is malleable and adaptable; assimilation fits right in with that idea. And a certain degree of ethnic (racial) pluralism was clearly compatible with American democracy: Look at the Irish, the Jews, the Italians … (Glazer and Moynihan 1970 [1963]); why not the Negroes as well?

The appearance of Gunnar Myrdal's *An American Dilemma* (1944) marked the ascent of the ethnicity paradigm to a position of theoretical dominance. This monumental study, funded by the Carnegie Commission, was the product of the labors not only of its director and principal author, but also of an wide array of talented students of racial issues in the United States.[26] Myrdal both challenged biologistic theories of racism and asserted the desirability of assimilation for blacks (Myrdal 1962 [1944], 929). He argued that there was an "American Creed" of democracy, equality, and justice, that was fundamentally in conflict with black inequality, segregation, and racial prejudice in general.[27] In order to resolve this conflict, America would be called upon, sooner or later, to extend its "creed" to include blacks. Myrdal's assessment was optimistic about the ultimate resolution of this battle—in his view racial domination would eventually give way to racial equality and the integration of blacks into the mainstream of American life.

Rather than presenting his "dilemma" as something endemic and foundational in U.S. society and culture, Myrdal framed racial injustice as an aberration, a retardation and obstacle besetting the higher virtues of U.S. democracy. He combined this account with a Fabian faith in progress over the historical medium to long term, which he saw as a process of "cumulative and circular development."[28] He would later apply this approach to global problems of poverty and economic development as well (Myrdal 1963). Myrdal also presented assimilation as an unproblematic objective of racial reform, a position that surely differed with the views of many of his black informants and collaborators. In short, Myrdal's devotion to the cause of racial reform—the product of many determinations and influences—drove his project at its most fundamental level. Writing during the World War II and desirous of contributing to an Allied victory, Myrdal idealized the "creed" and minimized the very real obstacles to its achievement:

> If America in actual practice could show the world a progressive trend by which the Negro finally became integrated into modern democracy, all mankind would be given faith again—it would have reason to believe that peace, progress, and order are feasible.... America is free to choose whether the Negro shall remain her liability or become her opportunity.
>
> (Myrdal 1962 [1944], 1021–1022)

Assimilation was simply the most logical and "natural" response to the "dilemma," which was the anachronistic and baleful legacy of slavery, a hindrance to both white and black development. While there was no doubt that whites must repudiate racial prejudice (Myrdal did not use the term "racism"), blacks had also to rise to the occasion and demonstrate their worthiness. Indeed Myrdal, drawing on the work of E. Franklin Frazier (as Daniel Patrick Moynihan was to do 20 years later), suggested that there was a "pathological" aspect to black culture which only full assimilation could cure.[29]

Elevated to theoretical dominance by the Myrdal study, ethnicity theory derived its agenda from the political imperatives of the period: to condemn in the liberal terms of the war years the phenomenon of racial inequality, which smacked of the kinds of despotism the United States fought against in Europe; to modernize and mobilize

American society in preparation for its postwar role of world leadership; and to distribute the seemingly limitless resources deriving from U.S. hegemony—resources which were not only economic, but also political and cultural—to all at home, even as they were to be offered abroad to American allies (and to the vanquished Axis powers as well). The ethnicity-based theoretical tradition, derived from the experiences of European immigrants, was thus extended in the conclusions of *An American Dilemma* so that it might include blacks.

And indeed, in the aftermath of the war, racial reforms became imperative. A "second" migration during the war years had brought millions of blacks and Latinos to the North and West; these were voters who identified with the New Deal and began to challenge Dixiecrat power in the Democratic Party, as well as to influence the Republicans. In the liberal view of the time, in short, these were black (and brown) "immigrants" whose conditions could be equated to the Italians, Jews, Polish peasants, Greeks, and others whose earlier arrivals had created 20th-century ethnicity in the first place.

Desegregation of the armed forces, which began in 1948, and the contested 1948 Democratic Party convention, also challenged racial divisions at home. The term "civil rights" returned to the political scene after World War II. Congress had passed civil rights acts in 1866, 1871, and 1875, during the Reconstruction years. Not until 1957 would it pass another such act. The Cold War and the rising tide of anti-imperialism in the global South brought Myrdal's prescriptions into sharper focus. Racial politics became central issues: At the United Nations, in the anti-colonial wars taking place in the Maghreb and Southeast Asia, and in a sharpening U.S. political debate that combined red-baiting as well as black-baiting, global and domestic racial concerns began to overlap. This rising phase of the trajectory of racial politics is discussed more fully in Chapter 6.

Ethnicity-based racial theory took off after World War II, driven by developing debates and controversies in everyday life and mainstream politics, drawing on the Myrdal study, and influenced by a range of recent social scientific work on race. In a 1947–1948 series of lectures on "Discrimination and National Welfare" offered at the Jewish Theological Seminary in New York, influential social scientists sought to apply Myrdal's analysis, not only domestically but internationally. Prominent New Dealer and Latin Americanist A.A. Berle, Jr. discussed "Race Discrimination and the Good Neighbor Policy"; Roger Baldwin, founder of the ACLU, lectured on "Our Standing in the Orient"; big-time Columbia sociologist Robert MacIver's talk was titled "Our Strengths and Our Weaknesses"; and a young Robert Merton presented a paper, still frequently cited, on "Discrimination and the American Creed."[30]

Social scientific studies of race based in the ethnicity model developed dramatically after World War II. In sociology, the disciplinary center of gravity moved east from Chicago to Harvard and Columbia, where structural-functionalism took over from Chicago School pragmatism. The structural-functionalist framework stressed the unifying role of culture, and particularly American values, in regulating and resolving conflicts. This approach was notably in evidence in respect to the sociology of race. It overlapped significantly with the argument of the Myrdal study—the "American creed." Myrdal and Talcott Parsons, Myrdal and Robert Merton, influenced each other. As for "who zoomed who?" we don't need to worry about that too much here. Parsons was a racial liberal and Merton had been involved in civil rights activity since his undergraduate days at Temple University[31]—but, in any case, the consensual political climate of the war years provided an appropriate moment for calls for racial reform. This was a point Myrdal had made clear in his book's concluding pages, pointing out the inconsistencies and contradictions inherent in a racially exclusionary and discriminatory society's leading a war for democracy.[32]

Another major sociological study that tackled race issues at this time, and that resonated very deeply with the structural-functionalist perspective, was Samuel Stouffer et al.'s *The American Soldier* (1949–1950; see also Ryan 2013). Research for this project was initiated in 1941 with War Department support; it was published in 1949–1950. The Stouffer study devoted significant attention to racial attitudes in the wartime military, and to the experiences of the over one million black members of the U.S. armed forces. In its explicit examination of the tensions of racial segregation and the aspirations for racial progress that characterized the wartime armed forces, *The American Soldier* strongly paralleled the Myrdal study, which had preceded it by some five years. In Stouffer et al.'s interviews, white soldiers continued to express their Negrophobia, while blacks articulated their expectations—as they had during World War I—that their sacrifices in wartime would be recognized and rewarded later. Stouffer et al. suggested that the war reduced the degree of white racism. While not a vacuous claim, the extent of this meliorism has since been called into question. To be sure, the armed forces remained segregated through the war years, various race riots (and even black–white gun battles) took place on U.S. bases, and U.S. servicemen of color were often discriminated against and assaulted, sometimes even while in uniform.[33]

Although Myrdal's was the predominant voice in the 1940s sociology of race, Stouffer et al.'s influence was also significant, especially since the latter work appeared at roughly the same moment that the U.S. military was finally being desegregated. Both studies departed from the conflict-oriented approach that had largely informed the sociology of race into the 1930s. Viewed in conjunction with other mainstream sociological work of the period (notably MacIver, ed. 1949), these works must be seen as definitively introducing an integration-oriented perspective on U.S. racial dynamics into mainstream sociology.

While recognizing the gravity of segregation and racial prejudice, the structural-functionalist view of race consistently stressed the integrative qualities of U.S. society; thus the overlap of the two uses of the term "integration"—one that summarized the key civil rights demands of the era, and one that framed sociological explanations in terms of social unity and commonality—is more than a casual synecdoche. Deep-seated conflicts were not amenable to the structural-functionalist account; at most they could appear as "social problems," or be understood as having "latent" functions (Coser 1956) of an integrative sort. An understanding of race and racial injustice as foundational elements in U.S. society and culture (not to mention as world-historically significant issues) was not possible within this viewpoint, which thus tended to marginalize radical accounts such as those deriving from the Duboisian tradition, anticolonialist and pan-African thought, or Marxism.

Once properly reconceptualized as symptoms of the tensions inherent in societal self-regulation, however, racial matters could be understood as amenable to reform. Racial conflict received little attention in Parsons's early work, but after the appearance of *An American Dilemma*, he began writing more about race. Drawing on the work of his Harvard colleague, the psychologist Gordon Allport, and focusing largely upon micro-sociological phenomena, Parsons began thinking about prejudice as a problem of values (in other words white values) in the late 1940s. The edited work *Toward a General Theory of Action* (Parsons and Shils, eds. 1951) contained a substantial essay by Allport taking this approach.[34] Parsons began the essay "Full Citizenship for the Negro American? A Sociological Problem," written for *The Negro American* (Parsons and Clark, eds. 1967) at the height of the civil rights struggle, by arguing social-psychologically. He recognized the values-conflict that exclusion and the experience of white prejudice engender in blacks, echoing Myrdal's diagnosis of the "dilemma." A reform-oriented transition was underway, he suggested, in which inclusion would first be advanced by legal action, then by politics, and finally by state-based guarantees of social citizenship and even redistribution of resources (Parsons in Parsons and Clark 1967, 718). The informed reader must have struggled with this even in 1967, notably with its underestimation of the white resistance—from overt "backlash" politics on down to limited reform—that such a program would face, and indeed was already confronting "up South" (for example, in the North, in places like the Chicago neighborhood of Cicero) as well as "down South."

Looking back on Parsons's account of race, what is most striking is his ungainly combination of sympathy ("moderate," to be sure) with the civil rights movement and his striking unfamiliarity with the nonwhite world. He did manage some criticism of white prejudice and discrimination, but he depicted U.S. "race relations" as undergoing a steady progress toward inclusion of blacks, a condition which he seemed to think was on the verge of accomplishment in 1966. A deeper interest in black life and thought, not to mention black experience, eluded him.

Parsons's co-editor was the eminent black psychologist Kenneth B. Clark, whose work in *The Negro American* took a much less rosy view of mid-1960s U.S. racial politics.[35] Clark's book *Dark Ghetto* appeared in 1965, with an epigraph by Du Bois and an introduction by Myrdal. In that work Clark was already reassessing what had been a lifelong commitment to integration. Clark's analysis of black exclusion and white racism invoked the "internal colonialism" framework; his influential book anticipated Blauner's important radical analyses (1972) that extended and popularized the concept several years later. Clark had been the first tenured black professor at City College of

New York, where he began teaching in 1942. He is perhaps best known for the influence his early work on internalized prejudice (the famous "doll experiments," the use of dolls to determine a child's racial attitude; carried out in collaboration with his wife Mamie Phipps Clark) had on the Supreme Court's 1954 *Brown* decision. His social psychological approach to racism and black identity, both collective and individual, has shaped thinking about racial "identity politics" more generally, right down to the present day. In rough parallel to Du Bois's trajectory, Clark's early work envisioned racial progress as occurring through integration and the extension of rational and democratic norms to U.S. blacks; we can see his affinities with the Myrdal model, as well as with Parsons's attempted systematization, through this lens. But his doubts were already visible in the mid-1960s and became more pronounced throughout his later work. He turned to more radical—and in some respects more "nationalist"—positions as similar tendencies gained increasing traction in the black community.

In the 1960s and 1970s, Nathan Glazer and Daniel Patrick Moynihan attempted a further innovation in ethnicity theory. Stimulated by the burgeoning civil rights movement, and threatened with being outflanked on their left, these two Harvard sociologists wished both to validate the assimilationist bent of previous ethnic group-based theory, and to reintroduce the theme of "ongoing ethnicity" or cultural pluralism. In *Beyond The Melting Pot* they sought to link cultural pluralism with political pluralism, the dominant construct in American political science, and thus seemingly to reconcile the paradigm's problem of ethnic group identity—assimilation vs. cultural pluralism, incorporation vs. preservation—at a stroke. This volume's title itself encapsulates the ethnicity paradigm's perspective on race; the book's two editions bracket the paradigm's triumphal moment and the onset of its downfall.

Glazer and Moynihan argued that immigrating groups were transformed, if hardly "melted," by their experiences in New York, emerging as communities distinct not only from each other and their pre-existing socio-cultural *milieux*, but also from their communities of origin.

> Ethnic groups, then, even after distinctive language, customs, and culture are lost ... are continually recreated by new experiences in America. The mere existence of a name itself is perhaps sufficient to form group character in new situations, for the name associates an individual, who actually can be anything, with a certain past, country, or race.
>
> (Glazer and Moynihan 1970 [1963], 17)

Assimilation, they argued, does take place as individuals acculturate and groups enter the political arena. Yet out of this very process a separate identity emerges, which must sustain itself culturally and deliver tangible political gains (as well as—ultimately—economic gains, "upward mobility") to the group. Thus, fundamental political interests, rather than factors such as primordial ties, cultural differences, or majoritarian resistance to incorporation, were ultimately decisive in the maintenance of ethnic identities. Continuing with the same passage:

> But as a matter of fact, someone who is Irish or Jewish or Italian generally has other traits than the mere existence of the name that associates him [sic] with other people attached to the group. A man is connected to his group by ties of family and friendship. But he is also connected by *ties of interest*. The ethnic groups in New York are also interest groups.
>
> (Ibid, emphasis original)

This political focus initially seemed quite compatible with the racial conflicts of the 1950s and early 1960s. At that time ethnicity theory was grappling with black attempts to achieve equality through the civil rights movement. As seen through the lens of ethnicity, the civil rights movement was a drive for black integration and for the removal of any remaining forms of institutional/legal discrimination. From the perspective of writers such as Glazer and Moynihan or Milton Gordon (1964), civil rights demands were intelligible and comprehensible within the ethnicity framework, and thus deserving of support. The civil rights movement was trying to create for blacks the same conditions that white ethnics had found: "opportunity" and relative equality, the absence of formal discriminatory barriers, however much attitudinal prejudice may have existed (Glazer 1987 [1975], 25–27).

Although virulent forms of racism persisted in the South, the remedies for segregation were clear. The North, though, presented a different set of problems for ethnicity theorists. At first glance, it was assumed that black equality had already been achieved there:

> One looked at the demands of the civil rights movement in 1963—equality in the vote, equality in the courts, equality in representation in public life, equality in accommodations—saw that they existed more or less in New York City, and concluded that the political course of the Northern Negro would be quite different from that of the Southern Negro. He [sic] would become part of the game of accommodation politics—he already was—in which posts and benefits were distributed to groups on the basis of struggle, of course, but also on the basis of votes, money, and political talent, and one concluded that in this game Negroes would not do so badly.
>
> (Glazer and Moynihan 1970 [1963], x)

In other words, blacks already had equal opportunity in the North; what more could they demand? Once equal opportunity legislation along with its judicial and administrative enforcement were accomplished facts, it fell to blacks to follow in their "predecessors'" footsteps. Through hard work, patience, and delayed gratification, blacks could carve out their own rightful place in American society. In the North, where blacks were still recent "immigrants" (from the South), this would involve some degree of assimilation (Glazer 1983). It would involve the development of a new post-immigration cultural identity, and it would require engagement in mainstream pluralist politics. Race relations would thus continue in what Nathan Glazer called the "American ethnic pattern."

So, ethnicity theory assigned to blacks and other people of color the roles which earlier generations of European immigrants had played in the great waves of the "Atlantic migration" of the 19th and early 20th centuries. *But both whites and people of color refused to play their assigned roles.* Structural barriers continued to render the immigrant analogy inappropriate; the trajectory of incorporation did not develop as the ethnicity paradigm had envisioned. Large-scale obtacles blocked the path to inclusion. (We discuss structural racism later in this book, but for now think of red-lining, racial steering and residential segregation, school segregration, hiring patterns, imprisonment.) In the face of these concrete practices of states, corporations, and millions of whites, many blacks (and later, many Latin@s, Native Americans, and Asian Americans as well) rejected ethnic identity and the false promise of inclusion, in favor of a more radical racial identity which demanded group rights and recognition. Given these developments, ethnicity theory found itself increasingly in opposition to the demands of anti-racist movements. The ethnicity paradigm had to be reworked once again. The result was the phenomenon of neoconservatism.

Not long after ethnicity theorists' embrace of civil rights came a new round of racial conflicts: above all, the black power revolt and its cousins, brown power, yellow power, and red power. These poked significant holes in the liberal framework of integration through values-convergence, aka the culturalism of ethnicity theory, aka the structural-functionalist sociology of race. In addition, race began to appear as a global issue, not just a U.S. domestic problem. Earlier sociological paradigms had recognized this better than the post-World War II approaches did: For all their limits, the biologistic approach had located race in the sphere of "development," and the Chicago pragmatists had at least hinted at its intimate connections with nascent U.S. imperialism.[36] By the mid-1960s, then, ethnicity theory and its liberal stalwarts were beginning to part company with the race radicals, nationalists and leftists alike, who had been at least tacit allies earlier. These were the seeds of ethnicity theory's decline and its hastening turn to the right.

The combination of post-World War II racial issues—the crisis of the Jim Crow regime at home and the breakdown of empire and neocolonialism abroad—all in the context of the Cold War and the "communist threat"—exceeded the tolerance level of the racial moderates. Where was the immigrant analogy now? How could the "free world" and the New Deal coalition address these new conditions? Sociology's leading lights were cold warriors; they had taken up the civil rights banner at a time when segregation, lynching, and discrimination against people of color had become deep embarrassments for the United States around the world. Did Parsons read Fanon or even Du Bois? Did Merton consider the sociology of African development proposed by his one-time junior colleague Immanuel Wallerstein? Did Kingsley Davis—who wrote on population in South Asia, comparative urbanization, and the sociology of the family and reproduction in global perspective—ever address anticolonialism? According to Lipset at least (1994), these leading figures, and many others as well, came to sociology after youthful involvements with socialism and communism. No doubt they were nervous in the late 1940s and 1950s. This was quite logical: Many of them were being watched.[37]

From the vantage point of the present, racial dynamics can be seen as deeply structuring all these issues. But during the 1950s and 1960s, racial issues appeared largely to be U.S. domestic problems. They were not to be confused with the battle against communism. Racial integration was supported while the purges and witch-hunting that stigmatized and disemployed some of the field's most active advocates for racial justice were condoned, at least in part.[38] The major figures associated with the structural-functionalist paradigm of race did not oppose the Vietnam War or consider its racial implications.[39] King's 1967 denunciation of the war from the pulpit of New York's Riverside Church was condemned by such "moderate" sociologists of race as Daniel Moynihan, as it was by such "moderate" civil rights leaders as Roy Wilkins and Whitney Young. In the 1960s such figures as Milton Gordon and Nathan Glazer combined support for the "moderate" tendencies in the civil rights movement and rejection of "positive" discrimination (aka affirmative action). Thus they first prefigured and soon after launched the neoconservative racial reaction and the "colorblind" resurgence of the "post-civil rights" era (Steinberg 2001).

The elective affinity between movement-oriented racial reformism and the sociological critique of racial prejudice and discrimination, then, only operated until the mid-1960s or so. The assimilationism advocated so unequivocally by Myrdal and the integrationism put forward by Parsons and Clark were soon exceeded by the vast agenda that meaningful racial reform entailed. This was a point made forcefully by the new wave of race riots beginning in Harlem in 1964 and Watts in 1965, by the assassinations of Malcolm and Martin, by the resurgence of black nationalism and the "black power revolt," and also—as Dr. King pointed out so powerfully—by the doomed U.S. defense of neocolonialism in Asia and elsewhere. Although Parsons, Merton, and other moderates tried valiantly to advocate an incrementalist and integrationist view of race and civil rights, by the later 1960s the reassertion of a conflict-oriented sociology of race (Ladner, ed. 1973) and the emergence of identity politics were well advanced.

Decline and Fall

Although the ethnicity paradigm of race began as a progressive and liberal challenge to racial biologism, eugenics, and white racial nationalism, it has shifted since the enactment of civil rights reforms in the mid-1960s. The core concepts of the paradigm—the immigrant analogy, cultural determinism, and the denial of the corporeal and "ocular" dimensions of raciality—have become the principal intellectual apparatus of the neoconservative and now "colorblind" racial project. Most of the paradigm's proponents have moved rightward, locating their arguments within an individualist problematic that has more in common with the white racial nationalism their predecessors once attacked than with the civil rights movement those same predecessors once supported. In many ways this shift is a consequence of efforts to understand race as a cultural phenomenon.

Once Chicago sociology had discarded the biological determinism of Sumner, Spencer, Madison Grant, Social Darwinism, and eugenics, the mainstream sociology of race dismissed the corporeal dimensions of race rather comprehensively. The body all but disappeared from the sociology of race, as it did from the cultural anthropology of race (post-Boas), and from other social scientific discussions as well, for example Myrdal's study. This was a *reductionist* view of race, one that neglected the importance of the body as a signifier of status, and as signifier of group belonging (Blumer 1958) in its own right. The racial body had served from the earliest days of conquest, and still serves today, as an imperfect but effective tool and marker: for both domination and resistance, for the assignment of identity and the recognition of difference, for the maintenance of social control and the drawing of boundaries among groups, and for claims of solidarity made both by the powerful and the powerless.

To understand race as a variety of ethnicity, then, was to neglect stigma, exclusion, privilege, and violence, all characteristics inherent in "the mark of race," the phenomic, "ocular" dimension of racial belonging. It was to adopt the immigrant analogy: the assumption that racially identified individuals and groups, like immigrants, could adapt to new circumstances (say, the urban settings of the North or West rather than the rural settings of the South, or industrial labor rather than agricultural labor). Just as immigrant ethnic groups learned a new language and new customs, eating and speaking (and perhaps worshipping) differently, so too could blacks, Asians, and Latin American immigrants. Indeed becoming "ethnic groups" at all, acquiring the hyphenated identity that marked ethnicity—Italian-American, Jewish-American, Mexican-American, Negro-American (or later, African-American)—was what ethnicity was all about (Glazer and Moynihan, eds. 1975). Both assimilation and cultural pluralism involved obtaining this ethnic option (Waters 1990) that was the mark of inclusion. Achieving ethnic identity might be an uneven and prolonged process that required several generations; it might not eliminate all status differentials, hierarchies, and prejudice; and indeed it might not render all groups equally permeable in the melting pot (or equally tasty in the "salad bowl"). But it would go a long way toward reducing remaining inequalities and differences.

Concerned that the incorporative consequences of immigration (assimilation and cultural pluralism once again) might not apply fully enough to racially "different"—that is, not white—groups, ethnicity theorists had struggled to keep up with the racial upheavals of the post-World War II period, in which the legacies of slavery and empire were central, and immigration was secondary. The capture, transport, mass murder, and chattelization of millions of Africans[40] could not easily be explained within the immigration analogy, though Kristol, Glazer and Moynihan, and others tried their best to locate it within their framework of immigrant inclusion and urban ethnic politics. Nor was the problem of the displacement, removal, and genocide of the pre-existing native inhabitants of the Americas a major concern of ethnicity theorists.[41] The "immigrant analogy" obviously did not work here. Or maybe it only worked in reverse: with the immigrants/settlers playing the dominant role.

The radical charge that the construction of American economies, cultures, and states, both in North America and elsewhere in the hemisphere, depended on slavery and empire. Indeed the fact that these imperial projects and subsequent American nations were intrinsically racist projects themselves, was discomfiting for ethnicity theorists (Drinnon 1997; Stoler, ed. 2006). From the 1960s on, the dominant ethnicity paradigm was confronted with radical critique from the left. Politically it was upset by the embrace of various Marxisms in the black movement and other anti-racist movements. It was hostile to the black power movement (Van DeBurg 1992; Joseph 2006), as well as to such related radical and nationalist organizations as the Black Panthers, the Young Lords, the American Indian Movement, and the Partido de la Raza Unida. None of these were comfortable political bedfellows for ethnicity theorists of race.

Confronted with the intractability of racial difference and the resilience of racial inequality in the aftermath of civil rights legislation and Supreme Court rulings that favored inclusive social policies, ethnicity theorists faced a stark choice. Broadly speaking, there were two possible reasons why reform did not effectively reduce racial inequality and difference and facilitate social and political inclusion under the "American creed": Either U.S. society was unwilling to tackle the endemic racial injustices that prevailed within it, or people of color were unwilling to grasp the opportunities newly becoming available. Ethnicity-based approaches could not accept the former view; was this not what the Panthers and other radicals were claiming? Calls for "positive" or "affirmative" anti-discrimination policies, for example, assumed the existence a far more entrenched system of racial injustice than ethnicity theorists such as Glazer, Moynihan, Charles Murray, and Thomas Sowell were willing to recognize. After all, earlier generations of immigrants had not required special policies or treatments; why should blacks? State activities should be restricted, they argued, to guarantees of formal equality for individuals.

This position was not new. Milton Gordon had argued something similar as early as 1964. But the *doyens* of the ethnicity school, Glazer and Moynihan, were ambivalent about the group rights question in the 1960s. Indeed, Moynihan had endorsed positive anti-discrimination measures ("equality of result") in his famous "Report" (Rainwater and Yancey 1967, 49); Moynihan also coauthored Lyndon Johnson's Howard University speech "To Fulfll these Rights" (June 5, 1964):

> You do not take a person who, for years, has been hobbled by chains and liberate him [sic], bring him up to the starting line of a race and then say, "you are free to compete with all the others," and still justly believe that you have been completely fair.
>
> (Ibid)

For his part Glazer had warned about group rights early on. He argued, also in 1965, that a "new national interest" in "the final liquidation of Negro separation" was being defined, and that blacks themselves had best not oppose it, for "When an ethnic group interest has clashed with a national interest, we have been quite ruthless and even extreme in overriding the group interest" (Glazer 1983, 27).[42]

During its long reign, ethnicity theory has frequently been modified as its advocates attempted to account for new empirical phenomena or to address competing theoretical approaches. In the early postwar period, the ethnicity model encountered its main opponents in conservative quarters. Explicitly racist perspectives, rooted in the formerly dominant biologistic, hierarchical, and religious beliefs of the prewar era, maintained their hold, especially in the South but also on a national level. (Think KKK.) The early civil rights movement in the South, and the mobilization of Mexican Americans in the Southwest, evoked overt expressions of hardcore white supremacy and violence in the 1960s, although reforms slowly took some hold in these regions as well.

The ethnicity paradigm was still on board the movement train in the early 1960s, operating as its "mainstream" explanatory voice. Until roughly 1966, ethnicity theorists supported the "moderate" desegregation policies of the Johnson presidency and Warren Court. Subsequently, in the wake of Goldwater's 1964 defeat, the Voting Rights Act (1965), and George Wallace's campaigns, and as a consequence of Nixon's (1968) "southern strategy" and party realignment, ethnicity theory was pushed to the right. By the early 1970s, it had been transformed into neoconservatism. Today, that political current is seen chiefly through its neo-imperial agenda in Iraq and its alliance with the right-wing Israeli Likud Party, but we should remember that it began as a center-right racial realignment after breaking with the civil rights movement, not only the black power movement, but also the movement of Martin Luther King, Jr.

The ethnicity-based, neoconservative approach to race had three main problems: 1) the social scientific, indeed methodological, limitations encountered by the ethnicity paradigm in its attempt to reduce race to an element of ethnicity; 2) the paradigm's consequent inability to deal with the particular characteristics of racially-defined groups as a direct consequence of this reductionism; and 3) the ethnicity paradigm's reliance on a single historical case in its use of the great wave of European migration at the turn of the 20th century to develop its "immigrant analogy." The first of these problems we call the "Bootstraps Model"; the second we refer to as "They All Look Alike"; the third we label "Once Is Not Enough."

The "Bootstraps Model": As we have noted, substantial reworking of the ethnicity paradigm took place in the later 1960s and early 1970s. By 1975 Glazer and Moynihan felt themselves able to offer a general hypothesis on the dynamics of group incorporation:

> Ethnic groups bring different norms to bear on common circumstances with consequent different levels of success—hence group differences in status.
>
> (Glazer and Moynihan, eds. 1975, 7)

The "group norms/common circumstances" correlation raises multiple problems, which can be traced back to the immigrant analogy. The key factor in explaining the success that an ethnic group will have in becoming incorporated into "normalized"[43] white society (a goal whose desirability is unquestioned) is the values or "norms" which the group brings to bear on the general social circumstances it faces, just as all other minorities have done. Since the independent variable is the "norms," the idea that "differences in status" could be affected by factors outside or even unrelated to the group is ruled out at the level of assumptions. Everything is mediated through "norms" internal to the group. If Chican@s don't do well in school, this cannot, even hypothetically, be due to low-quality education; it has instead to do with Chican@ values. After all, Jews and Japanese Americans did well in inferior schools, so why can't other groups? Ongoing processes of discrimination, shifts in the prevailing economic climate, the development of a sophisticated racial ideology of "conservative egalitarianism"—in other words, all the concrete sociopolitical dynamics within which racial phenomena operate in the United States—are ignored in this approach.[44]

"Common circumstances," by contrast, are relegated to the dependent variable. These are the universal conditions to which each ethnic group must accommodate. The assumption is that each racialized "ethnic group" faces the normalized white society in the same way that its predecessors did; furthermore it is assumed that each group confronts that majority society *alone*, unaffected by the histories, accomplishments, or misfortunes of previous ethnic/racial groups. The experiences of immigrants who previously arrived in the United States, or those of other racially defined minorities, are not considered relevant in the Glazer/Moynihan model. The achievement of mobility—the group-status dependent variable—reflects group willingness and ability to accept presumptive white norms and values. The "difference" that characterizes a racialized "ethnic group," once that group is incorporated, will be outweighed by the "commonality" it shares with whites.

In other words, something akin to Milton Gordon's notion of "structural assimilation" (1964, 70) is assumed to take place as immigrant groups pass beyond their "fresh off the boat" status and gain the acceptance of whites. Yet this assumption is quite unwarranted with respect to people of color, whose distance from the normalized whiteness valorized by the model has generally not been appreciably lessened by adoption of the dominant (white) norms and values of American society, something that actually occurs quite a lot, though obviously unevenly. A large literature on discrimination bears this out: Returns to education are not equivalent across racial lines, for example; employment levels and wage rates vary considerably even when we control for everything but race; the same may be said for access to credit, access to equivalent housing, and numerous other patterns of discrimination.

The entire model for comparing and evaluating the success of ethnic groups—in achieving higher status or in being incorporated into normalized white society—is thus limited by an unwillingness to consider whether there might be any *special circumstances* which racially defined minorities encounter in the United States, circumstances which definitively distinguish their experiences from those of earlier European immigrants, and make the injunction to "pull yourselves up by your own bootstraps" impossible to fulfill.

In addition, the "bootstraps" model is *dated.* The trend toward a "majority-minority" demographic is advancing in the United States. In other words, a situation is emerging in which no single racially defined group, including those considered white, will be a majority in the country. This inexorable transition casts the assimilationist premises of the "bootstraps" model, as well as the immigrant analogy, into considerable doubt. In practical terms, there is no longer a clear-cut set of "common circumstances" into which a given ethnic group can possibly blend its cultural values and norms. Race *exceeds* ethnicity in many respects, as it has done for centuries: Black immigrants from the Caribbean or Africa, for example, blend into U.S. blackness, perhaps retaining some cultural (that is, ethnic) differences, but unable and maybe unwilling to escape the all-inclusive framework of race (Waters 2000). Recent work on Mexican Americans suggests that broadly similar processes of racialization are operating in respect to that community as well (Telles and Ortiz 2009).

"They All Look Alike": In what sense can groups of color be considered in ethnic group terms? In what sense is the category "black," for example, equivalent to the categories "Irish" or "Jewish"? "Blacks" in ethnic terms are as diverse as "whites." Latin@s as well, Asian Americans and Native Americans too. Since ethnicity theory focuses on cultural identity and difference, its practitioners should go much deeper than they generally do. How might ethnicity theory address the range of subgroupings represented in the U.S. black community? What distinctions might it employ? Haitians? Jamaicans? Francophones? Georgians? Northern/southern? The black community has been intensively studied from an ethnographic standpoint, so there is no lack of materials for analysis.[45] Latin@ communities vary as well: by language, religion, place of origin; for example, in the United States there are substantial communities of indigenous people of Mexican origin whose first (and sometimes only) language is not Spanish but Maya, Mixtec, or Nahuatl (Fox and Rivera-Salgado, eds. 2004). Large numbers of Latin@s are phenotypically black, *Afro-descendientes*, while many others are visually indistinguishable from North American whites (Montalvo and Codina 2001; Rodriguez 2000).

Ethnicity theory has not delved to any significant extent into the meaning of these distinctions. There is a racist element in this substitution—in which whites are seen as variegated in terms of group identities, but blacks, Latin@s, Native Americans, and Asian Americans "all look alike." In our view, this is the effect of the application of a paradigm based in white ethnic history to a variety of racially defined groups. Indeed, in sharp contrast to the lack of interest among ethnicity theorists (and their neoconservative successors) in this issue of intra-racial distinctions, an important race-studies literature on *panethnicity* has developed over the past few decades. Racial formation always involves "lumping"; racialization proceeds through a combination of centripetal and centrifugal forces. Despite the presence of different cultural orientations and sometimes long-standing antagonisms—this is the "centrifugal" force—ethnic groups may be pressured into allying and "bridging" because of the common presssures they face: exclusion, discrimination, violence against them; such circumstances constitute "centripetal" forces (Calderón 1992; Espiritu 1993; Jones-Correa and Leal 1996; Okamoto 2006).

Once is Not Enough: The ethnicity paradigm was initially developed in reference to an unprecedented and perhaps unique period of U.S. immigration history: the arrival and eventual inclusion of vast waves of Southern and Eastern European immigrants before and after the turn of the 20th century, roughly 1880–1924. Though popularly regarded as a general theory of ethnic group incorporation, the paradigm might simply be characteristic of specific historical circumstances that may never be repeated again.

The dynamics of immigration have shifted dramatically between the turn of the 20th century and the present. The United States now relates to the global South and global East through a master-policy of "accumulation by dispossession." Displaced and impoverished workers and peasants from Latin America and the Caribbean, as well as from the Pacific Rim, continue to immigrate, their human flow modulated but hardly contained by boom and bust, "bubble" and recession. And the United States has also become more racially predatory domestically, practicing a similar policy of "accumulation by dispossession" at home as well. Consider post-Katrina New Orleans or the subprime housing crisis—to pick just two prominent examples. So is the country less able to integrate immigrants than it was in previous historical periods?

Where will the United States find another "engine of mobility" to parallel that of the late 19th and early 20th centuries, the epoch of mass labor recruitment to the industrial economy? The country's economic capacity to absorb enormous numbers of immigrants—low-wage workers and their families, and a new globally based (and very female) servant class (Glenn 2002)—without generating the sort of established subaltern groups we associate with the terms "race" and "racism," seems to us more limited than was the "whitening" of Europeans a century earlier, this argument's key precedent.

We suggest that the ethnicity paradigm's use of an "immigrant analogy" in an attempt to make sense of the post-World War II black movement upsurge, was fundamentally flawed. Most criticism to date has focused on the differences between the situations faced by European immigrants c. 1900 and blacks who sought integration post-1945. Perhaps an even more telling critique, however, is political-economic. The integration of the European immigrants *may have been a one-off.* The ethnicity paradigm's efforts to apply turn-of-the-20th-century accounts of European immigration and integration to the post-World War II United States may thus be a classical case of bad social science: the conception and (highly influential) divulgation of a theory based on little more than a single very limited case study and a good deal of ideological wishful thinking.

In sum, the logic of assimilation, the default to whiteness—whether conscious or unconscious—is an inherent part of ethnicity theories of race (Jung 2009). As U.S. society transitions from the substantial and largely unquestioned white majorities of the past, to an increasingly majority-minority demographic pattern, the normalization of whiteness that has been an assumed constant of ethnicity-based theories of race may be eroding.

Ethnicity-based approaches have lost social scientific coherence as they capitulated to neoconservative political priorities, insisting that in the "post-civil rights" era a new framework of "colorblindness" could replace race-consciousness. We discuss colorblind racial ideology at greater length in subsequent chapters; here it is sufficient to note that far from moving in an egalitarian and inclusive direction, far from achieving the "dream" of extending democracy across the color-line that was the elemental heart of the civil rights and allied movements in the early post-World War II period, American society has in many ways moved in the opposite direction. It has become more segregated and more racially unequal. Because on the most practical level these developments are perfectly visible, they undercut all claims that the significance of race is declining, and deeply undermine the idea of the United States as a colorblind or race-neutral society.

Under these conditions, the default to whiteness has gradually been revealed as the true message of the ethnicity paradigm of racial theory. Being "ethnic" turns out to be about whether and how much an individual or group can assimilate into or hybridize with whiteness. Being "racial" is about how much difference there is between an individual or a group and their white counterparts.

Notes

1. Max Weber's early concept of *ethnie* as a form of status, shaped by "honor"—a cultural construct—is frequently applied to racial matters. Weber also recognized racism, notably anti-black racism in the United States. See his remarks on U.S. racial attitudes in Gerth and Mills, eds. 1958, 177, 405–406. Weber's sensitivity to U.S. racial matters may be attributed, at least in part, to the orientation provided him by W.E.B. Du Bois (Lewis 1993, 225, 277). For critical remarks on Weber's treatment of race and ethnicity see Banton 2007.
2. The assignment of membership in a given racial group was, of course, problematic in itself. The existence and characteristics of supposed human groups, the boundaries of the groups, the groups' locations in the "great chain of being," and so on, were all debated.
3. All these themes had extensive intellectual histories, generally flowing from Enlightenment discussions of race: Linnaean, Kantian. Jefferson's reflections on such issues as the beauty and smell of black people may be contemplated in his *Notes on the State of Virginia* (Jefferson 1984 [1785]).
4. In fact what became "development theory" had its origins in race-based (and racist) scholarship: in anthropology, sociology, history, and beyond (Vitalis 2010).
5. Although these currents were often at odds with one another, they were all committed to the idea of racial hierarchy, with guess who at the top and bottom? Indeed, a great deal of

inflammatory "theoretical" material appeared on this topic as the biologistic paradigm consolidated its intellectual hegemony and achieved the status of "common sense" (Grant 1916; Stoddard 1920; Davenport 1972 [1911]). On eugenics, see Chase 1980; Kevles 1998; Spiro 2009.

6. In 1879 the black activist and scholar Martin R. Delaney attacked the early physical anthropology of Africa for its racial bias, with a book entitled *Principia of Ethnology* (Delaney 2009 [1879]). Du Bois's 1897 essay "The Conservation of Races" attempted a "transvaluation" of the racial hierarchy implicit in eugenics (Du Bois 1995 [1897]). Kelly Miller, Professor of Mathematics at Howard University, reviewed economist Frederick L. Hoffman's 1897 *Race Traits and Tendencies of the American Negro*, one of the leading eugenics-based works to argue for the innate inferiority of African Americans, using census data to argue that Hoffman's claims were statistically flawed. See Miller 1897; Stepan and Gilman 1993.
7. Witch-burning—the 250-year (c. 1450–1700) mass assault on women and the mass killings and torture that it involved—remains a sociologically undertheorized territory. Federici's audacious treatment (2004) is an erudite and crucial intersectional contribution to this necessary work. See also Lerner 1987.
8. The New England Puritans were slaveholders as well, but on a much smaller scale than the southern planters. There were also significant religious differences between the two settler groups.
9. Southern (white) Baptism is the world's largest Baptist denomination and the second largest U.S. church after Roman Catholicism. Religious adherence remains quite segregated in the United States today. Though various currents jostle within U.S. white Protestantism—some of them "liberal" (center-left) and some of them racially diverse—the majority of the national Protestant congregation is "conservative" (center-right), retains a "born again" theology and strong evangelical dimensions, and is in many ways still southern. Here we have all the basic elements for a politico-religious white racial nationalism: a civil religion (Bellah 2005) largely inclined to the right and still linked with theological, not to mention biological, racism. Witness the racial tensions in contemporary American Protestantism: traditionally white-black, but now augmented by substantial numbers of Latin@ and Asian American congregations as well (Wuthnow 2011).
10. The ethnicity paradigm continues today in sociology and other fields as well under a social psychological banner: "ethnicity as cognition" (Brubaker, Loveman, and Stamatov 2004).
11. This relatively innocuous notion tends to mask the underlying realities of U.S. imperialism, which was particularly active in the Pacific during the years when the Chicago School sociology of race was developing. Park's notion of an American "racial frontier" also gestures in this direction. As the early Chicago work was being carried out, U.S. troops were still pursuing the brutal subjugation of the Philippines, a war that was explicitly presented as a racial project (Kramer 2006). Hawai'i's annexation was still relatively recent, increasing Japanese power in the region was becoming a concern in Washington, and U.S. competition with various European powers for "spheres of influence" in China was well underway. In general, immigration—the matter of persons travelling *into one's country*—should be seen as producing only one-half of the issue known as "race contact"; the other half is produced by imperial travel *out from one's country*, notably in projects of settlement and conquest.
12. A little-remembered feature of Washington's famous Atlanta Exposition speech of 1895 was its anti-immigrant message. His plea to white elites was that they prefer blacks over

immigrants in their industrial employment practices and thus open the door to inclusion (Washington 2010 [1895]). That's what "Cast down your buckets where you are" is all about.

13. Here too Du Bois preceded the Chicago sociologists. Du Bois had been a student at Harvard of William James, one of the founding fathers of pragmatist philosophy.
14. Johnson was hired by Park to investigate the 1919 race riot in Chicago, probably the worst of that "Red Summer's" series of attacks by white mobs on black communities.
15. Roosevelt sought to mediate between his friend Madison Grant's biologistic (and in some ways proto-fascist) Aryanism, on the one hand, and the radical potentialities he saw in mass movements of immigrants on the other. Hence TR urged deliberate "Americanization" programs through schooling and other public policies, and embraced the "melting pot." Roosevelt's anti-black racism was mild, far less than that of his fellow progressive Woodrow Wilson, who was still fighting the Civil War as the Virginia confederate he had been in his youth. Wilson not only celebrated the film *Birth of a Nation* in 1915, but the following year ran for reelection on a nativist platform, calling for restrictions on immigration and explicitly red-baiting immigrant groups and organizations. For Wilson too, only immigrants who adapted to "true American" cultural norms could be accepted.
16. Kallen was a lifelong advocate of Jewish causes and a strong early Zionist. One of the founders of the New School for Social Research, he was also close friends with Alain Locke, whom he knew from Harvard and later worked with in New York. The origins of the term "cultural pluralism," and Kallen's own beginnings with the idea, are linked to Jewish student struggles for recognition around the turn of the 20th century (Greene 2011). Despite his celebration of what we today would call "diversity" and his apparent lack of personal racism, Kallen never addressed African-American issues or took a pro-civil rights stand. "Kallen's 'symphony of civilizations,' despite its apparent inclusiveness, excluded people of color—African Americans, Latinos, Asian Americans, and Native Americans," writes Gerald Meyer (2012).
17. At the American Museum of Natural History Boas had to combat the eugenicism of Madison Grant and the elite racism of Henry Fairfield Osborn, the paleontologist who became the Museum's President and chief primatologist (Haraway 1990). For a history of race in American anthropology, see Baker 1998.
18. Achieving whiteness serves as the desirable end-state of immigration, as it did for Park's cycle. This "default" operates in cultural pluralism accounts as well; there the desirable end-state is white recognition and tolerance for the former "others"; multiculturalism and diversity programs work in this direction as well. See Jung 2009.
19. The racial orientation of the New Deal was contradictory at best. FDR's coalition included both northern liberals and southern Dixiecrats. Roosevelt sought to accommodate both groups. He placated the South (and other racist allies) by excluding blacks from Social Security and the Wagner Act in 1935, exempting domestic and agricultural workers from labor regulation, resisting anti-lynching law proposals, and limiting the scope of welfare. He also maintained restrictive and racist immigration controls. Roosevelt gestured toward racial liberals by taking small steps toward integration, particularly as the war approached: most notably, he integrated defense industries by executive order, a move prompted by threats of black protest led by trade unionist A. Philip Randolph. As industrial employment and the demand for black and brown labor increased in the North and West, a combination of demographic shifts, unionization of blacks and Latinos in the CIO,

women's entry into industrial work, and linked voting shifts outside the South, deepened the Democratic Party's racial divisions. See Katnelson 2013; Klinkner and Smith 2002; Sitkoff 1978; Vargas 2007; Weiss 1983.

20. In the United States, World War II was anti-racist on the Atlantic front but decidedly racist on the Pacific front. See our discussion of Myrdal's *An American Dilemma*, below.
21. Unless otherwise stated, we use the term "liberal" here in the colloquial U.S. sense, meaning "center-left."
22. The Magnuson Act was a complex business. On the one hand, it recognized China as an ally in the anti-Japanese war; refocusing anti-Asian racism away from Chinese and more intensely onto Japanese and Japanese Americans. In no way, however, did it relax the anti-Asian Johnson–Reed immigration law, which had been in effect since 1924 and allowed only 105 Chinese immigrants to enter the country per year. Asian exclusion was not reduced until the passage of the Immigration and Nationality Act of 1965 (Hart–Celler). See Ngai 2005. Notably, numerous states (including California) maintained anti-miscegenation laws that prohibited Asians from marrying whites. Some of these laws were repealed or struck down in the late 1940s; some lasted until the U.S. Supreme Court struck down all anti-miscegenation laws in *Loving v. Virginia* (1967). See Spiro 2009.
23. Kikuchi had been a student at Berkeley—he was expelled in 1942 and was subsequently interned under EO 9066 (Briones 2013).
24. On these heroic figures, see Hirabayashi 1999.
25. The U.S. Congress passed, and President Ronald Reagan signed, the Civil Liberties Act of 1988, which stated that Executive Order 9066 was "unjust and motivated by racism rather than real military necessity." A second apology and further reparations were issued in 1992. For a good general account see Weglyn 1996 (1976).
26. The study has a monumental history of its own. See Stanfield 1985; Southern 1987; Jackson 1990. Black reaction to the Myrdal volume varied significantly. E. Franklin Frazier heaped praise upon the work. Myrdal, he wrote, "revealed a remarkable facility for getting the feel of the racial situation in the United States. His objectivity was apparent from the very beginning in his relations with Negroes. They were simply people to him" (Frazier 1945, 557). Ralph Ellison's review—written in 1944 but not published until 1964 in Ellison's *Shadow and Act*—was deeply critical: "It does not occur to Myrdal," Ellison writes, "that many of the Negro cultural manifestations which he considers merely reflective might also embody a *rejection* of what he considers 'higher values.'" Du Bois had been largely excluded from the project due to his radicalism; he was properly offended. The study's collaborators included, among many others, Arnold Rose and Richard Sterner (Myrdal's secondary authors), Ralph Bunche (Myrdal's principal associate and guide), Doxey Wilkerson, Sterling A. Brown, St. Clair Drake, E. Franklin Frazier, Melville J. Herskovits, Otto Klineberg, Edward Shils, and Louis Wirth. Consultants acknowledged were W.E.B. Du Bois, Horace Cayton, Robert E. Park, W.I. Thomas, Hortense Powdermaker, John Dollard, Alain Locke, Walter White, Abram L. Harris, and Ruth Benedict.
27. The Myrdal book was explicitly about "the Negro problem"; Myrdal only discussed blacks and whites; he had nothing to say about other racialized groups.
28. Myrdal's theory of "cumulative and circular development" appeared in an early form in *An American Dilemma* (1962 [1944]), 1065–1070. It was developed further in later writings on global inequality (Myrdal 1963) and as an economic analysis oriented toward progressive

redistribution of resources. Explicitly pragmatist, this account is counterposed to "vicious circle" explanations of racism ("prejudice") and poverty. Though primarily crafted to urge intervention against inequality, the theory also seeks to explain the breakdown of political systems based on unstable equilibria, and the reiterative dynamics of struggles against them.

29. See Myrdal 927ff. Frazier remained both a radical and a committed assimilationist:

    > Since the institutions, the social stratification, and the culture of the Negro community are essentially the same as those of the larger community, it is not strange that the Negro minority belongs among the assimilationist rather than the pluralist, secessionist, or militant minorities. It is seldom that one finds Negroes who think of themselves as possessing a different culture from whites and that their culture should be preserved. (Frazier 1957a, 681)

    His position derived from an insistence on political engagement with the questions of race and racism, which he traced back to Du Bois. See Platt 1991.
30. The papers were published under MacIver's editorship in 1949.
31. Robert Merton, personal communication.
32. Portions of this section appeared in different form in Winant 2007.
33. For additional commentary see Kryder 2001; for a valuable fictionalized account, see Killens 1983 (1963).
34. This essay, "Prejudice: A Problem in Psychological and Social Causation," is an early version of Allport's *The Nature of Prejudice* (1979 [1954]), a work that was to have a significant impact in social psychology.
35. *The Negro American* (1967) was initially a two-issue collection published in the journal *Daedalus.* It later went through several book-length editions. References here are to the 1967 Beacon edition. The contrast between the perspectives of black and white contributors to the book is quite notable. Clark's introduction to the volume, *The Dilemma of Power*, and John Hope Franklin's essay in the volume, *The Two Worlds of Race*, are standouts. Other critical black voices included are those of Martin Kilson, St. Clair Drake, and Whitney Young. Only Young, Director of the National Urban League, takes a "moderate" position.
36. Du Bois had never hesitated to make this connection, and had particularly emphasized it in *Black Reconstruction* (2007 [1935]).
37. The scandalous McCarthyite harassment (and at one point, indictment) of the octogenarian Du Bois in the 1950s occurred without notable protest from within the field. FBI surveillance extended to such mainstream figures as Samuel Stouffer, Herbert Blumer, Robert Bellah, Robert and Helen Lynd, E. Franklin Frazier, Alfred McClung Lee, and, of course, C. Wright Mills. Some leading sociologists, we know, cooperated with witch-hunters, most notably Pitirim Sorokin; but most remained cautious, at least through the late 1940s and 1950s (Lipset 1994; Keen 1999). Mass dismissals did occur on occasion and surveillance was very widespread (Slaughter 1980). Particular attention was being paid to area studies: notably Russia and China, but also to the insurgent "third world" (Simpson, ed., 1999; for parallels in anthropology, see Price 2004). A striking aspect of a great deal of this late 1940s–1950s academic repression and red-baiting was how much of it related to race. A major signal to the FBI, HUAC, and other similar agencies that a given scholar or teacher was ripe for purging, or at least needed watching, was that he or she participated in anti-racist activities or attended mixed-race events. A certain cold-war orthodoxy was

mandatory; this in itself resulted in a muting of sociological criticism of U.S. racism. For larger treatments of the links between the Cold War and the civil rights movement, see Kelley 2008 (1999); Borstelmann 2003; Dudziak 2011.

38. The battles of the McCarthy period lamentably engulfed the black movement as well, as W.E.B. Du Bois, Paul Robeson, and others were denounced as pariah figures, and racial "moderates" strove to distance themselves from them.
39. In a later edited work, Glazer and Moynihan (1975) did try to address the comparative sociology of race (in their framework, "ethnicity"). By this time, structural-functionalist approaches to race were effectively dead, though. Neoconservatism was emerging as the inheritor of both Parsons and Myrdal.
40. A partial exception here was the very controversial 1965 "Moynihan Report," formally titled "The Negro Family: The Case For National Action," and prepared by then-Assistant Secretary of Labor Daniel Patrick Moynihan (Rainwater and Yancey, eds. 1967). Moynihan provided a stilted reading of an important study by E. Franklin Frazier to argue that female-dominated black families did not adequately socialize young black men to the work ethic, leading to high rates of black male unemployment and crime. The source of this problem was traced to slavery's assault on the black family. Although appropriately attacked on numerous grounds—for misreading Frazier, for misunderstanding the strength of black family ties under and after slavery (Gutman 1976; see also Wilson 2009b), for "blaming the victim," for gender bias, and for neglecting larger social structures of racism, the report was at its core a proper liberal document, urging the Johnson administration to focus energy and attention on job-creation and job-training in the ghetto.
41. In fact it is striking how little attention ethnicity-based theories of race have devoted to the American Indian. See Rogin 1996; Drinnon 1997.
42. Still later, writing in retirement, Glazer (1997) provided some self-criticism of his own earlier racial views.
43. Not the "majority." In many areas of the country, whites are no longer the majority. Even if the local or regional population is not majority white, however, conformity with white norms is still understood as a prerequisite for assimilation under the colorblind standards of neoconservatism, the contemporary form of the ethnicity-based theory of race. For this reason we refer here to "normalized" white society, rather than uncritically adopting the white majority/nonwhite minority framework.
44. Probably the most straightforward application of this set of assumptions is Sowell 1995. Sowell treats racial/ethnic groups as equivalent and internally homogeneous; in a largely decontextualized fashion. He equates the cultural norms attributed to various groups with their access (or lack of access) to "human capital," seen as the key to well-being and prosperity. Though Sowell's treatment of these issues is quite shallow, he is far from alone in his insistence on the "bootstraps model."
45. See among a welter of possible sources, Clark 1965; Stack 1974; Gwaltney 1980; Kasinitz 1992; Gregory 1998; Bobo et al., eds. 2002.

CHAPTER 2

Class

Introduction

The class paradigm of race includes those approaches which, in Stuart Hall's characterization, argue that "Social divisions which assume a distinctively racial or ethnic character can be attributed or explained principally by reference to economic structures and processes" (Hall 1980, 306). The class paradigm of race includes schools of thought running from right to left, but they all afford primacy to economic relationships: market exchange, distribution, production. A central objective of this chapter is to review and critique class-based theories of race.

Our adoption of Hall's formulation truly opens up a Pandora's box. To equate his "economic structures and processes" with class, whether understood in the Marxian sense of relationship to the means of production, or in the Weberian sense of relationship to the mode of distribution (giving rise to particular "life chances"), is to make a certain analytic leap (Gerth and Mills 1958, 181–183). Indeed there is a significant economic literature on race, exemplified by the "neoclassical" approach of Nobel laureate Gary Becker and many other Chicago economists, that does not recognize the existence of classes at all, but confines itself narrowly to market relationships. This view overlaps with the paleoeconomic "Austrian"[1] perspective of Hayek, Friedman[2] et al., also tied to Chicago, that has informed the anti-statism of neoliberalism.

How, then, do we define the class paradigm of race, and how can the variety of approaches which emphasize "economic structures and processes" in their analyses of racial phenomena be categorized, linked, and compared?[3] Once we recognize that class theories principally explain race by reference to economic processes, understood in the standard sense of the production, exchange, and consumption of commodities, that brings inequality to the table. Once we are dealing with any sort of inequality—unequal exchange, unequal allocation of resources, exploitation in labor, or equivalent relationships—we have a "class" system, although particular analysts might prefer not to use this designation. Therefore, in the broad terms we have employed to describe the paradigm, these are class theories, even if the authors assume the existence of a totally free market (Becker's starting point is international trade!). Such "institutional" economists as Joseph Stiglitz, Paul Krugman, and Jeffrey Sachs clearly recognize this (Stiglitz 2001 [1944]; Krugman 2008).

This is how the class paradigm of race is constituted, in the broadest possible sense. We suggest that there are three general approaches to racial formation contained within it. We designate these as the market, stratification, and class conflict approaches. These three approaches ground themselves in the different economic spheres: in exchange relationships (markets), in systems of distribution (stratification), and in conflict over production processes (in Marxist terms, conflict over the "social relations of production"), to provide their respective frameworks of analysis.

In this chapter we review and critique class-based theories of race, moving through the class paradigm's varieties: market-, stratification-, and production/labor-based accounts. These roughly correspond to a right-to-left political spectrum: neoliberal theories ("Austrian," Chicago-based) emphasize the significance of exchange relationships and market-based approaches in explaining racial inequality; Marxism-based theories focus more on the role of production relationships and labor in shaping race; while U.S. "liberals"—mostly located on the center-left—focus on stratification/inequality-based accounts of race that emphasize distribution and the role of the state.

But this is only a rough correspondence. A number of civil rights organizations are oriented to markets, for example, the PUSH organization and the Urban League. These groups and parallel organizations in Latin@ communities represent the substantial black and brown business sectors and their markets, the professional and "striving" sectors, and even some of the "coping stratum" (Kilson and Cottingham 1991) of blacks and Latin@s today. On the Marxist left today (and throughout the left's history), there have been "colorblind" currents that seek to minimize or even ignore racial inequality, instead focusing their attention entirely (or nearly entirely) on class. Across the ideological spectrum from right to left there are peculiar overlaps and concurrences about the relationship between race and class. Eliminating or minimizing the significance of race is a feature of the *laissez-faire* positions associated with neoliberalism and Chicago economics. This idea is also associated with "colorblind" racial ideology and was featured in some pioneering civil rights movement positions. Class-based theories of race, in short, traverse the political spectrum.

The Market Relations Approach

Market relations approaches deal with the social *exchange* of resources such as labor and credit. Racial inequality—like all forms of inequality—is anomalous in market settings. In the 1950s and 1960s, debates around the nature of racial inequality in the United States revealed some glaring problems in market-based economic models: They lacked the capacity to explain racial discrimination as a market phenomenon. Indeed, the predominant economic model of the time, neoclassical theory, suggested that the market itself, unhampered by an interventionist state, would eliminate racial discrimination. Writers such as Milton Friedman argued that this was in fact taking place (Friedman 2002 [1962], 108–110).

A more accurate account would note that race was simply outside the awareness of the economics field. As elsewhere, racial inequality was an assumed condition, beneath the interest of economic explanation. To cite but one (prominent) example:

In his extremely well-known article, "Economic Development with Unlimited Supplies of Labor" (1954, 139–191), W. Arthur Lewis did not emphasize the means by which these unlimited supplies became available.[4] The discovery of the problem of racial discrimination came later; economics, which had largely seen inequality as eternal and natural where race was concerned, was finally troubled by the civil rights movement, but only in the 1960s.

The field was challenged by the upheavals of the postwar civil rights struggle, but civil rights introduced political variables that could not be accommodated within the "neoclassical" model. Three sources of market disequilibrium, potentially capable of generating racial inequality, were proposed: an irrational prejudice or "taste for discrimination"; monopolistic practices, which grant "privileges" or "special benefits" to strategically placed groups, and hence create various interests and incentives for maintaining (or transforming) racial inequality; and disruptive state practices which interfere with the supposed equilibrating tendencies of the market (Becker 1971 [1957]; Williams 1982).

Focus on each of these three destabilizing forces generated three different (but related) accounts of the social dynamics of race. Note that all these accounts introduce a non-economic independent variable, which they argue disrupts the "normal" equilibrium of the market.

The *irrational prejudice model* attributes inequality to a white "taste for discrimination," essentially a sociocultural variable. In the socially disembedded economy presumed by neoclassical economics, discrimination would be irrational and costly to its practitioners. Therefore this model suggests that a society segregated into black and white sectors, linked as "trading partners" but separated by white "distaste" for blacks,[5] will be gradually integrated by market pressures. This was the analysis offered by (Nobel laureate) Gary Becker (1971 [1957]; see also Friedman 2002 [1962]). Perhaps the most "liberally" inclined Chicago-school economics don, Becker further amended his markets-only orientation in the 1971 revision of his book, to suggest that this "natural" overcoming of the "taste" will occur only if countervailing irrationalities can be tamed by limited and judicious state interventionism. Becker's model thus includes a place for the state to intervene usefully—though still on the side of re-equilibrating markets, of course. This puts him on the "left" side of market-based approaches to race.[6]

The *monopolistic practices model* suggests a society structured in the interests of all whites, who gain through a systematic transfer of resources from nonwhites in a wide variety of fields. Whites, for example, can receive wages above the marginal utility rate for their labor and benefit from discriminatory pricing practices. Whites become de facto *rentiers* (landlords) who derive benefits from their ownership or control of resources: access to jobs, business licenses, union cards, and the like. Whiteness is itself a resource: there is a white monopoly or "cartel" that operates comprehensively across U.S. society, as much locally as nationally. It imposes inequalities in labor, capital, and consumption goods markets in order to maximize white gain.

Competition over scarce resources motivates whites to act in exclusionary or discriminatory ways (i.e., monopolistically) toward people of color. This combines with such extra-economic resources as the authorized use of violence (racial harassment and profiling; state-based violence via policing, courts, prison) to place obstacles between people of color and access to a "free" market. All forms of exchange are involved: Access to food, housing, and basic services, for example, is truncated; what is available is elevated in price ("the poor pay more," and poverty is more prevalent among people of color). This amounts to a "race tax" that directs benefits to whites: for example, higher rents collected by white landlords, or steeper credit terms of mortgage rates offered to blacks or Latin@s, or real estate "steering."[7] Furthermore, the stresses and vulnerabilities associated with these practices—fear of public officials or police, anticipation of profiling or stereotype threat, pressure to "act white" (Steele 2010; Carbado and Gulati 2013)—also impose costs. According to this model various racial inequalities—even seeming political or cultural conflicts about affirmative action, profiling, or racial disparities in sentencing practices—can be explained by reference to imputed monopolistic market-based interests.[8]

In the *disruptive state interventionism* model, class/racial inequality is generated by state action on behalf of some racially defined group. There are several different versions of this account, each with its own ideological baggage. A *laissez-faire*, free market account accuses state policies such as minimum wage laws, labor laws, licensing procedures in labor-intensive trades (barbering, taxi-driving, trucking), and importantly, affirmative action, of disrupting market equilibrium and depriving people of the opportunity to compete fairly (Williams 1982; see also Katznelson 2005).[9] Such policies are to distort the market—here the labor market—on behalf of powerful political actors. Historically, they developed to assist whites in insulating their jobs from nonwhite competition; today in the form of affirmative action, they operate to assist nonwhites. In this account, people of color and capital share an interest in free market economics, which the state and white workers act to obstruct. Partially overlapping with this is the "split labor-market" account, a neo-Marxist position that also emphasizes the actions of "dominant" (white) workers in protecting their jobs and wages from "subordinate" (nonwhite) workers' competition. We discuss this below in the section about class conflict-based class theories of race.

Historically, struggles over control of labor, as well as over taxes, property rights, and other principally economic matters"—"political class struggle"—developed as industrial capitalism took hold in the United States. In this country—perhaps above all others—these conflicts were racially inflected. Before the Civil War, there was only a nascent working class in the strict sense of the term; white men were yeomen in the rural areas and artisans in the towns; work for wages emerged out of contract labor. Workshops and sweatshops appeared in the 1820s in New England, New York, and elsewhere (Dawley 2000 [1975]; Wilentz 2004 [1984]). There was a large number of enslaved black laborers, and (from the 1840s on) a semi-racialized group of impoverished and barely integrated immigrants, the Irish. "Native" white workers had been mobilized in the 1840s and 1850s against the Irish. After emancipation, both they and the (now-integrated) Irish feared competition from cheap black labor. In the West, Asian immigrants played the same threatening role. By the end of Reconstruction in 1877, each of these potentially explosive conflicts had been contained by a combination of state action and state-sanctioned political violence.

In the United States, the state has always regulated capitalist development by means of race-based law and racial policy-making. This has been evident in labor law, but operates in other spheres as well. For example, many previously marginalized Irish immigrants had fought in the Civil War,[10] obtaining citizenship and state recognition as a result. New York, Philadelphia, and Boston, among other cities, incorporated them into the Democratic Party machine politics of the period, directing city jobs their way and harvesting their votes in return (Katznelson 2005; Roediger 2005). Efforts to regulate labor conditions, form trade unions, and discipline capital were struck down by the Supreme Court—for example, in the *Lochner* case (U.S. Supreme Court 1905)—based on due-process arguments grounded in the 14th amendment, which had been designed to protect emancipated slaves' citizenship rights. Anti-Chinese riots on the West Coast in 1877 were quickly translated into state policy: The Chinese Exclusion Act was signed in 1882[11] and the California Chinese were driven out of hundreds of cities and towns by armed mobs, often led by police and state officials with torches and pitchforks ready to hand (Pfaelzer 2008). Exclusionist policies vis-à-vis Asian labor were soon firmly in place. After the *Plessy* decision in 1896 (and in many ways before), Jim Crow was institutionalized as state racial policy, severely curtailing black labor's competitive threat to whites (and also holding down white wages). In the South after Reconstruction's end in 1877, convict leasing was institutionalized by the state as a form of peonage on farms and in factories (Blackmon 2009).

Market exchange theories of race necessarily try to reconcile racial inequality with the equilibrium assumptions of their model, but as we show here, this is not really possible. In market theories, discrimination is irrational because it increases labor costs, so it should be driven out of the market by the force of competition itself. Its persistence can only be explained, therefore, by the extra-economic dimensions of racial formation: notably coercion and state action. Market approaches conceive of racial phenomena rather monolithically in terms of (in)equality and discrimination in exchange. Racial interests are either cast in these terms or assumed to be irrational.

Certain elements of the market-based approach overlap with views deriving from other paradigms. For example, the disruptive state interventionism model agrees with "colorblind" theories that racial policies should be guided by principles of individualism, and opposes demands for "equality of result." In similar fashion, the monopolistic practices model shares certain elements with nation-based analyses of race, especially those that stress the operation of "white privilege" or of a "colonial labor principle" which allocates rights and resources differentially to groups on the basis of race. There are innumerable theoretical coincidences, along with patterns of agreement and influence, in the vast literature on race. These resemblances, however, should not be mistaken for theoretical accord. Market-based theories (which are class-oriented, economic theories) are based on quite different perceptions of what race means than are ethnicity- or nation-based approaches.

Stratification Theory

Stratification approaches deal with the social *distribution* of resources—chiefly though not exclusively economic ones. Individuals receiving roughly equal incomes, or partaking of equal quantities of wealth, are deemed to have similar "life chances" and located in similar positions in the ranked hierarchy of classes.[12] Varying degrees of social mobility are postulated among the ranks of a racial hierarchy and numerous non-economic factors are seen as shaping the stratification system's maintenance and modification over time. Social networks, informal ties, elite recruitment, caste-like barriers or other forms of extra-market means of allocation of resources, often play a role here.

Politics are also a crucial factor. In stratification theory the relationships of elites and masses, the dynamics of authority systems and forms of domination, and the overall shape of sociopolitical conflict are central preoccupations. In most respects these extra-economic factors reinforce the distribution dynamic. Patterns of elite rule, for example, are frequently traced back to the distribution of economic resources.

Especially since the civil rights movement challenged the racial inequality that had been taken for granted (especially by whites) throughout U.S. history, there has been unending debate on the dynamics of racial stratification. What accounts for its persistence and depth? In what ways does it parallel and in what ways does it diverge from class stratification? There is no real dispute on its extent and depth: In a deeply unequal society, whose class-based disparities in wealth and income distribution greatly exceed all other countries at equivalent levels of "development"—Western Europe, Japan, Canada, Australia—inequalities along racial lines are far greater still. Whatever variable one chooses: wealth/income (in)equality, health outcomes, access to/returns to education, segregation by residence or occupation, rates of surveillance or punishment by the criminal "justice" system, or many other indicators that compare racial "life-chances," one finds strikingly persistent patterns. Black unemployment and poverty are consistently double that of whites (and increase greatly if we factor in incarceration). Median black wealth now stands at about 5 percent of white wealth, an appalling statistic. Disparities between whites and Latin@s, whites and Native Americans, and whites and some (not all) Asian American groups also remain very deep.[13]

Almost all the discussion of racial stratification is framed along the *race versus class* divide, although serious efforts have been made in sociology to synthesize the two axes of inequality in various theories of "eth-classes"; these run all the way from Milton Gordon's assimilation-oriented account (1964) to James Geschwender's neo-Marxist one (1977). There is a profound tendency to reify these two dimensions of inequality, which makes synthesis difficult social scientifically.

In experiential terms, of course, inequality is not differentiated by race or class. Impoverishment is concretely about suffering, whether it derives from race-based discrimination or class-based unemployment or superexploitation, or as is more likely, from a combination of the two. We consider all stratification-based accounts to be located within the class paradigm of race, because they all seek to explain measurable differences in "life-chances" by race. Here we compare two leading currents: class-based accounts, represented by the extensive work of William J. Wilson on this subject; versus race-based accounts, as embodied by the equally large body of work on this theme by Douglas S. Massey. These distinguished researchers' positions define the parameters of the stratification approach and encompass much, if not all, of the key work on racial inequality in the contemporary United States.

William J. Wilson made his foundational statement with *The Declining Significance of Race* (2012 [1978]), which he then followed up with *The Truly Disadvantaged* (2012 [1987]). His earlier work on race, *Power, Racism, and Privilege*, had been political sociological and comparative, with the United States and South Africa serving as his principal cases (Wilson 1973).[14] But *Declining Significance* shifted the focus in the later 1970s toward a center-left class analysis, and set the stage for Wilson's entire later *oeuvre.* The book addressed problems of racial inequality in the context of deindustrialization, as well as interpreting emerging class cleavages within the black community as functions of limited but real civil rights era reforms. Wilson accepted an economically determined theory of race-based stratification for previous epochs of U.S. history (an "economic system," he wrote, shaped the "polity" and thereby structured and enforced "racial norms"). He argued, however, that the civil rights reforms of the 1960s had allowed the state to develop "autonomy" in handling racial problems (2012 [1978], 17). According to Wilson, although black life-chances were formerly determined by racial stratification, after 1965 (that is, after the main civil rights reforms) they were shaped directly by class recomposition. After state-enforced racial inequality was eliminated by civil rights legislation, blacks were admitted to the society-wide system of stratification, rather than being confined by segregation and exclusion to limited numbers of jobs. But a mismatch arose in the cities, as manufacturing shrank and the remaining industrial work, as well as administrative labor, moved away. White flight, capital flight, and a widespread lack of both blue-collar and white-collar skills condemned most blacks to an "underclass" stranded in the ghetto. The black community was further stratified as well: A small privileged "class" emerged whose opportunities and status were effectively equivalent to those of whites with similar, high levels of training and skills. While a significant number of blacks obtained what were essentially middle-class jobs—many in the public sector—the massive black "underclass" was relegated to permanent marginality.

Echoing Bayard Rustin's "From Protest to Politics" (1964), Wilson argued that transracial alliances within the Democratic Party would best be able to combat the emerging austerity of the 1970s and 1980s, as well as to confront the developing racial reaction of the Republicans. By the time Wilson's book first appeared (1978), however, that reactionary trend had been underway for a decade at least. Nixon's "southern strategy" had driven a racial wedge into U.S. class politics, deepening political divisions that had long histories: white workers who had previously flirted with George Wallace and would soon become known as "Reagan democrats" were resonating with the Republicans' code words of "law and order" and anti-welfarism. They were not inclined to make common cause with inner-city blacks. Wilson's call for state policies that would counteract deepening class cleavages in the black community fell on deaf ears in the Democratic Party. For instance his support for an expansion of day care services available to low-income single mothers (Wilson 1980, 161) went nowhere. Cowed by Republican arguments against more state "giveaways" to be funded by hard working (i.e., white) people's tax dollars, destined for black "welfare queens," whose children's fathers were probably in jail or ought to be (Edsall and Edsall 1992; Hancock 2004), Democrats barely defended welfare rights or even civil rights after the advent of Reagan.

Leaving aside Wilson's framework of a 1960s shift from race-based to class-based explanations of black inequality (Pettigrew 1980; Steinberg 2001), other serious questions remain about *Declining Significance.* Wilson argued that since the mid-1960s a genuinely egalitarian racial state had existed in the United States, and that support for its policies was now a permanent feature of U.S. politics. If the turn to the right that began under "Nixonland" did not undermine this idea, later developments—such as Bill Clinton's 1996 "welfare reform"—did not reinforce Wilson's benign view of state racial policy either.[15]

Wilson's argument that the contemporary black community was now stratified into a relatively small privileged class and a large black "underclass" implied that race was no longer a salient linkage between those who have "made it" and their less fortunate "underclass" counterparts. While that position may have appeared plausible at the time, today the condition of the black middle class seems more fragile, not less, as job losses in the public sector have accelerated and the already huge chasms of income and wealth distribution have deepened enormously (Oliver and Shapiro 2006; Woldoff and Ovadia 2009; Rugh and Massey 2010; Squires and Hyra 2010; McKernan et al. 2011; Taylor et al. 2012). The distribution of wealth remains tied to race in increasingly brutal ways.

Wilson's empirical findings are not really in dispute. It is his conceptual framework that has attracted opposition: the notion that class divides have superseded racial ones within the black community. In more recent books and articles, Wilson has focused on what happens "when work disappears" (1997). A tremendous amount of literature has documented urban poverty and explored the conditions of the urban poor in the aftermath of deindustrialization (Edin and Lein 1997; Brown 1999; Duneier 2000; Newman 2000; Anderson 2009; Conley 2009). Even before the massive job losses and regressive redistributions of wealth that accompanied the Great

Recession after 2008, black (and brown) positions in the U.S. stratification system were shaky, both for middle- and lower-strata households. As middle-class, "coping stratum" teachers, postal workers, and other public-sector workers faced cutbacks, low- and semi-skilled workers in the private sector were decimated by outsourcing. The educational and job opportunities available to middle-class blacks are located disproportionately in the public sector. These positions were largely created as a result of civil rights reforms as well as other 1960s shifts to more inclusive social policies and redistributive measures.[16] Furthermore, many middle-class blacks work in industries and economic sectors whose economic and political *raison d'être* is linked to those masses. Government workers, educators, and other tertiary sector workers, for example, may have achieved middle-class status and incomes, but their employment relates directly to the management, marketing, and servicing of the black community as a whole.[17] In addition, the repressive state apparatus (to borrow Althusser's phrase) employs millions of people of color, mainly with the purpose of controlling or brutalizing other people of color. Lots of whites are employed in this work too, of course; we're talking about the police, prison guards, and the armed forces, together with their huge infrastructural and logistical bases.[18]

Black personal, familial, and community ties, not class-based ones, continue to connect the middle-class (or formerly middle-class) and lower-class strata, though Wilson's claims about deepening stratification within the black community remain accurate. Feeble attempts on the part of a few neoconservative black intellectuals to rally better-off blacks to the conservative banner have not availed.[19] Forty years of neoliberalism, first appearing during the Nixon years and then continuing largely unchecked—though mildly impeded by Carter, Clinton, and Obama—until the onset of the Great Recession in 2008, have massively eroded whatever evidence existed for black upward mobility. Ongoing assaults on the welfare state (by Democrats as well as Republicans), underfunding of public education, and restriction of health and social security benefits as well have proven detrimental, not only to the black "underclass," but to middle-class blacks as well.[20]

In a recent book, *More Than Just Race* (2009a), Wilson has largely abandoned his agenda of a cross-class alliance against poverty, no doubt because of the deep political polarization that now shapes U.S. debates about such matters as redistribution and public investment. Written before the election of Obama, the book renews and deepens Wilson's long-standing argument that racial inequality (black poverty) is the consequence of deindustrialization and globalization, most notably induced by "impersonal economic forces, which sharply increased joblessness and declining real wages among many poor African Americans in the last several decades" (2009a, 6).

In other words, as Sidney Willhelm (1970) said a generation earlier, "who needs the negro?" In response to these conditions, Wilson argues, poor blacks have adopted a "culture of poverty": since there are no jobs, drug-dealing and other criminal vocations are the only alternatives for young men—with the very high likelihood of arrest and incarceration. For young women, pregnancy and subsequent dependence on what remains of the welfare state are all too often the only "careers" imaginable. Wilson explains these conditions as "cultural" adaptations to the harsh "structural" conditions of the ghetto (the "inner city"), explicitly invoking the legacies of Daniel Patrick Moynihan, as well as Oscar Lewis's "culture of poverty" theories. And, once again, he argues for "race neutral" policies to overcome these dire conditions: Minimum wage jobs programs akin to those of the New Deal, and vocational training efforts as well are about the only recommendations he can envision in the effort to overcome poverty and inequality. And while he recognizes that blacks are the main victims of this dire situation, the relationship between poverty and race seems almost incidental in his account: The global capitalist economy took the jobs away; only a hardheaded social policy aimed at instilling a culture of higher motivation and greater personal responsibility can restore hope in the ghetto.

In contrast to Wilson's class-based account of the sources of racial inequality, Douglas S. Massey offers a race-based view. Massey grounds his research in demographic and human geography-based approaches to race. Although his work has focused extensively on segregation and anti-black racism, his career's main thematic emphasis has been on migration, particularly Mexican immigration to the United States. Massey's book *American Apartheid* (co-authored with Nancy A. Denton 1993) was written as a fairly direct response to Wilson's *The Truly Disadvantaged.* This was a breakthrough work on the subject of residential segregation, addressing both its structure and consequences. Segregation was measured empirically, using dissimilarity indices that not only indicate the degree of black–white "apartness" in given geographic areas (principally cities), but also show segregation trends over time.

A few years earlier Massey had published an important book on immigration: *Return to Aztlán* (Massey et al. 1987). This work was grounded in a transborder stratification model, in which migrants were seen as situated, informed agents of their own mobility and to some extent that of their communities.

Both books had an "ethnographic" dimension, but the focus in *Apartheid* was on black isolation, exclusion, and separation, while that in *Return* was on brown initiative and mobility. Race was a more peripheral matter in *Return*; in *Apartheid* it was central.

We see these two books—and Massey's enormous subsequent work in both areas—as the foundations of his extensive—indeed, career-long—effort to rework the study of racial inequality in the United States. Both racial segregation and Mexican migration have experienced shifting trajectories over the last decades. Although there has been no qualitative shift in patterns of black–white racial segregation, moderate declines in dissimilarity indices did occur during the 1990s and 2000s; these were reversed after the crash of 2008 and the onset of the great recession, when black–white racial inequalities expanded greatly. On the immigration side, ongoing increases in the Latin@ population, led by Mexicans, have reshaped U.S. racial demography. The earlier immigration reforms of 1965 and 1986, which both combined elements of legalization with new restrictions, greatly increased the number of legal residents and citizens of Latin American ancestry. Legal immigration was restricted in 1996, as a new wave of anti-immigrant hostility gathered force on the right-wing. New restrictive policies enacted during that year in parallel with reductions in welfare programs—both policies supported by Bill Clinton as part of his "triangulation" strategy—resulted in a jump in the undocumented immigrant population.[21] Further crackdowns and cutbacks, the emergence of a mass immigrants rights movement (2006), and failed efforts at further immigration reform (2007) all complicated the situation. Latin@s also suffered disproportionately in the great recession, and in the present are experiencing levels of discrimination that parallel those of blacks, although nowhere near the same extent of residential segregation.

Massey developed a theoretically grounded account of the U.S. stratification system in his 2008 book *Categorically Unequal.* Here for the first time he comprehensively linked his understandings of anti-black and anti-brown racism, arguing that the ongoing system of stratification in the United States can be traced back to a systematic, "categorical" racial inequality that was endemic throughout U.S. history and that operated through a "socially defined process of exclusion" (6). Massey argued that poverty, injustice, and human suffering, though shifting over time in accord with state policy (levels of inequality substantially fell during the 1945–1975 period, he points out), nevertheless exhibit an ongoing longevity and depth that is largely intractable. Inequality is the result of a combination of practices that he documents in detail: Social groups are framed conceptually through deeply ingrained cognitive processes that in his view are of an intrinsic, biological nature. Massey's relatively recent turn to intrinsic/biological explanations for the operation of racial difference strikes us as problematic. Immediate and preconscious perception of race, he says, is rooted in the less evolved parts of the brain:

> Emotions stored in the limbic system may be positive or negative, but when they are associated with particular classes of people or objects they contribute to prejudice, which is a predetermined emotional orientation toward individuals or objects....
>
> (Massey 2008, 10, emphasis original; Wheeler and Fiske 2005)

Though closely tied to the *implicit bias* literature, Massey's account exceeds that framework by arguing that prejudice derives from ineluctable features of human biology and evolution, rather than patterns of socialization, however deeply ingrained over multiple generations. This is not a trivial difference; it suggests that racism (and other forms of bias as well) are permanent and ineradicable, casting a shadow of deep doubt over social construction-oriented accounts of race. We return to this debate—which is of course quite extensive—in Chapter 4.

On the social level, in Massey's account human groups are understood as deserving or underserving, capable or incapable, fully human or inferior and despicable. The latter "lend themselves to exploitation with relative impunity, [and] encounter few defenders in society" (2008, 244). Inequality is thus built into social geography, patterns of labor, education, law enforcement, and citizenship, largely through legitimated discrimination:

> [S]tratification—the unequal allocation of material, symbolic, and emotional resources among social categories—is accomplished by establishing social mechanisms that operate according to one of two templates: exploitation or opportunity hoarding. Exploitation is the expropriation of resources from an out-group by members of an in-group, such that out-group members receive less than full value for the resources they give up. Opportunity hoarding is the monopolization by in-group members of access to resources so as to keep it [sic] for themselves or charge rents to out-group members in return for access. In contemporary America, the most common form of exploitation is discrimination within markets, and the most common form of opportunity hoarding is exclusion from markets and resource-rich social settings.
>
> (2008, 244)

Massey includes patterns of gender inequality and class inequality ("defined by access to human capital, or more specifically, education" [2008, 252]) in his account, and looks at inequality largely in terms of income, not wealth.[22] His emphasis on long-standing, deeply entrenched patterns of inequality overlaps in many ways with our claim that in the United States race is a "master category" of domination and inequality. Where we differ is over his reliance on a biologically grounded, cognitively rooted basis for human equality, and indeed over his idea that inequality is the basic framework through which race (and gender as well) should be understood. In Massey's view, the sociopolitical dimensions of race and racism play a secondary role in structuring race; pride of place goes first to the biological/evolutionary dynamics of inequality (i.e., where the term "categorically" is grounded), with the economic determinations running close behind (that's the business about "discrimination within markets" and "opportunity hoarding").

As in the case of market-based theories, stratification theories overlap with viewpoints originating in other paradigms. Where they emphasize "caste," that is, the closing-off of "mobility" in a status order with racial characteristics, they resemble certain nation-based views that deny the potential for integration across racial (or colonizer/colonized) lines (Dollard 1937 and Warner and Srole 1976 [1947]). Massey's (2008) account of the "categorical" nature of inequality is an example here, especially since he relies on that stubborn limbic system.

Where the stratification-based approach focuses on those characteristics of the system which facilitate mobility, such as the avenues available to various minority groups for economic advancement, it resembles ethnicity-based views. Shifting cultural norms, adaptations to new conditions in the labor market or to new educational opportunities, can allow improvements in SES for individuals, households, or even whole communities (Blalock 1967; Banton 1980). Wilson's account is an example here, with its stress on the significance of the civil rights reforms and its call for cross-racial, class-based alliances.

A notable feature of stratification approaches is the absence of attention to the political agency of people of color. Wilson thinks of racial politics in terms of the elite-led class-based alliances he hoped to cultivate as an advisor to Clinton and later, Obama. Massey's views of Mexican immigrants as pragmatic opportunity-maximizers, emphasized in much of his work on patterns of settlement, remittances, labor patterns and the like, has more in common with rational choice approaches than social movement ones, and is largely eclipsed by his "categorical" view, which relegates more radical aspirations to the historical dustbin. The mass mobilizations that challenged the Jim Crow system, that put millions of demonstrators in the streets of hundreds of U.S. cities on May 1, 2006, to demand immigrants' rights, that began to shift U.S. voting patterns in a majority-minority direction well before the 2008 presidential election, do not figure in these accounts. Neither of these writers, despite their immense contributions, can explain how egalitarian or social justice-oriented transformations could ever occur, in the past, present, or future.

Class Conflict Theory

"Classical" Marxism never explicitly addressed issues of race and racial conflict, but it did consider the problems of division within the working class and the nature of "national oppression." Of course, Marxism has had a profound impact on the class-based paradigm of race. As the modern civil rights movement developed after World War II, its radical wing necessarily drew close to Marxist currents. The "old left," which included both the Communist Party and its rivals, had been deeply involved in anti-racist struggles for decades. The "new left" was as much an offshoot of the civil rights movement as it was a successor to communist and socialist currents of the past. For both these broad currents, race and racism were central issues.[23]

Despite their anti-racist orientation, however, Marxists had difficulties in explaining racial inequality and racial conflict. This was because of the *primacy of class* in Marxist theory. From a Marxist standpoint, the key relationship in capitalism is that of production, the social relationship between the capitalist class and the working class, the owners and the producers. Marxism explains racial conflict as occurring within the "social relations of production," that is, in terms of class conflict. So this form of class theory begins with a class reductionist model driven by what C. Wright Mills called a "labor metaphysic": Racial conflict improperly divides the working class, whose fundamental struggle requires solidarity. Workers of the world, unite!

Just as in the market-based approach racial division (discrimination) within the labor force (the working class) appears disruptive to market forces and distorts the price mechanism, so in the Marxist framework racial division (discrimination) within the working class disrupts the class struggle and undermines (distorts) the revolutionary process. Thus for decades the orthodox Marxist position was that "racism is the bosses' tool." Thus too the slogan, "Black and white, unite and fight."

In the "post-civil rights" period this analysis took the form of *labor market segmentation* studies. An exemplary book by Michael Reich, *Racial Inequality* (1981), measured the effects of racial (in)equality on wage levels and on the distribution of social spending in such areas as education and welfare. Reich showed that class cohesion across racial lines correlated to higher wages, and that class segmentation across racial lines depressed wages overall, though less so for whites than blacks. He attempted to synthesize the class conflict and neoclassical modes of analysis. Here as elsewhere, to develop this argument it was necessary to "bring the market back in." Concerned to emphasize the structural aspects of discrimination, Reich employed the concept of "bargaining power theory." Because a working class that lacks unity will exercise less leverage over employers, Reich argued, "Capitalists benefit from racial divisions whether or not they have individually or collectively practiced racial discrimination" (Reich 1981, 269; see also Franklin 1991; Goldfield 1997; Roemer 2000; Martinot 2002). This analysis had much in common with the structural racism accounts we discuss elsewhere in this book.

An alternative Marxist scenario was *split labor market* theory, which emphasized white labor's efforts to limit competition from lower-paid minority workers (Saxton 1971; Bonacich 1972). Where unemployment is higher and competition from low-waged labor greater, white workers tend to support discriminatory (or exclusionist) policies even at the price of receiving lower wages themselves. This account pointed to the extensive U.S. historical record of white working-class racism. Notably it recognized that under conditions of high unemployment and slack demand for labor—conditions that have become endemic in recent years—capitalists and nonwhite workers have a common interest in maintaining a low-waged labor market.

The debate on the left between segmented and split, or class conflict vs. race conflict, theories, has been around for decades. The resemblance of these approaches to market-based theories of racial inequality is not surprising, because both accounts rest upon extra-economic, coercive capabilities based not in the labor-capital relationship—the "social relations of production" themselves—but rather in the political power of one class or another, or one class segment or another, to intervene in the labor market in defense of its interests. Historically, corporate influence has achieved some victories in this structured-in conflict, and labor pressure has achieved others. It is not coincidental, for example, that most "right-to-work" states have been concentrated in the South; this was the result of the 1948 corporate victory of passing the Taft–Hartley Act, and of overriding Truman's veto of the law.[24] This reinforces the "divide-and-conquer" argument. On the other hand, immigration restriction has historically been a demand both of white mobs and white unions; this orientation only began to shift in the 1970s as the consequences of the civil rights reforms set in, especially the 1965 immigration reforms.[25] In the debates over immigration law taking place as we write, many unions have taken positions supporting reform, especially public-sector unions with large numbers of immigrant members. Other unions—notably craft unions, police unions, and prison guard unions in California—have maintained their restrictionist positions (Zimring, Hawkins, and Kamin 2003).

In most cases race conflict at the "point of production" is not involved in class conflict approaches; this is a major limit on these arguments. There are some situations, however, where class conflict and race conflict do overlap very closely. Discrimination at "the point of production" can be identified, for example in the assignment of more dangerous or dirty work to workers of color (Oppenheimer 1974). The huge struggles in the auto industry in the 1970s—mainly situated in Detroit—pitted radical black workers not only against the big three auto makers (Ford, General Motors, and Chrysler) but also against the white-led United Auto Workers union (Geschwender 1977; Georgakas and Surkin 2012 [1975]). The Justice for Janitors movement, based in the Service Employees International Union, conducted a series of strikes that were explicitly anti-racist (Greenhouse 2006; Zlolniski 2006).[26] Important as these combined race/class struggles have been, however, they were exceptions to the secular trends of deindustrialization, increasing polarization of the racial wealth/income gap, and relentless assaults upon unions that have characterized the U.S. since the 1980s.

Some Critical Reflections on the Class Paradigm of Race

All three class-based approaches to race are limited by economic determinism. All three approaches necessarily emphasize racial inequality as the defining feature of race and the core dimension of racism. Their task then becomes explaining how race operates economically, how it is generated and reproduced in the key economic relationships of market exchange, resource distribution, and class conflict in production itself. This is a valuable but more limited understanding of race, an approach that reduces its importance to an ancillary aspect of inequality, an epiphenomenon of class. While inequality is a fundamental dimension of race and racism, race can no more be reduced to an economic matter than it can to a cultural or national one. Political factors, violence, psychological elements, and numerous other social relationships shape economic life as much as they are shaped by it.

Still, the class paradigm makes indisputable contributions to racial formation theory, principally by linking racial identity and racial collectivity to the most material human questions: How do we create and sustain ourselves materially, practically? Labor, food, health, housing, and education are central to the class paradigm. But putting inequality at the center also has its limits. Class-based theories of race, whether right, left, or in between, all always forced to look *outside the economic sphere* to obtain their causal, or independent, variables. In order to explain racial inequality one must turn to social and political processes and practices. One must *re-embed* the economy in the society: Culture, politics, and collectivity all come back into play.

Labor, and particularly labor markets, play a central role in all three varieties of the class paradigm. This is undoubtedly a result of economic thinking itself. Mainstream economics, while riven by conflicting tendencies, while dreaming desperately and recurrently of achieving a unified theory of the field, some form of "synthesis" (the neoclassical synthesis, the Washington consensus), still clings to a view of markets as autonomous and self-regulated entities, "disembedded" as Karl Polanyi (2001 [1944]) famously argued, from social and political conditions. In the real world, markets cannot be understood in this way, especially after the Great Depression of the 1930s, the contributions of John Maynard Keynes, the emergence of social democracy throughout the "developed" capitalist world, and the rise of the New Deal. All the class-based approaches we have discussed—the market-, stratification-, and class-conflict approaches—focus their attention on the role played by labor-market processes in determining racial inequality.

Market/exchange-based approaches focus most directly on labor markets and try to explain why discrimination and exclusion continue when, in strict "supply and demand," disembedded economic terms, such practices are inefficient and therefore should be eliminated. Unable to account for these outcomes within their pure market model, even such hardcore market theorists as Gary Becker and Thomas Sowell have identified exogenous, non-economic causal or independent variables as shaping discrimination, exclusion, and thus racism. Looked at more deeply, this calls into question much of standard economic theory, not just racial theories of racial inequality.

Distribution/stratification-based approaches also focus on labor—on the demand for black and brown labor—also determined by extra-economic factors. In William J. Wilson's view global economic pressures, combined with anti-racist political conflict (the civil rights movement and its elimination of official discrimination) have reshaped the demand for black labor. In Douglas S. Massey's view a deeply ingrained, biologically based inequality shapes U.S. society (and human nature across the board), ultimately generating power-holders' strategies for the isolation of blacks and the super-exploitation of Latin@s. Blacks' labor is less required than it was previously; it is more profitable to exploit blacks via the housing market—especially by using their housing as poker-chips in global capital markets, and by stigmatizing, profiling, and punishing them—than it is to invest in their labor, even at low wages, or in their education. Latin@ labor is available at a bargain. It competes favorably with black labor because it is not native; it is reproduced at low cost in the periphery. Latin@s and Asians can integrate into U.S. society in ways that black people cannot, not only because they are a lower-cost labor force, not only because in many cases they are closer to phenotypic whiteness, but also because for many immigrants it is still possible to remit wages, to subsidize a family in Mexico, Egypt, or Vietnam, say.[27] Here, once again, extra-economic factors, such as global flows of immigrant labor and the centrality of race as a key social and political dimension of U.S. society, shape racial inequality.

Until quite recently, *class-conflict/production-based approaches* were also unduly focused on labor. Older Marxist frameworks have been particularly limited by economic determinism in their understanding of race. Because of the difficulty of locating racial dimensions in production processes themselves, many neo-Marxist approaches turned to class divisions produced by discrimination or exclusion as the key variables explaining racial inequality. Some theories cast the capitalist class in the role of racist villain, arguing that it seeks to divide and demobilize the workers' movement. Others assigned this role to the white working-class, since white workers seek to make use of their racial privileges to protect their jobs and status. Either way, the consequence was the same: Intra-class division and competition along racial lines were seen to undermine class struggle. In this way class conflict theories reproduced not only market-based approaches and their limits, but also fell victim to the "labor metaphysic."

Already more than a quarter-century ago, it was clear that this account did not correspond with economic realities: As the U.S. economy became less nationally self-contained, as it was more engulfed by the global economy, as it became ever-more deindustrialized and financialized, intra-class conflict along racial lines became less central to inequality. Once the turn away from the New Deal/social democracy had begun in the mid-1970s, followed shortly thereafter by the full flowering of neoliberalism, more abstract forms of racism and more predatory forms of inequality"—"accumulation by dispossession" (Harvey 2004) and colorblind racial ideology most notably—had emerged to plague workers across the board, especially people of color.

Notes

1. Although the "Austrian school," with its premises of antistatism and individualism, is associated most closely with Hayek and Mises, other Austrian economists such as Schumpeter, Hilferding, and Goldscheid had very different views. See Heilbroner 2000 [1953].
2. Milton Friedman's views differed in many ways from those of his mentor Hayek (2001 [1944]). In sharp contrast to Friedman's monetarism, Hayek went so far as to disapprove of the state's issuance of money.
3. "Mainstream" economics thinks of the economy as "disembedded," a set of relationships driven by the rational action of those engaged in market exchanges. Market events and practices are considered distinct and separate from other types of social relationships. The mainstream was roughly characterized by Paul Samuelson in the 1960s as a "neoclassical synthesis" of Walrasian equilibrium theory and Keynesian theory. The disembedded model of economic life has always been subject to criticism, notably from Marxist and institutional economists. Critics point out that a wide range of human needs and relationships inevitably impinge upon, or even dominate and structure, actual market relationships. Subsistence requirements, human creativity, political organization, psychological processes, and numerous institutional factors must be taken into account in meaningful economic accounts. Karl Polanyi (2001 [1944]) produced perhaps the most sophisticated critique of "disembedded" economics, emphasizing among many other factors the impossibility of rendering land, labor, or money as commodities equivalent to others (such as needles and pins) produced for sale at market. We cannot adequately address Polanyi's

insights here, but in this chapter we make extensive use of his concept of the economy as a necessarily complex social relationship, shaped by politics, culture, psychological factors, and self-reflective action of every sort.

Ernesto Laclau's remarks on this same topic, made without reference to Polanyi, seem prophetic today, and highly relevant to the race–class relationship:

> I think the critique of economism should have a much wider deconstructive effect on traditional Marxist theory. That is, we should no longer conceive the economy as a homogeneous milieu that follows its own endogenous laws of development.... Today we can see that the space which traditional Marxism designated "the economy" is in fact the terrain of a proliferation of discourses. We have discourses of authority, technical discourses, discourses of accountancy, discourses of information. Even categories such as profit can no longer be accepted as unequivocal. For instance, a multinational corporation today develops complex political and economic strategies within which the search for profit certainly plays a fundamental role, but does so within a whole policy of investment which can often require sacrificing immediate profits to wider strategic aims. The functioning of the economy itself is a political functioning, and cannot be understood in terms of a single logic. What we need today ... is a non-economistic understanding of the economy, one which introduces the primacy of politics at the level of the "infrastructure" itself. (Laclau and Mouffe 1982, 92; see also Mouffe 1983)

4. Sir William Arthur Lewis was another Nobelist (1979), an Afro-Caribbean (born in St. Lucia). A black intellectual pioneer, he was most certainly not oblivious to race. His early work on development has been applied to current conditions in China, Southeast Asia, and elsewhere. Where the "unlimited supplies of labor" are located, how they are recruited, and what their practical conditions are, are all consummately racial matters; indeed they are some of the core issues of the "modern world-system."
5. This "taste" business is merely a euphemism for prejudice or Negrophobia. We find it doubly unacceptable: as the bias that it embodies and as the crude disguise by which it is euphemized.
6. Becker's major innovation is introducing psychological factors into economic analysis, thus taking a step toward overcoming the image of a socially "disembedded" market. As the field has spiraled into deeper intellectual crisis, Becker has assumed higher status. The revised version of the book was undoubtedly influenced by the civil rights movement. On Becker's account, see Reich 1981, 86–88.
7. "Steering" is simply an economic form of profiling. Customers are steered—with race as a central orienting factor in the practice—to "appropriate" neighborhoods. Mortgage borrowers are steered to sub-prime and Alt-A loans—featuring deceptive interest rates, hidden "balloon" payments, "bundling" procedures, and extremely high foreclosure rates. These were particularly profitable during the real estate boom years of the late 1990s and 2000s. "Blockbusting" practices in the 1950s and 1960s were a more open form of steering. Such activities were supposedly outlawed by fair housing and fair credit legislation in the later years of the civil rights era. In more covert ways, however, many of these practices are still flourishing. See Satter 2009.
8. This account overlaps in numerous ways with white privilege theories (Allen 2012 [1994; 1997]; Wildman et al. 1996; Williams 2003; Lipsitz 2006).

9. "There is a 'moral [and] constitutional equivalence' between laws designed to subjugate a race and those that distribute benefits on the basis of race in order to foster some current notion of equality. Government cannot make us equal; it can only recognize, respect, and protect us as equal before the law. That [affirmative action] programs may have been motivated, in part, by good intentions cannot provide refuge from the principle that under our Constitution, the government may not make distinctions on the basis of race" (Thomas 1995).
10. Many young Irishmen were purchased as substitutes in the Union army draft by better-off citizens; many others were drafted; still others rioted in New York in 1863, attacking free blacks (blacks were excluded from the draft) and black neighborhoods. See Harris 2003.
11. The Act was supposed to suspend Chinese immigration for ten years; in fact it remained in effect for 60 years, until it was finally repealed by the Magnuson Act in 1943.
12. Stratification theories of class have their origins in Max Weber's critique of Marx; for Weber class position is shaped by relationship to the means of distribution, not production. It's income and wealth, baby: what you receive, not what you put into the economy, that shapes your class or "life-chances." See Gerth and Mills 1958.
13. For data on black–white economic inequality see Taylor et al. 2012; Oliver and Shapiro 2006. For good overview material on racial inequality, see O'Connor, Tilly, and Bobo, eds. 2001. For data on residential segregation, see Iceland, Weinberg, and Steinmetz 2002; Massey et al. 2009. For data on incarceration, see Mauer 2006. For data on educational segregation, see Frankenberg and Orfield, eds. 2012. For data on workplace segregation, see Hellerstein and Neumark 2005. For data on racial attitudes and racial politics, see Bobo 2001; Dawson 2003.
14. Racial stratification/inequality already received significant attention there, but largely as the outcome of despotic power relations organized along racial lines. Reflecting the influence of the civil rights movement, Wilson introduced his subject this way:

    > [C]onsidering the nature of both United States and South African race relations, I have given concepts of "racism" and "power" special attention in this study. In fact, the central arguments of this volume are (1) that a comprehensive account of the nature of race relations in these two societies must deal with the dimensions of power and their relation to dominant- and minority-group contact, and (2) that the dimensions of power cannot be completely understood if treated independently of the phenomenon of racism. (1973, 5)

    In this work Wilson not only also explored racial stratification, but also considered in depth the political conditions under which anti-racist protest operated in the two countries, the significance of biologistic racism, and a host of other topics that were largely left aside in his later work.
15. Wilson served as an adviser to Clinton, and has also consulted with Obama, whose "post-racial" efforts certainly resonate with Wilson's work.
16. Anti-poverty, Headstart, affirmative action programs, the rise of multiculturalism and diversity criteria in hiring, education, and public service provision, exemplified these shifts. Many such programs have been eviscerated under the neoliberal project, the decades-long right-wing effort to curtail social expenditures.
17. On this point Wilson's views converge with neocon/neoliberal abhorrence of "dependency" on the welfare state. Wilson argues that the black "underclass" is to some extent produced by this "dependency." While he notes that public sector employment has been

the chief route to black middle-class status, he does not engage the ongoing relationship of the black middle class and the "underclass."

18. On the situations of blacks and other people of color employed in the criminal "justice" system, see Ward 2006. On people of color in the military, see Latty and Tarver 2005. On black cops, see Bolton and Feagin 2004.
19. On this group, see Roberts 1996; Boston 1998; Ondaatje 2009. Some of the most durable black conservatives have been John McWhorter, Robert Woodson, Thomas Sowell, and Walter Williams. Economist Glenn Loury, after an early sojourn on the black right, moved back to the center in the Bush II years. It is instructive to compare the new ethos of "black conservatism" with classic works on the subject, notably Frazier 1957a.
20. In respect to health care, the Affordable Care Act ("Obamacare") may represent a partial reversal of the entrenched abandonment of the health rights of poor people (disproportionately black and brown). We must await the law's full implementation in 2014. In respect to welfare, it is important to note that despite Clinton's abandonment of cash-grant welfare (AFDC) in 1996, he did greatly expand the Earned Income Tax Credit (EITC) which was a substantial gain for the working poor.
21. By adopting a number of Republican-backed, racially inflected policies Clinton sought to immunize himself from white working-class voter discontent in the 1996 election year. This voting bloc—are they still the "Reagan Democrats"?—remains a significant force today: They are disproportionately male, blue-collar voters who have experienced increased economic vulnerability for decades; they are anti-welfare, anti-immigrant, right-wing populist, inclined toward the "Tea Party," and vote Republican (Frank 2005).
22. Perhaps because his book appeared before the onset of the great recession of 2008, Massey understates contemporary inequalities somewhat, especially with regard to recent developments such as loss of assets through foreclosure and sustained unemployment. In later work Massey has addressed foreclosure patterns and race (Rugh and Massey 2010).
23. The extensive history of "black–red" relationships, and also other communist and socialist relationships with anti-racist movements, is beyond our present scope. Some important contributions are Sale 1973; Allen 1974; Horne 1986; and Pulido 2006.
24. More recently the "right-to-work" (anti-union) strategy has been making gains outside the South, most notably in the intermountain West and in some midwestern states as well (Indiana and Michigan). Where this has occurred, there have been significant attacks against public-sector unions and against social "safety-net" programs, attacks that usually mobilize coded racist tropes (Fraser 2012). Taft–Hartley's original success in 1947 was based on a tactical alliance between Southern Dixiecrats (i.e., Democrats) and right-wing Republicans based in the Midwest.
25. The United Farmworkers—a very important case—supported immigration restrictions until after the death of Cesar Chavez in 1981. See Bardacke 2012.
26. In 2008 an explicitly anti-racist workers' movement carried out a sit-in against offshoring at the Chicago factory of Republic Windows and Doors, occupying the factory and forcing its reopening (Cullotta 2009).
27. Space is not available here to explore the role of the periphery in capitalist reproduction. World-system theory in general acknowledges the subsidization of the core global capitalist economy by its hinterlands, not only in terms of reducing the costs of labor reproduction but also by furnishing cheaper raw materials, absorbing pollution, and

externalizing other costs as well. This line of argument goes back through Immanuel Wallerstein to Rosa Luxemburg. Consider:

> The imperialist phase of capitalist accumulation which implies universal competition comprises the industrialization and capitalist emancipation of the *hinterland* where capital formerly realized its surplus value. Characteristic of this phase are: lending abroad, railroad constructions, revolutions, and wars. (Luxemburg 1973 (1913), 399; emphasis original; see also Schmidt 2010)

The hinterland today is the immigrant-sending area, whether in the periphery or the semiperiphery in Wallerstein's terms (1974–1989). Let us say that here in rural Zacatecas, a young migrant begins her journey to the lettuce-fields of Arizona or domestic service in Beverly Hills. To produce this worker has cost U.S.-based employers (and U.S. tax-payers) almost nothing. If formally employed and undocumented, her payroll tax payments accrue to the benefit of the Social Security Trust Fund, not to her future retirement income. If settlement in the United States is not an option after years of immigrant labor, her remittances and savings, accumulated in an immigrant household or community, might permit the construction of a cinderblock house with shingled roof, water well, and indoor plumbing where previously only a *bohio* (shack) had stood. On these issues, see in general Massey et al. 1987. The racialization of the periphery, the phenomic or diasporic link between the hinterlands of Mexico and the Mexican-American economy, needs greater attention than we can provide here.

CHAPTER 3

Nation

Introduction

The *nation-based paradigm* of race originates in seizures of territory by modern empires. The European conquest of the Western hemisphere, and the colonies that resulted, both extended the practice of "nation-building" that was central to imperial ventures,[1] and laid the groundwork for later, insurgent nationalist projects that would challenge and eventually overthrow these same empires.

In this chapter we explore the nation-based paradigm of race in the United States, focusing largely on post-World War II events. We begin by discussing *the white nation*, the historically dominant construct of the "American people." We note the centrality of whiteness in enabling the nation's expansion and rise to power on the world stage; we also recognize the instability and anxieties of white nationalism. Next, we discuss *race/class/gender/nation*, the intersectional cleavages and conflicts that shaped the white nation from its colonial origins through independence and beyond. From the beginning, there were *insurgent nationalisms* that were hallmarks of early resistance to the white nation, and that re-emerged among racially subaltern people in the postwar United States. Building on earlier religious, panethnic, and sometimes revolutionary forms of resistance, and linking their struggles to global anti-imperialism, new nationalist movements were launched after World War II. "Black power" nationalism was the most established and embedded form of these, but important nationalist projects were also developed during those years in Latin@, Native American, and Asian American communities as well (Pulido 2006; Joseph, ed. 2006).

The chapter concludes with *some critical remarks on the nation-based paradigm of race*. Here we focus on the limits of the race–nation equation, the nation-based paradigm's inherent incompleteness regarding race. We evaluate the uneven democratic commitments of nationalist politics; we consider the problem of transracial relations and alliances within the nation-based paradigm; and we reflect on the uncertain significance within it of class- or culture/ethnicity-based identities and social positions.

The White Nation

For five centuries the phrase "the American people" has been understood as an implicitly white designation. This understanding predates the achievement of national independence in the American Revolution and ignores or dismisses the continuing presence—in substantial numbers—of people not considered white. In other words, almost from the beginning of European settlement there has been a dominant white nation in North America. The colonies and the post-revolutionary independent U.S. state all explicitly celebrated their whiteness, and always took it for granted.

But the congruence of race and nation has never been a done deal, and periodically it has been necessary to tinker with the equation of whiteness and American identity. The United States has passed through numerous cycles of racial politics: Despotic moments have alternated with democratic ones; harder and softer racial regimes have taken the stage. Slavery, genocide, conquest, and empire all mess with the homogeneity implicit in the concept of a white nation. Immigration and exclusion also call the nation's assumed foundational whiteness into question. There have been various iterations of nativism and legalization, for example, and alternating trajectories of racial reform and backlash. These also parallel global developmental processes, in ways too complicated to detail here.[2]

White rule in North America, before and after 1776, has always been riven by racial conflict. The centrality of white/male/property-holders' rule has been both taken-for-granted and unstable. There have continually been two contradictory principles at work: national unity and racial division. To fuel and justify first the colonial impulse and later the nation-building process, race has served as what Antonio Gramsci called an ideological "glue" (Gramsci 1971, 328). Race operated as a multi-leveled organizing principle that established who was "civilized" and who was "savage," who was "free" (and hence human), and who was a slave (chattel, not a person). Race linked the corporeal/visible characteristics of different social groups to different sociopolitical statuses, and provided various religious and political principles for inclusion and exclusion from the imagined community (Anderson 2006) of the nation.

In the United States, the trope of the white nation—the forging of unity and solidarity among white rulers and their white subordinates—has time after time overwhelmed nonwhite or transnational (class-based, diasporic, hemispheric) conceptions of the nation and its peoples (Morgan 2003 [1975]). Oppositional nationalisms (from groups of color) have often faltered; they have repeatedly been subdued or absorbed. Yet uncertainty remains about the coherence of the "white nation" and white "peoplehood." The intelligibility and collectivity of whiteness were first cast into doubt after the Civil War, when the 14th Amendment to the U.S. Constitution extended U.S. citizenship and ostensible equality to the emancipated slaves. The white republic (Saxton 2003 [1990]) experienced numerous subsequent crises: over Asian immigration, relations with Latin America, and the extension of U.S. imperialism (previously a continental matter) overseas at the turn of the 20th century. The reactionary racism all this inspired continues to operate today.

During and after World War II, white peoplehood was problematized again, not only in the United States but on a worldwide level: by the traumatic and galvanizing experience of the war itself; by the rising tides of anticolonialism and anti-racism the war fostered; by the mass migrations it set in motion within the United States (and globally); and by the Cold War, which was waged on racial terrain in many ways; and above all by the political struggles for racial justice and democracy that took shape after World War II, not just in the United States but all over the world.[3]

So, white racial nationalism both built and fractured the United States. It unified whites across tremendous chasms of class and culture/ethnicity, precisely because it allowed them to claim their whiteness, sometimes with ease and sometimes only after passing through extended "probationary" periods. The racial cleavages we see in the nation are the products of the exploitative and exclusionist commitments of the white nation: its deracination of the indigenous inhabitants of North America; its capture, killing, transport in chains, and enslavement of millions of Africans; its conquest of adjacent territories and its relegation of their inhabitants to lesser status; and its massive dependence on immigration, mostly on the part of people not considered (or not yet considered) white. Thence cometh the divided and hierarchical peoplehood, the stratified and conflictual nation, the United States of America.

From the earliest days of U.S. national independence, Anglo-Saxonism and "anglo-conformity" helped create a norm of whiteness that shaped the national image and culture. State policy sometimes relaxed and sometimes tightened the boundaries of citizenship, but always reflected restrictive norms. Expansionism and economic interest linked "nation-building" and domestic labor recruitment to foreign policy and empire-building: Not only the "turning of Africa into a warren for the commercial hunting of black-skins" (Marx 1967, 351) but also Indian removal (i.e., ethnic cleansing; genocide) and hemispheric domination (after the 1823 Monroe Doctrine) were established principles by the early 19th century (Gonzalez 2011 [2001]).

Internally as well, citizenship was assigned or withheld according to racial criteria. The 14th Amendment notwithstanding, blacks only became citizens in a practical sense in the 1960s, and even then imperfectly; many Asians only achieved naturalization rights in the 1950s; and native peoples only received their citizenship in the 1920s. Stringent immigration restrictions were imposed on Asians after the upheavals of 1877, and on Europeans after the great influx that occurred around the turn of the 20th century. After World War I the screws were further tightened on immigration through highly restrictive policies that would endure for forty years. Mass deportations to Mexico occurred in the 1930s, with no regard given to whether the Latin@s rounded up (in Los Angeles and elsewhere) were U.S. citizens or not; a brown skin was all you needed to be placed on a sealed train to Jalisco or Michoacan (de Genova 2004; Balderrama and Rodriguez 2006 [1995]). Immigration raises large questions about national identity, about the meaning of citizenship, and about global inequality (Smith 2003; Massey, ed. 2008). Indeed the U.S. immigration regime has profoundly shaped the patterns of racial inclusion and exclusion

The common sense view of "the nation" has always been explicitly inflected by race. The United States was perceived as "a white man's country," a *herrenvolk* republic. This identification of the nation with whiteness (and maleness) was a nearly universal feature of imperial and settler nations.[4] Nativism (Higham 2002 [1955]; Saxton 1975) periodically flamed up when immigrants were seen as threats, just as anti-black racism and contempt for indigenous peoples underwrote state racial policy in both colony and metropole.[5] Despite the penchant for "exceptionalist" accounts of U.S. nationhood (Lind 1995; Zelinsky 1988; Lipset 2003 [1963]; Billig 1995 offers a good critique), the United States was no exception to this "rule of racialization" (Martinot 2002). Indeed, it was the rule's pioneer.

How white is the U.S. nation? The question of who makes up the American nation, indeed the question of what is the racial identity of the American nation remains unanswered. "Your country? How came it yours?" asked Du Bois in 1903. "Before the Pilgrims landed we were here. . . ." (Du Bois 2007 [1935], 162–163). And Native Americans had been "here" perhaps 25,000 years before that, according to paleoarchaeologists. Indeed, what we now call the United States of America only became "yours"—a white country—when first it fell under English imperial rule around the turn of the 17th century. It remained "yours" after it freed itself from that rule after 1776 in the first modern revolution. It is still "yours" in many respects. It has been a "white man's country" through conquest, settlement, and expansion, through slavery and emancipation, through continuing immigration, and through ascent to a global imperialism of its own, until finally becoming the greatest empire in world history.

But, white men, is the country still "yours"? Starting after World War II and in parallel with similar race-oriented conflicts elsewhere, the concept of "the American people" has become less white and less patriarchal. The United States is darkening, demographically speaking. Because of the black movement and the feminist movements it inspired—not only in the post-World War II period but continually since abolition—the country is less definitively a white male nation than it used to be, and that trend is continuing.[6] The U.S. racial regime has been losing momentum, both internally as a white republic, and globally, as the leading "developed" economic and military power. Patriarchal power is eroding as well. Of course, the age of the white and male nation is not over, at least not yet. But that nation is being undone; whether gradually or rapidly we do not know.

Especially since the imperial dawn, the ideas of race and nation have been deeply connected, mainly through concepts of *peoplehood.* Both as outposts of the British Empire (and to some extent of other European empires as well), and then as an independent nation-state, the United States (and its forerunners) identified itself as a *white nation.* This racial nationalism remains visible in the associations with whiteness that are implicit in such concepts as "the American people." The nation is gendered as well: the motherland, the fatherland, *patria o muerte.* Throughout the modern era the nation has been racialized. This proceeds from its imperial origins: its seizure of bodies (indigenous people, Africans), and of land as well, for purposes of primitive accumulation. Racialization is discussed in more detail in Chapter 4. Here it refers to the process of sorting out the bodies.

In the wake of the civil rights era, in the aftermath of the postwar racial "break," the meaning of the terms "nation" and "nation-state" in the United States must be carefully examined. What is in question here is "peoplehood." The general tendency is still to see the United States as a WASP nation, not only white, but Anglophilic and Protestant. U.S. national*ism* is still a strong tendency: particularly on the right, particularly in the "heartland" and in the "red" states, but not only there. Nationalism is also a civil religion and a working-class creed that cuts across racial lines.

At the same time, the standard racialized and gendered picture of the United States—as a "white man's country"—is breaking down. Significant portions of U.S. territory are now occupied in the majority by people who are not white. "Majority-minority" demographics now obtain in California as well as several other states and major cities, and in many other places that condition is not far off. A recent projection by the U.S. Department of the Census places the national transition to a "majority-minority" demographic in the year 2042 (U.S. Bureau of the Census 2008).

Race/Class/Gender/Nation

In early North America, race, class, and gender were deeply interlinked. Their amalgamation was established both by the necessity of developing a division of labor, an organized labor force; and by the necessity of supplying, through various forms of human trafficking (only some of which can be labeled as "voluntary immigration") the steady flow of actual human bodies (and souls) that would constitute the North American population.

An endemic and taken-for-granted national chauvinism consigned blacks and Indians to inferiority and subhumanity. This condition, this absence of fully human status, was supposedly permanent. As the settler nation expanded westward, the right of conquest and the license of the "pioneers" to deprive the Indians of life and land was never seriously questioned from within the white regime.[7] Although armed Indian resistance slowed the advance of the European-led tide, it could not, in the end, repel it. The centrality of slavery and the "primitive accumulation" of Indian lands in early American life meant that race and not class was the key social division both in the colonial period and after.[8]

What about other "others"? The Irish had been trafficked by the hundreds of thousands during the colonial period. In a British colonial outpost they were racialized as nonwhite, though generally subject to indenture, not chattelization (Jordan and Walsh 2008; Allen 2012 [1994; 1997]). The millions of Irish immigrants who arrived in the 1840s, driven by British-imposed famine, were exposed to the torches and pitchforks of mobs inflamed by nativism, and subject to racial discrimination as well. In the Civil War the Irish made good cannon fodder, especially in the North. Irish service in the Union armies (when they couldn't buy substitutes and anti-black riots didn't prevent their being drafted) finally launched them on the path to whiteness. The Civil War made many immigrant Irish members of the American nation.

The invasion of Mexico and subsequent incorporation of the Southwest, from the annexation of Texas in 1845 through the Treaty of Guadalupe Hidalgo in 1848, accomplished an enormous conquest of territory. Initially transferring their citizenship to the United States and retaining their land rights and titles, the Mexican population of this huge territory were progressively disenfranchised and stripped of their land (Pitt 1999 [1966]; Almaguer 2008 [1994]; Gomez 2008).

Post-Civil War industrialization augmented labor demand and European immigrant numbers increased. The floodgates would remain open to European arrivals for decades. But the ending of Reconstruction in 1877, the great railroad strike of that year, and the general economic crises of the 1870s combined with the rise of anti-Asian nativism to put new pressure on the white nation framework. Blacks were now citizens, but their labor (and that of Asians who were mere denizens, largely in the West) threatened the cross-class alliance that the white nation had maintained since colonial times. Additional threats came from mobilized white labor. Huge strikes and bitter labor conflict swept the nation, particularly in 1877 and 1894. Redrawing the boundaries of the white nation was essential for the development of U.S. capitalism. Class conflict could be controlled to some extent by the gradual whitening of European labor (Montgomery 1987; Saxton 2003 [1990]). This was not accomplished by any legislative decree or capitalist maneuvering to divide the working class, but rather by white workers themselves. Many of them were recent immigrants, who organized on ethnic lines as much as on traditionally defined class ones.

Race shaped class in America, then, because of the demand for territorial expansion, because racial slavery was crucial to the development of the early nation, and because whiteness played an important role in deterring rebellion and undermining popular transracial (i.e., class-based) solidarity (Morgan 2003 [1975]; Du Bois 2007 [1935]; Blight 2002).

Gendered practices were central to nation-building as well. Just as there was a "racial frontier" in the settlement of the United States, so too was there a "gender frontier."[9] As Ann Laura Stoler puts it, "Intimate domains—sex, sentiment, domestic arrangement, and child rearing—figure in the making of racial categories and in the management of imperial rule" (Stoler 2001, 829; see also Stoler 2002; Schiebinger 2004). In practice these two boundaries were often indistinguishable. From its earliest moments North American colonialism involved sexual encounters between Europeans and Indians; these became fodder for fiction and fantasy, and later for Hollywood films as well (Nash 1995). Some settlers "went native" (Torgovnick 1991; Ware 1992; McClintock 1995; Cooper and Stoler 1997; Caslin 2008). Miscegnation[10] was inevitable and widespread. Hence mixed-race children and families; hence the immediate problematization of racial categories.

The plantation, and African slavery overall, were also obviously gender frontiers (Williamson 1995). Rape and concubinage were commonplace. These practices were barely stigmatized because they were so widespread. Not unlike other colonial systems, U.S. nation-building from its earliest moments featured widespread interracial sex/racial hybridity/*mestizaje*/*métissage*.[11]

These currents have all continued up through the present. Still, the maintenance of "patriarchal authority and power, racial hierarchy, and white supremacy"

(Woodward 1998), for all its horrors, was never monolithic, never without opposition. Subversion, escape, revolt, and political mobilization (via abolitionism and, later, anti-imperialism and immigrants rights), all exposed the conflictual and indeed contradictory character of the white nation.

To the extent that the legitimacy of the white nation—with its almost unbroken history of structural racism, its history of slavery, violence, exclusion, and dispossession—is not accepted by racially subordinated groups, alternative national frameworks may be adopted by those groups as insurgent concepts, as an "imagined community" in rebellion.

Insurgent Nationalism

The national dimensions of nonwhite racial identities, the experience of collectivity and solidarity along racial lines, and the sense of collective identity ("peoplehood") among distinct—and often panethnic—peoples of color, were key dimensions of the national liberation and anticolonial struggles of the post-World War II period. The national impulse remains strong, as a form of cultural identification (where it overlaps with ethnicity); as the form of various nationalist movements; and as a general signifier of race-based community: the ghetto, the barrio, Koreatown. These recognitions—about the ever-problematic white nation and white nationalism, and about the continuing exclusion, denial of political and human rights, and discrimination experienced by peoples of color—all underlie the nation-based paradigm of racial formation.

So while white racial unity certainly fueled a great deal of nation-building zeal over the course of U.S. history, it also bred its own opposition. Perhaps ironically, some of the most committed adherents to the democratic ideals professed since the founding of the United States have been those to whom the white nation denied democratic rights and full membership; think again of Du Bois: "Your country? How came it yours...?" For those like Du Bois (especially the later Du Bois [Porter 2010]), Malcolm X, José Angel Gutiérrez, Russell Means, or Bobby Seale, inclusion in the white nation that was the United States, was never fully possible. Hence they saw themselves not only as Americans, but also as part of other, insurgent peoples, of various sorts: Pan-African, irredentist, anti-imperial, internally colonized.

As the limits of the civil rights reforms of the mid-1960s became clear, a substantial sector of the movement turned toward nationalist positions. This shift occurred first within the black movement, where long-standing discontent with civil rights moderates was most established, and where the immediate experience of betrayal was most galling: One example—out of many—was the experience of SNCC (Student Nonviolent Coordinating Committee) at the 1964 Democratic convention in Atlantic City, New Jersey.[12] SNCC's adoption in 1965 of a "black power" orientation was followed in the next few years by the emergence of red power, brown power, and yellow power movements.

The upsurge of black nationalism in the mid-1960s definitively ruptured the already tenuous unity of liberal and radical tendencies within the civil rights movement. It signaled a growing disillusionment with the moderate political agenda of non-violence and integration. The slogan "black power," and the growing popularity of black nationalism that it expressed, also initiated an intense theoretical and strategic debate about the nature of racism and the future of black politics in the United States. It followed the split in the Nation of Islam and the emergence of Malcolm X as the most visible black nationalist leader in the country.[13] It coincided with Lyndon Johnson's escalation of the Vietnam war and the emergence of the anti-war—and in a broader sense, anti-imperialist—movement. It also overlapped with a new phenomenon in U.S. racial politics: black-led, black-based ghetto rebellions (aka race riots), beginning with Harlem in 1964 and Watts in 1965.[14]

The nation-based analysis of black oppression and resistance had, of course, its historical antecedents. The refusal of assimilationism could be traced back at least to Ethiopianism and the repatriation movements of the mid-19th century, led by men such as Martin Delany, Edward Wilmot Blyden, and Paul Cuffe.[15] The Pan-Africanist and Marxist-Leninist traditions had also elaborated nationalist analyses, and a substantial current of cultural nationalism also existed whose components could be discerned in Du Bois's *The Souls of Black Folk* (1999 [1903]), in the Harlem Renaissance of the 1920s (Locke, ed. 1997 [1925]), and in the influential writings of Harold Cruse (1967, 1968), to name just a few sources. Strong nationalist traditions can also be found in all communities of color, notably among Puerto Ricans, Mexican Americans, and Native Americans.

The nation-based paradigm, to a far greater extent than the ethnicity- or class-based approaches, is a theoretical convergence, a resultant of disparate currents. Nationalist currents had always existed in the United States, notably in the black church (Rawick 1972; Moses 1998; Glaude 2000). Nation-based approaches to race also have a long theoretical fetch; this is the profound and variegated black political tradition, excluded for centuries from mainstream (white) intellectual and political discourse.

Rooted in the resistance to empire and colonialism, insurgent nationalisms logically invoke racial criteria in their efforts to theorize and mobilize opposition to white supremacist rule. Once again, "peoplehood" is a central concern. Who are black people, Latin@s, Native Americans, Asian Americans? In what historical, political-economic, and cultural conditions were these peoples created? In what ways are these groups' claims for self-rule, land, and freedom justified? How do imperial and colonial structures of power persist in the contemporary, ostensibly postcolonial world, the "modern world-system"?[16] How are they maintained, indeed, in the very contours of the international division of labor, based on unequal exchange and the domination of the "periphery" by the "core"? In the nation-based paradigm, racial dynamics are understood as products of colonialism and therefore as outcomes of relationships which are global and epochal in character.[17]

Framing the nation-based paradigm to emphasize "peoplehood" and post-coloniality has several advantages. First, it stresses the relationships among the different elements of racial oppression—inequality, political disenfranchisement, territorial and institutional segregation, cultural domination—in contrast to the ethnicity or class paradigms which focus on a few aspects (or even one "fundamental" aspect) of the social order in an attempt to explain racial dynamics. Recognition of the centrality of the colonial heritage also provides an alternative to other, more taxonomic approaches to nation-based theories of race. Many writers have delineated, for example, "varieties of black nationalism": bourgeois, proletarian, reformist, revolutionary, cultural, religious, economic, educational (Allen 1990 [1970]; Van Deburg 1996; Hanchard 2006). While efforts to catalog the range of nationalist positions within specific minority group traditions, and to trace debates within these traditions, obviously have merit, they often reveal a notable lack of specificity about the meaning of nation-based categories in such approaches. Nationalism is easily reduced to mere group militance or separatism if no effort is made to specify its historical and theoretical origins in particular racially defined peoples' experiences of colonialism.

Here we offer an all-too-brief examination of a few of the main insurgent nationalist approaches to race: Pan-Africanism, cultural nationalism, Marxist accounts of the "national question," and internal colonialism theory. We recognize the selective nature of focusing on these currents, still, we think that they encompass much of the broad sweep of nation-based paradigms of race.

While not comparable in many respects, we include these perspectives as varieties of insurgent nationalism that take shape within the nation-based paradigm of race. These approaches all share a reliance on concepts of *race as peoplehood* that derive from the meaning and uses of the race-concept prevalent in colonialism's heyday. Chief among these is the use of racial categories to distinguish members of the oppressor and oppressed "peoples"—the colonizers and the colonized, the "free" and the enslaved. Several consequences of these arguments may be specified: the explicit demand for organizations and movements uniformly composed of the "colonized" (the victims of racial oppression), the need for "cultural autonomy" to permit the development of those unique characteristics which the colonized group has developed or preserved through the ordeal of subjugation, and the necessity of "self-determination" to uproot the colonial heritage and restructure society on a non-racial basis.

Pan-Africanism: The roots of Pan-Africanism in the United States lie in the identities, principally collective identities—Yoruba, Bakongo, Asante—that enslaved Africans carried with them to the Western Hemisphere. In the 20th century, Pan-Africanism took shape on two fronts: The first was a series of international conferences held in Europe and the United States from 1900 to 1945, most of them organized by W.E.B. Du Bois.[18] These conferences were oriented primarily toward decolonization of Africa and had relatively little U.S. domestic impact.

The second front of Pan-Africanist activity was the formation, largely but not only in the United States, of the Universal Negro Improvement Association, led by Marcus Garvey. The UNIA (Universal Negro Improvement Association) had unprecedented success in mobilizing blacks, numbering millions of adherents at its height in the 1920s. Garvey sought to unite blacks throughout the world in a movement for the "redemption" of Africa, which he envisioned as a "racial empire." For him and his followers, Africa existed not only on the continent, but in the diaspora that slavery had visited on its inhabitants and their descendants. Thus the fates of blacks throughout the world were linked. The liberation and reconstruction of the African homeland would allow blacks finally to overcome the racial oppression that sustained colonialism (Hill and Bair, eds. 1988; Clarke 2011 [1974]; Taylor 2001).

Garvey was greatly influenced by the doctrines of Booker T. Washington, specifically those promoting separate economic development. Garvey's economic argument, however, went beyond Washington's in two respects: First, he denounced the exploitation of Africa and African labor throughout the world.[19] Second, he saw the black population of the United States not only in the "self-help" terms of Washington, but as

> a vanguard for Africa's redemption.... He believed that if the Negroes were economically strong in the United States, they would be able to redeem Africa and establish a worldwide confraternity of black people.
>
> (Essien-Udom 1962, 50)

For all its excesses and errors, the most notorious being its derelict business practices and its *rapprochement* with the Ku Klux Klan,[20] the Garvey movement represents one of the founding pillars of modern Pan-Africanism, and stands as a crucial source for much other black nationalism as well.[21] Indeed, it still represents the high-water mark of mass black political mobilization, rivaled only by the movements of the 1960s.

Pan-Africanism maintained a limited foothold in the United States through the contributions of W.E.B. Du Bois, George Padmore, and C.L.R. James. When Malcolm X broke with the Nation of Islam in 1964 to form the Organization of Afro-American Unity, making a series of well-publicized trips to Africa and the Middle East, and attempting to enlist the support of African governments in denouncing U.S. racism at the United Nations, he dramatically stimulated black interest in African issues. With the advent of black power, the contributions of Malcolm, Kwame Nkrumah, Frantz Fanon, and later, Amilcar Cabral and Walter Rodney received new attention in the United States, and contributed to the Pan-African canon. Kwame Ture (Stokely Carmichael) in particular moved to embrace Pan-Africanism after 1967.[22]

Beginning in the 1930s, political action in support of African independence became a focal point for U.S. Pan-Africanists. Before that, U.S. black activities in Africa had been largely confined to missionary work.[23] From Mussolini's invasion of Ethiopia in 1935 onward, U.S. black involvement with African politics confronted racism at home as much as imperialism on the continent, especially because the United States was often complicit in atrocities in Africa. During the Cold War, anti-imperialist struggles in Africa were linked quite closely to the anti-racist movement in the U.S. Africa (and the global "Third World" more broadly) became the sites of struggle for political influence between the U.S. and USSR. Pan-Africanism enjoyed a small renaissance in the United States when it became clear that Jim Crow practices were well understood on the continent, just as U.S. support for South African apartheid, the British war against the Mau-Mau in Kenya, the assassination of Patrice Lumumba in the Congo, and numerous other events were deeply resented by blacks in the United States (von Eschen 1997, 2006; Kelley 2003; Dudziak 2011). This connection began to wane in the 1970s as debates over the Angolan revolution divided left-wing Pan-Africanists, who supported the MPLA (People's Movement for the Liberation of Angola) and accepted (often dogmatically) some version of Marxism, from right-wing U.S. Pan-Africanists, who maintained an (equally dogmatic) Garveyish "race-first" position and sided with UNITA (Marable 1980, 86–88).[24] A final and largely symbolic iteration of this conflict took place in the United States over the downfall of the apartheid regime in South Africa in the early 1990s. In this instance, right-wing U.S. Pan-Africanists like Roy Innis sided with the South African Inkatha Freedom Party in opposition to the African National Congress, and Afrocentrists took up the causes of the South African Pan Africanist Congress (PAC—founded by Robert Sobukwe), and the Black Consciousness Movement (BCM—founded by Steven Biko).[25]

Pan-Africanist perspectives have lost ground in the post-cold war and post-apartheid periods. Africa is now wracked by civil wars sponsored by competing corporate (and to some extent, national) interests seeking unfettered access to such primary materials as coltan (Nest 2011), copper, and of course, petroleum. Wars and genocides in Eastern Congo, Southern Sudan, the Darfur region, and elsewhere have taken millions of lives and sparked horrifying atrocities such as rape epidemics. Chinese investment has skyrocketed, generating new claims of inter-imperial rivalries. Post-apartheid South Africa has emerged as an important regional power, operating through the New Partnership for Africa's Development (NEPAD).[26]

If Pan-Africanism retains any vitality in the wake of the massive transitions that Africa has undergone in recent decades, it would be based in its recognition of the continuity of the exploitation of Africa by the "developed" countries (China included). This is something that Du Bois denounced a century ago in his prescient 1915 article "The African Roots of the War" (Du Bois 1995 [1915]). Du Bois's vision of a unified African continent, which was in a broad sense also Nkrumah's vision, Garvey's vision (although Garvey and Du Bois were bitter opponents), Cheik Anta Diop's vision (Diop 1989, 1991), and the vision of what we today call Afrocentrism, was always a practical impossibility in a black diaspora riven in a thousand ways by rivalries and differences. Yet as a *cultural phenomenon*, Pan-Africanism still possesses considerable interpretive power; it still has the ability to link the specific forms of oppression which blacks face in various societies with the colonialist exploitation of Africa of past centuries. The impact this theoretical current has had in the United States stemmed from its argument that black identity conferred membership in a single worldwide black "nation"—the African diaspora itself.

Cultural Nationalism: The roots of cultural nationalism can be traced back at least to the Harlem Renaissance of the 1920s (Locke, ed. 1997 [1925]). As a broader phenomenon, however, cultural nationalist perspectives have been enunciated and practiced in nearly all U.S. communities of color. Because cultural nationalism has focused less on the political and economic elements of the nation-based approach—demands for statehood and self-determination within specific territorial boundaries for example—than it has on the cultural elements that give rise to collective identity, community, and a sense of "peoplehood," it exhibits certain overlaps with ethnicity-based theories of race.

Probably the most devoted and incisive cultural nationalist theorist has been Harold Cruse. In two early and highly original books (1967, 1968), Cruse argued that "The only observable way in which the Negro rebellion can become revolutionary in terms of American conditions is for the Negro movement to project the concept of Cultural Revolution" (1967, 111).

Cruse stressed the unique conditions facing American blacks, conditions which, while related to those encountered by other victims of colonialism, were unlike those of the African continent, the West Indies, or elsewhere. Cruse also accepted certain "domestic colonialism" concepts; indeed, he gave voice to them as early as 1962 (Cruse 1962). Anticipating the "black power" view, he criticized the civil rights movement in the early 1960s for being dominated by liberal ideas and demands:

> This Negro rebellion, mistakenly called by some the Negro revolution, is not revolutionary because it projects no new ideas beyond what have already been ratified in the democratic philosophy of the American Constitution.
>
> (Cruse 1967, 111–112)

He proposed that the movement "incorporate ... a cultural program along with its economic, social, and political programs" (ibid). A "cultural program," in Cruse's view, would recognize both the unique characteristics of black cultural traditions, and the essential part that these cultural elements—for example, in music, art, or language—played in the cultural life of the United States. Cruse suggested that the black movement focus its demands on "the creation and distribution of cultural production in America" (ibid, 117). The ultimate aim of this challenge, Cruse argued, was "the revolutionizing ... of the entire apparatus of cultural communication and placing it under public ownership" (ibid, 112).

This approach raised as many questions as it answered. How the cultural apparatus could be so transformed, how blacks could affect cultural production under the proposed new "revolutionary" conditions, and what would be the ultimate social and political impact of such changes, were only a few of the issues Cruse did not address. What was significant about his work, however, was not its immediate practical application. Rather, his accomplishment lay in the development of a culturally based radical perspective. His positions reframed debates between integrationists and nationalists in the later 1960s and 1970s. He re-opened questions that had lain dormant for nearly half a century.[27] In many ways Cruse explored the terrain upon which later figures of this current such as Maulana Karenga and Imamu Amiri Baraka would stand (on Karenga, see Brown 2003; on Baraka, see Benston 1976; Woodard 1999; Watts 2001.).

Many black nationalists embraced African values, traditions, culture, and language through Pan-Africanism, or became adherents of groups such as Karenga's US Organization or Baraka's Spirit House in Newark, New Jersey, without becoming Pan-Africanists politically. Cultural nationalism had many indirect effects on black "lifestyle": clothes, hair, language, and art reflected the perspective's upsurge. African heritage was often invoked to support domestic ideological and political aims.[28]

Cultural nationalism has taken a wide variety of forms among Latin@s, Asian Americans, and Native Americans as well. It has developed during the post-World War II period in rough correspondence with the rise and fall of racial justice movements, immigration rates and policies, and political-economic conditions. These racialized ethnic/national groups have undergone huge transformations over recent decades. To mention only a few of the major shifts:

- Latin@ and Asian immigration rates soared after passage of the 1965 Immigration and Nationality Act, dramatically changing U.S. racial demography over the medium to long term;
- U.S. wars and imperial adventures, notably in Asia, Central America, the Caribbean, and the Middle East, have focused attention and increased the numbers of such U.S.-based diasporic communities—Korean, Salvadoran, Vietnamese, and MEASA Americans, among others;[29]
- The linkage between U.S. domestic and global racial policies and the breakdown of moderate racial reformism after about 1970 generated a wide variety of radical movement groups across many communities of color; the legacy of SNCC and the influence of the Black Panther Party also were significant in this process, which generated the Young Lords, the Brown Berets, the American Indian Movement, the Asian American Political Alliance, and similar groups (Chávez 1998; Pulido 2006; Erick-Wanzer, ed. 2010; Ogbar 2001; Fujino 2012).

As anti-racist movements gained strength in the 1960s, they brought with them a sense of collective identity, race pride, and deepened interest in "roots" at various levels: family, community, and history. All these tendencies flowed together towards cultural nationalist politics, as larger numbers of people in communities of color moved to reject the assimilationism offered by mainstream (often white liberal), moderate currents in the civil rights movement and grounded in ethnicity theory. This was particularly true for youth and those influenced by student movements.

In the late 1960s and early 1970s, black student associations, deeply attuned to the civil rights and black power movements, as well as Latin@ student groups like the *Movimiento Estudiantil Chican@ de Aztlán* (MEChA), carried out numerous demonstrations and occupations on college campuses, demanding the creation of "ethnic studies" programs and the hiring of more faculty of color.[30] This movement began—as it usually does—in California, but soon became a national one, issuing a series of manifestos in support of black, brown, red, and yellow power,[31] and linking to anti-war movements and other national and international insurgencies as well. The year 1968, for example, was a moment of global student unrest in New York, Paris, Mexico City, Tokyo, Prague, and elsewhere.

Parallel to the occupations and conflicts that took place in the arena of higher education, a wide variety of other developments that occurred in the arts and mass media (popular music, film, TV)[32] from the mid-1960s onward may also be described as culturally nationalist: Various manifestos, arts movements, and media-based interventions advocating and celebrating the collective identities and insurgent histories of particular peoples of color appeared at this time, in some respects echoing Harold Cruse's call for cultural revolution. Such groups as the Black Arts Movement (Smethurst 2005), the Chican@ Asco group in East Los Angeles (Los Angeles County Museum of Art 2011), and the Asian American Kearny Street Workshop in San Francisco, to name but a few, built upon established national and ethnocultural traditions, both "highbrow" and popular, such as salsa, the vast black musical canon, the *muralista* movement in Mexico, and various literary and visual genres, all in the effort to express (and invent) emancipatory concepts of racial/national identity.

Yet for all its political aspirations, cultural nationalism was limited by its focus on expression rather than action. Although there were instances in which cultural action could be linked very directly to community-based action, such as the work of Sun Ra's Arkestra and Horace Tapscott's Pan Afrikan Peoples Arkestra, groups which combined jazz performance with music education and protest activity in Philadelphia and South Central Los Angeles respectively (on Sun Ra see Szwed 1998; on Tapscott see Tapscott 2001; Lipsitz 2007), much of black art or brown art could be coopted and commodified with relative ease. There was, it turned out, nothing inherently radical about dashikis, Kemet, or the concept of "soul," or for that matter about the Aztec heritage, pupusas, menudo, or fry bread. As Adolph L. Reed, Jr. noted in respect to black cultural nationalism:

> [T]he intellectual climate which came to pervade the movement was best summarized in the nationalists' exhortation to "think black".... Truth became a feature of the speaker's "blackness," i.e., validity claims were to be resolved not through discourse but by the claimant's manipulation of certain banal symbols of legitimacy.
>
> (Reed, in Glaude 2002, 52)

Demographic, economic, and political fissures within communities of color—whose "unity" and "peoplehood" had been central features of cultural nationalist theory—increasingly became too obvious to ignore. By the 1970s and 1980s, faced with some of these changes, leading adherents moved on to new political horizons. Some, notably Baraka, made spectacular and belated conversions to Marxism-Leninism and

Maoism, subsuming their original "racial" projects under broader "class" ones; these too would prove to have serious limits.

In sum, cultural nationalism built "countercultural" institutions, and wound up occupying a broad political spectrum that extended from the creation of small (though sometimes influential) alternative institutions like bookstores and schools, all the way to a "black capitalism" not too different from what Frazier had characterized in *Black Bourgeoisie* (1957a). Too often, though certainly not in all cases, cultural nationalist approaches neglected the key political determinants of race—the racial state, class conflict, the politics of alliance and coalitions—preferring expressive authenticity to political engagement.

The real accomplishment of cultural nationalist currents was in the nature of community service and education: "consciousness-raising." This is not to be sneezed at. An immense amount of interpretive and expressive work, and community organization based on culturally grounded themes such as music and art, has burst onto the American scene in recent decades. Making use of hiphop, Indian rock, punk rock, talk radio, music videos, and social media of various kinds, the cultural politics of race have been redefined since in the 1960s. Sun Ra and Horace Tapscott's work has been continued by George Clinton, Rage Against the Machine and Tom Morello, Lupe Fiasco, The Roots, Michael Franti, Das Racist, X-Clan, and innumerable others. Race-based cultural politics, and thus something very close to cultural nationalism, continues as a durable feature of American life. This underscores the centrality of cultural domination as a component of racial oppression, and stresses the importance of "cultures of resistance" in unifying and promoting collective identity among the oppressed.

The "National Question" and Marxism: Classical Marxism viewed nations and national boundaries as increasingly meaningless as world capitalism inexorably penetrated every corner of the planet. Marx and Engels stated this perspective clearly in *The Communist Manifesto* and viewed it as a "progressive" feature of the unfolding capitalist order:

> National differences and antagonisms between peoples are daily more and more vanishing, owing to the development of the bourgeoisie, to freedom of commerce, to the world market, to uniformity in the mode of production and in the conditions of life corresponding thereto.
>
> (Marx and Engels 1968 [1848], 55)

This was not their final word on the subject, though. Indeed the idea of a tendential abolition of national boundaries and antagonisms is undermined in other writings of Marx. For example, addressing the national question with specific reference to Ireland, Marx argues that the bourgeoisie not only maintains but *heightens* national antagonisms. National hostilities are engendered by

- The struggle to control world markets, which creates conflicts among capitalist powers;

- The exploitation of colonies, which creates antagonism between oppressed and oppressor nations; and
- The use of nationalism as an ideological tool to deflect proletarian attention away from class antagonisms (Marx and Engels 1972a,1972b; Lowy 1976).

This contradictory stance towards the persistence or demise of nations is further complicated by an implicit stage theory of development that views colonial penetration and plunder as progressive events: They are seen as rupturing traditional and "backward" social relations and supplanting them with modern capitalist ones.

Marx and Engels did not resolve the "national question," largely because it did not fit within the class struggle/mode of production problematic. Nationalism and empire occasioned significant debates during the period of the Second International.[33] An important polemical exchange between Lenin and Luxemburg, for example, revolves around the "right of nations to self-determination." Lenin argued that all nations should be free from national oppression and enjoy the right to determine their own destiny.[34] Luxemburg was critical of this "right to self-determination," which led in her view to a certain pandering to the aspirations of the national bourgeoisies of the "oppressed" countries. Both Lenin and Luxemburg attempted to steer a course between positions which asserted an unqualified right to national/cultural autonomy, and a position which completely denied the legitimacy of nationalist aspirations (Luxemburg 1976 [1909]).

The legacy of these debates on the national question was subsequently invoked to analyze the situation of blacks in the United States. Prior to 1928, the Communist Party of the United States had attributed no special role or status to blacks (or other "national minorities") within the general class struggle. Comintern (aka the Third International or the Communist International) discussions between 1928 and 1930, however, resulted in the "Black Nation Thesis": that blacks in the southern region known as the Black Belt (supposedly named for the soil) constituted a nation and were therefore entitled to "self-determination"—including the right of political secession. Blacks in the North were considered an oppressed "national minority" whose salvation was to be sought in solidarity with white workers in the struggle for socialism (Allen 1974).

The criteria for the thesis were drawn from a 1908 pamphlet by Joseph Stalin, who had proposed a formula of four defining characteristics of a nation:

> A nation is a historically constituted, stable community of people, formed on the basis of a common language, territory, economic life, and psychological make-up, manifested in a common culture.
>
> (Stalin 1975 [1908], 22)

In 1928 what Stalin said was not to be questioned. The Black Nation Thesis was both dogmatic and inapplicable to the United States, but it was adopted anyway, in an effort to resolve contradictions within the Communist Party due to racism. Most important, it was intended to help the party compete with Garveyism and other supposedly "bourgeois" separatist trends in the black community.

The Communist Party adhered only fitfully to this increasingly marginal analysis. Between 1936 and the early 1950s, the right to self-determination was subordinated to the New Deal and the war against fascism.[35] Between 1955 and 1959, the party moved to discard the thesis entirely, recognizing that black migration from the South had eroded its political viability. After dying this slow death, the thesis was exhumed by various Marxist-Leninist groups in the 1970s (Revolutionary Union n.d.; October League 1976). There never was any consensus about the application, or indeed the meaning, of the Black Nation Thesis on the Marxist-Leninist left.

Lacking an orthodox Marxist theory of racism, and unable to examine U.S. society without a comforting pillow of citations from the "classics," Marxists of all varieties have performed some strenuous theoretical labor in their efforts to apply the literature on the "national question" to racial dynamics in the United States. The general practice has been to substitute national categories for racial ones. The corresponding political rights, such as self-determination for "legitimate" nations, can then be asserted. The result has been confusion and endless debate over the appropriate criteria for "nationhood."[36] For Marxist-Leninists, nation-based approaches became little more than a convenient way to deal with the messy and undertheorized concepts of race and racism.

Internal Colonialism: The internal colonialism perspective has been applied to nationalist movements in many countries, among them France, Peru, South Africa, and Great Britain (Cotler 1970; Berger 1972; Wolpe 1975; Hechter 1998 [1975]). In the United States, the concept achieved great currency in the late 1960s and early 1970s (although earlier formulations, such as that of Cruse, can be found), when various writers employed it to account for the upsurge in racial minority militance. The radical nationalist movements that (re)surfaced in black, Latin@, Native American, and Asian American communities at this time generally rejected reform-oriented politics, preferring to link their struggles with those of such national liberation movements as the Vietnamese, Algerian, or Chinese revolutions.

Internal colonialism approaches attempted the synthesis of different aspects of racial oppression: economic, political, and cultural, through the invocation of a colonial model. In most cases they appealed as well to nationalist forms of mobilization against this generalized system of oppression. Among the elements of internal colonialism which analysts identified were:

- A colonial *geography* emphasizing the territoriality or spatial arrangement of population groups along racial lines;
- A dynamic of *cultural domination and resistance*, in which racial categories were utilized to distinguish between antagonistic colonizing and colonized groups, and conversely, to emphasize the essential cultural unity and autonomy of each;

- A system of *superexploitation*, understood as a process by which extra-economic coercion was applied to the racially identified colonized group, with the aim of increasing the economic resources appropriated by the colonizers.
- Institutionalization of *externally-based control*, such that the racially identified colonized group is organized in essential political and administrative aspects by the colonizers or their agents.

In some cases militant groups themselves adopted analyses of their conditions and demands based on internal colonialism arguments; in others, scholarly treatments brought these perspectives to bear. Notable studies were devoted to the black and Chican@ communities (Moore 1970; Barrera, Muñoz, and Ornelas 1972; Barrera 2002 [1979]; Flores 1973; Allen 1990 [1970]; Ture [Carmichael] and Hamilton 1992 [1967]).

Internal colonialists argued that the ghetto and barrio were in fact colonized territory (Boggs 1970). Robert Blauner's *Racial Oppression in America* is probably the most familiar general discussion of race in the U.S. written from an internal colonialism perspective, and the one most "tailored" to U.S. conditions (Blauner 2001 [1972], 2011).[37] Blauner had two central preoccupations: The first was to provide theoretical arguments with which to counter the dominant ethnicity paradigm of race in the United States. The second crucial commitment in Blauner's work was his identification with the radical nationalist politics of the 1960s. Blauner acknowledged the intellectual influence of movement theory and practice on his work, and counterposed its radical depth to the complacency of the ethnicity-oriented sociology he criticized.[38] He explicitly sought to deepen radical nationalist practice by grafting internal colonialism theory onto it.

Blauner employed the distinction between "colonized and immigrant minorities" to criticize the ethnic group paradigm. By "colonized" minorities he meant those whose presence in the United States was the result of "forced entry," a criterion that seeks to distinguish between those (Africans and Latin Americans) whose entry into the country was the direct result of processes of colonialism and slavery and those (Europeans) who "became ethnic groups and minorities within the United States by the essentially voluntary movements of individuals and families" (2001 [1972], 55). In using the distinction between coerced and voluntary migration, superimposing it, so to speak, on the race/ethnicity distinction, Blauner was on somewhat shaky ground. The line between coerced and voluntary migration is far from clear: consider the Irish emigrations in the 1840s, for example, or Jewish emigrations from Russia at the turn of the 20th century. In these cases, mass starvation (imposed by the British as a form of what we today might call "ethnic cleansing") and widespread pogroms (organized campaigns of murder, rape, and expulsions of impoverished and stigmatized people), seem to be sufficiently violent, and to cause sufficient desperation, to qualify as coercive practices, even if their monstrosity does not fully attain the levels of predation and mass murder achieved by the

Atlantic slave trade.[39] Further problems arise when we consider Asian immigration: coerced or voluntary, racial or ethnic? When we apply the Blauner's approach to contemporary patterns of global racism and migration, still other difficulties arise, for example: massive trafficking of living human bodies (preponderantly women) to the United States that combines coerced and voluntary dimensions; refugee and asylum policies shaped by U.S. government *realpolitik;* and post-1965 shifts in "voluntary" immigration from Africa, the Philippines, the Caribbean, and China (Zolberg 2008).

In respect to Blauner's second point of emphasis, derived chiefly from the militant black politics of the late 1960s—his "basic thesis that the most important expressions of protest in the black community reflect the colonized status of Afro-America" (2001 [1972], 89)—the internal colonialism approach also fares poorly, especially in a more contemporary perspective. None of the protest phenomena Blauner cites (ghetto riots, cultural nationalism, ghetto-based "community control" movements) necessitates the internal colonialism perspective as an analytical framework. For example, ghetto uprisings have been explained as an extension of "normal" politics when institutionalized channels of political expression are blocked (Piven and Cloward 1978). As the 1992 Los Angeles riots showed, urban revolt is now a multiracial phenomenon: black, brown, and even a bit white, and with Asians often targeted along with whites (Rutten 1992; Gooding-Williams 1993; Kim 2008).

What is "nationalist" about race-based social movements is a matter of considerable ambiguity and debate. Ghetto community control demands have proved subject to quite moderate (or "reformist") interpretation, besides proving to be at best "too little, too late" as key decisions about the cities' fate are made elsewhere. There is nothing inherently democratic about "community control"; it should be remembered that Richard Nixon was a major proponent of affirmative action, community control, and black capitalism, all of which he rearticulated to serve as "divide and conquer" strategies for the diffusion and demobilization of the black power movement (Perlstein 2008; Goldberg and Griffey, eds. 2010; Hill and Rabig, eds. 2012). At best, such programs can provide employment and training, and, of course, support for progressive sectors of the "black bourgeoisie" (see Cross 1974). At worst, such demands provide grounds for rearticulation in new right or neoconservative analyses and programs, for example to provide code words for opposition to busing or welfare rights.

Blauner's internal colonialism approach neglected the cleavages that exist within communities of color, notably class- and gender-based ones. He did not address inter-group rivalries either: "black–brown" and black–Asian conflicts, for example. Finally, the extensive "hybridization" of racial cultures in the U.S. societies went largely untheorized. Though it is hardly as complete as an ethnicity theorist like Glazer might wish to argue, the extensive mixture of racial identities and communities in the (still very segregated) United States casts doubt on the internal colonialism analogy in respect to territoriality, at the very least.[40] Racial hybridity also suggests limits to other elements of the nation-based paradigm in the U.S. context. The cultural domination/cultural autonomy tension so central to cultural nationalism, for example, appears to be but one element of a broader cultural dynamic that includes both the distinctiveness and the interaction of whiteness, blackness, and brownness, at a minimum. In the same way, the concept of "superexploitation," something central to Marxist accounts of race and nation, does not adequately address contemporary economic developments which include marginalization and permanent dependency for many, on the one hand, and significant "upward mobility" for some, on the other.

In many respects, then, there are limits to nation-based approaches to race. It is quite understandable why the epochal history of racial nationalism—notably black nationalism—was grafted onto or analogized to the national liberation struggles that swept the planet during the post-World War II period. The political affinities between domestic, U.S.-based racial freedom struggles and the anti-colonial battles of Vietnam, Algeria, and elsewhere, were linkages and overlaps of great resonance and importance. But because accords were grounded in political considerations and not theoretically or analytically worked out, they could not sustain the internal colonialist version of nation-based racial theory.

Some Critical Remarks on the Nation-Based Paradigm

How effectively does the nation-based paradigm account for racial dynamics? In fact, the connection is tenuous. Both the U.S. system of racial oppression and colonial systems of racial rule composed of colonizers and colonized made use of racial distinctions. But in the present period the two cannot be compared in more than a general way. All the specifically national aspects of the internal colonialism perspective (geography, culture, extra-economic coercion, and external political rule), while remaining true in a general fashion, are contradictory and problematic when examined in detail. While segregation is still extensive, it varies widely by class and racial category; culture is racially hybridized to an unprecedented degree. As we have already noted, extra-economic coercion, what David Harvey calls "accumulation by dispossession" (Harvey 2004) is a general feature of neoliberalism, and not only a matter of structural racism; and external political rule also operates fairly comprehensively under the present-day oligarchical regime of the United States.

Racial oppression and white supremacy retain their power, but these patterns and social structures have been reorganized and rearticulated over the post-World War II period, and especially since the late 1960s, in ways that render the nation-based paradigm of race problematic. As applied to the contemporary United States (with significant if partial exceptions such as Native American conditions or the cases of Puerto Rico and Hawai'i), the appeal of nationalism, in political practice or in theory, appears to be limited. This is true across the board: for the various cultural nationalisms, for Marxist accounts, and for internal colonialism theories as well. In our view, the nation-based paradigm of race is an important component of our understanding of race: in highlighting "peoplehood," collective identity, it "invents tradition" (Hobsbawm and Ranger, eds. 1983) and "imagines community" (Anderson 1998). Nation-based understandings of race provide affective identification: They promise a sense of ineffable connection within racially identified groups; they engage in "collective representation" (Durkheim 2014). The tropes of "soul," of "folk," of *hermanos/hermanas unidos/unidas* uphold Duboisian themes. They channel Martí's hemispheric consciousness (Martí 1977 [1899]); and Vasconcelos's ideas of *la raza cosmica* (1979; Stavans 2011). In communities and movements, in the arts and popular media, as well as universities and colleges (especially in ethnic studies) these frameworks of peoplehood play a vital part in maintaining a sense of racial solidarity, however uneven or partial.

So the nation-based paradigm remains valuable, but cannot capture the complexity of U.S. racial dynamics across the board. In this respect it parallels the other two paradigms we have discussed: ethnicity-based theory and class-based theory. Because it is based on a reductionism of race—in this case to the idea of "peoplehood"—it cannot grasp the phenomenon comprehensively.

Unlike many of the old colonial nations, and possibly because it was created in an anti-colonial revolution, the U.S. political scene allows insurgent racial nationalisms little space. It does preserve and protect *white* racial nationalism, not only as a popular ideology, but as a respectable intellectual position. This is visible not only on the political and academic right-wing (Swain 2002; Walters 2003), but also among centrist and liberal scholars, including those identified with the ethnicity paradigm (Glazer 1997; Thernstrom and Thernstrom 1999; Lipset 2003 [1963]). White racial nationalism remains the bedrock of the U.S. right wing, and much of its liberal center as well (Amadae 2003). This normalization of whiteness is often quite invisible to leading U.S. nationalists, who prefer to celebrate "western civilization" and the "triumph of democracy" (Smith 2003).[41]

Insurgent nationalisms tend to *reduce* race to a taken-for-granted "peoplehood," but they do take it seriously. They do not dismiss it as a mask for something else, as do both the ethnicity- and class-based approaches. Yet insurgent variants of the nation-based paradigm of race fail to demonstrate the existence of relatively homogeneous black, brown, or other colonized "nations," notably internally colonized peoples whose claims to "self-determination" in the United States might be logical and workable.[42] Despite the ongoing realities of structural racism, the vast increase in the incarcerated black and brown population over the past three decades, and the deepening of economic inequality since the onset of the great recession in 2008, U.S. communities of color remain highly stratified by class and gender, vastly differentiated by age cohorts, and more hybridized culturally—as well as through mixed-race relationships and identities—than was ever the case before. Therefore nation-based accounts cannot sustain the argument that the ghettos and barrios are so thoroughly and structurally separated from U.S. society overall that they could be reorganized in democratic and egalitarian fashion along the lines of "self-determination "and "community control." While these notions may have some emotional resonance for those who are simply "sick and tired of being sick and tired" (Nappy Roots 2003), in practical terms such measures would represent the opposite of an emancipatory solution to problems of segregation, isolation, and exploitation. Not that practical measures of this type are feasible, but if they were, they would more likely take the form of South African "bantustans" or "townships" than they would of liberated territory.

Nation-based theories of race still practice epiphenomenalism. They treat race as a manifestation of "peoplehood"—and thus still reduce it to a something supposedly more fundamental. We argue that race is not a mask for something else. It cannot be reduced to the "true" national identity of a racially categorized people—as the nation-based paradigm would claim. It cannot be reduced to cultural differences—as the ethnicity-based paradigm suggests. And it cannot be reduced to a type of inequality either—as the class-based paradigm suggests. Although race contains all these dimensions, it exceeds them all as well.

Perhaps it is the very inability of the nation-based account to specify precisely what exactly is "national" about racial oppression in the United States that leads it to lend a certain primacy and integrity to racial phenomena. The ethnicity and class paradigms, working from more secure assumptions about the "primacy" of their paradigmatic categories, tend to dissolve the unity of racially constituted groups more easily than the nation paradigm does.

Notes

1. Imperialism and conquest had been inherent in the making of modern European nations themselves. Even today many European nations are uneasy aggregations of distinct peoples forged by conquest: consider Scots or Catalan nationalisms today, for example. The transoceanic imperial adventures of the European powers were therefore extensions of earlier transitions to nation-states. Though that process was already well underway, it was expanded significantly after the politically foundational Treaties of Westphalia ended the Thirty-Years War in 1648 (Bobbitt 2002; Geary 2002).
2. For an overview of the linkages between U.S. and global racial politics, see Winant 2001. A substantial literature now links domestic racial policy and U.S. foreign policy in respect to the international coordination of racial rule. For example, the CIA worked with the BOSS, the apartheid-era South African secret police. On the flip side of this, these linkages were also recognized by radical democratic oppositions: SNCC, the South African ANC or Algerian FLN, and many other anti-racist and antiwar organizations around the world explicitly made these connections, especially during the 1960s (Dudziak 2011; Kelley 2003; Singh 2004; Hanchard 2006; Prashad 2007). Movement efforts to identify anti-imperial struggles in the "Third World" (the then-current term for the Global South), with anti-racism politics on the domestic front ("in the belly of the beast") have a very long history.
3. Debates on the dynamics of whiteness are extensive. We recognize the importance of "privilege" in the constitution of whiteness, but resist the reduction of white identity to

nothing more than privilege. We note that while whites generally benefit materially from racism and thus have an interest in perpetuating it (Harris 1993; Lipsitz 2006), they are also hurt by racism and therefore have contrary interests in reducing or ending it. Consider: about 750,000 Americans died in the Civil War, for example; the majority of them were white (Faust 2009; Gugliotta 2012).

4. In Europe as well, citizenship rights were only gradually extended (and even more gradually granted in practice) to immigrants, Jews, and nonwhites. In Germany *jus sanguinis* policies were continued from the formation of the nation, through the Third Reich, and into the establishment of the EU, when they were finally relaxed only in the 1990s (Brubaker 1992). French "racial differentialism" (Taguieff 1999, 2001) struggles in vain to reconcile the exclusion and despair of the *banlieues* with the Jacobin/Napoleonic legacies of assimilationism and secularism (Wieviorka 1995; Noiriel 1996; Silverstein 2004).
5. South Africa explicitly institutionalized the *herrenvolk* model, first piecemeal, and then systematically after 1948. All the European empires struggled to distinguish between metropolitans/citizens and colonials/natives, especially as mixed-race populations expanded, miscegenation became commonplace, and "creoles," "wogs," "kaffirs," "beurs," and "Indos" established themselves in London, Paris, Lisbon, Amsterdam, and elsewhere (Stoler 2002).
6. There are more women than men in the United States, and for the first time, more women than men in the U.S. labor force.
7. What few legal, political, or cultural constraints there were on Indian expulsions or land seizures were ignored in practice. The most famous case was Andrew Jackson defiance of the Supreme Court's ruling in *Worcester v Georgia* (31 U.S. 515, 1832): writing for the Court, Chief Justice John Marshall ruled that the Cherokee were a sovereign nation and therefore not subject to the Indian Removal Act, which Jackson supported. Jackson's famous response was, "Justice Marshall has made his decision. Let him enforce it now if he can." Jackson's defiance paved the way for the "Trail of Tears" forced march of the Cherokee from their homes in Georgia to the Oklahoma territory. See Rogin 1991.
8. Neither race nor class were ever fully worked-out and definitive characteristics of the early U.S. social system: from the early days the presence of free blacks, the abolitionist impulse, and the extensive overlap between the categories of "servant" and "slave" had both intensified and muddied the waters of racial despotism (Roediger 2007 [1991]). And the ill-defined and preliminary forms of capitalist development also vitiated clear distinctions of class: who or what was a "worker" and who a "servant" was being determined in the shoe factories of Lynn, Massachusetts, at the same time that the slave system was shaping U.S. exports, shipping, and investment opportunities (Dawley 2000 [1975]). Although most slaves were rural laborers, there was also industrial slavery (Starobin 1970) and of course extensive domestic slavery (mainly but not entirely female).
9. Brown (1998) provides a good overview of the historiography of gender and race in early North America, focusing on its late emergence under the influence of the civil rights and second-wave feminist movements. See also Hodes 1997; Gordon 2001; Gilmore 1996; and Bederman 1996 on the intersections of race, gender, and national identity in the United States. Mosse 1997 (1981); Radhakrishnan 1992; Stoler 2002; and McClintock 1995 link race, gender, and nation in the global context of imperialism.
10. A word to which we object, since it signifies "misbreeding." It was "coined in the election of 1864 by Northern Democrats, who used it to denounce Lincoln Republicans as advocates of interracial sex" (Woodward 1998).

11. As Martha Hodes (1997) has shown, in the slave South before the Civil War, there existed many varieties of intimate relationships, including marriages, between white women and black men. After the war, the southern regime became far more brutal and terroristic, in the age of the KKK and under the command of Judge Lynch. By then a great deal of interracial breeding had occurred. Mixed-race identity undermined and threatened the system of racial classification on which slavery and Jim Crow were based. After the war interracial liaisons grew far more dangerous, and white antagonism to them became ever more irrational and violent. See also Williamson 1986.
12. Urged on by the Kennedy administration and various liberal foundations and policy groups, SNCC had deeply committed itself to voter registration work in Mississippi. In return it was subject to unremitting KKK violence. The torture and murders of the three SNCC workers Chaney, Goodman, and Schwerner during the 1964 SNCC-led "Freedom Summer" project—a voting rights effort—were just the most publicized of these vicious reprisals. The Johnson administration, focused on the 1964 election and still pandering to the South, offered very little support and almost no protection to the effort its predecessor—especially Robert Kennedy—had sponsored. When the SNCC-led alternate Mississippi delegation to the national convention, known as the Mississippi Freedom Democratic Party, arrived in Atlantic City, it was rudely dismissed. Offered two seats in the state delegation, the MFDP (Mississippi Freedom Democratic Party)—led by civil rights hero Fannie Lou Hamer—criticized Lyndon Johnson ferociously and publically. SNCC went on to complete its turn, already well underway, to black power and the anti-imperialist left. See Payne 2007 (1995); Lee 2000; Carson 1995 (1981).
13. Malcolm's assassination in February of 1965 (at the age of 40) significantly narrowed the prospects for the creative development of black nationalist politics in the U.S. In Malcolm's final few years he had not only developed his own independent political orientation, but had also crafted the beginnings of a creative and autonomous black nationalist politics that combined internationalism, socialism, religious syncretism, and anti-racism. That approach to black nationalism would never come to fruition. See Marable 2011.
14. All previous race riots in U.S. history had been white attacks on people of color and their communities (Rucker and Upton, eds. 2006).
15. In 1854, for example, a National Emigration Convention was held at Pittsburgh, with Delany in the leadership, which called for emigration "towards those places where the black and colored man [sic] comprise, by population ... the ruling element of the body politic" (Bracey, Meier, and Rudwick, eds. 1970, 93).
16. Immanuel Wallerstein's term has now entered the social scientific canon; it intersects with race theory at multiple points. Original an anti-colonial sociologist of Africa, Wallerstein has written on race and racism fairly extensively. See Balibar and Wallerstein 2011, among other sources.
17. Peruvian sociologist Anibal Quijano (2000; see also Mignolo 2011) has developed a theory of "the coloniality of power" to account for the persistence of structures of unequal power in postcolonial societies. Quijano asks how racism, and racial categories themselves, managed to survive and indeed deepen in the aftermath of colonial rule throughout the global South. What accounts for the resilience, not only of racial inequality and exclusion from the political process of, say, indigenous and African people in Peru, long after the end of Spanish colonialism there?

18. A sixth (or seventh, depending on which events are counted) Pan-African Congress was held in Tanzania in 1974.
19. Garvey's origins were as a labor insurgent in Jamaica. See among many statements his "Speech at Royal Albert Hall." In Clarke 2011 (1974), 284–299.
20. Garvey visited Ku Klux Klan headquarters in June, 1922, and subsequently declared his agreement with the Klan that "this is a white man's country." He also flirted with the Anglo-Saxon Clubs of America, a white supremacist group led by one John Powell. His connection with such groups was certainly ill-advised, but his motivation in making these contacts has never been sufficiently explained. He was obviously not in agreement with such groups on white supremacy itself. See Moore in Clarke, ed. 2011 (1974), 225, 233–234. For a strong contemporary critique of authoritarianism in Garvey—and in black nationalism more generally—see Gilroy 2000.
21. Even opposing tendencies of black nationalism were influenced. For example, it is unlikely that the Communist Party would have adopted its "black nation" approach in 1928 had not Party leaders both in the United States and in Moscow become alarmed at Garvey's successes.
22. On Carmichael's 1967 meetings with Sekou Toure and Kwame Nkrumah, see Carson 1995 (1981), 276. Carmichael later founded a small Pan-Africanist party in the United States, the All African Peoples Revolutionary Party.
23. See Fredrickson 1995; Comaroff and Comaroff 1991, 1997. Of course, there were some exceptions. We have already mentioned U.S. black colonization movements. The early involvement of George Washington Williams—an extraordinary 19th-century U.S. black activist and intellectual—in the effort to curtail the genocidal practices in the Congo of King Leopold II of Belgium, also deserves notice. See Hochschild 1998; Franklin 1998 (1985).
24. In Angola, the U.S. and the USSR fought a "hot" proxy war for a quarter-century: from 1975 to 2002. Angola, a major oil-producing state, became independent in 1975 after Portugal's decrepit fascist regime was overthrown, largely by colonial soldiers disgusted with counterinsurgency warfare in Portugal's African colonies. Two anti-imperialist Angolan movements, the MPLA and the National Union for the Total Independence of Angola (UNITA), then commenced a brutal civil war for control of the resource-rich country. The MPLA, a Marxist group, received support from the USSR; the UNITA declared itself "anti-communist" and gained U.S. backing. Neighboring South Africa—a U.S. ally and then still an apartheid state—invaded in support of UNITA. Cuba, a USSR ally, sent in troops in support of the MPLA. The MPLA achieved victory only in 2002; an estimated 500,000 people died, and the country was largely destroyed.
25. The U.S. steadily backed the apartheid regime on Cold War grounds, branding the opposition ANC as communist, maintaining clandestine CIA ties with BOSS (the South Africa Bureau of State Security), and resisting a rising movement for democratization at home that included an anti-corporate boycott campaign and extensive civil disobedience. The fall of the regime was met with great excitement in the U.S., especially in the black community. Still, within the Pan-Africanist current there were echoes of the divisions that had arisen over Angola: right-wing support for Inkatha, and Afrocentrist support for the South African Pan-Africanist Congress, the organization founded by Robert Sobukwe in opposition to the "non-racialism" of the ANC. On Sobukwe see Pogrund 1991; Fredrickson 1991.

26. NEPAD has been strongly criticized from the left as a new sub-imperialist cartel in which South Africa dominates but Nigeria, Algeria, and the Organization of African Unity (OAU) also play important roles (Bond 2002, 2010).
27. Cruse's contention that the demand for "public ownership" of the cultural apparatus formed the basis for a new revolutionary nationalist politics was unrealistic. The *integration* of the U.S. cultural apparatus, on the other hand, proved possible, though not without ongoing struggle. A more conservative version of black cultural nationalism, akin to notions of "black capitalism," may be seen here. Robert Allen has noted the hegemonic dimensions of this process (Allen 1990 [1970], 179). Political battles within hip-hop, and struggles over TV and Hollywood "production values" with respect to race/class/gender, were all prefigured in Cruse's work.
28. A vast cultural nationalist literature seeks to establish links between U.S. black *habitus* and the (sometimes idealized and stereotyped) African motherland. Discussions here often intersect with long-standing debates in the anthropology of race. See Asante 1998; Moses 1998; Glaude, ed. 2002.
29. For a systematic treatment of the relationship over historical time between U.S. imperialism in Latin America and the emergence of Latin@ politics at home, see Gonzalez 2011 [2001].
30. To a large extent the presence on U.S. college and university campuses of ethnic studies departments and programs, multicultural centers, and recognized race-based organizations of various kinds is the product of these actions. Though still uneven and sometimes beleaguered in budgetary battles and ideological disputes, the institutionalization of ethnic studies has been a tremendous political and cultural accomplishment, responsible for reshaping the race consciousness of millions of U.S. students, by no means only students of color, across the United States for nearly half a century. Today, ethnic studies—and the teaching about race and racism in general—faces new challenges, and new attempts to curtail it as well. See Winant 2006; Alcoff 2012).
31. See *El Plan de Santa Barbara*, adopted April 1969 (Chican@ Coordinating Council on Higher Education, 1969).
32. Marlon Riggs's documentary film *Color Adjustment* (1992) traces the transformation of U.S. television from its all-white beginnings in the late 1940s through its various racial conflicts and accommodations up to the late 1980s.
33. The European "empires within" (Austria-Hungary and Tsarist Russia particularly) were the main objects of these debates. External colonies drew less attention, but were certainly not ignored, especially in the work of Luxemburg.
34. Lenin sought to place these "national" conflicts in their international "class" context: the relationship between the proletariat of the "oppressor" nation and the proletariat of the "oppressed" nation (the so-called "aristocracy of labor") was also one of exploitation (Lenin 1970 [1915]). Lenin's ideas on self-determination are productively compared to Woodrow Wilson's—who made this concept central to his position at the 1919 Versailles conference—by Nikhil Pal Singh (2004, 31).
35. As is well-known, the CPUSA undertook some torturous reversals during these years, moving from sectarian attacks on other leftist groups during 1928–1935, then embracing its former rivals in a "popular front" posture until 1939, then attacking them again during the period of the Hitler–Stalin pact (1939–1941), and then making common cause

with leftists and liberals after Germany attacked the Soviet Union in June of 1941. These reversals alienated many left-oriented black nationalists, as they did other anti-racists and progressives. See Robinson 2000 (1983) for the definitive analysis and background on these matters.

36. Some of the analyses are tragically humorous. The Communist Labor Party, a Marxist-Leninist group, understood the black nation in the following manner:

    > Owing to the specifics of the rise of USNA [United States of North America] imperialism and the history of the Black Belt of the South, there arose a nation, oppressed by USNA imperialism, whose social root and base was the aforementioned Negro people ... Now, when referring to the nation, we use the term Negro and mean national and not color ... In the sense of national, Negroes are both the "black" majority and "white" minority. (Peery 1975, 11)

    One can well imagine the success of efforts to organize both blacks and whites in the South on the basis of their common identity as "Negroes."

37. Blauner's approach influenced us very deeply. We pay tribute to him in Omi and Winant 2012. Of course this work, like other "internal colonialism" analyses, can be criticized as well. Blauner departs from the original meaning of the term "colonialism," as Michael Burawoy (1974, 546) has argued. Burawoy offers a definition of colonialism that reasserts the criterion of territoriality in terms which no "internal" application can satisfy:

    > Colonialism may be defined as the conquest and administration by a "metropolitan country" of a geographically separate territory in order to utilize available resources (usually human or natural) for the creation of surplus which is repatriated to the metropolis.

38. "My own developing framework," Blauner writes, "probably owes more to the social movements of the oppressed than to standard sociology" (2001 [1972], viii).

39. Blauner is not unaware that economic suffering and political persecution in their countries of origin impelled much immigration to the United States, but he notes that these problems, however dire, did not force their victims to come to the U.S. *specifically*. Many European emigrants headed for South America, for example. This seems to us an inadequate foundation on which to rest so important a distinction.

40. Ralph Ellison writes,

    > What, by the way, are we to make of a white youngster who, with a transistor radio screaming a Stevie Wonder tune glued to his ear, shouts racial epithets at black youngsters trying to swim at a public beach—and this in the name of the ethnic sanctity of what has been declared a neighborhood turf? (1995 [1986])

    Charles Gallagher writes,

    > An adolescent white male at a bar mitzvah wears a FUBU shirt while his white friend preens his tightly set, perfectly braided corn rows. A black model dressed in yachting attire peddles a New England yuppie boating look in Nautica advertisements. It is quite unremarkable to observe whites, Asians, or African Americans with dyed purple, blond, or red hair. White, black, and Asian students decorate their bodies with tattoos of Chinese characters and symbols. In cities and suburbs, young adults across the color line wear hip-hop clothing and listen to white rapper

Eminem and black rapper Jay-Z. A north Georgia branch of the NAACP installs a white biology professor as its president. The music of Jimi Hendrix is used to sell Apple Computers. Du-Rag kits [sic], complete with bandana headscarf and elastic headband are on sale for $2.95 at hip-hop clothing stores and theme parks like Six Flags. Salsa has replaced ketchup as the best-selling condiment in the United States … (2003, 22–23; see also Wimsatt 1994)

41. Some writers—for example, Samuel P. Huntington—do argue unabashedly that U.S. civic culture was founded on White Anglo-Saxon Protestant values, and that the ticket for inclusion in "our" society remains full adherence to those values (Huntington 2005).
42. With the partial exceptions of the Puerto Rican, Native Hawai'ian, and Native American peoples, who have more credible claims as racialized nations because of their history of U.S. occupation.

PART II

Racial Formation

CHAPTER 4

The Theory of Racial Formation

Race is a way of "making up people."[1] The very act of defining racial groups is a process fraught with confusion, contradiction, and unintended consequences. Concepts of race prove to be unreliable as supposed boundaries shift, slippages occur, realignments become evident, and new collectivities emerge. State-imposed classifications of race, for example, face continuing challenges by individuals and groups who seek to assert distinctive racial categories and identities. Historical shifts in scientific knowledge, in fields ranging from physical anthropology to the genomic sciences, fuel continuing debates about what race may or may not mean as an indicator of human variation. While such debates and reformulations regarding the concept of race initially occur in specific institutional arenas, public spaces, or academic fields, their consequences are often dramatic and reverberate broadly throughout society.

Race-making can also be understood as a process of "othering." Defining groups of people as "other" is obviously not restricted to distinctions based on race. Gender, class, sexuality, religion, culture, language, nationality, and age, among other perceived distinctions, are frequently evoked to justify structures of inequality, differential treatment, subordinate status, and in some cases violent conflict and war. Classifying people as other, and making use of various perceived attributes in order to do so, is a universal phenomenon that also classifies (and works to amalgamate and homogenize) those who do the classifying (Blumer 1958). "Making up people" is both basic and ubiquitous. As social beings, we must categorize people so as to be able to "navigate" in the world—to discern quickly who may be friend or foe, to position and situate ourselves within prevailing social hierarchies, and to provide clues that guide our social interactions with the individuals and groups we encounter.

But while the act of categorizing people and assigning different attributes to such categories may be universal, the categories themselves are subject to enormous variation over historical time and space. The definitions, meanings, and overall coherence of prevailing social categories are always subject to multiple interpretations. No social category rises to the level of being understood as a fixed, objective, social fact.

One might imagine, for example, that the category of a person's "age" (as measured in years) is an objective social category. But even this familiar concept's meaning varies across time and space. In many societies where the elderly are venerated and highly valued as leaders and living repositories of wisdom, individuals tend to overstate their age in years. By contrast, people in the youth-oriented United States tend to understate how old they are. Processes of classification, including self-classification, are reflective of specific social structures, cultural meanings and practices, and of broader power relations as well.

The definitions of specific categories are framed and contested from "above" and "below." The social identities of marginalized and subordinate groups, for example, are both imposed from above by dominant social groups and/or state institutions, and constituted from below by these groups themselves as expressions of self-identification and resistance to dominant forms of categorization. In any given historical moment, one can understand a social category's prevailing meaning, but such understandings can also be erroneous or transitory. They are often no more than the unstable and tentative result of the dynamic engagement between "elite" and "street" definitions and meanings.

Race as a Master Category

It is now widely accepted in most scholarly fields that race is a *social construction.* Simply stating that race is socially constructed, however, begs a number of important questions. How is race constructed? How and why do racial definitions and meanings change over time and place? And perhaps most important, what role does race play within the broader social system in which it is embedded?

With respect to this last question, we advance what may seem an audacious claim. We assert that in the United States, *race is a master category*—a fundamental concept that has profoundly shaped, and continues to shape, the history, polity, economic structure, and culture of the United States. Obviously, some clarification is in order. We are not suggesting that race is a transcendent category—something that stands above or apart from class, gender, or other axes of inequality and difference. The literature on intersectionality has clearly demonstrated the mutual determination and co-constitution of the categories of race, class, gender, and sexual orientation. It is not possible to understand the (il)logic of any form of social stratification, any practice of cultural marginalization, or any type of inequality or human variation, without appreciating the deep, complex, comingling, interpenetration of race, class, gender, and sexuality. In the cauldron of social life, these categories come together; they are profoundly transformed in the process.[2]

We hold these truths of intersectional analysis to be self-evident. But we also believe that race has played a unique role in the formation and historical development of the United States. Since the historical encounter of the hemispheres and the onset of transatlantic enslavement were the fundamental acts of race-making, since they launched a global and world-historical process of "making up people" that constituted the modern world, race has become the *template* of both difference and inequality. This is a world-historical claim, but here we develop it only in the context of the United States.

We suggest that the establishment and reproduction of different regimes of domination, inequality, and difference in the United States have consciously drawn upon concepts of difference, hierarchy, and marginalization based on race. The genocidal policies and practices directed towards indigenous peoples in the conquest and settlement of the "new world," and towards African peoples in the organization of racial slavery, combined to form a template, a master frame, that has perniciously shaped the treatment and experiences of other subordinated groups as well. This template includes not only the technologies (economic, political, cultural) of exploitation, domination, and deracination; it also includes the technologies of resistance: self-activity (James et al., 1958); "*liberté, égalité, fraternité*," sisterhood, and abolition democracy (Du Bois 2007 [1935]).

Consider the questions of class and gender. Historically in the United States, race has provided a master category for understanding the definition of class and the patterns of class consciousness, mobilization, and organization. Class stratification in the United States has been profoundly affected by race and racism, and the reproduction of class inequalities is inextricably linked to the maintenance of white supremacy. Race has shaped the meaning of such concepts as work and worker, labor and employment, master and servant, supervisor and subordinate (Roediger 2007 [1991]). Race is a fundamental organizing principle of social stratification. It has influenced the definition of rights and privileges, the distribution of resources, and the ideologies and practices of subordination and oppression. The concept of race as a marker of difference has permeated all forms of social relations. It is a template for the processes of marginalization that continue to shape social structures as well as collective and individual psyches. Drawing upon social psychology and mind science research that explores mechanisms of "othering," john a. powell and Stephen Menendian assert: "Without being identical, most of the forms of marginalization and stratification in society share a common set of heuristics and structure, which is patterned on race" (powell and Menendian n.d.).

From conquest and slavery on, racial parallels and racial "crossings" have shaped gender relations. Women and slaves were at best lower-status humans, at worst not human at all. They were both subject to chattelization. Their labor was coerced and unremunerated; they were physically brutalized. Although there were, of course, very distinct and widely varied experiences of subordination among different classes of women and of blacks, the objectification of both groups was near-total. Repression of women's autonomy, intellect, and bodily integrity was obsessive and often violent (Beauvoir 1989; Federici 2004). Blacks, Indians, and women were afforded very little recognition: Their entry into the public sphere, corporeal integrity, and intellectual capacity was strenuously denied. In political and legal theory, the sexual contract and the racial contract have been extensively compared (Goldman 1911; Rubin 1975; Pateman 1988; Mills 1999).

The corporeal distinction between white men and the others over whom they ruled as patriarchs and masters, then, links race to gender, and people of color to women. Whether they were defined by their racial status (as enslaved or "free," black, Indian, *mestiz@*), or by the patriarchal family (as daughters, wives, mothers), they were corporeally stigmatized, permanently rendered as "other than," and the possessions of, the white men who ruled. As in the case of class distinctions, evolving gender distinctions coincided in important ways with racial ones. In part, this too was corporeal: Perhaps at the core of intersectionality practice, as well as theory, is the "mixed-race" category. Well, how does it come about that people can be "mixed"? What does the presence of mixed people mean for both white and male supremacy?

In short, the master category of race profoundly shaped gender oppression. It is fascinating that this pattern of combined political influence and political tension, which was established in the antebellum intersection between abolitionism and early feminism and reproduced during the struggle for women's suffrage and against Jim Crow at the turn of the 20th century, was then reiterated again in the post-World War II years in "intersectional" alliance and conflict between the civil rights movement and "second-wave" feminism. To be sure, there were many "intersections" between the two patterns described here. The tense and ultimately ruptural relationship between "first-wave" feminism and the black freedom movement around the turn of the 20th century is perhaps the best-known example: The (white) women's suffrage movement broke with its former black allies, abandoning black women (and black men too) in the process, as the Jim Crow system was institutionalized in the United States. Southern states' ratification of the 19th Amendment was conditional on their continued denial of black voting rights. Such black women activists as Ida B. Wells, Mary Church Terrell, and Anna Julia Cooper, as well as many lesser-known figures, fiercely denounced this as a betrayal. Of course, it reflected the pervasive white racism of the epoch (see Crenshaw 1991; Cooper 1998; Collins 2008 [1999]; Davis 2011 [1983]).

While race is a template for the subordination and oppression of different social groups, we emphasize that it is also a template for resistance to many forms of marginalization and domination. The new social movements of the 1960s and 1970s, for example—the women's movement, the student movement, the anti-war movement, the gay liberation movement—were inspired by and consciously drew upon the black movement's theoretical insights, strategies, and tactics to organize their specific constituencies, make political demands, and challenge existing practices of exclusion and subordination. These movement challenges underscore the dual-edged and dynamic qualities that inhere in the social category of race. These qualities are, once again, economic, political, and cultural technologies. They involve asserting previously stigmatized identities, "fusing" previously "serialized" groups (Sartre 2004), creating "commons" where resources can be shared. "Making up people" racially, then, has been "portable" across U.S. history. It has spread from one oppressed group to another and proved transferable to other marginalized identities, social cleavages, and political struggles.

Before we can consider and fully evaluate the notion of race as a master category of social organization in the United States, we need to think about how race itself is defined, what meanings are attached to it, and how it is deployed to create, reproduce, or challenge racist structures. The process of race making, and its reverberations throughout the social order, is what we call *racial formation*. We define racial formation as *the sociohistorical process by which racial identities are created, lived out, transformed, and destroyed.*

Our presentation of racial formation theory proceeds in several steps. First, we provide a concept of *racialization* to emphasize how the phenomic, the corporeal dimension of human bodies, acquires meaning in social life. How are corporeal differences among humans apprehended and given meaning? Next, we advance the concept of *racial projects* to capture the simultaneous and co-constitutive ways that racial meanings are translated into social structures and become racially signified. Then, we discuss the problem of *racism* in an attempt to specify under what conditions a racial project can be defined as *racist*. Finally, we discuss *racial politics*, the way society is racially organized and ruled. Here, we consider *racial despotism, racial democracy, and racial hegemony* as frameworks for racial rule and racial resistance. We suggest that in the early 21st century the hegemonic concept of race in U.S. society is that of "colorblindness." The ideological hegemony of colorblindness, however, is extremely contradictory and shallow. It confronts widespread resistance and falls short of achieving the political stability that hegemonic projects are supposed to deliver. This chapter ends there; the post-World War II political trajectory of race is treated in detail in the chapters that follow.

Racialization

Race is often seen as a social category that is either objective or illusory. When viewed as an objective matter, race is usually understood as rooted in biological differences, ranging from such familiar phenomic markers as skin color, hair texture, or eye shape, to more obscure human variations occurring at the genetic or genomic levels. When viewed as an illusion, race is usually understood as an ideological construct, something that masks a more fundamental material distinction or axis of identity: our three paradigms of ethnicity, class, and nation typify such approaches. Thus race is often treated as a metonym or epiphenomenon of culture (in the ethnicity paradigm), inequality and stratification (in the class paradigm), or primordial peoplehood (in the nation paradigm).

On the "objective" side, race is often regarded as an *essence*, as something fixed and concrete. The three main racial classifications of humans once posed (and now largely rejected) by physical anthropology—Negroid, Caucasoid, and Mongoloid—are examples of such an essentialist perspective. Another example is "mixed-race" identity: To consider an individual or group as "multiracial" or mixed race presupposes the existence of clear, discernible, and discrete races that have subsequently been combined to create a hybrid, or perhaps mongrel, identity. Here race is functioning as a metonym for "species," although that connection is generally not admitted in the present day.

While race is still popularly understood as essence, it has also been viewed as a mere *illusion*, especially in more recent accounts. As a purely ideological construct, race is considered to be unreal, a product of "false consciousness." As we have seen in our discussion of class paradigms of race, both orthodox (neoclassical) economics and orthodox Marxism viewed race this way. For the former, it was an irrational distraction from pure, market-based considerations of value in exchange; for the latter it was an ideological tool that capitalists (or sometimes privileged white workers) deployed to prevent the emergence of a unified working-class movement. In the current period, colorblind ideology—expressed, for example, in affirmative action debates—argues that any form of racial classification is itself inherently racist since race is not "real."

We are critical of both positions: race as essence and race as illusion. Race is not something rooted in nature, something that reflects clear and discrete variations in human identity. But race is also not an illusion. While it may not be "real" in a biological sense, race is indeed real as a social category with definite social consequences. The family, as a social concept, provides an intriguing analogy to grasp the "reality" of race:

> We know that families take many forms … Some family categories correspond to biological categories; others do not. Moreover, boundaries of family membership vary, depending on individual and institutional factors. Yet regardless of whether families correspond to biological definitions, social scientists study families and use membership in family categories in their study of other phenomena, such as well-being. Similarly, racial statuses, although not representing biological differences, are of sociological interest in their form, their changes, and their consequences.
>
> (American Sociological Association 2003, 5)

We cannot dismiss race as a legitimate category of social analysis by simply stating that race is not real. With respect to race, the Thomases's sociological dictum is still in force: "It is not important whether or not the interpretation is correct—if men [sic] define situations as real, they are real in their consequences" (Thomas and Thomas 1928, pp. 571–572).

One of our aims here is to disrupt and reorganize the rigid and antinomic framework of essence-versus-illusion in which race is theorized and debated. We understand race as an unstable and "decentered" complex of social meanings constantly being transformed by political struggle. With this in mind, we advance the following definition: *Race is a concept that signifies and symbolizes social conflicts and interests by referring to different types of human bodies.* Although the concept of race invokes seemingly biologically based human characteristics (so-called phenotypes), selection of these particular human features for purposes of racial signification is always and necessarily a social and historical process. Indeed, the categories employed to differentiate among human beings along racial lines reveal themselves, upon serious examination, to be at best imprecise, and at worst completely arbitrary. They may be arbitrary, but they are not meaningless. Race is strategic; race does ideological and political work.

Despite the problematic nature of racial categorization, it should be apparent that there is a crucial and non-reducible *visual dimension* to the definition and understanding of racial categories. Bodies are visually read and narrated in ways that draw upon an ensemble of symbolic meanings and associations. Corporeal distinctions are common; they become essentialized. Perceived differences in skin color, physical build, hair texture, the structure of cheek bones, the shape of the nose, or the presence/absence of an epicanthic fold are understood as the manifestations of more profound differences that are situated *within* racially identified persons: differences in such qualities as intelligence, athletic ability, temperament, and sexuality, among other traits.

Through a complex process of selection, human physical characteristics ("real" or imagined) become the basis to justify or reinforce social differentiation. Conscious or unconscious, deeply ingrained or reinvented, the making of race, the "othering" of social groups by means of the invocation of physical distinctions, is a key component of modern societies. "Making up people," once again. This process of selection, of imparting social and symbolic meaning to perceived phenotypical differences, is the core, constitutive element of what we term "racialization."

We define racialization as *the extension of racial meaning to a previously racially unclassified relationship, social practice, or group.* Racialization occurs in large-scale and small-scale ways, macro- and micro-socially. In large-scale, even world-historical settings, racialization can be observed in the foundation and consolidation of the modern world-system: The conquest and settlement of the western hemisphere, the development of African slavery, and the rise of abolitionism, all involved profuse and profound extension of racial meanings into new social terrain. In smaller-scale settings as well, "making up people" or racial interpellation (a concept drawn from Althusser 2001 (1971) also operates as a quotidian form of racialization: Racial profiling for example, may be understood as a form of racialization. Racial categories, and the meanings attached to them, are often constructed from pre-existing conceptual or discursive elements that have crystallized through the genealogies of competing religious, scientific, and political ideologies and projects. These are so to speak the raw materials of racialization.

To summarize thus far: Race is a concept, a representation or signification of identity that refers to different types of human bodies, to the perceived corporeal and phenotypic markers of difference and the meanings and social practices that are ascribed to these differences.

It is important to emphasize that once specific concepts of race are widely circulated and accepted as a social reality, racial difference is not dependent on visual observation alone. Legal scholar Osagie Obasogie makes the intriguing point that iterative social practices give rise to "visual" understandings of race, even among those who cannot see. The respondents in his study, blind since birth, "see" race through interpersonal and institutional socializations and practices that shape their perceptions of what race is (Obasogie 2013). Thus race is neither self-evident nor obvious as an ocular phenomenon. Instead racialization depends on meanings and associations that permit phenotypic distinction among human bodies.

Some may argue that if the concept of race is so nebulous, so indeterminate, so flexible, and so susceptible to strategic manipulation by a range of political projects, why don't we simply dispense with it? Can we not get "beyond" race? Can we not see it as an illusory thing? Don't we see how much mischief has occurred in its name? These questions have been posed with tremendous frequency in both popular and academic discourse.[3] An affirmative answer would of course present obvious practical difficulties: It is rather difficult to jettison widely held beliefs, beliefs which moreover are central to everyone's identity and understanding of the social world. So the attempt to banish the concept as an archaism is at best counterintuitive. But a deeper difficulty, we believe, is inherent in the very formulation of this schema, in its way of posing race as a *problem*, a misconception left over from the past, a concept no longer relevant to a "post-racial" society.

A more effective starting point is the recognition that despite its uncertainties and contradictions, the concept of race continues to play a fundamental role in structuring and representing the social world. The task for theory is to capture this situation and avoid both the utopian framework that sees race as an illusion we can somehow "get beyond," as well as the essentialist formulation that sees race as something objective and fixed, a biological given. We should think of race as an element of social structure rather than as an irregularity within it; we should see race as a dimension of human representation rather than an illusion. Such a perspective informs what we mean by racial formation.

Since racial formation is always historically situated, understandings of the meaning of race, and of the way race structures society, have changed enormously over time. We now turn to a historical survey of the race concept and the domains in which it has been defined and debated, consolidated and contested. Our effort here is to outline a genealogy of racialization that proceeds from religion to science to politics. Such a trajectory is by no means linear or progressive; rather it consists of the accretion of racialized experiences that are uneven and often incompatible. But it does allow us roughly to map and situate the development of the race concept, and to underscore its still unstable and ambiguous character.

The Evolution of Race Consciousness

How do perceived differences between groups of people become racialized? The identification of distinctive human groups, and their association with differences in physical appearance, goes back to prehistory, and can be found in the earliest documents—in the Bible, for example, or in Herodotus. But the emergence of a modern conception of race does not occur until the rise of Europe and the arrival of Europeans in the Americas. Even the hostility and suspicion with which Christian Europe viewed its two significant non-Christian "others"—the Muslims and the Jews—cannot be understood as more than a rehearsal for racial formation, since these antagonisms, for all their bloodletting and chauvinism, were always and everywhere religiously interpreted.[4]

It was only when European explorers reached the Western Hemisphere, when the oceanic seal separating the "old" and the "new" worlds was breached, that the distinctions and categorizations fundamental to a racialized social structure, and to a discourse of race, began to appear. The European explorers were the advance guard of merchant capitalism, which sought new openings for trade. What they found exceeded their wildest dreams, for never before and never again in human history has an opportunity for the appropriation of wealth, for predation or "primitive accumulation" remotely approached that presented by the "discovery."[5] Modern capitalism could not have come into being without this grand infusion of stolen wealth: a seemingly limitless reservoir of treasure—land, labor, lives by the millions—to do with as one willed.

But the Europeans also "discovered" people, people who looked and acted differently. These "natives" challenged their discoverers' preexisting conceptions of the origins and possibilities of the human species (Jordan 2012 [1968], 3–43). The representation and interpretation of the meaning of the indigenous peoples' existence became a crucial matter, one that would affect not only the outcome of conquest but the future of empire and thus the development of the modern world. For the "discovery" raised disturbing questions as to whether *all* could be considered part of the same "family of man," and more practically, the extent to which native peoples could be exploited and enslaved. Thus "discovery," conquest, and soon enough, enslavement, launched not only the headlong rush toward modernity, but also debates over human nature, philosophical anthropology. Such questions as: "What is a human being?" and "What is the nature of human difference?" were posed repeatedly as rulers and their advisers sought to organize and exercise control over their new dominions and new subjects.[6]

In practice, of course, the seizure of territories and goods, the introduction of slavery through the *encomienda* and other forms of coerced native labor, and then through the organization of the African slave trade—not to mention the practice of outright extermination—all presupposed a worldview which distinguished Europeans, as children of God and fully-fledged human beings, from "others." Given the dimensions and the ineluctability of the European onslaught, given the conquerors' determination to appropriate labor, land, and goods, and given the presence of an axiomatic and unquestioned Christianity among them, the ferocious division of society into Europeans and "others" soon coalesced. This was true despite the famous 16th-century theological and philosophical debates about the identity of indigenous peoples.[7] In fact it ran right over whatever cautionary notes religious ethicists like las Casas, or later Antonio Vieira (Blackburn 1997; Cohen 1998), William Wilberforce, or Henry Ward Beecher might have sounded.

Indeed, debates about the nature of the "others" reached their practical limits with a certain dispatch. Plainly, they would never touch the essential: Nothing, after all, would induce the Europeans to pack up and go home. The "discovery" signaled a break from the previous proto-racial awareness by which Europe had contemplated its "others" in a relatively disorganized fashion. The "conquest of America" was not simply an epochal historical event—however unparalleled in importance. It was also the advent of a consolidated social structure of exploitation, appropriation, domination, and signification. Its representation, first in religious terms, but later in scientific and political ones, initiated modern racial awareness. It was the inauguration of racialization on a world-historical scale.

The conquest, therefore, was the first—and given the dramatic nature of the case, perhaps the greatest—racial formation project. Together with African slavery it produced the master category of race, the racial template we have discussed. Its significance was by no means limited to the Western Hemisphere, for it also began the work of constituting Europe as the metropole, the center, of a series of empires which could take, as Marx would later write, "the globe for a theater" (Marx 1967, 751). This new imperial structure was represented as a struggle between civilization and barbarism, and implicated in this representation all the great European philosophies, literary traditions, and social theories of the modern age (Said 1993).

The immensity of this historical arc, the *longue durée* of racial formation from religion to science to politics, also underlies our claim that race provided a master concept for our understanding of oppression and resistance. But it is worth noting that right from the beginning of this historical journey, something like the social construction of race was *already* present. Before the white talking heads had debated the philosophical anthropology of Native Americans, or Africans,[8] well before that in fact, *the immediate need to classify and categorize, to "make up people," had already surfaced:* Who was a European, a settler, a free man, and who was an *Indio*, an African, a slave? As a practical matter, something relatively devoid of theology or philosophy, the exercise of power required these distinctions.[9] The main criteria available for this purpose were phenomic: the visual appearance of the bodies that had to be judged, sometimes under great pressure and with speed—for violence was omnipresent—as like or unlike, similar or different. This social (or more properly, this power-oriented, political) construction, this phenomic categorical imperative, would soon enough be reprocessed in the discourse available at the time: primarily and for a long time to come, theological discourse.

Only in later epochs would other ways of knowing supplant theological understandings: First scientific, and later, political accounts of race would be offered. Still the earlier religious and scientific frameworks, though losing influence, would never be fully eliminated, never really die. Thus do we arrive at our own time, our own knowledge of race, our own insistence on the social construction of race, with its unstable combination of corporeal and performative elements, its inherent biosociality. We are still on this journey. We should be clear-sighted enough to recognize that these components, most centrally the political technology of the body, were there from the beginning. In short, just as the noise of the "big bang" still resonates through the universe, so the overdetermined construction of world "civilization" as a biosocial manifestation of European subjugation and the resistance of the rest of us still defines the race concept in the present.

From Religion to Science

After the initial depredations of conquest, religious justifications for racial difference gradually gave way to scientific ones. By the time of the Enlightenment, a general awareness of race was pervasive, and most of the great philosophers of Europe, such as Hegel, Kant, Voltaire, and Locke, were issuing virulently racist opinions (Count, ed. 1950; Eze, ed. 1997; Bernasconi and Lott, eds. 2000).

The problem posed by race during the late 18th century was markedly different than it had been in the earlier stages of conquest and enslavement. The social structures through which race operated were no longer primarily those of violent subjugation and plunder, nor of the establishment of thin beachheads of settlement on the edge of what had once seemed a limitless wilderness. Now the issues were much more complicated: nation-building, establishment of national economies in the world trading system, resistance to the arbitrary authority of monarchs, and the assertion of the "natural rights" of "man," including the right of revolution (Davis 1999 [1975]). In such a situation, racially organized exploitation in the form of slavery, the expansion of colonies, and the continuing expulsion of native peoples, was both necessary and newly difficult to justify.

Early Iterations of Scientific Racism: The invocation of scientific criteria to demonstrate the "natural" basis of racial hierarchy was both a logical consequence of the rise of this form of knowledge, and an attempt to provide a more subtle and nuanced account of human complexity in the new, "enlightened" age. Spurred on by the classificatory scheme of living organisms devised by Linnaeus in *Systema Naturae* (1735), many scholars in the eighteenth and nineteenth centuries dedicated themselves to the identification and ranking of variations in humankind. Race was conceived as a *biological* concept, a matter of species. Voltaire wrote that "The negro race is a species of men [sic] as different from ours ... as the breed of spaniels is from that of greyhounds," and in a formulation echoing down from his century to our own, declared that

> If their understanding is not of a different nature from ours ..., it is at least greatly inferior. They are not capable of any great application or association of ideas, and seem formed neither for the advantages nor the abuses of philosophy.
>
> (Voltaire, in Gossett 1997 [1965], 45)

Jefferson, the preeminent exponent of the Enlightenment doctrine of "the rights of man" on North American shores, echoed these sentiments:

> In general their existence appears to participate more of sensation than reflection. … [I]n memory they are equal to whites, in reason much inferior … [and] in imagination they are dull, tasteless, and anomalous.… I advance it therefore … that the blacks, whether originally a different race, or made distinct by time and circumstances, are inferior to the whites.… Will not a lover of natural history, then, one who views the gradations in all the animals with the eye of philosophy, excuse an effort to keep those in the department of Man [sic] as distinct as nature has formed them?
>
> (Jefferson 1984 [1785], 264–266, 270)

Such crackpot claims of species distinctiveness among humans justified the inequitable allocation of political and social rights, while still upholding the doctrine of "the rights of man." They rationalized the rapacious treatment to which the racial "others" were subjected, and even justified it as the unfortunate byproducts of development. You can still hear these arguments today: "Sure, these natives and slaves might be suffering now, but that is still preferable to being condemned to the eternal darkness of primitiveness and superstition.…" The frequent resort to familial metaphors ("Our slaves are like our children; they must be taught to obey …"), and the mad search for scientific justifications for unequal treatment—in phrenology and craniometry, for example, and then in evolution—all attest to the overarching importance of racial rule in the genealogy of the modern world.

Indeed the quest to obtain a precise scientific definition of race generated debates which continue to rage today, reiterated in the genomic, the criminological, and the humanistic approaches to race that we take for granted. Yet despite efforts to define race scientifically, ranging from Dr. Samuel Morton's studies of cranial capacity[10] to contemporary attempts in the genomic sciences, the concept of race has defied biological precision.

In the mid-19th century, Count Joseph Arthur de Gobineau drew upon the most respected scientific studies of his day to compose his four-volume *Essay on the Inequality of Races* (Biddiss 1970; Gobineau 1999 [1853–1855]; Todorov 1993). He not only greatly influenced the racial thinking of the period, but his themes would be echoed in the racist ideologies of the next one hundred years: beliefs that superior races produced superior cultures and that racial intermixtures resulted in the degradation of the superior racial stock. These ideas found expression, for instance, in the eugenics movement launched by Darwin's cousin, Francis Galton, which had an immense impact on scientific and sociopolitical thought in Europe and the United States (Chase 1980; Kevles 1998; Graves 2001; Black 2012). In the wake of civil war and emancipation, and with immigration from Southern and Eastern Europe as well as East Asia running high, the United States was particularly fertile ground for notions such as Social Darwinism and eugenics. Within this context, racial difference became the rationale for discriminatory policies and practices of immigrant exclusion, naturalization rights, residential segregation, and forced sterilization.

Although black scholars like Kelly Miller, William Monroe Trotter, and W.E.B. Du Bois had questioned biologistic racism at the end of the 19th century, and Chicago sociologists had cast doubt on evolution-based accounts of racial difference in the 1920s, it was not until after World War II that a sustained attack on the notion of race as a biological concept emerged and gained widespread acceptance. Only after eugenics had been discredited as the basis for racial science in Nazi Germany—eugenics had, of course, flourished in the United States as well—did scientific critiques of biologistic racism become prominent. The 1950 UNESCO "Statement on Race"[11] boldly asserted that race was not a biological fact but a social myth. During this period, social and cultural conceptions of race became ascendant and it was optimistically assumed that the death knell of scientific racism had been rung. But had it?

Contemporary Reiterations of Scientific Racism: Over the past decades, the study of human variation in a number of fields has often defaulted to, and indeed relied upon, biological concepts of race in research on "population groups." Default to the race concept remains pervasive. After the launching of the Human Genome Project, for example, geneticists have engaged in vigorous debate about whether race is a meaningful and useful genetic concept. But they can't get rid of it. The notion of race as a discernible "biological category" has not been relegated to the proverbial dustbin of history.

Geneticist Neil Risch contends that genetic differences have arisen among people from different continents and uses the term "race" to categorize and cluster the human population into five major groups. This recognition of race, he contends, is important for understanding genetic susceptibility to certain diseases and receptivity to medical interventions such as drug treatments (Wade 2002). Indeed, the linkage between race and genetics finds its sharpest expression in the field of pharmacogenomics. The ultimate goal of pharmacogenomics is to be able to deliver the precise type of medication—and precise dose—to a patient based on their individual genome. Its goal is to tailor-make drugs to treat a specific condition. Because it is not yet practical to sequence each individual's genome in a quick and cost-effective manner, much less to do drug design on this level, race often serves as a "proxy" for determining how treatment with a specific drug might be targeted, if not at individuals, then at identifiable groups. And not surprisingly, race is the descriptor employed to select such groups (Lee 2005).

Consider the introduction of BiDil as the first "ethnic designer drug." Originally produced by the now defunct biotech firm NitroMed, BiDil was marketed to African Americans who suffer from congestive heart failure, despite serious doubts that arose in clinical trials about the distinctive racial claims being made for the drug. Yet it was released anyway, and prescribed for African Americans. Some medical researchers feared that BiDil sets a dangerous precedent by linking race and genetics in ways that could distract from alternative ways of understanding the causes of a disease and the means to treat it (Kahn 2012).

The issue of race and genetics is a contentious one that finds expression in different sites and arenas.

- In 2010, PBS aired *Faces of America with Henry Louis Gates, Jr.*, a four-episode documentary series that traced the ancestral roots of prominent celebrities through "genealogy and genetics." An extension of earlier shows focused on famous African Americans, the series reflects a growing popular quest by individuals to find their "roots" through allegedly scientific means.
- In the field of forensics, Tony Frudakis of DNAPrint Genomics, a molecular biologist who came to fame in a Baton Rouge serial killer case in 2003, claims that he can determine a murderer's race by analyzing his or her DNA (Wade 2003; Quan 2011; Obasogie 2013).
- DNA testing has increasingly been used by individuals and groups to claim Native American tribal membership. The Meskwaki Nation in Iowa utilized genetic-ancestry testing as a way to screen out individuals who sought tribal affiliation in order to share in the tribe's casino profits. The Mashantucket Pequot Tribal Nation of Connecticut, which controls the huge Foxwoods casino, requires DNA testing of newborns. Both the Cherokee and Seminole nations/tribes have been embroiled in conflicts with blacks who claim tribal ancestry and seek access to court-ordered monetary judgments. In these cases disputes have revolved around the "blood quantum" system of measuring Indian belonging (put in place by the Dawes Act of 1887), and have also involved tribal attitudes toward DNA testing of present-day claimants (Tallbear 2003; Indians.com 2005; Kaplan 2005; Koerner 2005).[12]

Henry Louis Gates, Jr. has said: "We are living through an era of the ascendance of biology, and we have to be very careful. We will all be walking a fine line between using biology and allowing it to be abused" (Harmon 2007). There is indeed a fine line. Our individual sense of racial identity, the system of racial classification we employ, the meanings we ascribe to racial categories, and their use in social analysis and policy formation are rendered more complex, indeterminate, and muddy with the increasing re-biologization of race.

In psychology too, the cognitive presence of race, the immediacy of race that is seemingly rooted in perception rather than reasoning, leads researchers to think of it as an essence, something innate. Cognitive psychology and related fields have sought to uncover forms of racial animus that function "below the radar" of the conscious mind. Studies on the mechanisms and processes that affect perception, interpretation, memory, and decision-making have convincingly demonstrated that people harbor "implicit biases" and possess "racial schemas" that strongly influence perceptions and behaviors.[13] Implicit biases can influence or shape various forms of individual or institutional racial discrimination. Such discrimination, therefore, can occur in the absence of conscious intent, explicit prejudice, or racial animus. Thus the pervasiveness of racial meanings and their significance goes deep, very deep (Hirschfeld 1973 (1938); Eberhardt and Fiske, eds. 1998; Goff et al. 2008; Marsh, Mendoza-Denton, and Smith, eds. 2010). Notions of race do not only inform our conscious understanding of the social world; they also permeate our unconscious minds—shaping our perceptions and attitudes, and influencing our actions.

For all its obvious importance, this approach also raises troubling questions: Are those cultural formations not themselves constructed? Are those "aggregate relations of power" impervious to challenge? Social constructions like race (or gender, or countless other human qualities) are of course composed of layered attributes that human beings *understand* as essences, but that does not make race, or gender an essence *in reality*, does it? (What would W.I. Thomas reply to that question?) If in practice race remains flexible and unstable, how does that instability affect the "racial schemas" that structure immediate perceptions? What is the essence of blackness or whiteness? Of maleness or femaleness (Butler 1993; Butler 2006 [1990]; Shelby 2007)?

There is a very strong temptation to derive racial distinctions, and perforce racism, from biological or evolutionary sources. This tendency is not limited to reactionary or conservative thinkers, but also affects progressive and egalitarian analysts, as we have seen in Douglas S. Massey's "categorical" approach to inequality (discussed in Chapter 2). No doubt there is irony in contemporary attempts to provide a seemingly objective and scientific definition of race, and of the boundaries and contents (the essences) of racial categories as well. In previous historical periods, scientific racism provided the rationale for the subordination, if not elimination, of what were seen as undesirable, "mongrel," and threatening racially identified groups. In the current period, biological/genetic definitions of race are mobilized to improve the treatment of diseases and minimize health disparities, to serve justice by providing "hard evidence" in criminal cases, to help individuals find their ancestral "roots," and in the case of cognitive psychology, to reveal the deep mental structures of racism. While often motivated by good intentions, the premises behind these examples share an underlying logic with the racist frameworks of the historical past: a quest for some fundamental quality of racial identity, if not skin or hair, then genomic or limbic.

The recourse to "human nature," to philosophical anthropology, to explain the supposed differences and "natural" biases entailed by race, has been a constant feature of human thought, especially in western civilization.[14] It is tempting to extrapolate from implicit bias research: to conclude that race thinking is an innate part of human consciousness—something to which we are intrinsically and naturally predisposed. In clear disagreement with such views we insist that the "racial schemas" that structure immediate perceptions are also cultural formations; they may be deeply embedded as a result of centuries of reiteration in various forms. Yet they remain socially, not biologically, given. They remain subject to change. We are not biologically "hardwired" to be racist. We reject any default to an essentialist and intrinsically unprovable notion of race. Yet resisting the temptation to racial biologism, whether conscious or unconscious, remains as difficult in science as it once was in religion.

From Science to Politics

Efforts to "re-biologize" race suggest that the understanding of race as a preeminently social concept remains an embattled and contested notion. While we acknowledge this ongoing tension, we suggest that conflicts and controversies about the meaning of race are principally framed on the terrain of politics. By privileging politics, we do not mean to suggest that race has been displaced as a concern of scientific inquiry, or for that matter as a theological question. Nor do we claim that struggles over cultural representation are less significant than political ones in shaping prevailing patterns of race and racism. We do argue, however, that race is now a preeminently political phenomenon.

Toward Social Construction: The historical trend towards recognizing race as a social and political construction has been slow and uneven. While critiques of race as a biological concept were more evident and ascendant in the early post-World War II period, there were previous historical precedents for understanding race as a social and political category. For example, Max Weber discounted biological explanations for racial conflict and instead highlighted the social and political factors that engendered it (Weber 2008, 385–387; Manasse 1947). Du Bois too wrestled with the conflict between a fully sociohistorical conception of race, and the more essentialized and deterministic vision he encountered as a student in Berlin.[15] Pioneering cultural anthropologist Franz Boas rejected attempts to link racial characteristics to biological or evolutionist schemas, labeling as pseudoscientific any assumption of a continuum of "higher" and "lower" cultural groups, and allying with Du Bois quite early on (Boas 1969 [1945], 1962; Baker 1998).[16]

Du Bois and many prominent black scholars, for example, Alain Leroy Locke, philosopher and theorist of the Harlem Renaissance, had switched the focus of race studies definitively away from biologistic accounts and towards sociopolitical explanatory frameworks, almost before modern sociology even existed in the United States. Black voices were ignored, however, until white exponents of socially based views of race like Robert E. Park, one of the founders of the "Chicago School" of sociology, reinvented a socially grounded account of it in the 1920s. Park combined the standard German training in sociology with a history of eight years as journalist and publicist for Booker T. Washington. After his substantial career at Chicago, Park's last job was at Fisk University, the leading historically black college (Du Bois's *alma mater* as well).[17]

Perhaps more important than these and subsequent intellectual efforts, however, were the political struggles of people of color themselves. Waged all around the globe under a variety of banners such as anti-colonialism and civil rights, these battles to challenge various structural and cultural racisms have been a major feature of 20th-century politics. The racial horrors of the 20th century—colonial slaughter and apartheid, the genocide of the Holocaust, and the massive bloodlettings required to end these evils—have also indelibly marked the theme of race as a sociopolitical issue *par excellence.*

Racial Politics: Our notion of racial formation foregrounds the ongoing political contestation that takes place between the state and civil society—across the political spectrum—to define and redefine the very meaning of race. This is a good example of the way race operates across micro–macro linkages: The persistent and continuing controversies regarding state-based racial classification provide a particularly apt illustration of racial formation.

Over the last several centuries, the designation of racial categories by the state—the political dimensions of state assignment of racial identity—has provoked intense disputes in the United States. Who was considered "free" and who "unfree"? Who could be a naturalized citizen (Carbado 2005)? Who could marry whom? In this last regard, it is sobering to think that it was not until 1967 that all state anti-miscegenation laws were ruled unconstitutional in *Loving v. Virginia.* The state wields enormous power in defining what race is. Through its powers of racial classification, the state fundamentally shapes one's social status, access to economic opportunities, political rights, and indeed one's identity itself.

In 2003, former University of California Regent Ward Connerly introduced a measure popularly known as the Racial Privacy Initiative (Proposition 54) before California voters. Proposition 54 sought to amend the California State Constitution by enacting a ban on racial data collection by the state. Connerly (2003) asserted that relying on racial classification and maintaining race-based remedies to racial inequalities would only "give credence to the dangerous view held by many that 'race' is a fixed biological reality."[18]

The discrepancies, gaps, and contradictions between state definitions and individual and collective racial identities are no more evident than in the racial and ethnic categories employed by the U.S. Census. Among others, the U.S. Census establishes categories based on nativity, citizenship status, age, household income, and marital status. None of these categories, however, has been subject to such intense scrutiny, vigorous debate, and political controversy as that of race.

The race questions on the U.S. Census have been shaped by the political and social agenda of the historical period in question. The first census in 1790 distinguished holders of the franchise, namely tax-paying white males, from the general population. The practice of slavery motivated changes in categorization such as grouping blacks into free and slave populations. Prior to the 1960s, census categories were utilized politically to disenfranchise and discriminate against groups defined as nonwhite, a practice that has diminished but not entirely ceased in the "post-civil rights" era. From restrictions on, naturalization rights to the setting of national quotas in the 1924 National Origins Immigration Act, census categories were routinely and strategically deployed to circumscribe the political, economic, and social rights of people of color and immigrants. By the 1960s, the idea of race as a biological construct was widely discredited in academic and scientific circles, and the race question would have been excluded from the 1970 census had it not been for the passage of civil rights and equal opportunity legislation. The new laws required federal agencies to compile data, look for patterns of discrimination, and selectively redress them through various programs and initiatives. This made it necessary to continue to employ forms of racial classification and statistics (Prewitt 2013).

In 1977, the Office of Management and Budget (OMB) issued Statistical Directive No. 15 that fostered the creation of "compatible, nonduplicated, exchangeable racial and ethnic data by Federal agencies." The directive defined the basic racial and ethnic categories to be utilized by the federal government for three reporting purposes: statistical, administrative, and civil rights compliance. The five standard categories were American Indian or Alaskan Native, Asian or Pacific Islander, Black, White, and Hispanic (U.S. Office of Management and Budget 1994).

These racial categories are rife with inconsistencies and lack parallel construction. Only one category is specifically racial, only one is cultural, and only one relies on a notion of affiliation or community recognition. Directive No. 15 defines a black person as one who has his or her "origins in any of the black racial groups of Africa," but it does not define a white person with reference to any of the white racial groups of Europe, North Africa, or the Middle East. Indeed "Black" is the only category that is defined with an explicit "racial" designator—one which is quite problematic. What, we might ask, are the "black racial groups of Africa"? Hispanics are not considered or classified as a "race," but as an "ethnic group." The Hispanic category is, in fact, the only "ethnicity" that the state is interested in explicitly identifying and classifying. The category is defined through a combined national/ethnic designator—a person of "Mexican, Puerto Rican, Cuban, Central or South American or other Spanish culture or origin." In this definition, Hispanics can be of any race.[19] The category of "American Indian or Alaskan Native" complicates matters further. To be counted as part of the group, individuals must not only trace their origins in any of the original peoples of North America, but they must also maintain "cultural identification through tribal affiliation or community recognition." This is a condition that the state does not require of any of the other groups.

While originally narrowly conceived to provide consistent categories for use by federal agencies, Directive No. 15 had the unintended consequence of reshaping much of the discourse of race in the United States. These categories have become the *de facto* standard for state and local agencies, the private and nonprofit sectors, and the research community. Social scientists and policy analysts have widely adopted census directives since data is organized under these rubrics. The social and cultural impact of these categories is readily apparent. They inordinately shape both group identities and community-formation patterns. Largely in response to these categories, new organizations have emerged representing the interests of "Asian and Pacific Islanders" or "Hispanics" in a variety of forms from service providers to professional caucuses. Census categories have played a pivotal role in the emergence and sustaining of panethnic forms of social organization and consciousness. The Census has become the primary site within the U.S. state where competing political claims for group recognition by race and ethnicity are advanced, and where classifications are established in response to statistical needs, administrative recordkeeping practices, and legal requirements. Racially identified groups realize the political value of racial categorization, along with the strategic deployment of "numbers," in highlighting inequalities, arguing for resources, and lobbying for specific redistricting plans, among other demands. Electoral districts, for example, are drawn on the basis of census data.

Despite attempts to achieve standardized and generally understood racial categories, all such forms of classification are fundamentally unstable. One problem is the persistent gap between state definitions and individual/group forms of self-identification. According to the U.S. Census Bureau, over the last four Censuses (from 1980 to 2010) at least 40 percent of "Hispanics" failed to answer either the race question and/or the ethnicity question. Correspondingly, over 95 percent of individuals who mark the "Some Other Race" box were classified Hispanic by the Census. This reflects individual, group, and/or national differences in conceptualizing race. Immigrant groups who come from societies organized around different concepts of race and ethnicity often have difficulty navigating and situating themselves within U.S. racial categories.

Groups continually contest the existing system of racial classification. Arab Americans, currently classified as "white," have argued for a distinctive category to capture forms of discrimination exemplified by the hate crimes and profiling that have occurred as a result of the "War on Terror" and continuing political instability in the Middle East. Taiwanese Americans have been lobbying for a distinctive category as Taiwanese, separate from that of Chinese under the Asian or Pacific Islander category. In both these instances, racial and ethnic consciousness is being fueled in large part by geopolitical transformations that affect how groups see themselves as well as how they are viewed by others.

Multiracial Identity: The debate surrounding the establishment of a multiracial category in the U.S. Census illustrates how some groups contest the existing framework of racial classification, how other groups seek to preserve it, and how the power of the state is employed to adjudicate different racial claims.

For the past 100 years or so, the U.S. Census has assumed that each individual possessed a clear, singular, and monoracial identity. Earlier census enumeration schedules, by contrast, recognized "mixed race" individuals. The 1890 Census listed "mulatto, quadroon, and octoroon" along with "white, black, Chinese, Japanese, and Indian." These mixed race categories eventually disappeared from the census, but the "one-drop rule" of racial descent and the imposition of an arbitrary monoracial identity on individuals of racially mixed parentage remained in place. The 1920 census stipulated that "any mixture of White and some other race was to be reported according to the race of the person who was not White." In 1977, OMB Directive 15 stated that "[t]he category which most closely reflects the individual's recognition in his community should be used for purposes of reporting on persons who are of mixed racial and/or ethnic origins."

In an attempt to assert their multiracial heritage, some individuals ignored census instructions to "[f]ill ONE circle for the race that the person considers himself/herself to be," by marking two or more boxes. However, since the census scanners are designed to read only one marked box, these people were reclassified as monoracial, based on whichever box was marked more firmly. In addition, individuals specifying the "Other" category are routinely reassigned to one of the OMB's distinct racial categories based on the first race listed.

Beginning in the 1970s, various individuals and groups formally protested the notion of mutually exclusive racial categories embodied in the "single-race checkoff" policy. Much of the public pressure came from the parents of school-age multiracial children. In the public schools, a multiracial child is often faced with the dilemma of having to choose one race, and constantly risks being misclassified in this setting.

After several years of intense debate, the OMB's Interagency Committee for the Review of the Racial and Ethnic Standards rejected the proposal to add a separate multiracial category. Instead, in July 1997, the 30-agency task force recommended that Directive 15 be amended to permit multiracial Americans to "mark one or more" racial category when identifying themselves for the census and other government programs. At first, most of the major civil rights organizations, such as the Urban League and the National Council of La Raza, along with groups such as the National Coalition for an Accurate Count of Asians and Pacific Islanders, opposed a multiracial category. These groups feared a diminution in their numbers, and worried that a multiracial category would spur debates regarding the "protected status" of groups and individuals. According to various estimates, from 75 to 90 percent of those who checked the "black" box could potentially check a multiracial one if it were an option. Concerned about the possible reductions in group numbers, civil rights groups argued that existing federal civil rights laws and programs were based on exclusive membership in a defined racial/ethnic group. It would be difficult, if not impossible, from this angle, to assess the salience of multiraciality in relationship to these laws and programs. The "mark one or more" option was adopted in Census 2000.

Racial Projects

Race is a "crossroads" where social structure and cultural representation meet. Too often, the attempt is made to understand race simply or primarily in terms of only one of these two analytical dimensions. For example, efforts to explain racial inequality as a purely social structural phenomenon either neglect or are unable to account for the origins, patterning, and transformation of racial meanings, representations, and social identities. Conversely, many examinations of race as a system of signification, identity, or cultural attribution fail adequately to articulate these phenomena with evolving social structures (such as segregation or stratification) and institutions (such as prisons, schools, or the labor market).

Race can never be merely a concept or idea, a representation or signification alone. Indeed race cannot be discussed, cannot even be *noticed*, without reference—however explicit or implicit—to social structure. To identify an individual or group racially is to locate them within a socially and historically demarcated set of demographic and cultural boundaries, state activities, "life-chances," and tropes of identity/difference/(in)equality. Race is both a social/historical structure and a set of accumulated signifiers that suffuse individual and collective identities, inform social practices, shape institutions and communities, demarcate social boundaries, and organize the distribution of resources. We cannot understand how racial representations set up patterns of residential segregation, for example, without considering how segregation reciprocally shapes and reinforces the meaning of race itself.

We conceive of racial formation processes as occurring through a linkage between structure and signification. *Racial projects* do both the ideological and the practical "work" of making these links and articulating the connection between them. *A racial project is simultaneously an interpretation, representation, or explanation of racial identities and meanings, and an effort to organize and distribute resources (economic, political, cultural) along particular racial lines.* Racial projects connect what race *means* in a particular discursive or ideological practice and the ways in which both social structures and everyday experiences are racially *organized*, based upon that meaning. Racial projects are attempts both to shape the ways in which social structures are racially signified and the ways that racial meanings are embedded in social structures.

Racial projects occur at varying scales, both large and small. Projects take shape not only at the macro-level of racial policy-making, state activity, and collective action, but also at the level of everyday experience and personal interaction. Both dominant and subordinate groups and individual actors, both institutions and persons, carry out racial projects. The imposition of restrictive state voting rights laws, organizing work for immigrants', prisoners', and community health rights in the ghetto or barrio are all examples of racial projects. Individuals' practices may be seen as racial projects as well: The cop who "stops and frisks" a young pedestrian, the student who joins a memorial march for the slain teenager Trayvon Martin, even the decision to wear dreadlocks, can all be understood as racial projects. Such projects should not, however, be simply regarded and analyzed as discrete, separate, and autonomous ideas and actions. Every racial project is both a reflection of and response to the broader patterning of race in the overall social system. In turn, every racial project attempts to reproduce, extend, subvert, or directly challenge that system.

Racial projects are not necessarily confined to particular domains. They can, for example, "jump" scale in their impact and significance. Projects framed at the local level, for example, can end up influencing national policies and initiatives. Correspondingly, projects at the national or even global level can be creatively and strategically recast at regional and local levels. Projects "travel" as well. Consider how migration recasts concepts of race, racial meaning, and racial identity: Immigrants' notions of race are often shaped in reference to, and in dialogue with, concepts of race in both their countries of origin and settlement. Thus migrants can maintain, adopt, and strategically utilize different concepts of race in transnational space (Kim 2008; Roth 2012).

At any given historical moment, racial projects compete and overlap, evincing varying capacity either to maintain or to challenge the prevailing racial system. A good example is the current debate over the relevance of "colorblind" ideology, policy, and practice; this provides a study of overlapping and competing racial projects. We discuss the hegemony of colorblindness in the concluding section of this book.

Racial projects link signification and structure not only in order to shape policy or exercise political influence, but also to organize our understandings of race as everyday "common sense." To see racial projects operating at the level of everyday life, we have only to examine the many ways in which we "notice" race, often unconsciously.

One of the first things we notice about people when we meet them (along with their sex) is their race. We utilize race to provide clues about *who* a person is. This fact is made painfully obvious when we encounter someone whom we cannot conveniently racially categorize—someone who is, for example, racially "mixed" or of an ethnic/racial group with which we are not familiar. Such an encounter becomes a source of discomfort and momentarily a crisis of racial meaning.

Our ability to interpret racial meanings depends on preconceived notions of a racialized social structure. Comments such as "Funny, you don't look black" betray an underlying image of what black should look like. We expect people to act out their apparent racial identities. Phenotype and performativity should match up. Indeed we become disoriented and anxious when they do not. Encounters with the black person who can't dance, the Asian American not proficient in math and science, or the Latin@ who can't speak Spanish all momentarily confound our racial reading of the social world and how we navigate within it. The whole gamut of racial stereotypes testifies to the way a racialized social structure shapes racial experience and socializes racial meanings. Analysis of prevailing stereotypes reveals the always present, already active link between our view of the social structure—its demography, its laws, its customs, its threats—and our conception of what race means.

Conversely, the way we interpret our experience in racial terms shapes and reflects our relations to the institutions and organizations through which we are embedded in the social structure. Thus we expect racially coded human characteristics to explain social differences. "Making up people" once again. Temperament, sexuality, intelligence, athletic ability, aesthetic preferences are presumed to be fixed and discernible from the palpable mark of race. Such diverse questions as our confidence and trust in others (for example, salespeople, teachers, media figures, and neighbors), our sexual preferences and romantic images, our tastes in music, films, dance, or sports, and our very ways of talking, walking, eating, and dreaming become racially coded simply because we live in a society where racial awareness is so pervasive.

To summarize the argument so far: The theory of racial formation suggests that society is suffused with racial projects, large and small, to which all are subjected. This racial "subjection" is quintessentially ideological. Everybody learns some combination, some version, of the rules of racial classification, and of their own racial identity, often without obvious teaching or conscious inculcation. Thus are we inserted in a comprehensively racialized social structure. Race becomes "common sense"—a way of comprehending, explaining, and acting in the world. A vast web of racial projects mediates between the discursive or representational means in which race is identified and signified on the one hand, and the institutional and organizational forms in which it is routinized and standardized on the other. The interaction and accumulation of these projects are the heart of the racial formation process.

Because of the pervasion of society by race, because of its operation over the *longue durée* as a master category of difference and inequality, it is not possible to represent race discursively without simultaneously locating it, explicitly or implicitly, in a social structural (and historical) context. Nor is it possible to organize, maintain, or transform social structures without simultaneously engaging, once more either explicitly or implicitly, in racial signification. Racial formation, therefore, is *a synthesis, a constantly reiterated outcome*, of the interaction of racial projects on a society-wide level. These projects are, of course, vastly different in scope and effect. They include large-scale public action, state activities, and interpretations of racial conditions in political, artistic, journalistic, or academic fora,[20] as well as the seemingly infinite number of racial judgments and practices, conscious and unconscious, that we carry out as part of our individual experience.

The concept of racial projects can be understood and applied across historical time to identify patterns in the *longue durée* of racial formation, both nationally and the entire modern world. At any particular historical moment, one racial project can be hegemonic while others are subservient, marginal, or oppositional to it. White supremacy is the obvious example of this: an evolving hegemonic racial project that has taken different forms from the colonial era to the present. In the chapters that follow, we utilize the concept of racial projects to examine the political trajectory of race over the past six decades in the United States.

But we are not done with racial formation yet. Before we get to the recent history of racial politics, and with the foregoing account of racial formation in mind, we must turn our attention to the problem of *racism*. Racial politics are necessarily deeply bound up with this topic. But race and racism are not the same thing. What is the relationship between them?

Racism

Magnus Hirschfeld, a German physician and sexologist of the Weimar era who was an early advocate of gay and transgender rights, initially gave currency to the term "racism." Published posthumously, Hirschfeld's book *Rassismus* (*Racism*; 1938) provided a history, analysis, and critical refutation of Nazi racial doctrines. Since the 1930s, the concept of racism has undergone significant changes in scope, meaning, and application. As historian George Fredrickson observes, "Although commonly used, 'racism' has become a loaded and ambiguous term" (2002, 151). While ideological notions of race have been directly tied to practices ranging from social segregation, exclusion from political participation, restrictive access to economic opportunities and resources, and genocide, the precise definition and significance of *racism* has been subject to enormous debate.

Robert Miles (1989) has argued that the term "racism" has been conceptually "inflated" to the point where it has lost its precision. While the problem of conceptual inflation and its political implications are evident in an era of colorblindness, the term "racism" is also subject to conceptual *de*flation. That is, what is considered racist is often defined very narrowly, in ways that obscure rather than reveal the pervasiveness and persistence of racial inequality in the United States For example, racism has been popularly and narrowly conceived as racial *hate*. The category of "hate crimes" has been introduced in many states as a specific offense with enhanced sentencing consequence, and many colleges and universities have instituted "hate speech" codes to regulate expression and behavior both inside and outside of the classroom. Dramatic acts of racial violence are given considerable play in the mass media, and are the subject of extensive condemnation by political elites. But as critical race scholar David Theo Goldberg (1997) has pointed out, the conceptual and political reduction of racism to hate both limits our understanding of racism and of the ways to challenge it. Racist acts are seen as "crimes of passion"—abnormal, unusual, and irrational deeds that we popularly consider offensive. Missing from such a narrow interpretation of racism are the ideologies, policies, and practices in a variety of institutional arenas that normalize and reproduce racial inequality and domination.

How should we understand racism today? We have argued that race has no fixed meaning, that it is constructed and transformed sociohistorically through the cumulative convergence and conflict of racial projects that reciprocally structure and signify race. Our emphasis on racial projects allows us to advance a definition of racism as well. A racial project can be defined as racist if it *creates or reproduces structures of domination based on racial significations and identities.*

Rather than envisioning a single, monolithic, and dominant racist project, we suggest that racist projects exist in a dense matrix, operating at varying scales, networked with each other in formally and informally organized ways, enveloping and penetrating contemporary social relations, institutions, identities, and experiences. Like other racial projects, racist projects too converge and conflict, accumulate and interact with one another.

Complex and embedded as this web of racist projects is—remember, projects both signify and structure relationships, practices, and institutions—it is not the whole story. Powerful as racism is, it does not exhaust race. It does not crowd out anti-racism or eliminate the emancipatory dimensions of racial identity, racial solidarity, or racially conscious agency, both individual and collective. Indeed race is so profoundly a lived-in and lived-out part of both social structure and identity that it *exceeds and transcends* racism—thereby allowing for resistance to racism. Race, therefore, is *more* than racism; it is a fully-fledged "social fact" like sex/gender or class. From this perspective, race shapes racism as much as racism shapes race.

That said, a number of questions remain to be addressed. Our discussion has focused on racist projects, but are there also anti-racist projects? Can groups of color advance racist projects?

Are there anti-racist projects? On some level, this question answers itself. Millions of people in the United States (and elsewhere) have committed their actions, intellects, emotions, and in many cases their lives, to the cause of ending, or at least reducing, racism. Numerous individuals and groups continue to mobilize against racism. They seek to respond to racist attacks: assaults and murder, often by the police, on black and brown people, racial "steering" in housing and credit markets, racially biased sentencing practices in criminal courts ... the list is seemingly endless. They act to resist institutionalized racist practices, such as "stop and frisk" policies targeting black and brown youth;[21] to educate and organize against racism through media, research, legal and political action; and to disrupt and counter racist practices in everyday life. Continuing the argument advanced throughout this chapter, we define anti-racist projects as those that *undo or resist structures of domination based on racial significations and identities.*

Anti-racism has been the subject of seemingly endless discussion, especially through the rise and fall of the post-World War II political trajectory of race. It has become much more difficult to understand anti-racism since racism went "underground" at the end of the 1960s; since the racist practices and the meaning of racism have changed from "old school" explicit discourses and white supremacist actions like lynchings and cross-burnings. Instead, racism now takes more implicit, deniable, and often unconscious forms. Because the law continues to understand racism (racial discrimination) in the old way—as an explicit, intentional, *invidious* distinction based on race—legal remedies have been sharply curtailed.[22] By restricting its understanding of discrimination in this way, the Supreme Court has permitted and tacitly encouraged denial and concealment of racist practices.

If racism is not merely a matter of explicit beliefs or attitudes—significations or identities, in our vocabulary—but also and necessarily involves the production and maintenance of social structures of domination, then the denial of invidious intent is clearly insufficient to undo it. The absence of invidious intent does little or nothing to unwind the social structures through which racism flourishes and is reproduced. In the "post-civil rights" era, racism has been largely—though not entirely, to be sure—detached from its perpetrators. In its most advanced forms, indeed, it has no perpetrators; it is a nearly invisible, taken-for granted, common-sense feature of everyday life and social structure. This is the situation that has allowed U.S. courts and mainstream political discourse to block race-conscious reparative measures such as affirmative action, to proclaim the United States a "colorblind" society, and to stigmatize anti-racist activists and intellectuals—legal practitioners, community organizations, school systems and universities, and other individuals and institutions seeking to overturn structures of racial exclusion and discrimination—as "playing the race card," as the "real racists."

Can Groups of Color Advance Racist Projects? Some scholars and activists have defined racism as "prejudice plus power."[23] Using this formula, they argue that people of color can't be racist since they don't have power. But things are not that simple. "Power" cannot be reified as a thing that some possess and others do not; instead it constitutes a relational field. Furthermore, unless one is prepared to argue that there has been no transformation of the U.S. racial order in the past several decades, it is difficult to contend that groups of color have attained *no* power or influence. To do so risks dismissing the political agency of people of color.[24]

Racialized groups are positioned in unequal ways in a racially stratified society. Racial hierarchy pervades the contemporary United States; that hierarchy is preponderantly white supremacist, but it is not always that way. There are some exceptions, specific urban areas where groups of color have achieved local power, for example, in the administration of social services and distribution of economic resources. In cities like Oakland and Miami, this has led to conflicts between blacks and Latin@s over educational programs, minority business opportunities, and political power, with dramatically different results depending on which group held relative power. In these cases, some groups of color are promoting racial projects that subordinate other groups of color. While such exceptions do not negate the overarching reality of white supremacy, they do suggest that differences in racial power persist among groups of color. Inter-group racial conflict is not unidimensional; it is not solely whites vs. people of color, though whiteness still rules, OK?

Racial Politics: Despotism, Democracy, and Hegemony

For most of its existence, both as a European colony and, as an independent nation, the United States was a *racial despotism.* In many ways it remains racially despotic today. Progress towards political standing and the empowerment of people of color, for example, has been painfully slow and highly uneven. It took over 160 years, from the passage of the Naturalization Law of 1790 to the 1952 McCarran–Walter Act, to abolish racial restrictions regarding naturalization (well, not totally).[25] After the civil war, there was the brief democratic experiment of Reconstruction that terminated ignominiously in 1877. In its wake there followed almost a century of legally sanctioned segregation and wholesale denial of the vote. While the civil rights movement and its allies made significant strides towards enhancing formal political rights, obstacles to effective political participation have remained stubbornly persistent, as recent legal decisions jeopardizing voting rights have revealed (U.S. Supreme Court 2013).

It is important, therefore, to recognize that in many respects, racial despotism is the norm against which all U.S. politics must be measured. Centuries of U.S.

racial despotism have had three important and dramatic consequences. First, they defined "American" identity as white: as the negation of racialized "otherness"—initially African and indigenous, later Latin American and Asian as well (Rogin 1991; Morrison 1993; Drinnon 1997). This negation took shape in both law and custom, in public institutions and in forms of cultural representation. It became the archetype of racial domination in the United States. It melded with the conquest and slavery as the "master" racial project.

Second, racial despotism organized—albeit sometimes in an incoherent and contradictory fashion—the "color line," rendering racial division the fundamental schism in U.S. society. The despotism of the color line also demanded an ongoing and intensive policing of racial boundaries, an ongoing racialization effort that ran not only between various groups and people, but also *through* them. In other words, racial despotism did not only elaborate, articulate, and drive racial divisions institutionally; it also hammered them into our psyches, causing untold fear and suffering, and extending, up to the moment in which you are reading this, the racial obsessions and oppressions of the conquest and slavery periods.

Third, racial despotism consolidated oppositional racial consciousness and organization. Originally framed by slave revolts and *marronage*,[26] by indigenous resistance, and by nationalisms of various sorts, and later by nationalist and equalitarian racial freedom movements, oppositional racial consciousness took on permanence and depth as *racial resistance*. Just as racial despotism reinforced white supremacy as the master category of racial domination, so too it forged racial unity among the oppressed: first native peoples assaulted and displaced by armed settlers, later Africans and their descendants kidnapped and reduced to mere chattel, and then conquered Latin@s/*mestiz@s* and superexploited Asian immigrants. Racial despotism generated racial resistance: Just as the conquest created the "Indian" where once there had been Pequot, Iroquois, or Tutelo, so too it created the "Black" where once there had been Asante or Ovimbundu, Yoruba, or Bakongo. What had once been tribal or ethnic consciousness—among enslaved Africans, Native Americans "removed" to reservations or decimated by settler violence, Latin@s forcibly denationalized and stripped of their lands, and Asian immigrants subjected to virtual *corvee* labor and then violently expelled from the communities they had created—ultimately became oppositional *race consciousness* and *racial resistance*. Thus in many ways racial despotism laid the groundwork for the creation of the racially based movements of today.

These patterns are now understood as "panethnicizing" processes. (Every racially defined group is a panethnic group.) They comprise not only the shared experience of suffering and the unifying pressures it brings to bear, but also the concerted self-activity of the oppressed to confront their tormentors and change their conditions. Panethnicity is a type of racialization; it is not without internal tension and conflict; it is often uneven and incomplete; it often does not liquidate ethnic difference but subsumes it; above all, it is a product of racial despotism.

The transition from racial despotism to *racial democracy* has been a slow, painful, and contentious one; it remains far from complete. A recognition of the abiding presence of racial despotism, we contend, is crucial for the development of a theory of racial formation in the U.S. It is also crucial to the task of relating racial formation to racial resistance, the broader current of political practice, organization, and change.

Over extended periods of time, and as a result of resistance of disparate types, the balance of coercion and consent began to change, to move *from domination to hegemony.* It is possible to locate the origins of hegemony right within the heart of racial despotism, for the effort to possess the master's tools—religion and philosophy in this case—was crucial to emancipation and to "freedom dreams" (Kelley 2003), crucial to efforts both individual and collective to possess oneself, so to speak, to achieve some degree of "self-determination" as a people. As Ralph Ellison reminds us, "The slaves often took the essence of the aristocratic ideal (as they took Christianity) with far more seriousness than their masters" (1964, xiv). In their language, in their religion with its focus on the Exodus theme and on Jesus's tribulations (Glaude 2000), in their music with its figuring of suffering, resistance, perseverance, and transcendence (Du Bois 2007 (1935), in their interrogation of a political philosophy which sought perpetually to rationalize their bondage in a supposedly "free" society (Douglass 2000 [1852]), enslaved Africans and their descendants incorporated elements of racial rule into their thought and practice, turning them against their original bearers.

Racial rule can be understood as a slow and uneven historical process that has moved from despotism to democracy, from domination to hegemony. In this transition, hegemonic forms of racial rule—those based on consent—eventually came to supplant those based on coercion. But only to some extent, only partially. By no means has the United States established racial democracy in the 21st century, and by no means is coercion a thing of the past. But the sheer complexity of the racial questions U.S. society confronts today, the welter of competing racial projects and contradictory racial experiences which Americans undergo, suggests that hegemony is a useful and appropriate term with which to characterize contemporary racial rule.

What form does racial hegemony take today? In the aftermath of the epochal struggles of the post-World War II period, under the conditions of chronic crisis of racial meaning to which U.S. society has grown accustomed, we suggest that a new and highly unstable form of racial hegemony has emerged, that of *colorblindness.* In the following chapters, we discuss the post-World War II political trajectory of racial formation that has brought us to this point.

Notes

1. Ian Hacking (2006; 1999) has given us the phrase "making up people" to explain how the human sciences operate, but Hacking doesn't stop there: he discusses medicine, education, ideology, law, art, and state institutions as they do this work.

2. The notion of *intersectionality* was advanced by legal scholar Kimberlé W. Crenshaw, who argued that both oppression and resistance are always situated in multiple categories of difference (Crenshaw 1989). Failure to grasp how categories of race, gender, sexuality, and class dynamically interact and shape one another, she asserted, led to a fragmented politics:

    > Feminist efforts to politicize experiences of women and anti-racist efforts to politicize experiences of people of color have frequently proceeded as though the issues and experiences they each detail occur on mutually exclusive terrains. (Crenshaw 1991, 1242)

    Two other key intersectionality theorists should be mentioned. Patricia Hill Collins emphasizes the mutual determination of race, gender, and class in her survey and theoretical synthesis of the themes and issues of black feminist thought. Collins invented the phrase "matrix of domination" to describe the "overall social organization within which intersecting oppressions originate, develop, and are contained" (Collins 2008 [1999] 227–228). Evelyn Nakano Glenn argues that race and gender are relational concepts in an interlocking system, providing a historical examination of citizenship and labor in the United States between 1870 and 1930. Glenn argues that these categories cannot be understood separately, but are defined and given meaning in relationship to each other: "Race and gender share three key features as analytic concepts: (1) they are relational concepts whose construction involves (2) representation and material relations and (3) in which power is a constitutive element" (Glenn 2002, 12–13). In many respects, race is gendered and gender is racialized. Inequality is always racialized and gendered as well. There are no clear boundaries between the "regions" of hegemony, so political conflicts will often invoke some or all these themes simultaneously.

3. "The truth is that there are no races; there is nothing in the world that can do all we ask race to do for us.... The evil that is done is done by the concept, and by easy—yet impossible—assumptions as to its application" (Appiah 1992, 45). Appiah's eloquent and learned book fails, in our view, to dispense with the race concept, despite its anguished attempt to do so; this indeed is the source of its author's anguish. We agree with him as to the non-objective character of race, but fail to see how this recognition justifies its abandonment.

4. George L. Mosse (1985) argues that anti-semitism only began to be racialized in the 18th century. For a competing view, see Thomas 2010.

5. As Marx put it:

    > The discovery of gold and silver in America, the extirpation, enslavement, and entombment in mines of the aboriginal population, the beginning of the conquest and looting of the East Indies, the turning of Africa into a warren for the commercial hunting of blackskins, signalized the rosy dawn of the era of capitalist production. These idyllic proceedings are the chief momenta of primitive accumulation. (1967, 75)

    David E. Stannard (1992) argues that the wholesale slaughter perpetrated upon the native peoples of the Western hemisphere is unequalled in history, even in our own bloody century. See also Lovejoy and Rogers, eds. 1994.

6. Debates of a similar nature also took place among the subjects of conquest and enslavement. On Native American perspectives, see Calloway 1994; Richter 2003; White 2010. On African perspectives, see Opoku-Agyemang et al., eds. 2008; Thornton 2012.

7. In Virginia, for example, it took about two decades after the establishment of European colonies to extirpate the indigenous people of the greater vicinity; 50 years after the establishment of the first colonies, the elaboration of slave codes establishing race as *prima facie* evidence for enslaved status was well under way. See Jordan (2012 [1968]).
8. In 1550-1551 two Spanish Dominicans, Bartolomeo de las Casas and Juan Ginés de Sepúlveda, conducted a prolonged theological debate in Valladolid, Spain, about the humanity and spiritual status of Spain's Native American subjects. The debate was carried out at the behest of the Spanish king, Charles V, and in the shadow of the Inquisition. While ostensibly theological, and thus focused on such questions as the status—or even presence—of the souls of the Indians, the debate also addressed questions of Spanish imperial development strategy, notably the scope and legitimacy of slavery and the status of the *encomienda* system vis-à-vis religious and royal authority. See Hanke 1974; Todorov 1984.
9. For a pointed, parallel demonstration of the imperative of racial classification during relatively early stages of conquest, see the genre of Mexican *casta* paintings (Denver Art Museum 2004; Katzew 2005).
10. Proslavery physician Samuel George Morton (1799-1851) compiled a collection of 800 crania from all parts of the world, which formed the sample for his studies of race. Assuming that the larger the size of the cranium translated into greater intelligence, Morton established a relationship between race and skull capacity. Gossett reports that "In 1849, one of his studies included the following results: the English skulls in his collection proved to be the largest, with an average cranial capacity of 96 cubic inches. The Americans and Germans were rather poor seconds, both with cranial capacities of 90 cubic inches. At the bottom of the list were the Negroes with 83 cubic inches, the Chinese with 82, and the Indians with 79" (Gossett 1997 [1965], 74). When Steven Jay Gould reexamined Morton's research, he found that the data were deeply, though probably unconsciously, manipulated to agree with his "a priori conviction about racial ranking" (1981, 50-69).
11. See UNESCO 1950/1951. The production of the documents was coordinated by Alfred Metraux (1951). The 1950 authors included Professors Ernest Beaglehole (New Zealand), Juan Comas (Mexico), E. Franklin Frazier (U.S.), Humayun Kabir (India), Claude Levi-Strauss (France), Morris Ginsberg (United Kingdom), and Ashley Montagu (U.S.). It was revised by Montagu "after criticism submitted by Professors Hadley Cantril, E. G. Conklin, Gunnar Dahlberg, Theodosius Dobzhansky, L. C. Dunn, Donald Hager, Julian S. Huxley, Otto Klineberg, Wilbert Moore, H. J. Mullet, Gunnar Myrdal, Joseph Needham, and Curt Stern" (ibid, 35). The 1950 document was criticized as excessively sociologically oriented; the 1951 revision included text drafted by anthopologists, geneticists, and biologists as well. On Metraux see Prins 2007.
12. These are complex cases. The Cherokee Freedmen are the descendants of black slaves owned by the Cherokee (Jones 2009). The Seminole Blacks are the descendants of U.S. maroons who fled slavery to tribal lands in Florida, Indian territory controlled by Spain until 1821. The U.S. fought two "Seminole Wars" (1817–1818 and 1835–1842) to recapture the area and reimpose slavery. Many Seminoles were transported (or fled) to the Oklahoma territory, but some remained in Florida. In 1849, threatened by slave-raiders, *c.*200 armed Black Seminoles under the leadership of John Horse escaped from Florida and conducted a heroic "long march" across slave-holding Alabama, Louisiana, and Texas.

Accompanied by some traditional (i.e., non-black) Seminole comrades led by the Seminole chief Coacochee. This amazing feat culminated in their crossing into abolitionist Mexico in July 1850; they formed a community in Coahuila that is still called *Nacimiento de los Negros*. See Mulroy 2007.

13. The Implicit Bias Test (IAT) was developed in the mid-1990s by experimental/social psychologist Anthony G. Greenwald. It has spawned a large literature and been applied to various issues of bias (notably race, gender, and stereotyping of various types) in numerous settings, particularly educational, political, and legal. For a small sample of relevant work by Greenwald and collaborators, see Greenwald et al. 2003; Greenwald et al. 2009; Kang et al. 2012.
14. The legacy of Kant is particularly evident here (McCarthy 2009), but sociological and psychological concepts such as "consciousness of kind" (Giddings 1932) have also acquired great followings over the years.
15. See "The Conservation of Races" (1993 [1897]), an early statement that has occasioned much debate among Du Bois scholars (Marable 1986, 35-38; Appiah 1992, 28–46; Lewis 1993, 372–373; Reed 1997a).
16. Boas's work has drawn contemporary criticism for its residual essentialism; his early physical anthropology at times overwhelmed his vaunted cultural relativism (Boas 1912a, 1912b; Williams 1996).
17. Park's *Race and Culture* (1950) is still useful; see also Lyman 1992; Steinberg 2007. Locke's 1915 lectures at Howard University, unpublished until 1992, bear a remarkable resemblance to contemporary racial theories and comparative historical sociologies of race (Locke 1992 [1915]).
18. Proposition 54 was defeated, less because voters wished to preserve racial categorization as an overall state practice, but rather because in a few particular areas of state activity they had been convinced that maintaining racially based data was good for society overall. A particularly crucial source of Connerly's defeat was a series of campaign ads run by medical societies arguing that collecting racial data was important for public health purposes (HoSang 2010).
19. In August, 2012 the Bureau announced that it was considering redefining the Top of Form-Bottom of Form "Hispanic" category to the status of a racial category, possibly called "Hispanic/Latino," that would be equivalent on the form to white or black. See Cohn 2012.
20. We are not unaware, for example, that publishing this work is itself a racial project.
21. *Floyd, et al. v. City of New York, et al.*, a class action suit brought by the Center for Constitutional Rights on behalf of victims of "stop and frisk" racial profiling by New York City police, was decided on August 12, 2013. Federal judge Shira Scheindlin decided for the plaintiffs and ordered a series of modification and reforms of "stop and frisk." See Center for Constitutional Rights 2013. Challenges to the decision suggest that the case's ultimate outcome remains in doubt.
22. Racial jurisprudence largely relies on the Equal Protection Clause of the 14th Amendment and on the 1964 Civil Rights Act. The full extent of Supreme Court rulings on the nature of racism cannot be addressed here. An exemplary decision is *Washington v. Davis* (U.S. Supreme Court 1976), which established the rule of "invidious discriminatory purpose" as the criterion for determining if discrimination had occurred. The Court understood "purpose" as "intent" and refused to extend its concept of discrimination to include "disparate

impact"; in other words the consequences of practices alleged to be discriminatory were officially ignored. See Pillai 2001.

23. Bonilla-Silva defines this view as an "institutionalist perspective," in which "racism is defined as a combination of prejudice and power that allows the dominant race to institutionalize its dominance at all levels in a society (Bonilla-Silva 1997, 466). See also Katz 2003.
24. See our debate with Joe Feagin and Chris Elias over these issues: Feagin and Elias 2013; Omi and Winant 2013.
25. In practice, this just means rendering the racial dimensions of race informal, outside explicit legal regulation, but still subject to political pressures, and thus to racist projects and anti-racist ones as well. Thus it may be an overstatement to say that such restrictions were "abolished."
26. This term refers to the practice, widespread throughout the Americas, whereby runaway slaves formed communities in remote areas, such as swamps, mountains, or forests, often in alliance with dispossessed indigenous peoples. The Black Seminoles discussed above were a maroon people.

CHAPTER 5

Racial Politics and the Racial State

"[H]istorical reality is completely obfuscated in the myth of an all-inclusive contract creating a sociopolitical order presided over by a neutral state equally responsive to all its colorless citizens."

—Charles W. Mills[1]

Introduction

Race is consummately political. The instability of the race concept and the controversies it generates are emblematic of the racially contradictory society in which we live. In the United States, a system of racial rule has always been in place, operating not merely through macro-level, large-scale activities, but also through micro-level, small-scale practices. The racial regime is enforced and challenged in the schoolyard, on the dance floor, on talk radio, and in the classroom as much as it is in the Supreme Court, electoral politics, or on the battlefield of Helmand province. Because racial formation processes are dynamic, the racial regime remains unstable and contested. We cannot step outside of race and racism, since our society and our identities are constituted by them; we live in racial history.

Race is a vast and variegated theme. Any racial theory is a work-in-progress. Race is a factor not only in politics and history, but also in economy, culture, experience ...; it is a fully-fledged *social fact* like class or gender. Like those other large markers race is an unstable set of *collective representations* as well.[2] We focus here on racial politics and the racial state because through politics, through struggles over power and freedom, we can see race and racism being remade both social structurally and experientially. What we call racial projects have interacted over half a millennium to build up the *social structures* of race and racism. A parallel *experiential dimension* exists as well: The short-term, present-tense experience of racial subjectivity, in which new racial projects are being launched and interacting all the time.[3]

Looking at racial politics in general and the racial state in particular also allows us to consider the state–civil society distinction: The state may represent the core of a given racial regime, but no state can encompass all of civil society. People conceive of, operate, and inhabit their own racial projects (within broader constraints) and "experience" race in distinct and varied ways.

To theorize racial politics and the racial state, then, is to enter the complex territory where structural racism encounters self-reflective action, the radical pragmatism of people of color (and their white allies) in the United States[4] It is to confront the instability of the U.S. system of racial hegemony, in which despotism and democracy coexist in seemingly permanent conflict. It is to understand that the boundary between state and civil society is necessarily porous and uncertain where race is concerned. Emphasizing the political dimensions of race and racism allows us to discern the contours of the racial system, to understand what racial hegemony looks like, to specify its contradictions, and to envision alternative scenarios.

Racial politics are bigger than the state. They involve civil society, political socialization and thus race-consciousness, racial identity-making (both individual- and group-based), and group boundary formation (Barth, ed. 1998 [1969]) as well. The enmeshment of the state in our everyday lives means that all racial identities are contradictory and "hybrid"; it means that uncertain group boundaries are regulated and often tightened and enforced by the state. We make our racial identities, both individually and collectively, but not under conditions of our own choosing.

Racial formation theory approaches politics as an uneasy combination of despotic and democratic practices, of self-reflective action undertaken both with and against established social structures. Why, for example, are racial attributions so prone to violence, so "hot," so fiercely upheld and contested, so necessary in the modern world as components of both self and social structure? Why is race so available as a "scavenger concept": a default variable on the basis of which so many disparate phenomena are supposedly explained?[5] How can a social distinction be both so determining—of life chances and status, of freedom, of economic, political, and social institutions, and indeed of identity itself—and at the same time so undetermined, inchoate, and indeed unreal on so many levels?

The modern state makes use of ideology—racial ideology in this case—to "glue" together contradictory practices and structures: despotism and democracy, coercion and consent, formal equality and substantive inequality, identity and difference.[6] The racial state does not have precise boundaries. Although based in formally constituted institutions and grounded in a contentious historical process, the state extends beyond administrative, legislative, or judicial forms of activity. It inhabits and indeed organizes large segments of social and indeed psychological identity, as well as everyday life. Internalizing and "living out" a particular racial identity, for example, is in some ways internalizing the state; post-structuralist theorists might describe this in terms of "governmentality" (Foucault 1991, 1997). From a Freudian point of view, we might understand the racial state in terms of "introjection": another form of internalization in which rules and constraints become mechanisms of psychological self-defense. Still another way in which the racial state casts its net over our identities, our everyday experiences, is through the process Althusser called "interpellation": the way the state "notices" us, "hails" us. In Althusser's account, a police officer calls out "Hey! You there!" and we instantly flinch; we turn to face the state that is already within us:

> [I]deology "acts" or "functions" in such a way that it "recruits" subjects among the individuals (it recruits them all), or "transforms" the individuals

> into subjects (it transforms them all) by that very precise operation which I have called interpellation or hailing, and which can be imagined along the lines of the most commonplace everyday police (or other) hailing: "Hey, you there!"
>
> Assuming that the theoretical scene I have imagined takes place in the street, the hailed individual will turn round. By this mere one-hundred-and-eighty-degree physical conversion, he [sic] becomes a subject. Why? Because he has recognized that the hail was "really" addressed to him, and that "it was really him who was hailed" (and not someone else).
>
> (Althusser 2001 [1971], 174; see also Butler 1997a)

By *despotism* we refer to a familiar series of state practices: deprivation of life, liberty, or land; dispossession, violence, confinement, coerced labor, exclusion, and denial of rights or due process. The contemporary United States, and the colonial societies that preceded it in North America, were founded on these and related forms of despotism, all organized according to race. Although racial oppression has lessened over the years, and although some of these despotic practices have been significantly reduced if not eliminated (slavery is a good example here), others continue unabated and in some cases have even increased. For example, carceral practices today rival or exceed any previous period in both the proportions and absolute numbers of black and brown people held in confinement. The little-noticed development of a whole gulag of specialized immigration prisons has no precedent in U.S. history.

All right then, how about the *democratic dimensions* of the racial state? Though it is a constant and prominent feature of the racial state, despotism is not the only story that the state tells about race. "Freedom dreams" (Kelley 2003) rooted in racial politics are among the most enduring contributions to the foundation of democracy in the modern world; these "dreams" have constantly challenged the state, most famously in Martin Luther King, Jr.'s August 1963 speech, but on numerous other occasions as well. In fact the persistence and depth of social justice-oriented movements has been the chief source of popular democracy and indeed popular sovereignty in the United States. What W.E.B. Du Bois called "abolition democracy" is a clear instance of that movement challenge. In Du Bois's view, the American Revolution of 1776–1781 was only a partial and incomplete anti-imperial transformation, since it was dominated by elites and left slavery intact. The Civil War, and Reconstruction, abortive as it was, were the second phase of the American Revolution, based upon the expansion of the rights that abolition implied: the achievement by all of complete democracy and full citizenship (Du Bois 2007 [1935] 186; see also Lipsitz 2004; Davis 2005, 73–74).

To be sure, democratic movements have often been foreclosed by state-based coercion, as well as by reactionary practices based in civil society: mob violence and lynching, for example. Only under some circumstances has open and "free" political mobilization for democratic reform been possible for people of color: The two great moments of this mainstream political upsurge were, of course, the Reconstruction period (1865–1877) and the post-World War II civil rights period (1948–1970). At other times democratic political action had to take shape quite autonomously, beneath the radar of the state (and often beneath the social scientific radar as well). This suggests the subaltern character of racial democracy.[7]

* * *

In order to understand racial politics and to grasp the contradictory relationship between racial despotism and racial democracy, it is necessary to situate the racial state historically and account for its development over time. Here, we accomplish this by discussing the transition from *war of maneuver to war of position.* Next, we address the *racial body politic*, the corporeal or phenomic dimensions of raciality. Race and racism politicize the body, subjecting it to state control, surveillance, and violence. In the next section, *The Radical Pragmatist Politics of Race*, we consider the micro–macro linkages that operate in racial politics. We examine such matters as the way individuals and movements "navigate" in unstable and uncertain racial conditions, and the contradictions between racial despotism and racial democracy that continue to shape and reshape the racial state. We draw once again on the theories of the Italian neo-Marxist politician, theorist, and anti-fascist leader Antonio Gramsci. In the next section, we introduce the concept of *trajectories of racial politics.* Trajectories are shaped interactions, taking place over historical time, between the racial state and race-oriented social movements. Finally, we reflect upon racial politics in everyday life, discussing the *politicization of the social* that took place in the United States during the post-World War II years. We argue that anti-racist movements greatly expanded the political "space" available in the country, achieving an enormous deepening and broadening of political awareness. From (and within) race this "politics of identity" went everywhere: into personal relationships, family, sexuality, and "micro-political" interactions of all types. Prior to the 1970s, these identities and relationships were seen as mostly private matters, located outside the political sphere. Since the black movement challenge, they have "gone public"; awareness of racism, sexism, and homophobia cannot be removed from the public sphere.

From War of Maneuver to War of Position

There has been a racial system in North America since the earliest days of contact with and conquest by Europeans. This system has linked political rule to the racial classification of individuals and groups. The major institutions and social relationships of U.S. society—law, political organization, economic relationships, religion, cultural life, residential patterns—have been structured from the beginning by this system.

Clearly, the system was more monolithic, more absolute, at earlier historical moments. Despite its epochal revolutionary origins, the early U.S. maintained many of the residues of the absolutist system of monarchical rule from which it had emerged. Empire, slavery, and patrimonialism were some of these "birthmarks." Having thrown off the shackles of the British empire, "the first new nation" (Lipset 2003 [1963]) proceeded to establish itself as an empire of its own, seizing the land and labor of native peoples of North America (Kaplan 2005; Stoler, ed. 2006;). Having declared itself subject to a natural law in which "all men [sic] are created equal," the United States quite comprehensively disobeyed that law in practice: not only through its support for hereditary chattel slavery, but also through its severe restrictions on democratic participation.[8] The American Revolution was in many respects triggered by trade restrictions imposed by the "mother country";[9] the insurgent colonies were merchant capitalist, not yet industrial capitalist. They were patrimonial systems that were still marked by feudalism (Adams 2005). Not only did romantic racist ideology justifying slavery develop out of this political-economic complex—the plantation owner as the father, the slaves as children—but also the chattelization of both slaves and women was operating here (Pateman 1988; Mills 1999). Furthermore, because there was very little industrial production in the early decades of the nation's existence, property-less white men were uncertain about their status. The main "workers" were slaves, and white men, unwilling to accept the quasi-feudal status of "servant," were determined to distinguish themselves from slaves at all costs. David Roediger (2007 [1991]) finds deep roots for later U.S. racism in this unstable and conflictual situation. What about the slaves themselves? The 1790 census—the first ever taken in the country—counted roughly 20 percent of the U.S. population as enslaved (U.S. Bureau of the Census 1791). In Virginia, the principal slaveholding state of the time, the enslaved population was around 40 percent of the total.

Thus policing and controlling the enslaved population was a particular concern, especially in the South, where slaves were concentrated and represented the main source of labor. The U.S. Constitution reflected extensive experience in the surveillance and punishment of slaves, experience that had been acquired by Europeans over 250 years of colonization before the Constitution was even promulgated. Protection for "the peculiar institution" was provided by the document in numerous ways: notably in its provision for the return of escaped slaves, and in its ignominious "three-fifths clause," whereby the enslaved population, though obviously unrepresented in the legislature, could yet be counted as a component of the population for purposes of legislative enumeration.

For most of U.S. history, state racial policy's main objective was repression and exclusion. Congress' first attempt to define American citizenship, the Naturalization Law of 1790, declared that only free "white" immigrants could qualify. A persistent pattern of disenfranchisment targeted people of color. Before the Civil War, "free persons of color" were stripped of their right to vote—the key to citizenship status—in many states. The extension of eligibility to all racial groups has been slow indeed. Japanese, for example, could become naturalized citizens only after the passage of the McCarran–Walter Act of 1952.[10]

The state plays a crucial part in racialization, the extension of racial meaning to a previously racially unclassified relationship, social practice or group. Throughout the 19th century, many state and federal laws recognized only three racial categories: "white," "Negro," and "Indian." In California, the influx of Chinese and the debates surrounding the legal status of Mexicans provoked a brief juridical crisis of racial definition. California attempted to resolve this dilemma by classifying Mexicans and Chinese within the already existing framework of "legally defined" racial groups. After the Treaty of Guadalupe Hidalgo (1848), Mexicans were accorded the political-legal status of "free white persons," a fig-leaf placed by the U.S. conquerors over the realities of Mexican *mestizaje* and slave emancipation. State racialization of Asians was even more baroque: In 1854 the newly established California Supreme Court ruled in *People v. Hall* (CA Supreme Court 1854) that Chinese should be considered "Indian"[!] and denied the political rights accorded to whites.[11]

But even at its most oppressive, the racial order was unable to arrogate to itself the entire capacity for the production of racial meanings or the racial subjection of the population. Racially defined "others"—people of color—were always able to counterpose their own cultural traditions, their own forms of organization and identity, to the dehumanizing and enforced "invisibility" imposed by the majority society. As the voluminous literature on black culture under slavery shows, black slaves developed cultures of resistance based on music, religion, African traditions, and family ties, among other political technologies. By these means they sustained their own ideological project: the development of a "free" black identity, a sense of "peoplehood," and a collective dedication to emancipation.[12] Similar processes of cultural resistance developed among Native Americans, Latin@s, and Asians.[13]

Without reviewing the vast history of the U.S. racial order, it is still possible to make some general comments about the manner in which this order was historically consolidated. Gramsci's distinction between "war of maneuver" and "war of position" will prove useful here. In his account, *war of maneuver* is the form of politics appropriate to conditions of dictatorship or despotism, when no terrain is available for opposition inside the system. Resistance to the regime mobilizes outside the political arena, in the hinterlands, the slums and barracoons, the places of worship, the fields and mines and other workplaces, everywhere the subaltern strata are gathered. Once it has acquired the necessary force, resistance moves to the key locus of power, the capital, and seizes the key redoubts (the Bastille, the Winter Palace) from which oppressive power has been exercised.

War of position, by contrast, is the political form appropriate to hegemonic systems of rule that operate by incorporating their opposition, at least up to a point. Modern mass societies of both the fascist and the democratic type are the kinds of political systems Gramsci has in mind. Resistance to fascism combines the two forms of politics. Democratic states may be quite restrictive, but they still generally provide some space for challenge from within: legislative, electoral, or judicial processes, for example. In such societies the state is fortified (Gramsci calls it a system of "trenches")[14] by structures of legitimation and consent against insurrection or other direct challenges. The task faced by any oppositional movement engaged in a "war of position" is to delegitimate the hegemonic system and to erode or undermine consent. By rearticulating political and cultural "common sense" in such a way that the excluded, oppressed, and exploited sectors of society can achieve their own legitmacy, their own inclusion, the opposition develops *counter-hegemony*. It seeks to attain the rights, justice, and political power that its supporters had earlier been denied. "War of position" is thus a prolonged struggle for the adherence of the general population and the achievement of political power, generally without insurrection or armed struggle.[15]

For much of American history, no political legitimacy was conceded to alternative or oppositional racial projects. The absence of democratic rights, of material resources, and of political and ideological terrain upon which to challenge the monolithic character of the racial order, forced racially defined opposition both outward, to the margins of society, and inward, to the relative safety of self-defined communities. Slaves who escaped to the North or Canada, or who formed maroon communities in forests and swamps; Indians who made war on the United States in defense of their peoples and lands; Chinese and Filipin@s who drew together in Chinatowns and Manilatowns in order to gain some measure of collective control over their existence—these are some examples of the movement *outward*, away from political engagement with the racial state.

These same blacks, Indians, Asians (and many others), banned from the political system and relegated to what was supposed to be a permanently inferior sociocultural status, were also forced *inward* upon themselves as individuals, families, and communities. Tremendous cultural resources were nurtured among such communities; enormous labors were required to survive and to develop elements of an autonomy and opposition under such conditions. These circumstances can best be understood as combining with the violent clashes and necessity of resistance (to white-led race riots, military assaults) which characterized these periods, to constitute a racial war of maneuver.

War of maneuver was gradually replaced by *war of position* as racially defined minorities achieved political gains in the United States.[16] A strategy of war of position can only be predicated on political struggle—on the existence of diverse institutional and cultural terrains upon which oppositional political projects can be mounted. To the extent that you can confront the racial state from within the political system, to the degree that you possess political "voice" (Hirschman 1971), you are fighting a war of position. Prepared in large measure by the practices undertaken under conditions of war of maneuver, black movements and their allies were able to make sustained strategic incursions into the mainstream political process during the post-World War II years. "Opening up" the state was a process of democratization which had effects both on state structures and on racial meanings. The postwar black movement, later joined by other racially based minority movements, challenged the dominant racial ideology in the United States, insisting upon a more egalitarian and democratic concept of race. The state was the logical target for this effort.

The Racial Body Politic

Race and racism both define and disrupt the body politic of the nation-state.[17] As we saw in Chapter 3, concepts of the *nation* like "the American people" or "the French people" presuppose a degree of inclusion and commonality that is impossible to achieve in practice. States occasionally become the instruments of necessarily genocidal attempts to attain that level of uniformity ("purity"), which is usually framed in racial terms.[18] But more often they must manage the heterogeneity of the body politic, operating on the continuum of despotism–democracy that we have discussed. Therefore racial difference and racial inequality are fundamental dimensions of social organization. This is something that reductionist theoretical approaches to race and racism *just can't explain*. There is a persistent tendency to recur to other, supposedly more fundamental social forces like class and culture/ethnicity, in the effort to explain the persistence and breadth of race. Such accounts always neglect or dismiss the embeddedness of race in the modern world.

Foucault's concept of "biopower"[19] addresses some of the problems of this sort of management. Though he developed it in his later work on sexuality, Foucault also applied this term to issues of race and racism, especially in regard to colonialism and empire. The biopower concept is useful here because it allows us to see the normalization and comprehensiveness of race and racism in the modern world (and most certainly in the U.S.). With Foucault, we challenge the idea—found everywhere in both scholarly work and common sense—that human differentiation according to race is somehow aberrant, and that racism is an irrational deviation from such immutable principles as individualism, "*liberté, égalité, fraternité*," or the law of supply and demand. Foucault labels such accounts "scapegoat theories" of race. As Ann Laura Stoler writes,

> Scapegoat theories posit that under economic and social duress, particular subpopulations are cordoned off as intruders, invented to deflect anxieties, and conjured up precisely to nail blame. For Foucault, racism is more than an *ad hoc* response to crisis: It is a manifestation of preserved possibilities, the expression of an underlying discourse of permanent social war, nurtured by the biopolitical technologies of "incessant purification." Racism does not merely arise in moments of crisis, in sporadic cleansings. It is internal to the biopolitical state, woven into the weft of the social body, threaded through its fabric.
>
> (1995, 69)

From this standpoint the "scavenger concept" of race also acquires new focus and emphasis. The ready availability of race as an "explanation" for deviance from some attributed norm becomes more intelligible when we recognize both the ease with which racial distinctions are made—their "ocularity"—and when we simultaneously admit the breadth and depth of racial awareness in American society. With these political tools in view, with an awareness of biopower handy and Foucault by your side, consider once again the raciality of the body politic: the endless list of attributed variation by race that pervades the United States, and much of the rest of the world as well. Variation by race in scores on the SAT test? In evacuation rates by race from hurricane-flooded New Orleans? In different racial groups' commitments to "hard work"? In criminal propensities? How about in common-sense beliefs about sexual proclivities across racially defined groups (consider the word "vanilla" in this context)? This list can go on for days.

The phrase "body politic," of course, refers not only to the collective body, the "nation" or its equivalents; it also refers to the politicized body. Here we are arguing that the phenomic dimensions of race are among the central components of this phenomenon. Race and racism not only politicize the social but render up the human body into the burning heart of the state as material for the social control. State racial policy is directed against the racial body, in such forms as surveillance, profiling, policing, and confinement. This racial body politic is also gendered and classed: State violence against black men—against poor, dark, mainly male bodies—is one of the most continuous and seemingly central aspects of the U.S. racial system. Women of color are also targeted, especially by violence, discrimination, and assaults on their reproductive rights (Harris-Perry 2011); profiling is everywhere (Glover 2009).

Much recent scholarship has properly been devoted to "performing race" (Kondo 1997). In parallel fashion, critical studies of racism tend to see it as something that can be "performed' or not; for example we are urged to "interrupt" racism, or to "ally" against racism. We consider that both these dimensions of race—race as "performance" and race as "phenomics"—must be synthesized if we are to conceive fully of the racial politics of civil society. To be sure there is no easy separation of the racial state from the racial dimensions of identity and everyday life.

The body is the person. It is not news that racism derives much of its energy from the effort to control racially marked bodies. Nor is it surprising that despotism operates on the racial body, assaulting it, confining it, and profiling it.[20] Whether traditional or modern, whether religious or corporate, whether super-exploiting immigrant workers, profiling "suspicious" persons ("stop and frisk"; "show me your papers"), whether enforcing the boundaries of neighborhood segregation, policing school hallways in neighborhoods of color (Nolan 2011)—again the list is long—the convergence between despotism and the racial body is comprehensive. For this reason—as well as for reasons of gender and sexuality—the right of all human beings to control their own bodies is a fundamental democratic demand.

The Radical Pragmatist Politics of Race

Racial formation theory draws a great deal from the pragmatist philosophical tradition. Pragmatist concepts of self and society are based on the core idea of *self-reflective action.* This term means that both individually and collectively we are self-consciously cognizant of the social forces in which we are immersed, and through which we steer our individual and collective selves.[21] Consider racial formation as a continuous process of this type. It is not only a struggle over the meaning of one's own racial identity within a particular social context and defined set of relationships; it is also a conflict over the terms of collective self-definition carried out in the shadow of the state and its biopolitical capabilities. In the post-World War II period, these struggles have taken place in explicitly political terms, as an ongoing "war of position" between racial despotism and racial democracy.

A radical pragmatist approach allows us to analyze the interaction of the racialized self and the racialized social structure. At the "micro-level," each racial self engages in a certain amount of sociopolitical "navigation," so to speak. This activity takes place in everyday life and in political life, and requires what might be called racial "intelligence." When one acts self-reflectively in respect to race, she or he links the racial conditions of everyday life with those of the overall social structure. Often this racial intelligence is taken for granted, but it is also self-conscious much of the time, especially for people of color.

At the "macro-level," the radical pragmatism of racial formation theory allows us to understand why even in the present—in the post-civil rights, neoliberal era—racial politics are so intractable, why they consist of simultaneous advances and setbacks. At some moments and during some periods, projects for collective self-definition assume the utmost importance, while at others they are in relative abeyance. Under some conditions, when mobilization is sufficient—say in 1963 Birmingham, Alabama—movements and organizations are able to intervene politically and act strategically on behalf of insurgent groups of color. More often, self-reflective political activity is diffused and sporadic, less frequently concentrated in mass political undertakings. The Birmingham campaign or the August 1963 March on Washington were exceptional moments of collective mobilization. But self-reflective action is always present to some degree.

The state also operates this way. Indeed a radical pragmatist approach to racial politics also allows us to see the "life of the state" as Gramsci describes it, as

> a continuous process of formation and superseding of unstable equilibria ... between the interests of the fundamental group and those of the subordinate groups—equilibria in which the interests of the dominant group prevail, but only up to a certain point, i.e., stopping short of narrowly corporate economic interest.
>
> (1971, 182)

The framework here is Marxian class analysis, but if we think about this processual notion of "the life of the state" from a racial point of view it closely parallels the pragmatist concept. The "fundamental group" may be seen as whites—or more properly whites and others who benefit from white supremacy and racism—while the "subordinate groups" are people of color and their allies who are incorporated into the "unstable equilibrium," but only "up to a point." Racial politics are unstable because state and opposition are both the targets and operators of intersecting racial projects. In the old days, the racial state could be more overt and violent. In the "post-civil rights" era, the racial state cannot merely dominate; it must seek *hegemony.* It does this in two related ways; first by incorporating "subordinate" groups: the "sub-" others, in other words the *subaltern;* and second by creating and embodying racial "common sense," as we have discussed. Yet state violence, confinement, and aggressive and repressive policing of people of color all continue; this is how hegemony and subalternity are maintained: though a combination of repression and incorporation.

What is despotic, and what is democratic, about the U.S. racial state? Despite several historical "breaks"—when abolition of slavery, decolonization, and large-scale extensions of citizenship and civil rights took place—the contemporary world is still mired in the same racial history from which it originally sprang. The U.S. state was born out of white supremacy and still maintains it to a significant degree. Yet the state has been forced time and time again to make concessions to the racial "others": people of African descent, subjects of imperial conquest, indigenous people, and immigrants. The racial state has been transformed over and over in unending efforts to deal with its fundamental contradictions: Its concept of "freedom" included slavery. It is a racial despotism that also claims to be democratic. It is an empire that arose out of an anti-imperial revolution. It is a settler society (based on immigration) that is also exclusionist.

Colonial rule and slavocracy were systems whose fundamental political character was despotic. By seizure of territory, by kidnapping and theft, by coercive and authoritarian rule, Europe-based imperial regimes destroyed countless lives and sensibilities. No amount of rationalization, no invocation of themes of development and uplift, no efforts at historical relativization can justify these predations or deodorize their moral stink. So, racial politics and the racial state have their origins in the ravaging of the globe, in the consolidation of European rule, and in the classification of all humanity along racial lines. It is a bleak picture.

But not in every way. Racial politics also embody self-activity, resistance, and "situated creativity" (another pragmatist phrase; see Joas 1996). For the past half-millennium, refusal of slavery, resistance to colonialism, noncompliance with racial domination, fidelity to oppositional cultural traditions and alternative concepts of group and individual identity, and belief in racial solidarity have been some of the most crucial sources of insurgency, some of the central passions underlying emancipatory and democratic politics, both in the United States and around the world.

Trajectories of Racial Politics

What happens in racial politics when huge crises and racial "breaks"—matters of global and not just national significance for the most part—are *not* on the horizon? The 17 years of the Civil War/Reconstruction (1860–1877) and roughly 22 years (1948–1970) of the post-World War II racial "break" were exceptional periods. The brief and heroic latter period is now receding historically. As President Obama has noted—speaking about himself as well as other present-day black leaders—the "Moses" generation of Dr. King and his contemporaries has now been succeeded by the "Joshua" generation (Bobo and Dawson 2009). What do "normal" racial politics look like today?

Racial politics should be understood in terms of *trajectories*. In the post-World War II civil rights era and its aftermath, there have been a rising and a declining phase of this political trajectory. The trajectory proceeded from the relative abeyance of racial justice movements before the war; it was initiated during the war with the 1941 desegregation of the defense industries, and continued with the desegregation of the armed forces and the 1954 *Brown* decision; it reached its apogee with the upsurge of the civil rights, black power, and their allied movements in the 1960s. It began its decline after the adoption of civil rights reforms in the mid-1960s. A victim of its own (partial) success, the movement confronted the onset of racial reaction at the hands of the new right from about 1970 onward.

Applying Gramsci's approach, let us consider the U.S. racial system as an "unstable equilibrium." The idea of politics as "the continuous process of formation and superseding of unstable equilibria" has particular resonance in describing the operation of the racial state. The racial system is managed by the state—encoded in law, organized through policy-making, and enforced by a repressive apparatus. But the equilibrium thus achieved is unstable, for the great variety of conflicting interests encapsulated in racial meanings and identities can be no more than pacified by the state. Racial conflict persists at every level of society, varying over time and in respect to different groups, but ubiquitous. Indeed, the state is itself penetrated and structured by the very interests whose conflicts it seeks to stabilize and control.[22]

Disruption and restoration of the racial order suggest the type of reiterative movement or pattern we designate by the term "trajectory." Both racial movements and the racial state experience such transformations, passing through periods of rapid change and virtual stasis, through moments of massive mobilization and others of relative passivity. While the movement and regime versions of the overall trajectory are independently observable, they could not exist independently of each other. Racially based political movements are inconceivable without the racial state, which provides a focus for political demands and structures the racial order. The racial regime, in turn, has been historically constructed by racial movements; it consists of agencies and programs which are institutionalized responses to racially based movements of the past.

Our concept of the trajectory of racial politics thus links the two central actors in the drama of contemporary racial politics—the racial state and anti-racist social movements, the "dominant" and "subordinate" groups in Gramsci's account—and suggests a general pattern of interaction between them. Change in the racial order, in the social meaning and political role played by race, is achieved only when the state has initiated reforms, when it has generated new programs and agencies in response to movement demands. Movements capable of achieving such reforms only arise when there is significant "decay" in the capacities of pre-existing state programs and institutions to organize and enforce racial ideology. Contemporary patterns of change in the racial order illustrate this point clearly.

Taken as a whole, the anti-racist movements of the post-World War II period constitute a broad democratic upsurge, whose goals were a wide aggregation of "freedom dreams" (Kelley 2003) that ranged from moderate (voting rights) to radical (socialist revolution, national liberation). The state response to this challenge sought to contain it through reforms that would substitute a system of racial *hegemony* for the previous system of racial *domination.* The various civil rights acts and court decisions of the 1960s incorporated movement opposition. This involved making tangible concessions without altering the underlying structural racism that was characteristic of the United States. It also meant the marginalization and in some cases destruction of those sectors of racial opposition that were unwilling to accept limited (aka "moderate") reforms.

After the dust had settled from the titanic confrontation between the movement's radical propensities and the "establishment's" tremendous capacity for incorporative "moderate" reform, a great deal remained unresolved. The ambiguous and contradictory racial conditions in the nation today result from decades-long attempts simultaneously to ameliorate racial opposition and to placate and sustain the *ancien régime raciale.* The unending reiteration of these opposite gestures, these contradictory practices, itself testifies to the limitations of democracy and the continuing significance of race in the United States.

Where are we located today on this trajectory? Were the incorporative reforms effective in defusing the anti-racist movement? Of course, they were; let's not have any illusions about that. But the political processes we are discussing here proceed forward in time, driven in part by the very limitations of the reforms that shaped them. The trajectory of racial politics continues. Perhaps perversely, or at least ironically, the reforms which curtailed racial inequality and injustice's most despotic features have worked to reinforce the production and diffusion of "colorblindness" as the hegemonic U.S. racial ideology in the late 20th and early 21st centuries. In Chapters 7 (*Racial Reaction: Containment and Rearticulation*) and 8 (*Colorblindness, Neoliberalism, and Obama*), we consider the rise to hegemony of colorblind racial ideology, as well as its contradictions and vulnerabilities.

This is the racial crisis of the early 21st century. "[C]risis," Gramsci wrote, "consists precisely in the fact that the old is dying and the new cannot be born: in this interregnum, a great variety of morbid symptoms appear" (1971, 276). The significant advances made since World War II in overcoming the entrenched systems of U.S. racial despotism coexist with a system of ongoing racial stratification and injustice that manages to reproduce most of the conditions that have supposedly been abolished.

The Politicization of the Social

The race-based/anti-racism movements that arose after World War II were the first *new social movements* (Laraña, Johnston, and Gusfield, eds. 1994; Goodwin, Jasper, and Polletta, eds. 2001). They were the first systematically to expand the concerns of politics to the social sphere, to the terrain of everyday life and emotional life.[23] New social movement politics would later prove "contagious," leading to the mobilization of other people of color, as well as other groups whose concerns were principally social. The new social movements were inspired by the black movement—particularly in the United States but all around the world as well (Mullings 2009). These movements challenged the more limited notions of politics that had shaped "mainstream" understandings. They vastly enlarged and qualitatively transformed the classical definition of politics: "Who gets what, when, and how" (Lasswell 1950 [1936]).

What distinguishes the post-World War II racial regime, and the anti-racist initiatives of the mid-20th century, from previous periods of racial despotism and earlier attempts to create racial democracy? Of course, no historical period is completely different from those that preceded it; all political systems, all racial projects, bear the "birthmarks" of their epochs of origin. Even a radical "break," like the one described by Du Bois in *Black Reconstruction,* or the post-World War II upheaval in racial dynamics—which was a worldwide phenomenon, not just a U.S. one—preserves within itself substantial components of what went before.

How could it be otherwise? Enslaved people of African descent may have sought freedom, and indeed fought and died for it with all their hearts, but they nevertheless remained wounded and brutalized by the system they succeeded in overthrowing. And that system, however much it had been laid waste by Sherman's armies, and however much it had been chastened by Lincoln's poignant warning in his Second Inaugural Address (1864) that

> if God wills that it [the War] continue until all the wealth piled by the bondsman's two hundred and fifty years of unrequited toil shall be sunk, and ... every drop of blood drawn with the lash shall be paid by another drawn with the sword, as was said three thousand years ago, so still it must be said, "The judgments of the Lord are true and righteous altogether...,"

would still not emerge from the carnage and suffering of the Civil War as a truly free society.

The achievement of civil rights reforms was a great triumph, despite the limitations and compromises built into the reform legislation and the Supreme Court decisions involved (the *Brown* decision's "all deliberate speed" equivocation on desegregation was but one example of this). Yet the passage of civil rights laws in the mid-1960s was no more the creation of racial democracy than was the passage of civil rights laws in the late 1860s. The Supreme Court overturned the 1868 Civil Rights Act and other emancipatory Reconstruction-era measures, just as it has eviscerated the 1960s civil rights laws in the decades since their enactment.[24] The achievement of slavery's abolition was at best a hint of what "abolition democracy"—that quasi-revolutionary ideal that Du Bois identified as the heart of slaves' auto-emancipation during the Civil War—would have involved: redistribution of land, severe punishment for rebellious Confederates. Civil rights are not the same as democracy. They do not spell the end of racism; indeed they are marked by racism's continuity, not its elimination.

Yet the post-World War II racial upheavals in the United States, the anti-racist movements of that epoch, did indeed achieve something new and unprecedented. This was the *politicization of the social*: the overflow of political meaning and awareness into the arena of everyday and emotional life, which had up to then been a largely "private" and depoliticized sphere. This terrain had previously been seen as largely irrational, disembodied, unrelated to politics, unconnected to power, and outside the purview of the state.

Emerging from the territory of the everyday, lived experience of racism, and indeed embedded with that experience, the anti-racist movement was all about the ways race was conceived, constructed, and practiced at both the macro-level of institutional arrangements and social structure and the micro-level of everyday social relationships. The modern civil rights movement, and its allied anti-racist movements, were struggles over these concepts, practices, and structures; they were conflicts about the *social meaning of race*. It was their incursion into the nation's political life, and their achievements within it, that created what we call The Great Transformation—the shifts in racial awareness, racial meaning, racial subjectivity that were brought about by the black movement. Race is not only a matter of politics, economics, or culture, but operates simultaneously on all these levels of lived experience. It is a pre-eminently social phenomenon that suffuses each individual identity, each family and community, and that also penetrates state institutions and market relationships.

After World War II, the black movement *politicized the social*. It asserted the "fact of blackness" (Fanon 1967), a realization that erupted like a volcano onto the sleeping village below. The village of American social life—that is, the white "mainstream" of segregated American society—was turned inside out by this "social fact" (Durkheim 2014) after centuries of white obliviousness and dormant racial insurgency. The rise of the black movement eclipsed the ethnicity-based model of race and instituted a new model based on new understandings—what we call *rearticulations*—of key socio-political pillars of U.S. "common sense": democracy, state, and identity.

Because it represented a critical upheaval in the meaning of race and a far more profound understanding of the dynamics of racism, the politicization of the social was linked to the two challenging paradigms of racial formation that we have discussed here: the class-based paradigm and the nation-based paradigm. But it was only linked in part. Yes, the class-based and nation-based approaches to race and racism shared a rejection of the "moderate" orientation of the ethnicity paradigm. This drew them together in their quest for a more radical anti-racist position, and it suggested a deeper critique of race and racism in everyday life. For example, some class-based theories of race focused on the *experience* of inequality and superexploitation (Oppenheimer 1974). Cultural nationalist politics and theory focused on community, customs, and *peoplehood.*

But the challenging paradigms could not grasp the larger significance of the racial politics of everyday life, the social psychological and experiential dimensions of the politicized social. The class-based and nation-based paradigms of race, though critical and radical, relied on more traditional forms of politics—on economic determinism and anti-colonialism respectively. Because they were limited by their reductionism of race, even the radical varieties of the class-based and nation-based paradigms—Marxist accounts and internal colonialism accounts in particular—could not fully embrace the autonomy and *self-activity* of the new social movements.

We do not argue that the politicization of the social was a purely spontaneous phenomenon. Indeed it was *crafted* in part by movement activists and theorists, for example by Bayard Rustin (Rustin 2003 [1965]; D'Emilio 2004). We draw special attention, however, to the movement's ability to pay attention to its base, to "learn from its followers." This derived from its profound commitment to the complexities of race itself. This recognition of black "self-activity" (James et al. 2006 [1958]) bore a strong resemblance to the "situated creativity" highlighted in Dewey's political philosophy. We have discussed this *radical pragmatism of race.* The movement's immersion in the black religious tradition, its embrace of direct action, and its heteronomous adoption of such political tactics as the "sit-in" (based in the labor movement) and *satyagraha*/nonviolence (based in Gandhi's anti-colonial struggle in India; see Chabot 2011)[25] all undermined the racist barriers that had for so long separated the thoroughly racialized social life of American society from the exclusive white politics of the Jim Crow regime. A notable feature of the black movement's politicization of the social was the active role that youth, especially black youth, played in this transition. The willingness of young blacks to expose their bodies to the brutality of white racism—particularly in the South—was itself a rearticulation: a practical reinterpretation of the significance of the black body, as well as a defiance of the inherent violence of lynching.[26]

In short, racial identity, racial experience, racial politics, and the racial state itself were deeply transformed after World War II by the black movement and its allies. They were so profoundly reinvented and reinterpreted that the racial meanings established during this period continue to shape social and political life, even in the current period of reaction.

Furthermore, the politicization of the social spread across all of American life, highlighting the injustices, inequalities, and indignities that pervade U.S. society. The taken-for-granted unfreedom of women as a result of their sexual objectification and assumed unsuitability for the public sphere—in other words, the whole panoply of sexist practices and social structures—now became visible and a matter of contention, not only in the legislatures and courts but in the workplace and bedroom.[27] The assumed abnormality, perversion, deviance, and criminality of homosexuality—in other words, the unquestioned homophobia, ostracism, and discrimination experienced as a matter of course by anyone recognized as gay—now became a public political conflict, not only for those stigmatized as a result of their sexual identities, but for *everyone*, for the whole society.[28] Of course, these shifts did not take place overnight; they required years to unfold; indeed they are still very much sociopolitical battlefields and are likely to remain so, just as race and racism itself will remain a political "war zone," a field of profound conflict. But our point here is not that that these were "problems" that were "solved" in political life and everyday life. Indeed it is quite the opposite: that racism, sexism, and homophobia—and other society-wide conflicts as well—were *revealed and politicized* by the anti-racist movement that succeeded World War II. Henceforth these and related dimensions of injustice, inequality, and exclusion became public issues, ceasing forever to be relegated to the private and personal sphere, or worse yet, to be utterly denied and suppressed.

The radical upsurge of the anti-racist movement during the post-World War II years succeeded in disrupting white supremacy. It discredited the European immigrant-based model of race that had grounded ethnicity theory and had rationalized the racial "moderation" and complacency of white liberals. Anti-racist mobilization incentivized class-based and nation-based theories and analyses of race—the challenging paradigms we have discussed in Chapters 2 and 3. But although the movement launched a new political trajectory of conflict and reform, neither of the two challenging viewpoints could achieve hegemonic status. They suffered from serious deficiencies, largely because (as we have argued in Part I) of their reduction of race to other phenomena. The subsequent waning of the class- and nation-based viewpoints and organizations, grounded in challenging paradigms left a vacuum in racial theory and politics. This vacuum permitted the racial state to adopt new techniques of violence and repression, working under the "law and order" ideology of the new right. This vacuum also created the political space for the rearticulation and containment of movement demands under the ideology of colorblindness.

Despite these serious setbacks, the depth and breadth of "the Great Transformation" can hardly be exaggerated. *The forging of new collective racial identities during the 1950s and 1960s has been the single most enduring contribution of the anti-racist movement.* It is a set of political resources that endures today as a central component of the struggle for democracy in the United States. Today, the gains won in the past have been rolled back in many respects. Many anti-racist movement organizations have been forced onto the defensive: Rather than demanding increased racial justice, they have had to fight to uphold welfare state policies and liberal reforms—affirmative action is perhaps the best example—that they once condemned as inadequate and tokenistic at best. The trajectory of racial politics continues, but now in a prolonged downturn. Amidst these reversals, the persistence of the politicized social, the continuity and strength of the new racial identities forged by the anti-racist movement, stands out as the most formidable obstacle to the consolidation of a repressive racial order. Apparently, the movements themselves could be fragmented, many of the policies for which they fought could be reversed, and their leaders could be coopted or even assassinated; but the racial subjectivity and self-awareness that they developed have taken permanent hold, and no amount of repression or cooptation can change that.

Notes

1. Mills 2008, 1389.
2. Durkheim's theoretical claims about social facts and collective representations are conveniently assembled and discussed in Durkheim 2014.
3. Concepts of the subject, subjection, and subjectivity are usefully deconstructed in Butler 1997a. The experience/structure framework parallels Mills's "sociological imagination" (2000 [1959]), and also Levi-Strauss's (1966) concept of social structure as simultaneously synchronic and diachronic. All three of these accounts share central pragmatist tenets as well.
4. The concepts of "situated creativity" and "self-reflective action" are core ideas in the radical pragmatism of John Dewey (1933, 1948 [1919]). A parallel concept can be found in C.L.R. James's idea of "self-activity" and in Grace Lee's early work. The term "self-activity" was introduced into the political lexicon in *Facing Reality*, a theoretical text by C.L.R. James, Grace Lee, Martin Glaberman, and Cornelius Castoriadis that appeared in the 1950s. Because "self-activity" cannot be delegated to others, it embodies radical democracy. The authors write:

   > The end toward which mankind is inexorably developing by the constant overcoming of internal antagonisms is not the enjoyment, ownership, or use of goods, but self-realization, creativity based upon the incorporation into the individual personality of the whole previous development of humanity. Freedom is creative universality, not utility. (2006 [1958], 58)

   The radical pragmatist (and arguably Deweyan) framework here is quite palpable. See also Rawick 1972; Lawson and Koch, eds. 2004. Lee (later Grace Lee Boggs), still active today at age 95, remains a leading anti-racist radical activist and author. She received her Ph.D. in 1940 with a dissertation on George Herbert Mead and has written on Dewey as well.
5. The notion of racism as a "scavenger ideology" was first elaborated by George Mosse (1985, 213). It is also noted in Collins and Solomos 2010, 11; Fredrickson 2002.
6. On Gramsci's concept of ideology as "glue," see Gramsci 1971, 328.
7. In U.S. race studies the subalternity argument goes back through Robin D.G. Kelley to the "hidden transcripts" of James C. Scott. Scott in turn drew on the "subaltern studies" school of Ranajit Guha, Partha Chatterjee, and Gayatri Chakravorty Spivak, among others. The term "subaltern" comes from Gramsci. In our view, it pairs domination and "otherness," and thus addresses key race/racism issues. In important part of subalternity theories is the argument that it is difficult to govern subaltern peoples "all the way down."

Implicitly, "below" normal politics there is a level of autonomy available to such groups and individuals, an "infrapolitical" terrain beneath the radar of white supremacy, colonialism, slavocracy, or other authoritarian regimes. This theme relates to the theme of race/racism as the "politicization of the social" that we discuss later in this chapter.

8. The American Revolution was a bourgeois revolution, in the sense that it overthrew a feudal system and established a system of rule by a property-holding class of "commoners." The revolution thus repudiated not only absolutism and "divine right" but also nobility and aristocracy. But because it occurred in the early stages of capitalism's development, it initially recognized only the democratic rights of established (male, white) property-holders. The founding fathers' distaste for the "rabble," the masses, even those who were white and male, is well-known. Later, as capitalism developed, political rights could be extended (gradually to be sure) to the "middling sorts": small (white, male) property-holders. See Beckert 2001.
9. This is true of almost all the American anti-colonial revolutions: Beginning in the early 19th century, local ("creole") elites—Bolivar, Juarez, San Martin—sought to throw off the restrictive commercial practices demanded by colonial administrations based in Europe. They wanted to control their own exports—largely primary products—and sell to the world market, a form of "free trade" much encouraged by the superpower of that century: Great Britain. The one exception here is Haiti and even that epochal struggle was partially trade-based.
10. The ideological residue of these restrictions in naturalization and citizenship is the popular equation of the term "American" with "white." The emergence of the "birther" phenomenon in the aftermath of Barack Obama's election in 2008 has been cited as evidence of this. As pundit Andrew Sullivan writes:

    > The demographics tell the basic story: a black man is president and a large majority of white southerners cannot accept that, even in 2009. They grasp conspiracy theories to wish Obama—and the America he represents—away. Since white southerners comprise an increasing proportion of the 22% of Americans who still describe themselves as Republican, the GOP can neither dismiss the crankery nor move past it. The fringe defines what's left of the Republican center. (Sullivan 2009; see also Parker and Barreto 2013; Fang 2013)

11. For a comparative analysis of Mexican and Chinese experiences in 19th-century California see Almaguer 2008 [1994].
12. A brief selection of sources: Lester 1968a; Harding 1969; Rawick 1972; Gutman 1976; Aptheker 1983 (1963); Thompson 1983; Hahn 2003; Du Bois 2007 (1935).
13. The examples of Geronimo, Crazy Horse, and other Native American leaders were passed down from generation to generation as examples of resistance, and the Ghost Dance and Native American Church were employed by particular generations of Indians to maintain a resistance culture (Geronimo 2005 [1905]; Powers 2011; see also Snipp 1989). Rodolfo Acuña has pointed out how the same "bandits" against whom Anglo vigilantes mounted expeditions after the Treaty of Guadalupe Hidalgo—Tiburcio Vasquez and Joaquín Murieta are perhaps the most famous of these—became heroes in the Mexicano communities of the Southwest, remembered in folktales and celebrated in corridos (Acuña 2011 [1972]; see also Peña 1985). Chinese immigrants confined at Angel Island in the San Francisco Bay carved poetry in the walls of their cells, seeking not only to identify themselves

and their home villages, but also to memorialize their experiences and to inform their successor occupants of those same places of confinement (Lai, Lim, and Yung 1991; Huang 2008). We do not offer these examples to romanticize repression or to give the air of revolutionary struggle to what were often desperate acts; we simply seek to affirm that even in the most uncontested periods of American racism, oppositional cultures were able, often at very great cost, to maintain themselves.

14. "The massive structures of the modern democracies, both as State organisations, and as complexes of associations in civil society, constitute for the art of politics as it were the 'trenches' and the permanent fortifications of the front in the war of position: they render merely 'partial' the element of movement which before used to be 'the whole' of war" (Gramsci 1971, 503).
15. Gramsci's elliptical language, required by imprisonment in fascist Italy, makes concise citation difficult. For more details of his approach to the war of maneuver/war of position concepts, see "State and Civil Society," in Gramsci 1971, 445–557. The entire work (itself an edited selection) is useful for the student of race and racism.
16. Our treatment here is necessarily very brief. The contemporary configuration of racial politics is a major subject later on in this work.
17. We confine ourselves here to the issue of political uses of the racial body, which is what we mean by "the racial body politic." Originally the phrase "body politic" referred to absolutist political frameworks, in which the sovereign's body was conceived as dual. A mortal individual, the sovereign's political body was also divine. As a result of divine right, it incorporated (note the bodily etymology of this term) his or her people as well. Only because sovereignty embodied the divine in the mortal, only because of "the king's two bodies" could it exercise absolute power (Kantorowicz 1957; see also Allen 2004, 69–84).
18. Eric D. Weitz (2003) has traced a whole series of 20th-century genocides back to the attempt, which he calls "utopian," to achieve racial (or quasi-racial) homogeneity in particular nations or empires.
19. This term refers to the making of political distinctions among human bodies. This happens according to gender and race most centrally, but in respect to other phenomic characteristics as well. Such distinctions are not merely imposed from outside, but are seen as intrinsic by their bearers; they thus become essential to the political-economic and cultural self-discipline Foucault calls "governmentality." He refers to biopower as a political technology—that is, an apparatus of rule and subjection—that took the shape of "an explosion of numerous and diverse techniques for achieving the subjugations of bodies and the control of populations" (Foucault 1990 [1978], 140). See also Butler 1997a.
20. Similar patterns can be discerned in efforts to control the gendered body and the queer body: abortion restriction, gay-bashing, and numerous other repressive practices are clear examples.
21. This definition imperfectly renders some organized principles of pragmatist thought, notably its democratic currents. These proceed from Dewey 1933; see also Joas 1996.
22. The main means available to the state for the equilibration of conflicting interests is precisely their incorporation into the state in the form of policies, programs, patronage, etc. Gramsci argues that various forms of hegemony flow from this process of incorporation: "expansive" hegemony if state–society relations display sufficient dynamism and are not inordinately plagued by crisis conditions; or "reformist" hegemony (what he calls "transformism") if political stability requires continuing concessions to competing forces.

23. This is not strictly true, of course. From the onset of racial slavery there has always been a ferocious social critique not only of slavery itself, but of racism too, although that term was not yet used. This is evident in the writings and speeches of Douglass, Wells, Cooper. "First-wave" feminism also possessed a social critique: It was about women's lives, not just about the vote.

    Yet our claim holds, because by and large the earlier movements were far more constrained by the very laws, customs and conventions that they sought to oppose, than were the post-World War II movements. The appeal that the modern civil rights movement exercised, its penetration into the everyday, its appeal to youth, its institutional base ("resource mobilization") were unprecedented in earlier cycles of protest. We address this topic at greater length in Chapter 6.
24. This may be yet another example of Myrdal's "cumulative and circular development." On the SCOTUS annulment of the 1960s civil rights laws and the undoing of the Warren Court's own liberal race jurisprudence, see Kairys 1994; Alexander 2012. On the undoing of the Radical Republican civil rights laws of the 1860s, see Kaczorowski 1987.
25. The movement's early assertion of nonviolent resistance linked it to anti-colonialism well before civil rights and antiwar politics fused in the later 1960s.
26. Martin Luther King, Jr. wrote:

    > In 1960 an electrifying movement of Negro students shattered the placid surface of campuses and communities across the South. The young students of the South, through sit-ins and other demonstrations, gave America a glowing example of disciplined, dignified nonviolent action against the system of segregation. Though confronted in many places by hoodlums, police guns, tear gas, arrests, and jail sentences, the students tenaciously continued to sit down and demand equal service at variety store lunch counters, and they extended their protest from city to city. Spontaneously born, but guided by the theory of nonviolent resistance, the lunch counter sit-ins accomplished integration in hundreds of communities at the swiftest rate of change in the civil rights movement up to that time. In communities like Montgomery, Alabama, the whole student body rallied behind expelled students and staged a walkout while state government intimidation was unleashed with a display of military force appropriate to a wartime invasion. Nevertheless, the spirit of self- sacrifice and commitment remained firm, and the state governments found themselves dealing with students who had lost the fear of jail and physical injury.
    >
    > The campuses of Negro colleges were infused with a dynamism of both action and philosophical discussion. Even in the thirties, when the college campus was alive with social thought, only a minority were involved in action. During the sit-in phase, when a few students were suspended or expelled, more than one college saw the total student body involved in a walkout protest. This was a change in student activity of profound significance. Seldom, if ever, in American history had a student movement engulfed the whole student body of a college.
    >
    > Many of the students, when pressed to express their inner feelings, identified themselves with students in Africa, Asia, and South America. The liberation struggle in Africa was the great single international influence on American Negro students. Frequently, I heard them say that if their African brothers could break the bonds of colonialism, surely the American Negro could break Jim Crow (King 2001, 137–138; see also MLK Jr Research and Education Institute n.d.).

It is also vital to note the key role of Ella Baker in the emergence of the student-based components of the movement: in the 1960 Greensboro sit-ins and the Student Non-Violent Coordinating Committee (SNCC). In the 1964 Freedom Summer, students were the key activists (Carson 1995 [1981]; Ransby 2005).

27. The origins of "second-wave" feminism have been linked to the analyses and practice of key women activists in the civil rights movement. See Echols 1989; Curry 2000; Breines 2007.
28. Here too Bayard Rustin must be acknowledged. As a gay man Rustin was marginalized and discriminated against in the movement he did so much to found. See Rustin 2003; D'Emilio 2004.

PART III

Racial Politics Since World War II

CHAPTER 6

The Great Transformation

Introduction

The racial upsurges of the 1950s and 1960s were among the most tempestuous events in American history. The struggles for voting rights, the sit-ins, freedom rides, and boycotts to desegregate public facilities, the ghetto rebellions, armed standoffs (Wounded Knee, Tierra Amarilla, Alcatraz, Attica...), and the mobilizations of Latin@s, Indians, and Asian Americans dramatically transformed the political and cultural landscape of the United States. The postwar period has indeed been a racial crucible. During these decades, new conceptions of racial identity and its meaning, new modes of political organization and confrontation, and new definitions of the state's role in promoting and achieving equality were explored, debated, and fought out on the battlegrounds of institutionalized politics, the politics of law, and the politics of everyday life.

Beginning during World War II, movements for racial justice, led by the black movement, initiated a "second reconstruction," a Great Transformation (*pace* Polanyi),[1] an expansion of democracy that challenged some of the pillars of despotism in the United States. The black movement enlarged and deepened democracy, not only in terms of racial justice and equality, but in terms of *social* justice and equality. Over a mere quarter of a century, very real reforms were achieved, though there were numerous limits and indeed failures in this democratizing project.

We suggest that two important changes characterize postwar racial politics: *paradigm shift* and *new social movements.* Paradigm shift occurred as the hegemonic theory of race, based in the ethnicity paradigm of race, experienced increasing strain and opposition. This opposition gradually took shape within the civil rights movement, initially as a challenge against segregation in the South, and was subsequently transformed into a national movement against racism. The second change was the rise of *new social movements*, led by the black movement, as the primary means for contesting the nature of racial politics. These movements irreversibly expanded the terrain of political conflict, not only recentering and refiguring race, but also refiguring experience itself as a political matter, a matter of identity and self-conscious activity. They thus set the stage for a general reorganization of U.S. politics.

Paradigm Shift: The modern civil rights movement was initially organized *within* the dominant paradigm of ethnicity. The ethnicity perspective initially shaped the movement's political agenda. Early movement leaders were also assimilation-oriented and individualistic to a degree that appears a bit embarrassing today, but made more sense in the repressive and exclusive racial climate of the time. They were moderates who sought to end "race-thinking" and assure "equality" to each individual. The movement initially focused its energies on the South, the most racially reactionary region of the country. There the ethnicity paradigm of assimilation and group-oriented pluralism retained a critical edge in facing exclusion, segregation, and still-vibrant Jim-Crow racism.[2] "Civil rights" was then a radical challenge to explicit white supremacy. Later, when demands for racial reforms attained national scope and expanded beyond the black movement to other racially defined minorities, the limited explanatory abilities and programmatic usefulness of the ethnicity paradigm were revealed. The eclipse of this perspective led to a period where competing paradigms—the class- and nation-based views—flourished and contested for hegemony.

Although the challenging paradigms were not able to replace the dominant ethnicity-based view of race, they did manage to dislodge it for a while. When it regained its hegemony as the dominant paradigm, the ethnicity-based approach had been rearticulated, deeply transformed, emerging as the "colorblind" concept of race. It remains highly problematic and riven by contradictions, as we shall see in later chapters of this book.

New Social Movements: The upsurge of racially based movements that began in the 1950s was a contest over the *social meaning* of race. It was this battle that transformed racial awareness, racial politics, and racial identity. Race is not only a matter of politics, economics, or culture, but of all these "levels" of lived experience simultaneously. It is a pre-eminently *social* phenomenon, something which suffuses each individual identity, each family and community, yet equally penetrates state institutions and market relationships. The racial justice movements of the postwar period were the first *new social movements*—the first to expand the concerns of politics to the social, to the terrain of everyday life. New social movement politics would prove "portable," leading to the mobilization of other racial minorities, as well as other groups whose concerns were principally social. The black movement, in other words, made it possible for a wide range of movements to reframe social identities, both at the collective and individual level. It helped these movements connect with each other as well, though not always easily (Epstein 1987; Scott 1988; Morris and Mueller, eds. 1992; Polletta and Jasper 2001). An extensive literature that developed even before the development of "intersectionality" accounts drew upon the black struggle as an organizing framework, a "master narrative" of oppression and resistance. Both in political practice and in critical theory, then, the black movement's politicization of the social shaped the upsurges of the 1960s: anti-imperialist, student, feminist, and gay. As British playwright and activist David Edgar wrote, black mobilization was "a central organizational fact …, a defining political metaphor and inspiration" (1981, 222).

These two interrelated dimensions—the eclipse of the ethnicity paradigm and the emergence of new social movement politics—constitute an alternative framework by which to assess the racial politics of the Great Transformation. Racial identity, the racial state, and the very nature of racial politics as a whole were radically transformed during the 1960s—were transformed so profoundly that the racial meanings established during this period came to shape U.S. politics permanently, even after the movements peaked and entered a decades-long decline.

Although the ethnicity paradigm was weakened during the 1960s and the class-based and nation-based paradigms of race increased in strength, these two challenging viewpoints could not achieve hegemonic status. All three paradigms suffered from serious deficiencies, largely because their concepts of race were *reductionist*: They relied on other, supposedly more fundamental phenomena, such as culture (the ethnicity paradigm), inequality (the class paradigm), or "peoplehood" (the nation-based paradigm), to explain the social fact of race. The subsequent waning of class-based (generally Marxist) and nationalist movements, and of the specific organizations operating within these challenging paradigms, left a vacuum in racial theory and politics. This created the political space for the resurgence of neoconservatism, which developed in the 1970 and 1980s as a reworked, right-wing version of the ethnicity paradigm. This contributed to the rise of colorblind racial ideology.

Still, the depth and breadth of "the Great Transformation" can hardly be exaggerated. The forging of new collective racial identities during the 1950s and 1960s has been the enduring legacy of the new social movements pioneered by the black movement. Even though many anti-racist movement victories were rolled back, even though many movement organizations were marginalized by the combined powers of the racial state and racial reaction, the *politicization of the social* during this rising phase of the political trajectory of race has persisted. The deepening and broadening of racial politics in the sphere of everyday life stands out as the single truly formidable obstacle to the consolidation of a newly repressive racial order. Apparently, the movements of people of color themselves could be weakened, the policies for which they fought could be reframed and even reversed, and their leaders could be coopted or destroyed, but the racial subjectivity and self-awareness which they developed had taken permanent hold, and no amount of repression or cooptation could change that. The genie was out of the bottle.

The Emergence of the Civil Rights Movement

The moderate goals of the early civil rights movement did not challenge the nationally dominant paradigm of racial theory, the ethnicity perspective. Indeed, early movement rhetoric often explicitly appealed to the ideal of a "race-free" society, the centerpiece of the liberal ethnicity vision. This was consistent with the call for integration framed by Gunnar Myrdal in 1944, or with Nathan Glazer's description of the "national consensus" which abolished Jim Crow in the mid-1960s (Glazer 1975, 3).

Although its political goals were moderate, the black movement had to adopt radical tactics of disruption and direct action due to the "massive resistance" strategy of the South, a region that clung to the racist assumptions of the Jim Crow/*Plessy* era.[3] The modern civil rights movement came into being when southern black organizations, frustrated by Southern intransigence and drawing on both national and indigenous support bases, moved to mobilize a *mass* constituency in the South. They thus augmented the tactics of judicial/legislative activism—based in the elite politics that had previously characterized the civil rights struggle[4]—with those of direct action, which required an active "grass-roots" constituency. This was the key shift of the mid-1950s.

What made this change possible? After the civil rights upsurge, social movement studies have developed models of "political process" or "resource mobilization" to explain the emergence of significant struggles for change. Analyses of the formation of the modern civil rights movement in the mid-1950s are often based on these models (McAdam 1984; Morris 1984). Clearly, such approaches have their merits as they focus on essential conditions for the emergence of movements: the inadequacy of "normal" political channels to process demands, and the availability of material and political resources for the organization of movement constituencies. The monolithic southern resistance to desegregation is an instance of the failure of "normal" politics to respond to demands for change; white supremacist intransigence revealed the ossification and racial despotism of the political system in Dixie, generating a new political process and a new organizing vision (Payne 2007 [1995]). The role of such groups as the local NAACP chapters, and particularly the black churches, effectively documented by Aldon Morris, exemplifies the centrality of resource mobilization issues.

Although both the resistance to change and the availability of economic and political resources in the black community were essential components of the civil rights movement's shift to a direct action strategy, neither of these conditions were sufficient to spark the transition. After all, racial degradation, exclusion, and violence had been well-established in the region since Reconstruction's termination in 1877, and black mobilization had been continuous, even under severely repressive conditions (Hahn 2003). A third element was required. This was an ideological or cultural transformation, the politicization of black identity, the *rearticulation of black collective subjectivity*. It was this change that would eventually place radical objectives on the agenda of racial minority movements, facilitate the diffusion of racially based movement activity to other groups, and become anathema to the moderate advocates of civil rights operating within the ethnicity paradigm of race.

New Social Movement Politics: Identity and Rearticulation

Before the modern black movement's appearance on the political stage, the U.S. political system had not significantly changed since the New Deal. The Democratic Party had served as a repository of consensus ever since Roosevelt led it to power in the 1930s. Compromise and coalition-building among disparate interests, constituencies, and loyalties ("interest-group liberalism")[5] shaped national politics. "Interests" themselves were largely defined economically. Such a system had obvious limitations in its ability to respond to challenges that cut across class (or "status") lines. It was unable to confront an unjust social system which had not only economic but also political and cultural causes and consequences. The near-total disenfranchisement of black voters in the South, for example, not only underwrote the New Deal coalition and vastly increased the legislative power of Southern legislators in Congress (as it had done throughout U.S. history), but also undermined prospects for social legislation, not only in regard to civil rights but also in labor law, health, education, and other areas. A good example of this was Congress's overriding of Truman's veto of the Taft–Hartley Act in 1947, perhaps the single most telling setback of labor rights in U.S. history. This was accomplished by a coalition of Southern Democrats and right-wing, pro-business Republicans (Cockburn 2004).

In its efforts to transform precisely that social system, the black movement sought to *expand* the concerns of politics, without abandoning the earlier economically centered logic. The expansion of normal politics to include racial issues—a "common-sense" recognition of the political elements at the heart of racial identities and meanings—made possible the movement's greatest triumphs, its most permanent successes. These did not lie in its legislative accomplishments, but rather in its ability to create new racial "subjects." The black movement redefined the meaning of racial identity, and consequently of race itself, in American society.

Social movements create collective identity by offering their adherents a different view of themselves and their world; different, that is, from the worldview and self-concepts offered by the established social order. Movements take elements and themes of existing culture and traditions and infuse them with new meaning. This process of *rearticulation* produces new subjectivity by making use of information and knowledge already present in the subject's mind. Drawing once again on the insights of Antonio Gramsci, we define rearticulation as a *practice of discursive reorganization or reinterpretation of ideological themes and interests already present in subjects' consciousness, such that these elements obtain new meanings or coherence.* In Gramsci's account this practice is ordinarily the work of "intellectuals," those whose role is to interpret the social world for given subjects—religious leaders, entertainers, school teachers (Gramsci 1971, 3–23; Butler 1997b; Laclau and Mouffe 2001 [1985]; Visweswaran 2010).[6]

The movement's "intellectuals" were often preachers. They infused their activism with a well-known set of symbols and rhetorical tools.[7] The centuries-long black interrogation of biblical images of bondage and liberation—as embodied in the Exodus, for instance, or the theology of Christian redemption—had traditionally furnished a familiar vocabulary and textual reference-point for freedom struggle, a home-grown "liberation theology" (West 1982).

The civil rights movement rearticulated black collective subjectivity. It reframed traditional black cultural and religious themes to forge a new black politics. Its intellectuals augmented the already vast treasure-trove of emancipatory black historical and religious imagery with ideas, lessons, and strategies developed not only in North

America but in India, Africa, and Europe (in the experience of anti-Nazi resistance).[8] Martin Luther King, Jr.'s application of the Gandhian philosophy of *satyagraha* drew upon Bayard Rustin's involvement in the anti-colonial struggle in India (Anderson 1998; Rustin 2003; Prashad 2009).

The adoption of the "sit-in" as a tactic for forcing integration had deep roots not only in union battles against the repressive, post-*Lochner* U.S. labor regime in the early decades of the 20th century, but also in the legacy of enslaved people of African descent "sitting in" in the fields and slave quarters of the plantation and forcing their masters to negotiate over working conditions, time off, and the right to cultivate their own garden plots and sell their produce for money at town markets (Hahn 2003). Parallels drawn between the Civil Rights and Black Power movement struggles and those of African liberation movements also provided material for rearticulation as they invoked already known, long-standing cultural traditions that traversed the whole dark history of black oppression in the United States.

The formation of the modern civil rights movement is a classical illustration of rearticulation processes. In order to win mass black support for the tactics of direct action, it was necessary to replace the established cultural norms through which ordinary blacks, particularly in the South, had previously sought to ameliorate the impact of racial oppression: "shuckin' and jivin'," "putting on whitey," feigning ignorance and humility. These strategies had served in the past to limit the extent of white control, to insulate the black community and black institutions from white intrusion and surveillance, and to protect individual blacks who ran afoul of white authority. But they had also limited the extent and depth of black organization, organization that would be necessary to challenge the system of segregation. They represented a range of *subaltern* political adaptations, in effect both practical recognitions of powerlessness, and strategies for surviving it.[9]

But this is not the whole story. Researchers associated with the subaltern studies school have shown that even where political mobilization is highly restricted, a substantial reservoir of cultural resistance necessarily confronts racist regimes, peripheral or metropolitan, colonial or postcolonial. In their studies of colonial and postcolonial systems of rule in a variety of spatiotemporal contexts—India, Latin America, Southeast Asia, as well as the American South—they have demonstrated that where rule is highly despotic and racially exclusive, it cannot "go too deep." It generally must rely on "indirect" strategies of domination: collaborators, colonial administrators, agents, informers, and the like. Beneath this level, *infrapolitically* so to speak, an alternative and antagonistic culture of resistance takes hold, operating largely defensively, impenetrable from above (Bond-Graham 2010). The term "subaltern," after all, combines the meanings "subordinate" and "other" (alterity).[10]

Elsewhere in the book we have characterized the Jim Crow era as necessitating opposition in the form of "war of maneuver." Only in the post-World War II period did anything like normal politics—"war of position"—become possible on a mass scale. And given the degree of racial despotism that had to be overcome, even after

World War II, the achievements of the modern civil rights movement truly stand out as remarkable and heroic.

The movement sought not to survive racial oppression, but to overthrow it. Thus the traditional ideological themes of liberation and redemption, and the political tactics of protest derived from movements around the world were rearticulated: incorporated in the heat of political struggle as elements of a *transformed racial identity*, one of explicit collective opposition. According to Robert Parris Moses or Martin Luther King, Jr., blacks were, collectively, the moral, spiritual, and political leadership of American society. They represented not only their own centuries-long struggle for freedom, but the highest and noblest aspirations of white America as well.

Far from having to passively accept the "'bukes and scorns" of segregation and perhaps trying to outmaneuver "whitey," blacks were now called upon to oppose the system with righteous and disciplined action:

> To accept passively an unjust system is to cooperate with that system; thereby the oppressed become as evil as the oppressor. Noncooperation with evil is as much a moral obligation as cooperation with good.
>
> (King, quoted in Sitkoff 1981, 61)

Thus the old linkages of religious and cultural themes—for example, the Christian virtues of humility, of "turning the other cheek"—were not negated, but dramatically captured by the movement. The "culture of resistance" with which these virtues had previously been identified was displaced from an emphasis on individual survival to one of collective action. This process of rearticulation made the movement's political agenda possible, especially its challenge to the existing racial state.

Black Power

In subsequent stages of the movement's history, rearticulation processes continued to function as radical perspectives, filling the void created by the eclipse of the ethnicity paradigm. This is particularly true of the emergence of *black power.* When the moderate demands of the civil rights movement were realized—after a fashion—in 1964 with the passage of the Civil Rights Act, and in 1965 with the enactment of voting rights legislation, many black activists considered that their underlying ideals had not only gone unfulfilled, but had been betrayed. Not only had they failed to create a "beloved community" (which they now admitted had been a utopian vision; see Lester 1968b), but they had failed to achieve significant change in the overall social conditions faced by blacks. Kenneth Clark echoed these sentiments in 1967:

> The masses of Negroes are now starkly aware that recent civil rights victories benefited a very small number of middle-class Negroes while their predicament remained the same or worsened.
>
> (Clark, quoted in Wilson 1981, 28)

The radicalization of an important segment of the black movement took shape in the myriad disappointments and disillusionments that afflicted civil rights activists: the acrimonious division between SNCC (Student Nonviolent Coordinating Committee) and civil rights moderates amidst the ferocity of the Birmingham campaign of April–May, 1963, combined with the limited victory won there;[11] the conflicts during the preparations for the August, 1963 March on Washington;[12] the experience of the Mississippi Freedom Democratic Party, an SNCC-organized project to unseat the segregationist "regular" delegation at the 1964 Democratic Party convention in Atlantic City;[13] the onset of rioting in northern cities during the summer of 1964, followed by hundreds of riots during the next four years;[14] and the development of a new "backlash" politics in the middle 1960s, after the "massive resistance" strategy of the South had been broken. Backlash was epitomized by the appearance in the national spotlight of George Wallace, the segregationist Governor of Alabama. It also took the form of white counterdemonstrations and violence against civil rights marches, notably in 1966 in Cicero, Illinois, a white suburb of Chicago. Many movement radicals viewed white resistance (especially white resistance in the North) as decisive proof that non-violent strategy was ineffective in its efforts to lead not only blacks but whites toward greater racial equality and harmony.

By the time of the Selma campaign (February–March, 1965), no more than limited tactical cooperation existed between the radicals, led by SNCC, and the moderates, led by SCLC (Southern Christian Leadership Conference). Militants from SNCC were infuriated when King, maneuvering between Washington, the federal courts, and the marchers themselves, halted an attempt to march from Selma to Montgomery on March 10, 1965.[15] By June, 1966, when diverse civil rights groups came together to complete a march through Mississippi begun by James Meredith (who had been shot by a sniper), there was open competition between advocates of "black power" and supporters of integration.

Beginning with the Meredith march,[16] the more radical wing of the movement signaled its disillusionment with past emphases on civil rights and the transformative power of nonviolence. SNCC and CORE (Congress of Racial Equality), in particular, adopted the more militant positions associated with the slogan "Black Power."

Black power was a crystallization of numerous political and cultural tendencies, some of them quite venerable, within the black community and black history.[17] It was a flexible, even amorphous concept, but it was frequently interpreted to mean separatism. It was this connotation which the moderates, operating within the ethnicity paradigm, despised and strenuously denounced: "We of the NAACP will have none of this. It is the father of hatred and the mother of violence. Black power can mean in the end only black death" (Wilkins, quoted in Allen 1990 [1970], 78).

But the concept of black power was also a rearticulative move. It operated on a very practical level. It expressed black popular frustration—especially among young people—with the glacial pace of racial reform. The cry of "black power" was no more a complete break with the civil rights movement than that movement had been a break with the older "establishment" of civil rights organizations such as the NAACP and National Urban League. The concept of black power embraced a wide spectrum of political tendencies, extending from moderate "self-help" groups through reform-oriented advocates of "community control" to cultural and revolutionary nationalism and armed struggle. The concept's emergence as a nationalist ideology was an effort once more to rearticulate traditional themes of the black movement. The rearticulation of civil rights as black power invoked themes central to both the dominant ethnicity paradigm and the civil rights movement, while simultaneously rejecting their integrationist and assimilationist goals. It also vastly expanded the already resourceful black imagination: The postwar decades of black activism had rendered possible and had concretized a set of new political and economic strategies ranging from boycotts to sit-ins, from black business opportunities to insurrection, all situated somewhat uncomfortably under the black power umbrella.

Indeed black power had a mainstream political version: In the early 1960s the premier liberal ethnicity theorists, Nathan Glazer and Daniel P. Moynihan, mindful of their paradigm's origins in the experiences of white ethnic groups of previous generations, had suggested that blacks in the North, too, should be organized as an interest group (Glazer and Moynihan 1970 [1963], x). Much of the black power current could be understood as following this advice. The idea that the black community should patronize businesses owned by blacks, that it should adopt cooperative forms of organization, that it should mobilize politically at the local level ("community control") were concepts which borrowed as much from the tradition of Booker T. Washington as they did from those of Cyril Briggs, Marcus Garvey, or Malcolm X. Robert Allen notes that in many respects black power was "only another form of traditional ethnic group politics" (1990 [1970], 50; see also Ture (Carmichael) and Hamilton 1992 [1967], 44; Joseph 2006).

Despite its many "moderate" elements, black power drew an important line of demarcation within the black movement and deeply disturbed the dominant (i.e., white) political culture. White liberals reacted in horror when their ethnic prescriptions were put into practice by black militants; they quickly retreated into a fundamentalist individualism which would have embarrassed Adam Smith.

While liberals like Glazer and Moynihan sought to rearticulate the ethnicity paradigm, which was after all the dominant current in U.S. race-thinking during the mid-1960s, black power theorists were also breaking with it. They were reinvigorating black nationalism, a current that had far deeper roots, something that went back centuries in black America (Moses 1988 [1978]). Black power also repudiated the ethnicity paradigm by drawing upon colonial analogies to analyze the plight of blacks, and by focusing attention on racially based intra-class conflict. The political implications of this paradigmatic shift represented a distinct departure from the "interest group" politics of the ethnicity paradigm. Ture and Hamilton's work, for example, explicitly addressed black conditions from within the nationalist paradigm.[18] James

Boggs' essays (1970) focused on the role of black industrial workers and urban struggles from a perspective based in Marxism-Leninism.

A key figure in the transition from civil rights to black power was Malcolm X, who framed radical black nationalism with a political energy and coherence never seen before in the United States. Malcolm attracted mass black support that in some ways echoed the Garvey movement of the 1920s.[19] First as organizer and chief spokesperson for the Nation of Islam (NOI), and then, briefly, as founder of the Organization of Afro-American Unity, Malcolm played a unique role in the black community. Although he often derided the civil rights movement, referring to its organizations and leaders as "Uncle Toms," Malcolm also recognized the importance of raising civil rights demands, even while arguing that the United States could not meet them (Malcolm X 1964; 1990 [1965]).

After his 1963 break with the Nation of Islam, Malcolm moved closer to the radical wing of the movement and deeply influenced SNCC thinking, bringing a more internationalist orientation to the organization. In late 1964 he met with SNCC leaders in Nairobi, Kenya, where he stressed the importance of Pan-Africanism for U.S. blacks (Williams 1997). He also approached socialist positions in a number of respects (Malcolm X 1990 [1965]; Marable 2011). Malcolm formulated a radical challenge to the moderate agenda of the civil rights movement and prefigured the themes of black power. In February, 1965 he was assassinated at the Audubon Ballroom in Harlem, under circumstances that remain mysterious. Malcolm's chief bodyguard was later revealed to have been a police agent; his criticisms of the misdeeds of Elijah Muhammad, as well as his break with Elijah's politics, drew death threats from the NOI.

Black power advocates and adherents questioned the integrationist and assimilationist orientations pursued by the civil rights movement, especially by its moderate leadership and middle-class black adherents. In breaking away from the earlier black movement's struggle for a "raceless society" they anticipated—by several decades—later opposition to "colorblindness" as a supposedly anti-racist orientation. Integration, they powerfully argued, could only be a result of political power and equality, never its cause. The radicalization of the black movement appropriated and rearticulated the legacy of civil rights, much as the earlier movement had appropriated the legacy of the southern "culture of resistance" which had been nourished in the black church, in black music, in folklore and literature, even in food (Childs 1984).

In addition to the demand for social justice, black power advocates raised the question of "self-determination." This was not only a revindication of the centuries-long legacy of black nationalism, but also a convergence with the Marxist (and in some instances Leninist and Maoist) left. In the great debates about nationalism that had preoccupied the Second and Third Internationals, and that had drawn passionate polemics from Rosa Luxemburg, V.I. Lenin, the "Austro-Marxists," and Joseph Stalin, U.S. black radicals rediscovered the socialist and communist affinities that had preoccupied and confounded the black left in their grandparents' times (Luxemburg 1976 (1909); Naison 1983; James 1999; Robinson 2000 [1983]; Perry 2008; Kelley and Esch 2008 [1999]). The prospect of having not only "rights" but "power" once again rearticulated black cultural and political traditions, reviving themes from black political history. The cultural nationalism and black Marxism of the late-1960s were restatements of positions which harked back to the 1920s and 1930s, the days of the Harlem Renaissance, the African Blood Brotherhood, the Garvey movement, and the "black nation" thesis of the Communist Party. The nation-based paradigm was not, however, synonymous with radical politics. Less "progressive"—or, as Huey P. Newton, co-founder of the Black Panther Party, called them, "pork chop"—nationalists tended to dilute their vision of black power by ignoring its racial dimensions for a more limited, "ethnic" view of its meaning. These groups often adopted reformist orientations, embracing "black capitalism," for example (Allen 1990 [1970], 153–164, 210–238; Hill and Rabig, eds. 2012).

Encountering and Reforming the Racial State

There were two phases to the minority encounter with the state in the 1950s and 1960s. The first phase was shaped by the civil rights movement's mass mobilization in the South, a "direct action" political strategy aimed at desegregation that is usually seen as beginning in the mid-1950s with the Montgomery bus boycott. As we have seen, this already depended upon new social movement politics, on the "politics of identity," and rearticulation of racist tropes in new and insurgent directions.

Selection of this 1955 point of departure accepts the movement's decision to focus on desegregation, rather than labor injustice and superexploitation, as the cutting-edge issue in the civil rights struggle. That decision in turn was influenced by the NAACP's exercise of leadership in the early post-World War II years. Success in desegregating the armed forces and in the courts were crucial in shaping the turn toward desegregation as the major goal. Use of the "due process" clause of the 14th Amendment as a weapon against state-based, *de jure* segregation was the linchpin of NAACP attorney Thurgood Marshall's decades-long campaign for racial justice. An alternative strategy that had been equally successful but was not pursued involved labor rights. This was to attack racism via the 13th Amendment's prohibition of involuntary servitude, a situation that continued through peonage, convict leasing, and racist labor practices. This approach had been effectively supported by the Civil Rights Section of the Justice Department, but was dismissed by the NAACP (for this argument see Goluboff 2007).

The first phase resulted in the civil rights reforms of the mid-1960s. Through desegregation campaigns the black movement set in motion a reform-oriented, democratizing political process. The resulting concessions were limited but real: policy shifts through executive order and legislation, judicial action against specific racist practices, establishment of new state programs and agencies with "equal opportunity" mandates, and the election and the hiring of many black activists by state institutions. Civil rights reforms were crafted in numerous state settings: NAACP legal offices, the White House, the Congress, the federal courts. They were then implemented unevenly throughout the state apparatus at all levels: resisted, unevenly enforced, subverted even after adoption, sure, but also carried out to a significant extent. These victories ended the exceptional situation in the South by forcing that region to confront the nationally dominant racial ideology, as defined by the ethnicity paradigm. The reforms of the 1960s also signaled the fulfillment of that paradigm's vision of racial equality.

The second phase of the movement/state encounter was marked the onset of racial reaction. Indeed it was the reality of civil rights reforms—the moderate, limited, but nevertheless significant democratic concessions that the movement obtained—that allowed the racial reaction to consolidate. The capacity of the racial reaction to adjust to a somewhat democratized racial state, and to the national civil society's broad endorsement of limited racial reform, was what made possible the right-wing rearticulation of concepts of civil rights—notably racial equality and racial justice—in what would become the colorblind racial ideology we see all around us today.

We discuss racial reaction at length in later chapters of this work. Here we emphasize the fragmentation of the black movements into competing currents—entrists and radicals, most notably—in the aftermath of the adoption of the racial reforms of the mid-1960s. As the new reforms took hold, they transformed a part of the movement into a constituency for the new programs its efforts had won. They lent support to the assimilationist and pluralist policy orientations rooted in the ethnicity-based paradigm of race. At the same time, the inadequacy and limitations of the reforms reinforced the radical tendencies in the movement, accelerating the rise of the insurgent class- and nation-based paradigms of race, and fuelling radical and rebellious political approaches.

The state was the chief movement target for several reasons. The state, as the "factor of cohesion in society," gives shape to the racial system. State racial policy ultimately defines the extent and limits of racial democracy, of racial despotism and inequality, of racial inclusion or exclusion. The state is traversed by the same antagonisms that penetrate the entire society, antagonisms that are themselves the results of past cycles of racial struggle. The lukewarm commitments to desegregation in public employment and the armed forces extracted by A. Philip Randolph from Roosevelt and Truman, the use of the 14th Amendment by NAACP lawyer Thurgood Marshall to challenge school segregation, the freedom rides of the 1940s and 1960s (which probed the federal commitment to integration of interstate travel), and the voting rights drives in the South, were all examples of the small but significant "openings" through which the existing racial state was susceptible to challenge. Movement tactics often sought to make use of the state's internal racial contradictions. For example: The SNCC-led voting rights drives sought to induce confrontations between different branches of the state—the courts vs. state legislatures, federal police vs. local or state police. The idea was to force the federal government to defend civil rights from infringement by racist local and state agencies. In some respects SNCC's strategic turn to voting rights was fomented by the Kennedy administration, although the Justice Department (headed by Robert F. Kennedy) did not adequately protect the activists of the 1964 Freedom Summer campaign.[20]

By the latter stages of this process—the late 1960s—the reform-oriented program of the black movement was acquiring a foothold in state institutions, where movement activists were becoming officials: social service agencies, electorally based positions: legislators, mayors, elected judges and local officials. The numbers weren't large, but they were growing. This "entrism" was linked in important ways with such Great Society programs as Head Start, the War on Poverty (OEO),[21] massive new federal aid to education, new labor programs, and expansions in the welfare system (AFDC).[22] It amounted to a modest but real shift toward progressive redistribution, which would not only benefit people of color but be democratically directed by them, under the banner of "maximum feasible participation," a guiding principle of the Community Action Program, one of the most important components of the OEO.

In the racial minority movements of the period, the state confronted a new type of opposition, one that for a while deployed an "inside–outside" strategy. Numerous progressive initiatives were undertaken after the passage of the Civil Rights Act of 1964 and the Voting Rights Act of 1965; this was a moment of national remorse following the JFK assassination and the landslide victory of Lyndon Johnson in November, 1964. These were the first years of the "Great Society," when the black movement and its allies were at their apogee of political influence. They were able to challenge established racist practices simultaneously through direct action, through penetration of the mainstream political arena (electoral/institutional projects from voter registration to community organization, and other sorts of entrism as well), and through "ethical/political" tactics (taking the "moral initiative," developing "resistance cultures" and service projects). For a brief time the movement was able to link spontaneity and mass participation, on the one hand, with electoral/institutional politics, on the other. The unifying element in this opposition was at first the burgeoning collective subjectivity of blacks—and later that of other people of color—which connected demands for access to the state with more radical demands for freedom, "self-determination," cultural and organizational autonomy, "community control," and a host of other issues. The beginning of urban uprisings, the rise of black power, and the reorganization of right-wing opposition as well, all were looming up during this brief period, roughly 1964–1966.

By combining different oppositional tactics, the black movement of the 1960s initiated the reforms that eventually created a new racial state. This new state, however, was not the institutional fulfillment of the movements' ideals. Rather it held a cloudy mirror up to its antagonists, reflecting their demands (and indeed their rearticulated racial identities) in a distorted fashion.

At the same time, splits and divisions had surfaced in the movement, and in minority communities as well. These included inter-group rivalries, class divisions, controversies over strategy, and disputes over the meaning of race: notably racial integration and pluralism vs. black power and ghetto-based "community control." Malcolm's assassination in February 1965 was a huge blow to mass-oriented black radical organization; his nationalism, always clearly present, had been evolving steadily towards a more class-based and global orientation that had the potential to bridge across divisions among people of color, and even across the black–white divide, the core of the colorline. Martin Luther King, Jr.'s assassination in 1968 would remove many more possibilities for alliances across movements. As the 1960s wore on, class polarization deepened within communities of color. Those who were able to do so took advantage of new jobs and educational opportunities, while the majority of ghetto and barrio dwellers remained locked in poverty. The war on poverty was lost, as King had warned, on the battlefields of Vietnam.[23] Some formerly integrated movement organizations expelled their white members (SNCC did so in December of 1966); others that formed in the later 1960s were organized from the beginning as exclusively black, Mexican American, or Asian American.

Contesting Paradigms/Strategic Divisions

By the late 1960s, the fragmentation within the movement was clearly visible and shaped very distinct and sometimes antagonistic currents. New social movement politics had galvanized activists in their respective communities, but the lack of theoretical clarity about racial dynamics in the United States splintered political action. Although the ethnicity paradigm had been seriously challenged, it remained an important explanatory model, not only for academics, but also for movement activists who sought to work within the reformed racial state. The challenging paradigms—the class- and nation-based views—gave rise to counterposed strategic orientations. Strategic divisions also flowed from class cleavages internal to communities of color, from state repression that marginalized radical tendencies, and from the very effectiveness of state strategies of reform, which tended to replace movement perspectives with the constituency-based (and ethnicity paradigm-derived) viewpoints of "normal" politics.

Three broad political currents can be recognized within the racial minority movements of this period.[24] These were *electoral/institutional entrism*, *socialism*, and *nationalism*. Each recognized the incompleteness of the civil rights reforms. While distinct from one another both in their understandings of race and in their practical activities, the *entrists*, socialists, and nationalists were not diametrically opposed: They overlapped and drew upon each other's orientations. They had, after all, emerged from roughly similar movement experiences. Each tendency embodied and enacted a particular understanding of race, one of the three theoretical paradigms of race discussed here.

Electoral/Institutional Entrism reflected greater participation in existing political organizations and processes by movement activists. The electoral/institutional *entrists* were oriented by the ethnicity paradigm of race. Drawing upon the assimilationist and cultural pluralist frameworks that shaped the ethnicity paradigm (and that had always been in tension with one another as well), and recognizing that ethnic group mobilization had been essential to obtaining political power and access to the state for more than a century of U.S. history, they built political organizations that could win elections, penetrate and influence state bureaucracies, and either exercise power in the Democratic Party or openly compete with it.[25] By the 1970s, groups such as the Congressional Black Caucus and the Joint Center for Political Studies had achieved real influence on the national political scene, while local political machines developed under victorious black and Chican@ mayors in Atlanta, Newark, Gary, Birmingham, Denver, Detroit, Chicago (the important Harold Washington campaign), and San Antonio. These instrumentalities were in turn linked to the many civil rights, lobbying, and local political groups, including those at the neighborhood, social agency, union, or church level. Thus as a result of the 1960s movement victories, social programs and policies—with all their limitations—addressed the needs of minority communities as never before. The nascent influence of entrist activists of color made innovations not only in the obvious areas of policy—in employment, housing, education, health—but also in the less obvious such policy areas of foreign affairs, taxation, environment, science and arts support. The network of entrists as a whole played a key long-term role in maintaining minority viewpoints and positions—for example, the Congressional Black Caucus's annual alternative budget proposals—in the mainstream political process.

After the successes of the civil rights movement, pressures to include communities of color in the mainstream political process increased rapidly as voting patterns shifted, immigration expanded, and the "politics of turmoil" escalated. The ethnicity paradigm of race came under significant assault and for a time seemed in disarray. It ultimately re-emerged under the banner of neoconservatism and later "colorblindness." The permanently increased presence of people of color in elective or administrative office, while a clear victory for racial reform, did not signal the end, but only the limited democratization, of white supremacy in the United States. The ethnicity paradigm retained its grasp on racial hegemony, but only under conditions of ongoing tension and instability. Party politics, local government agencies, welfare state and poverty programs, and electoral campaigns were some sites for entrism. While this tendency was perhaps most closely associated with the reform orientation of moderate movement factions, more militant currents also experimented with entrist strategies, for example, in the campaigns of La Raza Unida Party Texas during the 1970s (Shockley 1974; Navarro 2000; Barrera 2002 [1979]; Acuña 2011 [1972], 329–331), and SNCC's organization of the campaigns of activist Julian Bond for the Georgia House of Representatives and later the Georgia Senate (Carson 1995 [1981], 167–168). Still later, the Black Panther Party engaged in entrism as well, first running the electoral campaign of Bobby Seale and later that of Elaine Brown for the mayoralty in Oakland, California. The necessity of "entering the mainstream" was advocated for the following reasons: to avoid marginalization, since no other historically continuous political terrain was available to minority activists; to achieve reforms such as redistribution of income, goods, and services; to obtain increased access to the racial state at all levels from municipal to national; and to educate and "raise consciousness" that would allow for further movement-building.

The *socialist* tendency was oriented by the class paradigm of race. Marxist (sometimes Marxist-Leninist) and social democratic trends were the main representatives of this current. These approaches emphasized the class dimensions of anti-racist struggles. They argued that racism is an indispensable support to advanced capitalism; that class cleavages exist within communities of color—this served to curb excessive nationalism and point out the dangers of multi-class alliances; and that it was essential to base organizational efforts on the (traditionally defined) working class. Somewhat paradoxically, Marxist-Leninist groups often successfully recruited minority memberships, particularly among students, even as they became increasingly marginal among working-class communities of color and on the U.S. political landscape in general (Pulido 2006).

Although Marxist-Leninists lost influence precipitously in the 1970s and by the 1980s had lost touch with communities of color as well, social democrats (aka democratic socialists) retained a certainly relevance at the left of the Democratic Party and in a wide range of movements. In trade unions, anti-war and anti-imperial movements, women's and gay movements, and in many local and issue-oriented social justice groups, these anti-racist activists and intellectuals dug in for the long-haul effort to revitalize and expand the welfare state and social rights (Marshall 1987 [1950]). In some sense they were successors to the New Deal and the Great Society. The former had abandoned blacks and people of color to obtain the support of the racist South; the latter had gestured in the direction of racial inclusion and racial justice, but had sacrificed those aims on the altars of the Cold War and imperial adventure. Such organizations as the Institute for Policy Studies, Children's Defense Fund, NAACP, ACLU, National Council of La Raza, various immigrant rights groups, and the National Organization for Woman—to name but a few—emerged from both the civil rights and anti-war movements with strong redistributionist agendas, anti-racist commitments, and sometimes with anti-war and anti-imperial agendas as well.[26] These groups and intellectuals—academic, religious, community-based—worked within the social democratic tradition and emphasized the class-based paradigm of race, at least implicitly if not explicitly. Although socialist organizations and intellectuals have made major contributions to the struggle for racial equality, they were relegated to the margins of mainstream politics quite rapidly after the success of the civil rights reforms in the mid-1960s.[27]

Under the banner of the class paradigm, some intellectuals and activists ultimately adopted a left-wing version of colorblindness, arguing that progressive redistribution of income across racial lines would ultimately erode racism in the United States. This was a reversion to old-school understandings of race/class intersectionality, on the model of the old slogan, "black and white, unite and fight," that had proved destructive to communities of color in the past. And indeed, in the era of colorblind racial hegemony, we see once again that the greatest suffering—in strictly economic terms—is experienced in communities of color, where the chasms of inequality in income, and especially in wealth, have yawned open dramatically just in the wake of the 2008 economic crash. It is vital to state, once again, that there is a huge difference between efforts to understand and challenge racial inequality by synthesizing race- and class-based forms of inequality on the one hand, and by denying the ongoing significance of race and racism by stressing the supposedly "fundamental" class conflict on the other hand. "Colorblindness" on the political left remains a major defect in the class-based paradigm of race.

Nationalism was a diverse current whose main strategic unity lay in rejection of the assimilationist and integrationist tendencies associated with the movement moderates. A tremendous diversity of political tendencies were understood in different communities of color under the "nationalist" label. In the black community the term referred not only to a legacy of radical opposition to assimilation, but also to the "separate development" strategy associated with Booker T. Washington, and to various Pan-Africanist currents that passed through Garvey and Du Bois. It also included a cultural nationalist current which was largely anti-political. In the Mexican American community, nationalism had its roots in Mexican revolutionary traditions, notably those of land struggles,[28] and confrontations at the border that went way beyond issues of migration.[29] Asian American nationalism, for the most part, centered on community issues. Native American, Puerto Rican, and Hawai'ian nationalisms focused to varying degrees on territorial autonomy, up to and including radical demands for independence.

Nationalists called on minority communities to develop their distinct collective identities and unique political agendas, based on their particular histories of oppression and resistance. Nationalists opposed both political frameworks of the dominant ethnicity paradigm—integrationism and cultural pluralism—arguing that these were formulas for tokenism and cooptation that fell far short of the self-determination sought by their particular communities of color. Nationalists had a more mixed relationship with the class paradigm of race: Some groups and thinkers, generally those on the left, embraced a synthesis of the nation- and class-based paradigms, often linking U.S. racial oppression to U.S. imperialism and colonial history via an "internal colonialism" analysis (Blauner 2001 [1972]; Allen 2005).

The nation-based paradigm generated the range of particularist racial movements we have described above—focused on the African diaspora, Aztlan, the Rez, or the ghetto/barrio as a locus of "community control." Embracing black, Latin@, or Native American particularity meant confronting major divisions and at times glaring contradictions: Black nationalists ranged from separatists like Revolutionary Action

Movement (RAM),[30] to internal colonialism theorists to black capitalists inspired by Booker T. Washington, and to bitter black conservatives (think Clarence Thomas). Native Americans ranged from AIM (American Indian Movement) activists to (somewhat later) casino operators. Cultural nationalist groups and intellectuals in every community also ranged from radical artists engaged in art-based social movement organizing (Lipsitz 2007) to radicals in the Harold Cruse tradition, to commercial operations selling dashikis (Reed 2002), to those who habitually repudiated political activism as "the white man's game."

Internal colonialist perspectives should also be included here. These approaches bridged between the socialist and nationalist paradigms, depicting racism as an ongoing historical process which contained *both* class- and nationally based elements. Racially defined communities within the United States were analogized to colonies, and said to face the same types of economic exploitation and cultural domination that the developed nations had visited on the underdeveloped ones. The internal colonialism rubric included a strategic spectrum running all the way from moderate reform initiatives to revolution and "national liberation." Demands for increases in the number of "natives" occupying key posts in businesses or state institutions (police, schools, social agencies), plans to achieve "community control" of the ghetto and barrio economies, and schemes for a two-stage revolutionary process analogous to the Guinea-Bissau or Vietnamese experiences were all put forward based on the internal colonialism analysis.[31]

And what about alliances? Conflicts among communities of color—black/brown or black/Asian American—frequently reduced nationalist politics to squabbling over political spoils, or worse, to racist stereotyping. And what about whites? Were alliances possible with anti-racist whites? Did anti-racists whites even exist? By focusing too intensely on "white privilege"—obviously, a crucial issue in white supremacist America—nationalists often abandoned alliances that were politically essential. Although there were numerous reasons to insist on organizational "purity" along racial lines, in practice all racial categories are panethnic and decentered, so that sort of homogeneity would be impossible to achieve, even if it were desirable. Indeed, important nationalist organizations, such as the Black Panther Party, did ally with other groups across racial lines, including white groups.

Although nationalist organizations challenged the ubiquity and despotism of white supremacy, made important contributions to community organization and community control efforts—sometimes taking a page from the entrist playbook as in the La Raza Unida electoral drive in Crystal City, TX, or the Bobby Seale/Black Panther Party campaign for the mayoralty of Oakland, California—and played an important role in advancing "identity politics," they were not able to develop the political alliances and mass base necessary to challenge the dominant racial paradigm in the United States.

Considered critically, none of these political projects succeeded even remotely in forging an oppositional racial ideology or movement capable of radically transforming the U.S. racial order. The electoral/institutional entrists succumbed to illusions about the malleability of the racial state and were forced into a new version of ethnic group pluralism—the idea that racial minorities, like the white ethnics of the past, could claim their rights through "normal" political channels. Marxists (and particularly Marxist-Leninists) could fight racism only by recourse to a futile dogma, and moreover one which consigned race to the terrain of "false consciousness," while social democrats were reduced to becoming an ineffective appendage of the Democratic Party. Internal colonialism critics, like an earlier generation of black (and other minority) nationalists, refused to recognize the particularities of the U.S. racial order and the limits of all analogies with revolutionary movements abroad. The cultural nationalists ignored the political sphere, and indeed heaped scorn upon both reform-oriented entrists and minority socialists.[32]

* * *

All these tendencies were at best partial assaults on the U.S. racial system and on white supremacy. All failed to grasp the comprehensive manner by which race is structured into the U.S. social fabric. All *reduced* race: to interest group/cultural identity, class inequality, or nationality. Perhaps most importantly, all these currents lacked adequate conceptions of racial politics and the racial state. In their radical as much as in their moderate phases, anti-racist movements neglected the state's capacity for adaptation under political pressure. And while the civil rights movement and its allies, both radical and moderate, had launched the politics of identity, had initiated the "politicization of the social," the movement and its allies could not manage the contradictions and uncertainties that these new identities and new political configurations generated.

The movement's limits also arose from the strategic divisions that befell it as a result of its own successes. Here the black movement's fate is illustrative. Only in the South, while fighting against a backward political structure and overt cultural oppression, had the black movement been able to maintain a decentered unity, even when internal debates were fierce. Once it moved north, the black movement began to split, because competing political projects, linked to different segments of the community, sought either integration in the (reformed) mainstream, or more radical transformation of the dominant racial system.

After initial victories against segregation were won, one sector of the movement was thus reconstituted as an interest group, seeking to enter the political fray and fulfill the "dream" of integration and cultural pluralism. Once it entered the state, this entrist current found itself locked in a bear hug with the state institutions whose reforms it had itself demanded, forced to compromise on basic demands, and—in what sometimes appeared to be a modern minstrel show—presented to the nation on the public stage in seeming proof of the state's openness and racial democracy.

The radical sectors of the movement were similarly marginalized on the left or in cultural arenas. Those who confronted the state from radical positions (SNCC, the Black Panther Party, the League of Revolutionary Black Workers, and others) were met with intense repression, and often succumbed to authoritarian and anti-democratic impulses. Socialists were relegated to the fringes of the Democratic Party. "Cultural revolution" might raise consciousness, but it did not move political power from white hands to darker ones. And indeed, many nationalists disdained engagement with the racial state.

Although the mass movement for racial justice that arose in the early postwar years and culminated in the 1960s would be contained by a combination of concessions and repression, the partial victories it won should not be condemned or dismissed. The movement persisted, decentered to be sure, but also broadened and deepened. As we have argued, the complex of racial meanings inherited from the Jim Crow era were irrevocably altered by years of political activity, by intense campaigns for racial equality and democracy, by the production of deeply transformed notions of "blackness," "whiteness," "*Latinidad*," and all other racial identities as well. The movement vastly expanded the terrain of politics, generating not only a new racial politics of identity, but a new *social* politics of identity: intersectional, conscious of sex/gender issues, and hungry for a new and radical democracy that would transform every facet of American experience. The specter of racial equality, and beyond that, of an end to race/class/gender oppression itself, continued to haunt American dreams and nightmares.

Notes

1. This phrase, of course, is Karl Polanyi's term for the transition to capitalism in England. Polanyi stresses the social embeddedness of the capitalist economy. We have appropriated his term—with appropriate apologies—to indicate the social embeddedness of the political system, a recognition brought home by the post-World War II black movement and its allies, in the United States.
2. Katznelson (2013) makes the important argument that the New Deal, while allied with Jim Crow, also undermined it by "nationalizing" and "uplifting" the South. The South was also transformed by the effects of enormous black emigration during World War II (family members voting and working in factories in Detroit, Chicago, Philadelphia and so on), by the 1948 desegregation of the U.S. armed forces (which caused great anxiety and conflict in the highly militarized South), by the return of hundreds of thousands of black soldiers, and by deepening political divisions in the Democratic Party over civil rights.
3. By no means was Jim Crow confined to the South. As James Loewen (2005) points out, cities and towns throughout the country had explicitly racist local laws. Many "sundown towns" (purposely all-white municipalities) were located in the Midwest, Pacific Northwest, and elsewhere.
4. Use of the term "elite" is not meant pejoratively. Although the prewar civil rights movement included some episodes of direct action and mass mobilization, notably during Reconstruction and in the aftermath of World War—for example, the Garvey movement—these were infrequent and antagonistic to moderate reforms. Even during the first decade of the post-World War II period strategies concentrated, for reasons of necessity, on lobbying,

use of the courts, and appeals to enlightened whites, tactics which depend on knowledgeable elites for leadership and render mass participation counterproductive. In addition, the straitened conditions facing blacks before World War II generated a survival-oriented ideology which did not adapt itself well to mass mobilization. For accounts of racial politics in the 1930s, see Weiss 1983; Rosengarten 2000 (1974); Katznelson 2013.

5. For representative statements from this period, see Dahl 1967; Rose 1967. Good contemporary critiques are Lowi 1969; Bachrach and Baratz 1970; Lukes 2005 (1974).
6. A little-known passage in Gramsci's short discussion on "Intellectuals" refers to American blacks, chiefly noting how they might provide leadership to the impoverished and then still-colonized masses in Africa. Rather amazingly, though, sitting in his dark cell in a fascist prison (in about 1930), Gramsci recognizes the black freedom struggle, "the formation of a surprising number of negro intellectuals who absorb American culture and technology." He continues:

   > It seems to me that, for the moment, American negroes have a national and racial spirit which is negative rather than positive, one which is a product of the struggle carried on by the whites in order to isolate and depress them. But was not this the case with the Jews up to and throughout the eighteenth century? (Gramsci 1971, 21)

7. For a startling and vivid evocation of that rhetorical toolkit, see Zora Neale Hurston, "The Sermon" (1984 [1929]). This is a transcribed field recording by Hurston, then an anthropology graduate student, of a sermon given by preacher C.C. Lovelace in a church in Eau Gallie, Florida, in 1929.
8. Robert Parris Moses drew important inspiration from Camus, for example Carson 1995 (1981).
9. Eugene Genovese has argued that the slavemasters' paternalism allowed a substantial black culture of resistance to develop, and that slavery was consequently rendered more benign. Against this view, Steven Hahn has documented deeply-rooted patterns of resistance and political struggle during the slavery era; and Walter Johnson has reasserted the savagery, not only of slavery's oppression and exploitation, but also of its militarism and expansionist ambitions (Genovese 1974; Hahn 2003; Johnson 2013).
10. "Subalternity" is also a term launched by Gramsci. See his "Notes on Italian History," "The Modern Prince," and elsewhere (Gramsci 1971). A few major sources in subaltern studies, by no means all consistently in agreement, are these: Guha and Spivak, eds. 1988; Scott 1990; Kelley 1996; Beverley 1999; Mignolo 2000; Chatterjee 2010.
11. White violence culminated a month after the campaign's end in the "Birmingham Sunday" bombing of the 16th Street Baptist Church (September 15, 1963), which killed four black children in an institution that had been the center of the Birmingham movement. On Birmingham, see King 1964; Greenberg 1980; Branch 1988, 1998; Garrow, ed. 1989; McWhorter 2001.
12. The march had been planned as a unified effort to demonstrate black and liberal support for national civil rights legislation. The SNCC speaker, John Lewis, was forced to censor his remarks by white and black moderates, but even the rewritten speech contrasted sharply with the self-congratulatory tone of the rest of the event: "The party of Kennedy is also the party of Eastland … the party of Javits is also the party of Goldwater. Where is our party?" (Moyers 2013).

13. At first promised and then denied white liberal support, the MFDP challengers left the convention profoundly disillusioned. On the MFDP, see Carson 1995 (1981).
14. The "long hot summers" of the middle 1960s were viewed by many blacks (and by the U.S. police at all levels) as a proto-revolutionary situation. Many activists saw the black underclass as "voting with shopping carts," taking what was deservedly theirs, and accelerating the unacceptably slow pace of reform. Moderates, by contrast, questioned the effectiveness of disruption and argued that riots discredited efforts to achieve political reforms. In retrospect we may discount the more extreme claims made by all sides during these years. Still, during the 1967–1968 period alone, some 384 "racial disorders" were recorded in 298 cities (McAdam 1984, 227). These can hardly be considered as unrelated to the atmosphere of black protest that engulfed the nation after 1964, not just the South. See also Rustin 2003 (1965), 1967; Feagin and Hahn 1973; Killian 1975; Button 1978; Piven and Cloward 1978 .
15. On March 7, 1965 some 2,000 marchers were ferociously attacked on the Pettus Bridge at Selma. For good analyses of the complexities of the Selma situation, which many see as the point at which southern intransigence was finally ruptured, see Garrow 1978; Carson 1995 (1981).
16. Many commentators date the black power phase of the movement from the "Meredith march" of June, 1966, though this is clearly a somewhat arbitrary periodization.
17. Richard Wright's *Black Power* appeared in 1954; Wright was certainly not the first to use the term. Over recent decades an enormous amount of writing has been produced on black power; our treatment here is necessarily brief. Some classic texts from the black power period are Boggs 1970; Allen 1990 [1970]; Ture (Carmichael) and Hamilton 1992 [1967]. Among the many contemporary contributions, see Van Deburg 1992; Tyson 1999; Woodard 1999; Robinson 2000 [1983]; Glaude, ed. 2002; Joseph 2006; Slate 2012.
18. Still Ture and Hamilton did not entirely burn their moderate bridges. Robert Allen wrote that *Black Power* "was largely an essay in liberal reformism" (Allen 1990 [1970], 247), a judgment based on the authors' lack of a "revolutionary" political program. Ture and Hamilton wanted to break with the ethnicity paradigm, but not with the mainstream aspirations of U.S. blacks.
19. Malcolm's own father was a UNIA activist who may have been lynched in Michigan in 1931 by a racist group called the Black Legion. See Marable 2011.
20. The vastness of the literature on Freedom Summer attests in its own right to the importance of this SNCC initiative in shaping U.S. racial history. That importance goes far beyond voting rights, important as those rights may be. See Belfrage 1965; Payne 2007 (1995); Martinez, ed. 2007 (1965); Watson 2010.
21. The "war on poverty" was launched by the Economic Opportunity Act of 1964, which set up the Office of Economic Opportunity. OEO was dismantled under the Nixon administration.
22. Piven and Cloward's 1965 call for additional redistribution of resources through the AFDC system helped set off the Welfare Rights Movement. See Cloward and Piven 1966.
23. Radical black organizations like SNCC opposed the war, while moderate groups like the Urban League supported it. King's late but fierce declaration of opposition was proclaimed in his Riverside Church speech, "A Time To Break Silence," on April 4, 1967, exactly one year before his assassination. This courageous act deeply embodied the split

in the movement, placed MLK Jr. solidly on the side of its radical wing, and undoubtedly contributed to his death, now credibly seen as an FBI murder (Pepper 2008).

24. None of these currents is by any means exclusive. Specific perspectives often contain elements of more than one current. Internal colonialism, for example, can be expressed in nationalist or socialist terms. The categories we employ are "ideal types"—they permit the classification of diverse tendencies for analytical purposes.
25. What about Republican "entrism"? After the New Deal came to power the GOP never regained the influence in communities of color—particularly black communities—that it earlier possessed as the "party of Lincoln." But it still held on until the 1960s, for example electing Edward Brooke to the Senate in 1966 as the first black senator seated in the 20th century(!). The Democrats were also the "Dixiecrats," let it be remembered (Weiss 1983), and civil rights found no secure home in either party until the 1960s, when the Republicans adopted the "southern strategy." Even with blacks gone, the GOP held onto a sizeable number of Latin@ and Asian American voters until it kissed them off with its support for the anti-immigrant Proposition 187 in California. Sporadic attempts to woo voters of color, and efforts to put on display such putatively attractive tokens as Sen. Marco Rubio, and former Secretaries of State Condoleeza Rice and Colin Powell, have not availed (Lusane 2006; Hattam and Lowndes 2013). The Republicans are now the white people's party, a fact they only intermittently bother to deny.
26. For example, the Children's Defense Fund is active in opposing the "school to prison pipeline" and in challenging the continuing and disgracefully high numbers of children in poverty in the U.S.; these social policies—which is what they are; they are not accidental—disproportionately destroy the lives of millions of children of color in the United States. See Edelman 2000, 1993.
27. Both Kennedy and Johnson harassed MLK Jr., abetted by J. Edgar Hoover who charged that King was under the influence of "the Communists." See Churchill and Vander Wall, 2001 (1988).
28. Land struggles were most strenuously pursued by the *Alianza Federal de Mercedes*, founded in 1963 by Reies Lopez Tijerina. The *Alianza* (later renamed *La Confederación de Pueblos Libres*) sought to restore lands originally held by Mexican Americans in northern New Mexico under grants dating from the conquest, and built upon regional traditions of struggle dating from the 19th century (Tijerina 1978; Nabokov 1969). Tijerina's politics have been the subject of some debate. His personalistic and confrontational style and his focus on the tactics of land occupation place him in a venerable Mexican revolutionary tradition. But Tijerina built upon and altered this legacy in the attempt to address modern U.S. conditions. He ran for Governor of New Mexico in 1968, joined Martin Luther King, Jr.'s Poor People's Crusade, and espoused a Pan American and Third Worldist revolutionary philosophy. After extensive harassment, Tijerina was jailed in 1969, and his movement dispersed.
29. Revolutionary nationalism in Latin@ communities has a long tradition. Chican@ nationalism, for example, was tied to the legacy of the Mexican revolution of 1910–1920, which both swept across the U.S. border and provoked U.S. military intervention into Mexico. Revolutionary movements in Mexico sparked early Mexican-American radical efforts, and linked to radical movements in the United States as well. For example, the Flores Magón brothers, Enrique and Ricardo, were both leaders of an anarchist tendency

in the Mexican Revolution and activists in the International Workers of the World, mainly in Southern California. Caught up in the Palmer raids of the 1920s, Ricardo Flores Magón was cruelly persecuted in the United States and died in Leavenworth Prison in Kansas (Gómez-Quiñones 1973). In Texas/Chihuahua, the El Paso-Juarez urban complex was also the site of significant Mexicano radical activity and U.S. repression (Romo 2005). The U.S. general John J. Pershing invaded Northern Mexico in 1916–1917 on a so-called punitive expedition against Mexican revolutionary general Pancho Villa, who had attacked a village on the New Mexico side of the border (Eisenhower 1995).

30. The RAM was a revolutionary black nationalist organization founded by Muhammad Ahmad (Max Stanford), who had been an associate of Malcolm X. Some of its members became active in SNCC in its later days, as well as in the Black Panther Party and the League of Revolutionary Black Workers. Other insurrectionary black nationalist groups that were linked with RAM include the African Peoples Party, the Black Liberation Army, the Black United Front, the Black Workers Congress, and the Republic of New Africa. See Ahmad, Allen, and Bracey, eds. n.d.
31. The first "stage" is the creation of a multi-class united front to liberate the colony; the second "stage" is the subsequent pursuit of socialist reconstruction and, presumably, class struggle. The internal colonialist orientation of the 1960s was often explicitly Maoist, as were many other Marxisms of the period.
32. See, for example, Moore 1974–1975.

CHAPTER 7

Racial Reaction: Containment and Rearticulation

Introduction

The black movement and its allied movements that emerged during the Great Transformation disrupted and reshaped American society. They called into question the logic and structure of racial segregation. They appealed for social justice and drew upon cherished principles of equality and freedom. The movements' demands for the elimination of racial discrimination became a broad-based challenge to racism across-the-board, and thus developed in radical and sometimes revolutionary ways. The revolutionary potential of the post-World War II Great Transformation cannot be understated. To shake up white supremacy as the black movement did was to reiterate the nightmare from which the racist system cannot awake: black insurgency. The Civil War was the first great assault on the U.S. racist system. The Great Transformation was the second great assault, the second anti-racist uprising. It revealed and called into question the fundamental limits of democracy in the United States.[1] The issues that were posed by the movement had deep and sustained reverberations throughout the world, not only in regard to race and racism but much more broadly.

The black movement and its allies confronted not only the state but the nation iself—"the American people."[2] The movement sought not only equality but also community. Equality could possibly, though by no means definitively, be enhanced through state-based reform policies. But to create community required a *social* reorientation, a reinterpretation or rearticulation of the very definition of the American nation and the American people. The movement asked, "Who is included, and who excluded, from our community?"

This remains a radical, even revolutionary question. When the movement demanded the incorporation of racially defined "others," the democratization of structurally racist institutions, it challenged both the state and civil society to recognize and validate racially defined experience and identity. This was the *politicization of the social*. It was transformative and attractive. It was contagious; you "caught" it. It spread from one person to another, from one group to another. This new emphasis on social identity came to frame emancipatory and democratic aspirations more generally. It arched over different issues, selves, groups, and conceptions of liberation. The "politics of identity" has been critiqued by both the political right and left. But that may be precisely the point: Over the past few decades *all* politics have become, to a large degree, "identity politics." The politicization of the social meant, above all, the recognition of a new depth of political life (Guigni 1988; Melucci 1989; Laraña, Johnston, and Gusfield, eds. 1994).

Consider the immensity of this recognition. No longer would it be sufficient to think of politics as a competition for resources regulated by a neutral legitimate arbiter, namely the state. The famous definition of politics as "who gets what, when, and how" (Lasswell 1950 [1936]) was now superseded. "The personal is political," a phrase often associated with second-wave feminism, was now in play; this concept too has its origins in the black movement (Hanisch 1969; Evans 1979). The post-World War II upsurge of racial subjectivity and self-awareness into the mainstream political arena set off this transformation that, in many ways, resonated with democratic impulses worldwide. The prevailing racial regime in the United States, then, was seriously challenged.

The racial reaction that emerged had an obvious central objective: the demobilization of the black movement and of the other anti-racist and new social movements that it had spawned. This was far from an easy task. Among many other reasons why the movement had to be stopped was that it consciously embodied a wide range of fundamental American ideals and cherished beliefs. The movement's demands could not be rejected out of hand, for this would have emboldened and radicalized it further, as well as risk drawing new supporters from varying quarters to movement ranks.

As a racial project, therefore, racial reaction had to combine different responses to the movement upsurge. Movement gains could not be easily halted, much less reversed. They had to be blunted and absorbed. The most immediate task was that of containment. Repression was present from the earliest stages of the movement upsurge: The coercive powers of the state were employed to disrupt, demobilize, and destroy by any means necessary (including murder) the more radical elements of the movement. Repression had dramatic results. Still, the insurgency moved fast in its early years. Even by the time of the March on Washington for Jobs and Freedom in 1963, a return to the past modalities of racial terror and oppression was no longer a serious option for the state at the federal level.

Nor could repression alone contain the movement. The key objective of the U.S. racial regime from the later 1960s onward was incorporation, not rollback. The incorporation of the movement's demands through civil rights reform legislation, through administrative maneuver, and through judicial action was already well under way when Martin Luther King, Jr. stood on the Lincoln Memorial steps in August 1963. Indeed, reform initiatives undertaken to incorporate movement demands bore a striking resemblance to state action undertaken a century before during the Reconstruction period. The enactment of "moderate" civil rights reforms, themselves painstakingly negotiated (Carmines and Stinson 1989; Lieberman 1998), and the Warren Court's piecemeal expansion of black citizenship rights as well (Kluger 2004 [1976]) were both reiterations of that earlier period of reform.

In the late 1860s, there had been conflicts between the vision, policies, and practices of "Presidential" Reconstruction and that of "Congressional" Reconstruction; these paralleled the debates, squabbles, and contradictory moves underway within the racial state during the 1960s. But things were also different during the "Second Reconstruction."

Nor was the combination of repression and incorporation adequate to the objective of containment. A third element was needed: the *rearticulation* of the movement's central themes and ideals—those of freedom and equality, and of what constitutes a fair and just society. The forces of racial reaction sought to reestablish racial hegemony by reinterpreting and reframing key civil rights principles and practices, through an ideologically driven process of rearticulation.[3] The racial meanings and identities, as well as the visions of equality advanced by movement activists and organizations, would eventually become subject to rearticulation by the political right. Yes, identities of emancipation, speaking broadly, could be rearticulated as identities of incorporation. Ideals of redistribution and justice, again speaking broadly, could be rearticulated as ideals of formal, but not substantive, equality.

In summary, containment of the movement, which was imperative to sustain the broader racial regime, involved outright state repression, selective incorporation of movement demands, and most important from our perspective, the rearticulation of the movement's identities and ideals.

The forces of racial reaction had both to affirm and to reject the movement's vision and demands. They had both to propose a system of racial rule broad enough to absorb the egalitarian and inclusive thrust of the black movement and its allied movements; and at the same time, incremental enough to preserve the entitlements of white supremacy that were the system's key features. This was obviously a contradictory racial project: often hypocritical, sometimes naive, but always deeply ideological.

In the next pages we discuss the early "post-civil rights" period, focusing on the development of projects to contain the movement in the late 1960s and 1970s. We begin with *incorporation and repression*; move through the two main *reactionary racial projects*, the new right and neoconservatism; and conclude the chapter with a working summary: *from code words to reverse racism to colorblindness*.

Incorporation and Repression

The brief period of moderate reform politics during the mid- to late-1960s was filled with irony and contradiction. Incorporation created a host of difficulties for movement groups and activists attempting to engage with and operate within the state—including those who were now directly employed by it. In the effort to adapt to the new racial politics it had created, the black movement lost its decentered political unity. Before the civil rights reforms, opposition to the backward and coercive racial order of the South had permitted a tenuous alliance between the moderate and radical currents of the movement. But after a modicum of reform had been achieved, that alliance was weakened. Working within the newly reformed racial state was more possible, and confronting it more difficult, than during the preceding period.

Many civil rights activists went to work in the housing, healthcare delivery, legal services, education, and "community action" programs set up as part of the Great Society (McAdam 1988). These people were the foot soldiers of service provision, advocacy, and to some extent mobilization. Programs such as the War on Poverty, Model Cities, and Head Start, among others, brought resources and jobs to the ghettos, barrios, and reservations. But reforms of this type could also be interpreted as classic examples of incorporation, at times resembling the "machine" politics of Chicago or Philadelphia more than the radical work of the black freedom movement in the South such as SNCC's "freedom schools," for example.[4] The landscape created by new reforms thus echoed the critical reflections originally posed by E. Franklin Frazier in his classic text *Black Bourgeoisie* (1957a). Frazier dissed his "bourgeoisie" as opportunists in the main: They were generally local black leaders, often preachers or local businessmen, whose relationships with white power structures allowed them to broker local resources in segregated cities. They found themselves torn between their loyalties to the black communities they "represented," and the white elites whose local clients and fixers they had become. Over time they vacillated between accommodation—when resources were forthcoming and they received respect from their white business and political counterparts—and opposition: turning to black nationalism, trade union, or protest politics when the needs of their communities were slighted or when they themselves felt disempowered and disrespected.

Movement activists and veterans of the "beautiful struggle" often felt the same way—"entrists" were torn between their roles as agents of change and incipient bureaucrats. Local power structures based in City Hall or the Board of Education sought to routinize or dismiss their work. Meanwhile, the supposed triumph of civil rights failed to placate radicals who sought not simply rights, but power, resources, and the broader goal of "self-determination." From the radical perspective, the conferring of formal rights or the provision of a job-training program did not appreciably change the circumstances of a black youth in Harlem or a *vato loco* in East Los Angeles. What were heralded as great victories by moderates appeared to radicals as merely more streamlined versions of racial oppression. As George Lipsitz reports, Malcolm X used to tell his followers that "Racism is like a Cadillac; they bring out a new model every year."[5]

In the immediate wake of civil rights reforms, the question of how to understand and conceptualize the meaning and significance of race and racism in a transformed political, social, and cultural landscape was one of overwhelming significance. Theories of race were reconsidered, debated, invented, and reinvented. The explanatory power and political efficacy of the ethnicity perspective—with its belief in the gradual assimilationist and cultural pluralist currents—was deeply debilitated, especially by the regime's repressive activities. Radical theories of race gained strength and adherence as liberal approaches lost their appeal and coherence. Embracing nation-based and class-based paradigms, groups like the Black Panther Party (founded in Oakland, California, in 1966) and the League of Revolutionary Black Workers (founded in Detroit. Michigan, in 1969) advanced radical demands for a more thoroughgoing restructuring of the social order—one which would recognize the pervasiveness of racial oppression not only in "normal" politics, but in the organization of the labor market, urban geography, and in the forms of cultural life (Boggs and Boggs 1966; see also Boggs 1970; Geschwender 1977; Hilliard 1993; Abu-Jamal 2008; Georgakas and Surkin 2012 [1975]).

Corresponding to the radicalization of parts of the movement, the racial regime was dramatically increasing its repression, notably its political policing, of the black movement and the black community. The FBI COINTELPRO (Counter-Intelligence Program) was the best-known and most extensive of these activities. Started by J. Edgar Hoover to monitor and disrupt the Communist Party USA, it was first expanded, and then shifted almost entirely toward, surveillance and harassment of the U.S. black movement (Churchill and Vander Wall 2001 [1988]; Weiner 2012). State agencies at all levels from the national to the local committed numerous crimes against movement activists and supporters, and against black communities as a whole (Irons 2010).

These crimes included assassinations, arson, torture, larceny, and fraud, among others (Haas 2011). COINTELPRO also fomented internecine conflicts in the movement, infiltrated movement organizations and hired *agents provocateurs*, and ran entrapment schemes to delegitimate and decimate radical opposition (Rosenfeld 2013). All this occurred during the very same period when the federal government was supposedly legislating and adjudicating the terms of the belated inclusion of blacks and others in the national polity. The "iron fist" of repression has always lurked beneath the "velvet glove" of reform and accommodation.[6]

Throughout this period, the spectrum of maneuver and manipulation on the part of the racial regime—ranging from democratic openings on the left to secret policing and covert action/state-based terrorism on the right—contained the movement by fragmenting it, keeping it off balance, and hindering its ability to maintain clear goals, principles, and focus. But attempts simply to contain the movement's challenge to the existing racial regime—through incorporation of political demands for formal/legal racial equality or through outright state repression—would simply not be enough, in the long run, to address what the movement had unleashed, what the millions of people whom it had touched were seeing, feeling, and thinking anew. "Freedom dreams" would not be forgotten, the yearning for a truly racially just society would remain undiminished, and the politicization of the social would not be restricted or restrained. The forces of racial reaction required stronger ideological weapons, more powerful castor oil, to counteract the indigestion that racism was now generating in the black community and beyond. The regime needed to combat the powerful medicine that the movement had produced in the form of politicized identities and collective mobilization. A thorough political and ideological rearticulation of the movement's understanding and vision of race and democracy was required—a rearticulation on the right that would recast themes of racial equality and justice in ways that would serve to rationalize and reinforce persistent patterns of racial inequality.

Reactionary Racial Projects

There were clear limits to any attempt to undo the effects of the Great Transformation. Racial equality had to be acknowledged as a desirable goal, but the *meaning* of equality, and the proper means for achieving it, had to be reopened for debate.

After the civil rights reforms and the anti-racist upsurge of the 1960s, the forces of racial reaction required time to regroup and develop a new strategic orientation. Existing racist projects were no longer sustainable and posed significant risks: of marginalization at the far right of the political spectrum, and of a further radicalization of the new social movements, now composed of a growing, though loose and uneven, alliance of anti-racist, second-wave feminist, and anti-war contingents. Still, white supremacy had hardly been overturned. However "shook up" it was—Elvis had been right about that—both everyday and structural racism still substantively shaped U.S. society and culture. White racial subjectivity, media-based representations of race, and the sheer cognitive incapacity of the white population—still over 80 percent of all Americans at that time—had not been significantly transformed. In fact, the ameliorative effects of the moderate civil rights reforms and of Supreme Court racial jurisprudence—sometimes gestural at best—were thought by many whites to be enough to solve "the race problem": with a few significant concessions to the demand for racial democracy, domestic tranquility could be restored.

Like other political projects to consolidate hegemony, racial reaction involved both the state and civil society. It was a concerted, sequentially developing response to the demand for "racial liberation" (Wolfenstein 1977) that had been posed by the black movement and its allies. Just as the movement developed through various stages, evolving from demands for inclusion to demands for community self-determination and radical redistribution of resources, so too did the racial reaction move along a historical trajectory. Its main players sought to accommodate and absorb movement demands with moderate reforms, attempting to rearticulate those radical demands in a conservative or even rightwing fashion. Like the black movement it followed, racial reaction was a combination of initiatives; it contained disparate "racial projects." Over time, some of these would succeed and others would fail; some would develop and others would atrophy. The racial reaction was by no means driven by a unified political orientation, ideology, or strategic approach. Emblematic of distinct approaches are the ideology and politics of the new right and that of neoconservatism. Both emerged as responses to the overall transformation of polity and culture in the wake of the new social movements of the 1960s, and both were centrally concerned with defining the limits of racial democracy.

The New Right: Authoritarian Populism and "Code Words"

Walter Dean Burnham noted that the political culture of the United States is highly influenced by the values of 17th-century dissenting Protestantism and that this has frequently become manifest in periods of transition and crisis:

> Whenever and wherever the pressures of "modernization"—secularity, urbanization, the growing importance of science—have become unusually intense, episodes of revivalism and culture-issue politics have swept over the American social landscape. In all such cases since at least the end of the Civil War, such movements have been more or less explicitly reactionary, and have frequently been linked with other kinds of reaction in explicitly political ways.
> (Burnham 1983, 125)

The new right emerged and developed in such a political space. It was an attempt to create an authoritarian, right-wing populism—a populism fuelled by resentment.

The political, economic, and social transformations and dislocations of the late-1960s and early-1970s called the "American Dream" into question and shook people's faith in their country. Apolitical, perpetually prosperous, militarily invincible, and deeply self-absorbed and self-righteous, mainstream American culture was shaken to its foundations by developments over this period. Economic stability and global military supremacy were perceived to be eroding. Commonly held concepts of nation, community, and family were transformed, and no new principle of cohesion, no new cultural center, emerged to replace them. In a period of dramatic political fragmentation, the mainstream was left with no clear notion of the "common good."[7]

In the face of these challenges, traditional conservatism seemed to have little to offer—society and politics, and the conventional way in which they were understood, had *already* been radically transformed. Only the appearance of the new right in the middle 1970s gave the millions of threatened members of what Richard Nixon called the "silent majority" a sense of cultural identity, renewed faith, and political hope. The new right was a well-organized alternative to the moral and existential chaos of the preceding decades: a network of conservative organizations with an aggressive political style, an outspoken religious and cultural traditionalism, and a clear populist commitment.

Gillian Peele defined the new right as "a loose movement of conservative politicians and a collection of general-purpose political organizations which have developed independently of the political parties" (1984, 52). The new right had its origins in the Barry Goldwater campaign of 1964 and the George Wallace campaign of 1968. An early achievement was influencing the Republican "Southern Strategy"; a project developed around the 1968 presidential election—and fully supported by the wily Richard Nixon—with the objective of repositioning white supremacism as a mainstream political initiative in the aftermath of the civil rights reforms (Phillips 1970; Perlstein 2008, 2009 [2001]).

The main new right affiliates emerged, for the most part, in the 1970s: the American Conservative Union, the National Conservative Political Action Committee (NCPAC), the Conservative Caucus, the Young Americans for Freedom, the Heritage Foundation, and a group of fundamentalist Protestant sects incorporating millions of adherents. Leading figures of the new right were fundraiser/publisher Richard A. Viguerie, Paul Weyrich (Committee for the Survival of a Free Congress), Howard Phillips (Conservative Caucus), and John T. Dolan (NCPAC), as well as activist Phyllis Schlafly (Eagle Forum, Stop-ERA) and fundamentalist evangelist Rev. Jerry Falwell (Moral Majority). Periodicals identified with the new right included the *Conservative Digest*, *Policy Review*, and *New Guard*. The key new right think tank was the Heritage Foundation, founded by brewer Joseph Coors and Paul Weyrich in 1973. Central to the new right's growth, as Alan Crawford notes, was the ramped-up use of direct-mail solicitation to build a movement:

> Collecting millions of dollars in small contributions from blue-collar workers and housewives, the new right feeds on discontent, anger, insecurity, and resentment, and flourishes on backlash politics.
>
> (1980, 5)[8]

The new right was not just a grassroots, right-wing populist movement. As Coors's early support already indicated, it was also an attempt by politically conservative corporate elite members to develop a mass base. These leaders faced a challenge in the political gains of the anti-racist movements. They sought to avoid large-scale redistribution, not only of state resources, but also of political power. The racial upheavals of the 1960s ruled out any attempt to return to legally enforced segregation. They also precluded mounting a defense of inequality rooted in the "scientific racism" of the immediate past.[9]

Since the political gains of anti-racist movements could not be easily reversed, they had to be *rearticulated*. The key device used by the new right to challenge these gains was the innovative use of "code words" in its political messaging. Code words are phrases and symbols that imply or refer indirectly to racial themes, but do not directly challenge popular democratic or egalitarian ideals such as justice and equal opportunity.

The issue of busing to achieve racial integration in the schools provides an example of how such code words were deployed. The new right framed its opposition to busing not as an overt effort to maintain residential or school segregation, but as an assault on "the community" and "the family." School integration, new right activists argued, meant that the state was usurping decision-making powers which should be vested in parents: deciding in what kind of communities their children would be raised and what kind of education their children will receive. As Linda Gordon and Allen Hunter observed, the link between family and community was clearly emphasized in anti-busing mobilization:

> The anti-busing movement is nourished by … fears for the loss of the family. The loss of neighborhood schools is perceived as a threat to community, and

therefore family stability by many people, particularly in cities where ethnically homogenous communities remain.

(2005, 239)

In similar fashion, the progressive theme of "community control" advanced earlier in the 1960s was recast to prevent school desegregation and to challenge fair housing initiatives. As HoSang notes, California opponents of the 1963 Rumford Act that outlawed housing discrimination succeeded in overturning it with the 1964 Proposition 14. They labeled the Rumford Act the "Forced Housing Act" and campaigned for their 1964 initiative, not by supporting residential segregation, but by avowing a "freedom to choose" on the part of the landlord or home-seller. In declaring this "right" (which did not exist in law and amounted to nothing more than the right to discriminate), they rearticulated civil rights doctrines of equality and community control, reframing them as property rights. This anticipated later campaigns against affirmative action ("reverse discrimination") and other reforms such as fair lending (HoSang 2010, 69). Many civil rights reforms proved vulnerable to strategically framed campaigns of rearticulation designed to blunt or avoid charges of explicit racism. Indeed one measure of the success of such coded language was the confusion it sowed even among left organizations during the Boston busing controversy of the 1970s.[10]

Beginning with the Wallace campaign of 1968, we can trace the pattern of new right experimentation with these code words, and with the rearticulation of racial meanings they attempt. The first rumblings of the new right agenda were heard in George Wallace's 1968 presidential bid. Wallace's initial role on the national political stage had been that of die-hard segregationist.[11] His entry into the presidential race was seen at first as a replay of the Dixiecrat strategy which had led to the candidacy of Strom Thurmond 20 years before. Few analysts expected Wallace to have mass appeal outside the South, yet in northern blue-collar strongholds like Milwaukee, Detroit, and Philadelphia, he demonstrated surprising strength.

Although Wallace's image as a racist politician had originally placed him in the national spotlight, it did not make good presidential politics, and he was forced to incorporate his racial message as a subtext, implicit but "coded," in a populist appeal. Wallace thus struck certain chords that anticipated the new right agenda—defense of traditional values, opposition to "big government," and patriotic and militaristic themes. But the centerpiece of his appeal was his racial politics. Wallace was a law-and-order candidate, an anti-statist, an inheritor of classical southern populist traditions. He called for the stepped-up use of force to repress ghetto rebellions, derided the black movement and the war on poverty, and attacked liberal politicians and intellectuals. Wallace departed from his early 1960s style, however, by avoiding direct race-baiting.

During the same campaign, political analyst Kevin Phillips, then a young aide to Nixon campaign manager John Mitchell, submitted a lengthy and rather scholarly analysis of U.S. voting trends to Nixon headquarters.[12] Phillips argued that a

Republican victory and long-term electoral realignment were possible on racial grounds. His subsequently published *The Emerging Republican Majority* suggested a turn to the right and the use of "coded" anti-black campaign rhetoric; he recognized quite accurately that a great majority of southern white voters had abandoned the Democratic Party, and that Negrophobia was alive and well, not only in the South but nationally. In fact what was "emerging" had been there all along: a massive racist complex of white resentment, dread, and shame that went back to slavery, the "lost cause," and reactionary political resentment.[13]

Wallace's success, the disarray in Democratic ranks caused by the "Negro socio-economic revolution," and polling data from blue-collar districts around the country convinced Phillips that a strategic approach of this kind—a "Southern Strategy"—could fundamentally shift political alignments which had been in effect since 1932. The Democratic "Solid South" could become the Republican "Solid South." And lo it came to pass ...

These innovations bore rich political fruit. They coincided with the fragmentation of the New Deal coalition, the "loss" of the war on poverty, and the decline of the black movement. They represented an apparent alternative to ghetto riots and white guilt, to the integration of northern schools and the onset of "stagflation." They effortlessly, if demagogically, appealed to a majority of the electorate, then more than 80 percent white—something that the black movement and its allies had not succeeded in doing.

By the early 1980s, the new right's dream seemed within reach: to consolidate a "new majority" which could dismantle the welfare state, legislate a return to "traditional morality," and stem the tide of political and cultural dislocation which the 1960s and 1970s represented. The new right project linked the assault on liberalism and "secular humanism," the obsession with individual guilt and responsibility where social questions were concerned (crime, sex, education, poverty), with a fierce anti-statism. The political strategy involved was populist. Use of the initiative process, especially in California, permitted well-funded campaigns of electoral mobilization in defense of (suitably coded) white privilege: on issues of housing, education, and especially taxation. Legislating through the ballot-box provided the new right a detour around the courts, the bureaucracy, state governments, and the Congress as well. Such strategies alienated traditional conservatives, who labeled the channeling of popular rage through direct democratic channels "antipolitical":

> A near-constant theme of conservative thought, from Edmund Burke to William Buckley, has been that unrestrained expressions of popular will militate against the orderly processes of government on which stable societies depend.... The new right, impatient for short-run results, has rejected this dominant theme of conservatism in favor of direct democracy, threatening to shatter the safeguards against political centralization and, therefore, freedom itself.
>
> (Crawford 1980, 311–312)

But they worked, so the new right pressed ahead with them, and the Republicans signed on.

Some analysts saw the new right as a status revolt[14] by those whom Ben Wattenberg called the "unyoung, unpoor and unblack" (Crawford 1980, 148), whose identities and interests were articulated *negatively* by the social movements of the 1960s and the crises of the 1970s. This newly identified "silent majority" resented any mobility on the part of lower-status groups, and demanded that the political process recognize the traditional values to which they subscribed. Their anger was directed at those who were "not like themselves"; this involved a racial dimension which they experienced as a cultural and political threat as much as an economic one:

> [T]he fear of black power, "reverse discrimination" at the community level—associated with fear of crime, property devaluation, dirtiness and noisiness—reflects not only the direct economic crunch on white working-class people but also a less tangible sense of cultural disintegration.
> (Gordon and Hunter 2005, 239; see also Rieder 1985)

The perceived failure of the Great Society and other liberal experiments focused the new right's wrath not only on the undeserving (and implicitly black) poor,[15] who had the nerve to demand "handouts," but also on the welfare state. That state was viewed as an alliance between the racially identified poor and a *new class* of educators, administrators, planners, consultants, and journalists, who advocated the expansion of welfare state policies. For the new right, the Great Society was not the continuation of the New Deal—from which many white working-class families had benefited greatly—but its opposite. The New Deal, let it be remembered, had largely excluded blacks and Latin@s. Wallace charged that "pointy-headed intellectuals," especially those based in universities and state institutions, were responsible for the prevailing political, economic, and cultural malaise. According to the new right, the state was recklessly allowed to expand and intervene in every aspect of social life, to threaten private property and individual rights—mainly the right to discriminate, although this was rarely acknowledged—and to dictate social policy, all with disastrous results. In particular, the state was accused of acceding to the demands of formerly stigmatized groups (people of color, women, gays and lesbians) at the expense of "real Americans," in other words white men. Charges flew that civil rights reforms were attacks on principles of merit and legitimate authority, that they established privileged access for people of color to jobs and social services. Ed Davis, a new right cult figure and former Chief of the Los Angeles Police Department, put it this way: "I always felt that the government really was out to force me to hire 4-foot-11 transvestite morons" (Evans and Novak 1978).[16]

The new right criticized liberal statism at every juncture. The Supreme Court was criticized for its liberal bias in matters of race relations. The electoral college system was opposed for restricting third-party efforts and, as Kevin Phillips suggested, maximizing the influence of a "Third World state"[17] such as California. While constantly calling for a return to the basics of the Constitution, new right activists were also intent on revising it through amendments to stop busing, prohibit abortions (after 1973), and encourage school prayer.

To summarize thus far: The new right's ascendance can be traced directly back to the late-1960s political reaction against the black movement and its allied new social movements. Both the Wallace and Nixon presidential campaigns of 1968 sought leverage from the national civil rights laws that were then in place: Wallace by launching a national, electorally oriented, reactionary populist movement; and Nixon by a more stealthy approach aimed at de-linking the formerly "solid South" from the Democratic Party.

Wallace's right-wing politics were aimed squarely at white working-class voters who were threatened both by economic crisis and by the social upheavals of black liberation, feminism, the student and antiwar movements, and other manifestations of the "counterculture." Through whatever optics political reaction employed—anti-communism, racism, southern chauvinism, states' rights doctrines going back to Calhoun, agrarian populism, nativism, America First isolationism—the Wallaceites and their numerous supporters grasped a deep truth: that white supremacy was not an excrescence on the basically egalitarian and democratic "American creed," but a fundamental component of U.S. society. To destroy it meant reinventing the social order, the state, and American national identity itself.

Nixon's strategy was to raise some of those same specters, but to employ a more moderate and more inclusive tone in doing so, recognizing the importance for his campaign of suburban, centrist, white voters—the "silent majority" as he was later to call them. Nixon was adroit enough to use the Vietnam War against the Democrats as well: Hapless Hubert Humphrey, the Democratic candidate, failed to distance himself from the outgoing President Lyndon Johnson's doomed Vietnam policies until the very end of the campaign, when it was too late to undo Nixon's phony efforts to present himself as the peace candidate.[18]

Nixon learned from Wallace but, unlike the guv-nah, he kept his racist pitch on the down-low. He countered the black movement's democratic and egalitarian appeal, as he did the anti-war appeal, in ways that would not leave him vulnerable to charges of explicit racism (or of excessive hawkishness). Building on the right-wing populism of Wallace, and exploiting the self-immolation of the Democrats—by highlighting black unrest, the antiwar demonstrations in Chicago and the predicament of the forlorn Humphrey—Nixon helped the new right develop a new subtextual approach to politics. This involved the *rearticulation* of white resentments against blacks, and soon enough against other insurgent groups as well: "second-wave" feminists, the antiwar movement, the counterculture, and the dawning gay rights movement. It did not, however, repudiate civil rights in its entirety, nor did it directly attack the new social movements. Instead of defending segregation, institutionalized discrimination, and white supremacy, the new right invoked the code words of "law and order"; instead of advocating for systemic patriarchy and justifying male chauvinism, it upheld "family values"; instead of justifying yet again the duplicitous and unpopular war in Vietnam (which, after the April 1968 Tet offensive and the massive anti-war demonstrations of Fall 1969, the U.S. was now clearly losing), the Nixon administration now claimed to be seeking "peace with honor."

These were the early days of racial rearticulation, when white supremacy was in the process of "going underground." In later stages of the process, the new right would *adopt* black demands, claiming that civil rights enforcement and efforts at racial redistribution constituted "racism in reverse." Still later, efforts at rearticulation would involve the wholesale denial of racial discrimination and indeed of racial identity itself.

But at the end of the turbulent 1960s, racial rearticulation was still in an early and experimental phase, still marked by the tumultuous period from which the United States was only just emerging. Indeed the new right itself was still wet behind the ears. The accomplishments of the civil rights movement, and the horrors of the assassinations of the two Kennedys and MLK Jr., were still fresh in the national memory; division and confusion beset not only the two national political parties but also the political alignments of both the liberal North and the reactionary South. In such a period of political transition, neither the outrages of racial injustice nor the requirements of significant racial reform could easily be defended. The consequences of any attempt to reinstate the *ancien régime raciale* were too horrifying to contemplate: Both the enactment of civil rights laws (however moderate) and the "long hot summers" from 1964 through 1968 had demonstrated that civil rights reform was ineluctable and that the strategy of "massive resistance" had failed.

At the same time, a serious program of racial democratization was equally unimaginable. At a minimum, such an effort would have included significant economic redistribution and official acknowledgement of the racially despotic dimensions of state power, not only in slavery times but in the present. Thus the risk posed by the black movement—material, political, and psychic—to the key institutions of the Pax Americana, not to mention the majority of the U.S. population, the white majority, was quite profound. The radical consequences of black demands for racial democracy continued to horrify whites, as they had for centuries.[19]

Under these conditions, the new right's adoption of racial "code words" and phrases like "law and order," "the right to life," and "family values" as strategies to maintain racial inequality and repression, as well as militaristic foreign policy, patriarchal rule, repressive forms of social control, and assaults on the welfare state, all made sense as strategies for political navigation. Nixon had won the 1968 election, but the South was not yet in the Republican column. George Wallace was still on the scene.[20] Because the Democrats were unable to move beyond their late 1960s crackup, the new right had a significant period in the 1970s during which it could consolidate itself institutionally (notably around the Heritage Foundation and other think tanks) and ideologically (more or less around the Southern Strategy). During that same period, the U.S. polity had to be steered away from the racist past whose repressive and indeed despotic policies had been discredited. The new right was groping and maneuvering toward a new racism—a new strategy of racial rearticulation—that could incorporate the civil rights "revolution" in an ideology of "colorblindness." This would emerge in a more developed form during the 1980s.

Neoconservatism

While the new right was experimenting with racial "code words," another approach was being developed by the neoconservatives, who in earlier incarnations had been Democratic racial "moderates": generally based in the North, white, and liberal supporters of civil rights. Some neocon leaders were ex-Marxists who had been traumatized by the McCarthy period and redefined themselves as anti-communist, which in practice meant anti-socialist as well. Supporters of the Vietnam war (a cold war, anti-communist conflict) and often Zionist,[21] they were also disaffected by the black movement's links to anti-colonialist struggles around the world, notably by Malcolm's turn to orthodox Islam and tours of Africa and the Middle East. Thus the black movement's radical turn in the mid-1960s, its affinity for socialism (including the developing political orientation of Dr. King), and its increasing black nationalism (embodied in black power) all raised red flags, so to speak, for such intellectuals as Irving Kristol, Norman Podhoretz, Sidney Hook, and others.[22] Marked by their white ethnicity, their experience as the children of immigrants, and in particular by their youthful leftism and their struggles against anti-semitism (many key neoconservatives were Jews), these thinkers and politicians had made visceral commitments to what they saw as the core political and cultural values of the United States: pluralism, consensus, gradualism, and individualism. Their opposition to outright state-supported discrimination, which had temporarily allied them with the pre-1965 civil rights movement, thus had very different sources from that of their former movement allies. The idea of white supremacy as an abiding presence in American life was troubling to the neoconservatives, for it called into question their idealized view of U.S. political culture.

Largely unwilling to engage in "coded" or subtextual race-baiting *á la* the new right, these activists and intellectuals took up centrist positions on the right of the Democratic and left of the Republican parties; over time they became more right-wing. They subscribed to an ethnicity-based model of race, derived quite consciously from the "immigrant analogy" (see Chapter 1).

Equally problematic was the fact that blacks and other people of color questioned the legitimacy of reforms based on the principle of individual equality and rights, calling instead for a radical collective equality. Both nationalist positions and Marxist/social democratic tendencies were oriented towards "group rights"—autonomy programs *á la* "community control" and redistributionist schemes such as a "Marshall plan for the inner cities."[23]

From the neoconservative standpoint—rooted in the ethnicity paradigm—group rights were anathematized as anti-democratic. To demand equality as an *outcome* of civil rights policies, or to frame measures of egalitarian reforms in terms of the policies' *results*, called into question the opportunity-based premises of the "American dream," what W.E.B. Du Bois in 1935 had called "the American assumption." By the 1970s, opposition to radical demands for equality of "outcomes" rather than "opportunities" had become a centerpiece of the neoconservative perspective. The ethnicity theorists associated with the current did not ground their arguments, as some in the new right did, on "white rights." Instead they restricted their opposition to racial discrimination to "negative" cases: exclusion, inequality, denial of opportunity to individuals, not to groups. To go farther than prohibiting these injustices, they argued, would be to indulge in "positive" discrimination (Gordon 1964). Nathan Glazer's objections to affirmative action (1987 [1975]) policies centered on their challenge to the fundamental civic ideals which had made the "American ethnic pattern" possible: individualism, market-based opportunity, and the curtailment of excessive state interventionism. Affirmative action, he wrote,

> has meant that we abandon the first principle of a liberal society, that the individual's interests and good and welfare are the test of a good society, for we now attach benefits and penalties to individuals simply on the basis of their race, color, and national origins. The implications of this new course are increasing consciousness of the significance of group membership, an increasing divisiveness on the basis of race, color, and national origin, and a spreading resentment among the disfavored groups against the favored ones. If the individual is the measure, however, our public concern is with the individual's capacity to work out an individual fate by means of education, work, and self-realization in the various spheres of life. Then how the figures add up on the basis of whatever measure of group we use may be interesting, but should be of no concern to public policy.
>
> (Glazer 1987 [1975], 220)

This position provided ideological grounding for racial reaction in a way that use of "code words" could never do. Eschewing the dissembling and disguised racism that appeals to "law and order" or "states' rights" involved, the neoconservative view was initially framed by moderates as a centrist but in their view pro-civil rights ideology. Its studious avoidance of the structural dimensions of white supremacy was still somewhat disingenuous. Notably Glazer did not argue that white resentment against such programs as affirmative action was justified—in the manner of a William Rusher (an advocate of postwar conservativism) or a George Wallace—only that it was inevitable. He even went so far as to suggest that if affirmative action programs were effective he might support them out of pragmatic commitment to equality:

> For me, no consideration of principle—such as that merit should be rewarded, or that governmental programs should not discriminate on the grounds of race or ethnic group—would stand in the way of a program of preferential

> hiring if it made some substantial progress in reducing the severe problems of the low-income black population and of the inner cities.
>
> (1987 [1975], 73)

This distinguished the neoconservative and new right oppositions to such policies: the neoconservatives feared the politics of resentment as an unwanted consequence of state over-involvement, while the new right mobilized precisely such sentiments.

The power of the neoconservative critique of affirmative action was based on the ability of writers such as Glazer to present themselves as simultaneously opposed both to discrimination *and* to anti-discrimination measures based on "group rights" principles. The neoconservatives thus refocused the debate on the question of what ideas and what means were best for achieving racial equality. Although they were children of the New Deal and not anti-welfare statists, in some ways the neocons adopted views quite close to market fundamentalism. According to the neoconservative argument, only individual rights exist, only individual opportunity can be guaranteed by law, and only "merit" justifies the granting of privilege. Yet even the most cursory examination of such arguments reveals their deeper political subtexts. Glazer's concern about the resentments and heightened racial polarization any abandonment of traditional liberalism would inspire, for example, does not extend to the resentments and polarization which adherence to liberalism entails. Morris Abram, a former liberal partisan of civil rights and early neocon who served on the U.S. Civil Rights Commission under Reagan, proposed the extension of unionization as a better remedy than affirmative action for alleviating minority poverty and powerlessness (Abram 1984, 60). Thereby he merely indicated which groups he considered acceptable vehicles for political demands. Workers were apparently free to have collective interests, but people of color were not. Concepts of "individual merit," as many writers shown, have the same shallowness. "Merit" is a construct too, as numerous studies of the SAT and similar exams have shown (Lemann 2000). Employers, schools, and state agencies need to legitimate the allocation of benefits, and to deny the validity of competing claims. But the means of judging merit remain questionable at best.[24]

By limiting themselves to considering discrimination against individuals, neoconservatives trivialized the problem of racial equality, and of equality in general. Discrimination never derived its main strength from individual actions or prejudices, however great these might have been or might still be. Racial inequality is deeply embedded in the very organization of the social order and reflected in all its political, economic, and social domains. The neoconservative concept of "reverse discrimination" took the political demand for equality presented by the black and allied racial justice movements of the 1960s and stood it on its head. Racial discrimination and racial equality—in the neoconservative model—were problems to be confronted *only* at an individual level, once legal systems of discrimination such as *de jure* segregation had been eliminated. Thus discrimination may be an illegitimate infringement on individual rights, but it can no longer be a legitimate source for group demands. What the neoconservatives opposed was therefore not racial equality, but racial collectivity.

Neoconservatives abhorred the arguments of black militants—for example, Malcolm's statement that "We don't see any American dream; we've experienced only the American nightmare" (Malcolm X 1964; variant version in Malcolm X 1990 [1965], 26). In a striking way, the neoconservatives reproduced the fearful and compensatory allegiance to whiteness exhibited in the United States in the late 19th century (Roediger and Esch 2012). Just as many whites in the 19th century had opposed slavery but resisted a comprehensive reorganization of their privileged status vis-á-vis emancipated blacks, so too the neoconservatives opposed overt discrimination, but resisted an in-depth confrontation with the enduring benefits that race conferred on whites. Thus they sought to confine the egalitarian upsurge, to reinterpret movement ideas more narrowly and individualistically, and to channel them in more gradualist directions. Their views aligned them with the white ethnics whose integration into mainstream American society had led them—especially after the New Deal—toward more conservative politics and a sense of "optional" ethnicity (Waters 1990). In its critique of race conscious policies and practices, neoconservativism laid the theoretical foundations and politico-moral justifications for the "colorblind" ideology that has been consolidated as the reigning racial "common sense" of the past several decades.

In contrast to the new right, the neoconservatives never had significant mass support or a major voting bloc that they could mobilize. The neocons were essentially a bunch of policy wonks. Their assaults on affirmative action and on welfare were important (Mead 1993; Murray 1996 [1984]), but after the Reagan years and with the Cold War's end they would largely abandon domestic policy for foreign policy. The term "neoconservatism" reappeared in the later Clinton years as a shorthand designation for an influential group of imperial hawks, organized in something called the Project for a New American Century and linked to the right-wing think tank the American Enterprise Institute. This group distinguished itself by providing the monumentally mendacious rationale for the 2003 U.S. invasion of Iraq (Mann 2004).

From Code Words to Reverse Racism to Colorblindness

So the containment of the black movement by the U.S. state was initially achieved through a contradictory political strategy that combined incorporation of movement demands and violent repression directed against movement organizations and leaders. Containment was largely accomplished by the mid-1970s, setting the stage for the protracted crisis of racial meaning that has preoccupied the country ever since.

Incorporation and repression were not enough to curtail the movement's political effects. Winning political demands is a contradictory experience. On the one hand, winning means the installation of movement objectives as components of state policy; on the other hand it has demobilizing consequences. The black movement, like other insurgent movements, demanded that the state act to achieve the movement's objectives: integration, redistribution, an end to racist violence, and equalization of political rights. The state was adjured not only to legislate these reforms but to enforce them practically. It was to *take over* for the movement, to institutionalize the movement. That this incorporation of the movement agenda was enacted in a series of compromises and "moderate" versions only reinforced the fact that although the movement's "victories" were substantial, they also involved defeats. Not only did civil rights become law in 1964 in a limited and toothless fashion—for example, discriminatory practices were not criminalized but only made subject to civil remedies—but also incorporation of movement demands subsequently rendered the movement less effectual in respect to the deeper conflicts that shaped its original demands. The black movement's successes in the 1960s can be compared to the labor movement's successes in the 1930s: Union rights were guaranteed by the Wagner Act, but organized labor paid the price of having to accept state regulation, to uphold and enforce labor contracts, to oppose wildcat strikes, and to all intents and purposes collaborate in enforcing labor law on their own members (Klare 1977–1978, 2004).

Incorporation rules, OK? Successful movements undermine the conditions for their own existence. Insurgent movements are generally split by their very achievements into accommodationist and radical fractions, and the gains thus achieved are purchased at the price of at least partial demobilization. For those who refuse the compromises that mainstream political achievements entail, marginalization and repression await.

Yet that is obviously not the whole story. Winning reforms is also empowering. It places activists in positions where they can themselves enforce their former demands: serving their communities (now their "constituents"), punishing their opponents, operating the levers of state power, and continuing to provide leadership. Winning demands advances the horizon of movement vision, both because when you move closer to achieving your goals, you have met certain democratic needs, and also because you have learned valuable lessons about how limited your former goals were. As we move toward the horizon, the horizon recedes before us.

Racial reaction, then, could not be accomplished simply by repression of its radical elements, because the incorporated components, the "entrists" who had now gained some measure of power, were not thereby rendered ineffective, even if they had been absorbed into the state. In fact, radicals were not neutralized by repression either; though they suffered and were subjected to brutal and illegal state practices, they were not destroyed. Reaction had to find other means to cope with the movement's successes: There had to be mobilization against the black movement's accomplishments.

"Code words" did some of the early work of reactionary mobilization. It was politically salutary for the new right to engage its supporters with calls of "law and order" and other similar appeals. These served the purpose of reinforcing white supremacy without explicitly advocating it, of motivating the right wing after the doctrine of "massive resistance" to civil rights reforms had collapsed.

But "code words" did not themselves provide doctrine. They were ideologically insufficient for the cause of racial reaction. What was required was ideologically grounded opposition to substantive racial reforms going forward in the early "post-civil rights" period: affirmative action, busing, "fair-housing" and "fair-lending," initiatives and so on. With the 1968 election of Richard Nixon, strategically guided by the Southern Strategy, it became possible to "mainstream" such an ideology, in the form of opposition to "reverse discrimination" (or "reverse racism"). A blizzard of academic treatises and law review articles debated the politics and constitutionality of these concepts, and political mobilization for and against them proliferated. Legal challenges multiplied, moving from the cautious upholding of affirmative action in the *Griggs* case (1971a), through the *Charlotte-Mecklenburg* school desegregation cases (1971b, 2001) and cresting with the *Bakke* case (1978).[25]

The Nixon administration played an important role in making this shift happen. Nixon's strategic orientation toward the electoral politics of race was of a piece with his approach to state racial policy. After his early years as a fire-breathing red-baiter, Richard Nixon had become something of a centrist in the 1960s. Defeated in his run for California governor in 1962 ("You won't have Nixon to kick around anymore" (Hill 1962; see also Perlstein 2008, 61), and chastened by the Goldwater debacle of 1964, Nixon had spent some years in the woodshed, reinventing himself as a mainstream, modern Republican. This was a stance that was indexed to the civil rights "revolution" in more ways than one. In Nixon's first term he tacked left from the Southern Strategy and away from "code words," advocating black capitalism, proposing a guaranteed annual income, minority enterprise zones, and affirmative action initiatives. These moves consolidated the coastal and northern moderates of the Republican Party. Influenced by Daniel P. Moynihan, the Nixon administration's initial racial maneuvering was actually to the "left" of the neoconservatives, for whom affirmative action was a particular anathema.[26] In his second term, though, Nixon moved sharply toward the new right and adopted a more authoritarian direction, disavowing his earlier interests in welfare reform and jousting with the unions whose support for his Vietnam strategy he had previously courted. His rightward shift during his second term was made possible by the dismantlement of the black movement under the twin pressures of incorporation and repression, by the effectiveness of the "code words'" appeal in cementing the new right to the Republican Party, and by Nixon's unwavering disposition toward divisive political tactics.[27]

> The Nixon administration's short-lived experiment with an authentic Southern Strategy backfired at the height of the busing controversy, but the alignment of federal desegregation policies with the grassroots demands of the Silent Majority established the spatial constraints on the scope of *Brown*.
> (Lassiter 2007, 19)

Nixon's resignation from office in August 1974; the ignominious U.S. withdrawal from Vietnam in 1975; and Jimmy Carter's defeat of Gerald Ford in 1976 seemed, at least on the surface, to suggest a new dawn. Carter himself seemed to embody the country's racial contradictions. A post-segregationist Southern governor and a "born again" Southern Baptist, Carter was solidly within the moderate civil rights camp and projected a certain political quiescence on racial terrain (Allitt 2005, 148–149).

But all was not well. The 1970s were the cradle years for the new right and for the neoconservatives who were directly responding to anti-racist movements' vision of racial democracy and the promotion of "group rights." The *Bakke* case (U.S. Supreme Court 1978) constituted a pivotal legal challenge that framed affirmative action as "affirmative discrimination." To anti-racist activists, the limits of the civil rights reforms of the mid-1960s were becoming increasingly apparent while persistent patterns of racial oppression and inequality remained and, in some cases, had become more glaring. The use of civil rights logic to protect whites from anti-racist reforms—the "reverse racism" argument as legal, academic, and above all political ideology—was a more effective *rearticulation* of the "post-civil rights" era than the new rights "code words" had been. It was to be followed by the revival of "colorblind" racial ideology, a further (and eventually hegemonic) rearticulation in the 1980s. We consider colorblindness in Chapter 8.

As we have argued throughout this book, the post-World War II anti-racist movement *politicized the social.* In the United States and around the world, overlapping movements demanded the inclusion of racially defined "others," the democratization of structurally racist societies, and the recognition and validation by both the state and civil society of racially defined experience and identity. These demands broadened and deepened the nature of democracy itself. They inspired a range of new social movements oriented to social equality, justice, and inclusion.

What goes around comes around. The political forms developed on the left were also adaptable by the right (Laclau 1978; Laclau and Mouffe 2001 [1985]). The vision, principles, and even language of the new social movements were soon rearticulated by right-wing reactions of various types, also overlapping in many ways: racist, anti-feminist, homophobic. These matured in the 1970s. Notions of "community control," the "right to life," and "traditional values" were used to beat back the fragile gains of the new social movements. Mobilization on the political right presented a partial and distorted mirror image of the black, feminist, and gay movements, but it was real enough and effective as hell. Both racial reaction and neoconservatism brought about setbacks in legislation, law, policing and punishment practices, and other state actions. Reaction also took cultural forms: moving from early recodings and rearticulations of anti-racist meanings to more ideologically grounded reactionary rearticulations as "reverse discrimination" and anti-statism.[28] Yet even the incorporation and containment of "identity politics" reveals the politically transformative character of the "politicization of the social." It was the long-delayed eruption into the mainstream political arena of racial subjectivity and politicized identity that set off this transformation, shaping both the democratic and anti-democratic social movements that today dominate American politics, and in a variety of ways transforming democratic impulses worldwide.[29]

We have argued that the *declining phase* of the political trajectory of racial politics started around 1970. History continued, not to repeat itself, but to rhyme (to quote, probably spuriously, Mark Twain). Despite the partial reforms accomplished at a tremendous human cost, the basic patterns of racial despotism remained unchanged. The First Reconstruction (after the Civil War) had not been able to undo white supremacy; the Second Reconstruction (after World War II) was not able to do so either. From about 1970, a racial reaction set in—a long, declining phase of the post-World War II political trajectory of race. We trace this trajectory further in the next chapter, centering in the emergence and consolidation of colorblindness as a hegemonic racial project, linked and in many ways overlapping with neoliberalism.

Notes

1. The Great Transformation was certainly not as enormous as the Civil War. It did not "tear the roof off the sucker," so to speak. But it was still a big challenge to white supremacy.
2. The Duboisian question—"An American, a Negro?"—is a permanent question.
3. Hegemony operates, Gramsci says, by incorporating opposition. Speaking the language of class, he writes, "Undoubtedly the fact of hegemony presupposes that account be taken of the interests and the tendencies of the groups over which hegemony is to be exercised, and that a certain compromise equilibrium should be formed—in other words, that the leading group should make sacrifices of an economic-corporate kind. But there is also no doubt that such sacrifices and such a compromise cannot touch the essential; for though hegemony is ethico-political, it must also be economic, must necessarily be based on the decisive function exercised by the leading group in the decisive nucleus of economic activity" (1971, 161).
4. On the Freedom Schools, see Payne 2007 (1995), 301–306.
5. George Lipsitz elaborates: "In [Malcolm X's] view, just as General Motors made adjustments in surface features of its automobiles, racism changed its contours and dimensions. The racism of 1964 might not look like the racism of 1954, but it was still racism. Malcolm X warned against thinking that racism had ended because it had changed its appearance, at the same time cautioning his listeners that they could not defeat today's racism with yesterday's slogans and analysis" (Lipsitz 1998, 182).
6. Elsewhere in this book we refer to the reiterative aspects of racial rule, invoking for example Myrdal's idea of "cumulative and circular development." Certainly in respect to repression there are ample instances of reiteration: convict labor and leasing; torture in various forms including mutilation as well as solitary confinement; this list could be extended. Mass incarceration organized along race lines, often for petty, victimless offenses, is an unprecedented development, resembling slavery more than any other mode of repression. Note the clause in the 13th Amendment outlawing slavery, "except as a punishment for crime whereof the party shall have been duly convicted...." In respect to repression of movements, John Adams arrested political opponents under the Sedition Act of 1790.
7. A parallel (and intersecting) case was the "second wave" feminist movement, which critiqued the patriarchal family, inequities in sex/gender relations, and women's lack of control over their own bodies (Baxandall and Gordon, eds. 2000).

8. The new right learned about direct mail from the New Left, or more accurately from the George McGovern campaign of 1972. As Richard Viguerie wrote:

   Direct mail is the advertising medium of the non-establishment candidate....

   George McGovern became the Democratic presidential nominee in 1972 because of direct mail.

   When he couldn't afford to advertise on television, McGovern could spend $200,000 (mostly on credit) to write to 1 million identified liberal Democrats, knowing that an appeal for money in the letters would bring in enough funds within 30 days to pay for the direct mail advertising.

   So George McGovern and his brilliant direct mail team of Morris Dees and Tom Collins used the mails to bypass the party bosses, the party establishment, and the smoke-filled rooms to go straight to the people.

   Most of the news media didn't understand political direct mail, until George McGovern came along that year and made it an acceptable political tool. (1981; 90–98)

9. Eugenics was hardly dead, though. It was always knocking around, appearing under the bylines of William Shockley, Hans Eysenck, and Roger Pearson (among many others), and receiving organization support and funding through the Pioneer Fund (Tucker 2007). It then made a massive splash with the publication of Herrnstein and Murray's *The Bell Curve* (Herrnstein and Murray 1994; see also Fraser, ed. 1995; Fischer et al. 1996). Like Malcolm X said, "Racism is like a Cadillac ... "
10. Certain left groups allied themselves with the anti-busing forces, arguing that the issue was one of class, rather than race (*Radical America* 1974, 1975).
11. As a young Alabama politician, Wallace was seen as something of a moderate. But after losing a close election early in his career he made a public vow to "never be outniggered again." He then rose to his second last stand, when as Governor of Alabama in 1962 he "stood in the schoolhouse door" to prevent integration. His third incarnation, as presidential candidate, required him to moderate his white supremacy and to experiment with "code words." His fourth and final identity, which appeared in the aftermath of the Voting Rights Act and of a 1972 assassination attempt, was once again "moderate."
12. Phillips's subsequent and somewhat iconoclastic journey leftward may be viewed as a prolonged atonement for this early and quite consequential political mistake; see 2007; 2004.
13. What Phillips was picking up on and framing politically was the emotional sociology of racism. As Scheff and Retzinger argue (1991), shame is an extremely difficult emotion to manage. It often transmogrifies into anger. The social fact of slavery, for all its rationalizations both ante- and post-bellum, produced great emotional stress and shame for whites. This is evident in the very need for a "psychological wage" (Du Bois 2007 [1935]; Roediger 2007 [1991]). In addition: the ever-present demand to exercise oppressive and violent control, the perceived necessity to mete out punishment; the requirement to patrol and police constantly. In addition: the fear of black revenge. What if they do to us what we've done to them? To say nothing of the Hegelian master–slave dialectic or of the immense greed, sexism, eroticism, or religious contortions that characterized the slavery complex...). This storm of terrifying emotions experienced by whites as a consequence of their deeply rooted racism—far more than a set of attitudes and beliefs; in fact a whole *Weltanschauung* and comprehensive social structure—was then subjected to the trauma of massive defeat and societal destruction in the

Civil War, followed by military occupation. After Sherman's tender mercies, for example, very little remained standing in many places. On top of that, the liberation of the former slaves and their elevation to a putatively equal status resulted—as is well-documented—in a boundless white rage and resentment that ultimately led to the Jim Crow system (Williamson 1986; Woodward 2002 [1955]; Hahn 2003).

14. The concept of "status revolution" has its origins in the liberal historian Richard Hofstadter's rejection of the class-based categories of Charles Beard and others whose work on U.S. social movements had reached its high point in the 1930s (Hofstadter 1965).
15. The majority of poor people in the United States were white in the 1960s and 1970s. This did not prevent the new right's identification of poverty and blackness, a trope that was quickly institutionalized and remains in force today.
16. This was all rather ironic, since police departments, licensing and zoning practices, municipal employment and service-provision in general, patronage and machine politics, and public subvention had been proprietary white ethnic zones for almost a century. See Katznelson 2005.
17. Phillips coined the term "Third World state" to describe states that had an increasing racial minority population. This anticipated the onset of a majority-minority" demographic. "Retention of the Electoral College," Phillips wrote, "would probably guarantee a minority-oriented presidential selection process for the 1980s" (Phillips 1977, cited in Crawford 1980, 324).
18. When Humphrey did manage to bleat softly against the war and thus crawl out from under Johnson's imperious shadow, about two weeks before election day, his poll numbers began to improve. In the end, Nixon's electoral margin was very thin.
19. That sort of transformation would also have required revising standard conceptions of the state: The Constitution would have had to be apprehended as a white supremacist and slavocratic document, a notion that brings to mind the abolitionist William Lloyd Garrison. At a public meeting in Boston on July 4, 1844, Garrison burned a copy of the Constitution on the stage, calling it a "covenant with death" and "an agreement with Hell" (Mayer 1998).
20. Wallace ran again for president in 1972. An attempted assassination during the campaign left him paralyzed and removed him from the national political stage. By 1972 he had begun to moderate his racial politics and reinvent himself as a centrist.
21. The Six-Day Israel–Arab war (June 1967) was viewed as a great triumph by many members of this group (Segev 2007).
22. On April 4, 1967, exactly one year before his murder, King denounced the Vietnam war in a magnificent speech at the Riverside Church in New York City. He immediately came under severe criticism not only from the right, but from "moderate" civil rights movement leaders as well (such as Roy Wilkins and Whitney Young). He was exceeding his mandate, they said; he should focus entirely on domestic issues. But by this time the antiwar movement and the more radical elements in the black movement (notably SNCC) were allied. King was following his movement—and his own deep ethical sense of course. Beyond that, as his speech itself made clear, the Vietnam war *was* a domestic issue; if there had ever been a gap between anti-racism at home and abroad, that gap had now ceased to exist.
23. A striking example of this trend was the presentation of a "Black Manifesto" at New York City's Riverside Church—where MLK's April 4, 1967, anti-Vietnam War speech had also

been delivered. On Sunday May 11, 1969, a group of activists led by SNCC President James Forman interrupted services at the church:

> Addressing himself to "the White Christian Churches and Jewish Synagogues in the United States of America and All Other Racist Institutions," [Forman] read a Black Manifesto which demanded that the churches and synagogues pay $500 million "as a beginning of the reparations due us as people who have been exploited and degraded, brutalized, killed and persecuted." The amount demanded by the Manifesto, which was adopted by the National Black Economic Development Conference before Forman's action was taken, was to be used to establish a Southern land bank, publishing and printing industries, four audio-visual networks, a research skills center, a training center for teaching skills in community organization and communications, a black labor strike and defense fund, a black university, and several other institutions. (Bittker 2003 [1973], 4)

Forman had also planned to carry out a parallel interruption two weeks later at the Saturday services of Congregation Emanu-El of the City of New York, perhaps the most prestigious Jewish synagogue in the United States. The action was called off after the Jewish Defense League, a radical right-wing Jewish organization led by Rabbi Meir Kahane, threatened to confront Forman and his group with violence. The JDL members assembled at the synagogue on Fifth Ave., carrying chains and clubs, and Forman did not appear at the synagogue.

24. It turns out that whites' commitment to meritocratic principles in higher education admissions varies depending on their perception of the "racial group threat" these principles pose. Using a survey-based experiment of California residents, Frank Samson (2013) found that when whites received a prompt that noted the high proportion of Asian American undergraduates in the University of California system, they decreased the importance they afforded to grade point averages in admissions decisions. This suggests that affirmative action in higher education should be understood in terms of "group position" (Blumer 1958) and access to resources more than in terms of "academic standards" and merit. Similar considerations may apply to affirmative action in other areas, such as employment, government contracting, and licensing (Katznelson 2005).
25. In *Griggs* (U.S. Supreme Court 1971a) the SCOTUS cautiously approved an employment-based affirmative action plan; in *Swann* (U.S. Supreme Court 1971b) they approved a school redistricting and busing plan that had been worked out by NGOs and local community/political alliances (somewhat transracial). The Swann decision was reversed in 2001 on appeal in the *Belk v. Charlotte-Mecklenburg* case, with the SCOTUS refusing certiorari (U.S. Supreme Court, 4th Circuit 2001). *Bakke* was a turning-point on affirmative action, in which the Court set restrictive limits to affirmative action by applying anti-discrimination law in favor of whites in such cases (U.S. Supreme Court 1978).
26. Although these were all developed as political "wedge" issues that would both fracture the Democratic Party's labor–black alliance and consolidate right-wing (and racist) anti-statism, some of these proposals had strategic advantages that the Democrats did not grasp. On the "failed" welfare reform initiatives of the 1970s—the "Family Assistance Plan" of Nixon (crafted by Moynihan) and the "Better Jobs and Income" plan of Carter—see Steensland 2007.
27. Nixon's personal racism has been well documented. "On April 28, 1969, [Nixon's Chief-of-Staff H.R.] Haldeman recorded: 'P [Nixon] emphasized that you have to face the fact

that the whole problem is really the blacks. The key is to devise a system that recognizes this while not appearing to.'" In the second term: "'Had me tell Mitchell not to open Southern offices and not to send his men down en masse, only when needed on a spot basis. Also set policy that we'll use no federal troops or marshals to enforce, must be done by locals ... We take a very conservative civil rights line,' Nixon instructed" (Graham 1996, 99).

28. In an argument parallel to ours, HoSang (2010) applies the term "political whiteness" to these projects, arguing that after the taken-for-granted previous meanings of whiteness had been called into question by civil rights struggles, a new framework had to be invented to advance exclusive and discriminatory white interests in such areas as housing, employment, and access to higher education.
29. One example of many that could be provided: In the "Bloody Sunday" demonstration in Derry, Northern Ireland (January 30, 1972), marchers sang "We Shall Overcome" and carried pictures of Martin Luther King, Jr. British troops fired on the protest, killing 13 unarmed demonstrators.

CHAPTER 8

Colorblindness, Neoliberalism, and Obama

Introduction

We have argued that the declining phase of the political trajectory of racial politics started around 1970. For all the ways that it had challenged the old Jim Crow-based, hegemonic system of white supremacy, for all the reforms and cultural recognition (and self-recognition) that it had won, the movement lacked the political support, particularly of white allies, that would have been needed to realize more of its demands. In many ways the standard pattern applied: partial reforms were accomplished at a tremendous human cost, but basic patterns of racial despotism remained unchanged. From about 1970 a "racial reaction" set in, a long, declining phase of the post-World War II political trajectory of race. Under Reagan, beginning in 1981, a new neoliberal administration came to power. Though not generally recognized as such, neoliberalism in the United States was very much a racial regime. This chapter concentrates on neoliberalism and race in the Reagan to Obama period.

In the chapter's next section, we discuss the *Rise of the Neoliberal Project*, focusing on neoliberalism's racial elements. Although they were not revolutionary in scope, the black movement and the new social movements did represent a radical threat to the limited and manipulated democracy that had previously operated as the political mainstream. It was the convergence of these movements, the rise of a radical, democratic, participatory culture, that neoliberalism had to overcome. Neoliberalism took charge under the banners of anti-statism and authoritarian populism. Although it was led by big capital, it owed its ascent to the mass electoral base that only the new right could provide. Neoliberalism was at its core a racial project as much as a capitalist accumulation project. Its central racial component was colorblind racial ideology. The hegemony of neoliberal economics is matched and underwritten by the racial hegemony of colorblindness.

The new right's authoritarian populism attracted mass white support. The competing tendency on the right, the neoconservatives, had never commanded a significant mass following. The new right could deploy a *politics of resentment* that flowed directly from the southern strategy—the subject of this chapter's next section. In its mobilization of white suburban tax-payers, in its hostility to integration, in its use of long-standing producerist ideology to distinguish between "deserving" and "undeserving" members of U.S. society, neoliberalism adapted the new right's deep-seated racist ideology to the "post-civil rights" era.

The *genealogy of colorblind politics* is the subject of the following section. The new right rearticulation of racial politics passed through several phases: a "code words" phase and a "reverse racism" phase, before finally landing on colorblindness. Colorblind racial ideology developed in league with neoliberalism from the Reagan years forward, until it got elected in the form of Barack Obama.

Neoliberalism too had its internal tensions, its competing political tendencies. It took center-right and center-left forms. In the next section of this chapter, *Long Road Out of Eden: Presidents and Race Politics*, we note the centrality of colorblind racial ideology to the neoliberal economic project; this is a connection that is not frequently made, and deserves serious exploration.

Through the whole "post-civil rights" era, through all that political waffling over race—three decades' worth—the anti-racist movement remained; critical race consciousness remained. Of course, its key ideals—of expanded democracy, inclusion, and egalitarian redistribution—took a beating, but they were not destroyed. Because it was impossible to repudiate the "dream," it was necessary to rearticulate it. A new racial ideology of colorblindness developed as Reagan and his successors worked to construct a new racial hegemony. The colorblind racial project fit in nicely with neoliberalism's emphasis on market relationships and privatization, but it clashed with neoliberalism's barely covert racism. In its anti-immigrant initiatives (California's 1994 Proposition 187); in its vindictive policies of racial profiling, mass incarceration, and disfranchisement of voters of color; in its assault on welfare (led by Bill Clinton in 1996); and in its systematic victimization of post-Katrina New Orleans under Bush II in 2005, the colorblind project ran into difficulties as well. The same regime that professed colorblindness, it turned out, also needed race to rule.

The election of Barack Obama, in the midst of a catastrophic recession and a tidal wave of anti-Bush II revulsion, seemed to portend a repudiation of neoliberalism and a reawakening of the inclusive ideals of the civil rights and Great Society era. But this promise was not to be fulfilled. Obama was a progressive alternative to his predecessor, but he has disappointed many of his supporters by maintaining the neoliberal regime he inherited. We discuss *Obama and Colorblindness* in a later section of the chapter,

We conclude this chapter with some reflections on contemporary political realignments, affording particular attention to the role of race. In *Where's the (Tea) Party?* we note the racial cleavages emerging in the U.S. political system in light of such matters as the hugely destructive Great Recession of 2008, the ongoing demographic shift to a "majority-minority" U.S. population, the heightening costs of repression, and the resurgence of the new social movements.

Rise of the Neoliberal Project

That U.S. neoliberalism would be racially reactionary is not a stretch. Rooted in possessive individualism and worshipful of the "free market," it ran counter to the state-centered, generally democratizing legacies of the New Deal, World War II, and the Great Society. These programs and policies had a lot of popular support; to roll them back required a great deal of political effort. Only by tapping into the deep current of white supremacy that was fundamental to U.S. development and that structured the country's political unconscious could an assault on the welfare state be mounted. Neoliberalism came to power at a moment when capital perceived itself to be facing a radical threat that was based in part on the political accomplishments of the new social movements of the 1960s. It must be recognized as part and parcel of the racial reaction that followed the Great Transformation. Indeed, civil rights, black power, red, brown, and yellow power, the antiwar movement, the feminist movement, and the student movement …, all menaced the oligarchic system that passed for democracy in the United States.

In 1971 Lewis F. Powell, corporate lawyer, former American Bar Association President, former Chairman of the (of course segregated) Richmond Virginia School Board, and future Supreme Court justice (he wrote the 1978 *Bakke* decision), sent a "Confidential Memorandum" to the U.S. Chamber of Commerce, with which he was closely connected. The memo was titled "Attack on the American Free Enterprise System" and outlined a plan for a new level of corporate political activism (Powell 1971). Powell proposed that business organizations move from their former, somewhat desultory style of lobbying to a much more engaged approach, mobilizing existing organizations like the Chamber itself, and also setting up new ones. Sparked in part by the Powell memo, there emerged an activist, corporate-led network of think tanks, campus and media activities, and lobbying. At the core of this initiative was a widespread and lavishly funded effort to support corporate interests against demands for redistribution of wealth and expansion of the welfare state. Although Powell's document—just eight pages in length—only glancingly acknowledged the civil rights movement, his hostility to the 1960s social movements and their political-economic consequences was palpable and comprehensive. Powell named adversaries: Ralph Nader, Eldridge Cleaver, William Kunstler, and Herbert Marcuse, among others (there were no women on his enemies list). His memo has become quite famous as the blueprint for the subsequent corporate turn to the right.[1]

Spurred by business's turn toward political activism and by Nixon's defeat of George McGovern in 1972, the corporate elite now moved to abandon whatever remaining agreement (or acquiescence) they had with the New Deal, in favor of a strategy of regressive redistribution and increased discipline for American workers. The collective bargaining accord with big labor—especially the UAW—that wages could rise in parallel with productivity and automation, was unceremoniously disavowed (Aronowitz 1991 [1973]; Stein 2010). The economy was entering recession, with unemployment rising and GDP dropping. As *Business Week* announced, "Some people will obviously have to do with less … Yet it will be a hard pill for many Americans to swallow—the idea of doing with less so that business can have more" (*Business*

Week 1974, 51–53; see also Perlstein 2008, 605; Cowie 2010, 224). Kim Phillips-Fein reports that

> Between September 1974 and September 1975 top corporate executives from firms such as IBM, Exxon, Bechtel, and Hughes Tool held eight three-day meetings to explore the role of business in American society. Most in this anxiety-ridden group believed that "the have-nots are gaining steadily more power to distribute the wealth downward. The masses have turned to a larger government." The businessmen believed that the government, responding to the have-nots, controlled and allocated too much of the nation's wealth. They feared that the trend toward government financing, subsidy, and control would end up socializing investment decisions.... Many thought that only a sharp recession would sober up their fellow citizens.
>
> (Phillips-Fein 2010, 123, citing Silk and Vogel 1976, 21–22)

They got that deep recession, starting in 1975. It combined with a rising rate of inflation, the "stagflation" phenomenon, which economists were at a loss to explain. Economic crisis ultimately doomed Carter, who could not extricate himself from the slowdown by the normal means of increasing government expenditure and expansion of the money supply. Indeed, on his watch inflation spiraled upward. In August 1979 Carter appointed Paul Volcker as Chairman of the Federal Reserve Board, with the commitment to wringing out inflation, which was nearing 13 percent as the 1980 election took place. Reagan trounced Carter.[2] The punishing recession Volcker engineered drove inflation down to 3.5 percent in 1981, when he was reappointed by Reagan as Fed Chair. Volcker's legacy was thus not only Reagan's but Carter's as well: low inflation, sure, but permanently higher unemployment, endemic wage stagnation, and the undoing of the post-World War II tradeoff between industrial capital and big labor of increasing wages in return for productivity gains. In a deep structural sense, working-class hostility to the Democrats proceeded from the annulment of this bargain. As liberalism and Keynesianism went out the window, neoliberalism came in the front door.

The Politics of Resentment

The racial regime that developed under Reagan involved a quite explicit ramping-up of what might be called the "politics of resentment." That resentment had been nurtured in the Wallace campaigns and Nixon's "Southern Strategy"; it underwrote Reagan's unsuccessful attempt to win the 1976 Republican nomination and his subsequent campaigns and elections in 1980 and 1984. Even before its arrival in Washington, neoliberalism was premised on racial resentment. Nixon had tried out anti-statism, particularly anti-welfare statism. He had begun to withdraw the state from social provisioning: in education, health care, and other state-based services as well. Under Reagan, neoliberalism was grounded more deeply. It was far more ideologically driven, far more right-wing. It took the form of market-worship and "devolution" of social policy: ideally to the private sector; if not, then at least to the states and local authorities. Reagan sought as far as possible to lessen government regulation of the economy, to reduce taxes, and to abandon the "social safety net" in favor of an "individual responsibility" ethos.

Two central aspects of U.S. neoliberalism had particularly clear overtones of racial resentment: *tax revolt* and *producerism.*

Tax revolt: In 1978 California enacted Proposition 13, a measure that severely restricted property taxes and limited the state's ability to tax. The initiative was racially driven from the start: It was a reaction by residents of wealthier school districts to civil rights-oriented court decisions that required the state to distribute funds to public schools equitably across the state. Its sharply deleterious consequences for public education, however, soon expanded to social expenditures of other types, particularly those that benefited lower-income citizens and people of color.

Tax revolt spread rapidly as a national movement. This was a delicious dish for the Republican Party to serve in the suburbs, since it focused (white) popular resentment on poor people, which in the national popular culture meant black people (Lo 1995; for a more sanguine assessment of Prop. 13, see Citrin 2009). Ever in search of a mass base for regressive redistribution of resources and curtailment of social expenditure, Republicans linked Prop. 13 and its successors to the new "political whiteness" that they had been practicing in California since the late 1940s (HoSang 2010).[3]

Producerism: The ideology of producerism lies at the heart of right-wing populism and is fertile ground for the politics of resentment. It has a long and twisted history going back to Jefferson. At its core is hostility to "nonproductive" classes, originally seen as both *rentier* interests living off unearned income (banks in particular), and the "undeserving poor" living off public outlays (Piven and Cloward 1993 [1971]; Block and Somers 2003). The latter category deeply overlaps with white supremacism: laziness, irresponsibility, difference in "intelligence," an orientation to "immediate gratification," and a vast set of (largely biologistic) racist tropes have long been associated with blackness. The "rentiers" have largely disappeared, although they still surface from time to time, for example, in Steinbeck's *The Grapes of Wrath* or in the 2011 Occupy movement.[4] In Jacksonian times, when industrial capitalism was in its infancy and there was no working class yet, producerism was explicitly racist. Berlet and Lyons note that "[P]roducerism bolstered White supremacy, blurred actual class divisions, and embraced some elite groups while scapegoating others" (Berlet and Lyons 2000; see also Saxton 1990; Kazin 1995; Roediger 2007 [1991]). By the "post-civil rights" era, of course, that racism had become more implicit; it was framed in "coded" terms. In 1975 new right publisher William Rusher wrote:

> A new economic division pits the producers—businessmen, manufacturers, hard-hats, blue-collar workers, and farmers—against a new and powerful class of non-producers comprised of a liberal verbalist elite (the dominant

> media, the major foundations and research institutions, the educational establishment, the federal and state bureaucracies) and a semipermanent welfare constituency, all coexisting happily in a state of mutually sustaining symbiosis.
> (Rusher 1975, 31)

Although Rusher's claim that this division was "new" was incorrect, he was accurate in his efforts to frame regressively redistributive economic policies as politically attractive to working-class and middle-class whites.[5]

Discipline and Punish: Neoliberalism has been distinctly despotic, both in the United States and globally. The U.S. defeat in Vietnam, which occurred in 1975 just as the neoliberal project was taking off, seemed to limit the country's global coercive capabilities somewhat. The armed enforcement of corporate interests certainly did not stop, however, the "Vietnam syndrome" notwithstanding. Indeed this was the period in which the Chilean "experiment" was underway (Klein 2008). That horrific assault on democracy was perhaps the prototypical test of the neoliberal model; it involved the kidnapping, torture, and summary execution of trade unionists, movement activists, and student leaders; the privatization of state-held enterprises and social services, and the gutting of the country's educational and health programs.[6]

In the United States, the project gestured in similar directions but concentrated its punitive attention on racial subjects and movement activists. A related set of repressive means were directed against political opponents. For these targets there was a vast repertoire of surveillance and disciplinary technologies available, much of it deriving from slavery and post-Reconstruction approaches to controlling blacks. What Rebecca M. McLennan (2008) labels the U.S. "mode of punishment"—an ongoing, contested, and unstable interaction of "forces of repression" on the one hand, with the "social relations of repression" on the other—entered a new phase. A massive increase in incarceration—unabashedly and disproportionately targeting black and brown men—began in the early 1980s and has continued until the present. The "race to incarcerate" was multiply determined: it afforded major opportunities for profit-making and privatization, it thrived on the politics of fear, and it was traditionally associated with racism (Mauer 2006 [1995]; Wacquant 2009; Soss et al. 2011). Perhaps the most important aspect of mass imprisonment, seen from the perspective of neoliberalism, is its anti-democratic effects: Not only does it banish millions of felons and ex-felons from the electoral rolls, but it comprehensively disadvantages low-income people of color on a mass scale. In stark contrast to our argument about the Great Transformation—that the black movement and its allied new social movements expanded the terrain of politics by politicizing identity—mass incarceration *depoliticizes* the social, removing the potential for political engagement and participation from those it confines and "supervises," and indeed from most who have ever come into contact with the carceral system (Weaver and Lerman 2010).

Both during the rising phase of the post-World War II movement trajectory, and during the neoliberal (right-wing) ascendance after 1973 or so, the government expanded its assaults against the black movement and other "new social movements" as well (Donner 1990; Rosenfeld 2013). Infiltration, disruption, and surveillance by police or other state agencies, deportation, assassination and disappearance (only occasional, unlike Chile, Brazil, and other dictatorships, where *desaparición* was standard operating procedure), profiling, counter-intelligence operations such as the FBI's COINTELPRO are all examples of repressive techniques introduced at this time. But then again, imprisonment is a type of disappearance, is it not? Of course, many of these despotic practices had extensive histories.[7]

The Genealogy of Colorblind Politics

We have argued that racial reaction has gone through a series of stages since the partial "victory" of the civil rights movement and the enactment of civil rights reforms in the mid-1960s. Our idea of the trajectory of postwar U.S. racial politics suggests that the apogee of democratizing, inclusionist, and egalitarian trends was reached around the middle of the decade, and that a "downward" trend (from the movement's perspective) had begun by about 1970.

Nothing in the early phases of racial reaction pointed toward what would become "colorblind" racial ideology.[8] The initial reaction to civil rights reform was driven by racist rage and full-throated rejectionism. That is hardly surprising. Well before the passage of civil rights and voting rights laws, the South was mobilizing—often violently—against civil rights. The movement "called the question" on the Democrats' racially split personality. On the one hand, the Democrats were grounded in the "solid South" where since the end of the Civil War whites were open in their negrophobia; and, on the other hand, they were dominant in the liberal North, to which millions of blacks had migrated, where they could vote and join unions, and where segregation, though still omnipresent, was less oppressive.

The Dixiecrat wing had broken with the Democratic Party before. Implacably opposed to a civil rights plank in the 1948 party platform, and incensed about the imminent desegregation of the U.S. armed forces, southern Democrats had bolted to run Strom Thurmond for president on an independent ticket. They had spent the 1950s murdering civil rights activists (and lynching ordinary black people like 14-year-old Emmett Till), and had implacably bottlenecked and filibustered the legislative civil rights agenda. In the aftermath of the Brown decision, they had developed the "massive resistance" strategy, which involved local obstructionism that sometimes approached insurrection. They had mercilessly harassed and degraded black people, and terrorized not only local communities but federal officials. Civil rights reforms been achieved in the teeth of these tactics. Furthermore, by the mid-1960s the black movement's political trajectory had been on a two-decade ascent and had achieved a practical alliance with other anti-racist currents, new social movements, the massive anti-war movement, and the left-wing, the social democratically inclined wing of the Democratic Party.

So opposition to civil rights reform in the form of "massive resistance" was actually a late stage of racist rejectionism. It involved defending segregation by such means as engineered closures of public school systems and the establishment of private (and, of course, all white) schools.[9] After the collapse of "massive resistance," opposition to civil rights reform evolved: It developed more sophisticated legal strategies for opposing school desegregation, for example.

Racial reaction had to win allies outside the South; it had to operate within the national party system (both parties). It had to make strategic concessions. At its core was the task of developing a new right. This required formidable political reinvention: making use of the deep-seated racism of the white working and middle classes, without explicitly advocating racial "backlash." Of course, diehard segregationists, white citizens groups, the KKK, biologistic racists, and other racial troglodytes still abounded; these had to be marginalized on the "far right." The rise of "code word" strategies was a logical next step, an effort to race-bait less explicitly, while making full use of the traditional stereotypes. "Code words" like "get tough on crime" and "welfare handouts" reasserted racist tropes of black violence and laziness without having to refer to race at all. As Lee Atwater put it:

> You start out in 1954 by saying, "Nigger, nigger, nigger." By 1968 you can't say "nigger"—that hurts you. Backfires. So you say stuff like forced busing, states' rights and all that stuff. You're getting so abstract now [that] you're talking about cutting taxes, and all these things you're talking about are totally economic things and a byproduct of them is [that] blacks get hurt worse than whites. And subconsciously maybe that is part of it. I'm not saying that. But I'm saying that if it is getting that abstract, and that coded, that we are doing away with the racial problem one way or the other. You follow me—because obviously sitting around saying, "We want to cut this," is much more abstract than even the busing thing, and a hell of a lot more abstract than "Nigger, nigger."
>
> (Perlstein 2012; see also Lamis et al. 1990; Herbert 2005; Brady 1997)[10]

"Code words" never disappeared and never lost their rearticulative utility. But their deployment was inadequate to the task of mobilizing an adequate mass base for racial reaction, especially one that could incorporate the political center, not just the whites of the Jim Crow South, but whites nationally as well.

In order to reach out further, the new right developed the ideologically grounded "reverse racism" allegation. This took shape over the 1970s. "Reverse racism" (or "reverse discrimination") had several advantages over "code words." First and most important of these was the claim that racially inclusive reform policies—notably affirmative action—were unfair to whites: They "punished" whites who were merely seeking a job, admission to a university, or a federal contract. In seeking to overcome the legacy of past racism, ostensibly anti-racist policy and state actions were engaging in racism themselves, racism against whites, "reverse racism."

In other words the implementation of civil rights policy was recast as an attack on whites. It was reframed as a redistribution of resources away from whites—deserving, hard-working, family-values whites—and towards people of color. The latter, of course, were undeserving, lazy, promiscuous, and criminal, but these stereotypes could be implied, not stated openly. "Reverse racism" had obviously not been foremost in anyone's mind—at least in no white people's minds—while racial discrimination was the law of the land. But now that a significant if partial attempt was underway to ameliorate it, whites' sensibilities and sensitivities were activated big time. White concern with supposed discrimination *against them* was in any case a complete red herring, since extensive research—exploring such matters as returns to education and racial "steering," looking at employment and housing rental practices via audits—showed that traditional patterns of white racism continued largely unabated in the "post-civil rights" era.

What was significant, however, was the reframing of racism as a "race-neutral" matter. Racism was now recast as something that could affect anyone; a century of white predication—whites as the subjects of racism, blacks and people of color as the objects—was thus peremptorily dismissed. And that was only taking the post-emancipation period into consideration; when the structural legacies of slavery were addressed—massive theft of life and labor, comprehensive appropriation of value added without compensation, ongoing denigration and exclusion, not to mention torture and terror past and present—the *chutzpah* of the "reverse racism" ideology mounted to the very heavens.

The ideology of "reverse racism" was presented to whites as an effort to protect them from "unfair" claims on the part of blacks or other people of color. In this respect it had some continuity with the previous "code words' approach. But there was obviously a deeper agenda, since "reverse racism" barely existed. That agenda was to consolidate and expand the new right's mass base among whites without appealing to racist tropes as the "code words" approach had done. It was to rearticulate "post-civil rights" racial politics in such a way that the democratizing and egalitarian effects of the movement could be more effectively contained. The new right shift from the somewhat defensive use of "code words" to the ideology of "reverse racism" reframed racism as a zero-sum game. "Reverse racism" was conceptualized as an issue of "fairness," thus rearticulating the central tenets of civil rights demands—equality and justice. This was an ideological appeal that seemed consistent with the anti-discrimination demands of the movement, yet simultaneously attacked the movement for "going too far" and indeed violating its own principles. Because "reverse racism" charges targeted policies that sought practically to overcome the legacies of racial discrimination, segregation, and exclusion, these attacks had the concrete consequences of impeding redistributive efforts in such areas as university admissions, employment, government contracting and licensing, and civil rights in general.

Attacking affirmative action as an unfair system of "racial quotas" worked to defend existing systems of racial inequality and domination much more effectively than use of "code words" could ever have done. Other civil rights efforts to overcome or at least mitigate established practices of discrimination were subject to the same charges. The new right could now present itself as anti-racist: To understand the "true meaning" of civil rights was to declare that race would henceforth be "irrelevant" to the distribution of scarce resources like jobs or college admissions.[11] The "reverse racism" charge also undercut movement advocates, who were depicted as serving their own "narrow interests"—not those of larger communities of color—by pressing demands for "equality of result," not equality of opportunity.

"Reverse racism" ideology already contained the seeds of the colorblind concept, since as noted it was premised on the concept of "race neutrality." A vast literature has successfully demonstrated the impossibility of viewing race "neutrally," in the sense of ignoring it or dismissing its sociohistorical significance (Brown et al. 2003; Carbado and Harris 2008; Roediger 2008; Sugrue 2010; powell 2012). Here we focus on the political *process* that established colorblindness as the hegemonic ideology of racial reaction in the United States, and on the political *consequences* that the attainment of colorblind racial hegemony entailed. We also explore the contradictory conditions that curtail and constrain colorblindness, even in its currently hegemonic form.

Colorblind racial ideology represented a step beyond "reverse discrimination" because it repudiated the concept of race itself. In certain respects the concept of race "neutrality" already does that ideological work. To dismiss the immense sociohistorical weight of race, to argue that it is somehow possible, indeed imperative, to refuse race consciousness and simply not take account of it,[12] is by any rational standard a fool's errand. Yet from a political point of view colorblind racial ideology has scored some successes, as well as taking some losses. It is worthwhile asking why.

In our view it is the convergence of colorblindness and neoliberalism that accounts for the success of both ideologies, for their conjoint rise to hegemonic positions, and for their eventual demise. These seemingly distinct theoretical and practical formulas are each politically indispensable for the success of the other. As we have noted, the rise of neoliberalism in the United States, and its attainment of hegemonic status as an accumulation project on a world scale (Jessop 1990) depended on the containment of the political challenge of the new social movements, led by the black movement. Containment meant more than restricting the reach of demands for greater racial equality and vastly expanded democracy; it also meant resisting the redistributive logic of the Great Society, which was an early effort to extend the New Deal to the lower strata of U.S. society, and especially to people of color. The threat that the black movement and its allies posed to the dominant power-bloc (or if you prefer, ruling class) was extremely severe: It involved the prospect of a fully-fledged social democratic system in the United States, serious commitments to full employment,[13] substantial curtailment of U.S. imperial adventures—the war on poverty, Dr. King famously said, was lost on the battlefields of Vietnam—and recognition of race- and gender-based demands for full-scale social equality and inclusion.

Neoliberalism was ideologically anti-statist, but in order to acquire a mass base it had to undo the New Deal coalition, which had held power—under both Democratic and Republican administrations—from the 1930s to the 1970s. This task, first envisioned under Nixon, was accomplished by Reagan. The New Deal had been politically and morally complicit with Jim Crow and indeed could not have been implemented without its deference to the "solid South" (Katznelson 2013). But in the post-World War II period, and in many ways because of the war itself, that complicity was no longer politically viable. The black movement challenged it and ultimately overthrew it, splitting the Democratic Party in the process and transferring the South, as Lyndon Johnson lamented, to the Republican column. This political shift in which the party of Lincoln became the party of Lee Atwater was a bitter historical irony, absolutely Hegelian in its dialectical cunning.

Even though the assault on the welfare state required containment of the black movement and its new social movement allies, even though derailing demands for expanded racial democracy and for increased racial equality were the *sine qua non* of the neoliberal agenda, that agenda could not be proposed in such an explicit form. It could not be presented as "backlash," rollback, or resegregation, although it was all those things. Indeed the racial reaction experimented with a series of ideological approaches for containment and rearticulation during the 1970s, as we have noted. Colorblindness would become the central component of the racial reaction, but its establishment as a new racial "common sense" was tendential, not immediate. The term, of course, had been around for nearly a century.

Long Road out of Eden: Presidents and Race Politics[14]

Combining repression with austerity, neoliberalism reiterates and reinvents the sordid and racist histories of slavery and empire; it rearticulates racist cultural tropes. In short, it is as much a racial project as a class project. The links between racism in the metropole and racism in the periphery remain in force under the neoliberal regime. Neoliberalism rose to prominence as doctrine and policy in response to the post-World War II global insurgencies of which the black movement and its allies—not just the "new social movements" at home but the anti-imperial insurgencies among "the darker nations"—were an integral part.

Issues of race were dramatically revived in the 1980s. The Reagan campaigns and administration spoke "backlash" fluently. Reagan characterized black welfare recipients as "welfare queens" and black men as "strapping young bucks." He invoked "states' rights" at a campaign stop in Philadelphia, Mississippi—site of the kidnapping and murder of the three civil rights workers Chaney, Goodman, and Schwerner in 1964. These were repudiations of civil rights and reminders to black voters of their powerlessness. Allying with the Christian right—the Moral Majority, the Christian Coalition, Focus on the Family, and the Family Research Council—Reagan attracted millions of Southern Baptists to the Republican Party. Up through

1976, the evangelical and increasingly fundamentalist Southern Baptist Convention had largely avoided involvement in electoral politics. Indeed many of these voters had been supporters of Jimmy Carter, a "born again" Southern Baptist himself.[15] But by 1980 the "solid South" was solid again, this time on the Republican side, despite the fact that blacks could now vote there. Even beyond Dixie, Reagan could appeal to former Democrats using racial "code words." An ex-New Deal Democrat and former union leader himself, a former media mouthpiece for the giant corporation General Electric, Reagan could strike some of the same notes that Wallace and Nixon did: pro-business, anti-welfare (i.e., anti-black), law and order (i.e., anti-black), anti-feminist, anti-hippie, anti-communist. He drew to the right wing the intellectual, academic, and other defectors from the "moderate" camp of the civil rights movement—the neoconservatives—to form an uneasy but powerful alliance that underwrote his administration's racial politics. In short, Reagan consolidated the Republican Party's authoritarian populist appeal; he was genial where Nixon had scowled; he inspired trust rather than mistrust, all the while repudiating the civil rights movement and the legacy of the Great Society, both largely associated with the Democrats.[16]

Reagan's neoliberal commitments were of a piece with his genial racism. His iconic comment in his 1981 Inaugural Address, "In this present crisis, government is not the solution to our problem; government *is* the problem," distilled a political orientation that was hostile to civil rights, hostile to the welfare state, hostile to taxation (though Reagan did raise taxes several times), and hostile to unions.[17] His successor George H.W. Bush developed a similar two-faced style: half patrician/Connecticut Yankee, half Texas oilman, Bush I maintained the simmering white coalition of Republicans on a wobbly bridge located between the gentility of Wall Street and the new right ferocity of his political gunslinger Lee Atwater, who became famous for the Willie Horton political ads (on behalf of Bush) and the "white hands" ads (on behalf of reactionary North Carolina Senator Jesse Helms). These race-baiting maneuvers stoked white fears of black crime, affirmative action, and the like.

In the 1990s the nation experienced a Democratic Party version of the same balancing act. The brilliant but troubled Bill Clinton, dubbed by Toni Morrison (no doubt to her later regret) "America's first black president," cultivated the black community effectively and understood the depths of southern racism better than any of his predecessors. Ever. A fabled policy wonk, former Rhodes scholar, and preternaturally talented politician, Clinton's chosen mission was to *centrify* the Democratic Party. The way he did that was by curtailing the influence of the black movement and the new social movements. Many movement veterans, choosing to take the moderate "entrism" route to achieving power, had acquired real influence in the party. They had to make their peace with Clinton, who could do the blue-eyed soul thing very well, who never repudiated and indeed identified with the civil rights movement, and who had after all, returned the White House to Democratic occupants.

Clinton's later career mirrored his early rise to power. Though he was never a movement activist, he had been an opponent of the Vietnam War. He had worked for

Arkansas Senator J. William Fulbright and had run (with Hillary) McGovern's 1972 campaign in Texas. Elected Governor of Arkansas at the age of 32, he had no problem playing a double game: he could be Bubba and a good ole boy when the occasion demanded it, and talk Southern Baptist when he needed to. To win the Democratic nomination in 1992, he spanked a symbolic negro, Sistah Souljah (Lisa Williamson).[18] Soon after taking office, he threw his friend the voting rights scholar, Lani Guinier, under the bus; he was unwilling to defend Guinier's nomination for the post of Assistant Attorney General for Civil Rights, notably distancing himself from her criticism of the racial gerrymandering taking place in the South.[19]

A third black woman to be repudiated by Clinton was Marion Wright Edelman, who was jettisoned in connection with the greatest racial injustice perpetrated by his administration: its abandonment of the Aid to Families with Dependent Children program (AFDC, commonly known as "welfare") in 1996. Clinton campaigned for reelection on a promise to "end welfare as we know it." He set his sights on AFDC. The program had evolved out of the New Deal Social Security Act of 1935, slowly developing over the decades into its Great Society version, which after years of exclusion and continuous neglect was finally extended to blacks and other people of color (Quadagno 1994). AFDC remained punitive and was subject to constant right-wing stigma,[20] but it stood in sharp contrast to the 1935 law, which had been crafted by Dixiecrats to exclude black recipients, in provisions FDR had never questioned. Clinton's proposal substituted for AFDC the much more punitive Personal Responsibility and Work Opportunity Act (PWORA).[21] PWORA limited cash payments (renamed Temporary Assistance to Needy Families—TANF) and attached them to work requirements, often at below-minimum wage levels. The attack on AFDC was a significant concession to neoliberal market-oriented ideology (Block et al., 1987). In abandoning public assistance, Clinton took a page from Reagan's playbook; as early as 1982 Reagan had proposed "devolution" as a way to limit the federal government's powers of market regulation and countercyclical economic policy-making. Reagan had argued that welfare provision should be a state responsibility, not a federal one.[22]

Clinton embraced a great deal of neoliberal ideology beyond the attack on welfare. By the time he took office, the influence of the 1960s movements was receding in memory, though there was still plenty of racial discontent to go around. The Los Angeles race riots that occurred during the 1992 campaign—after the police officers who had savagely beaten Rodney King were acquitted in a rigged trial—reminded the nation that the racial cauldron continued to bubble; but they drew only ritual condemnations from candidates Bush I and Clinton (and no notice to speak of from potential spoiler Ross Perot). Though police beatings and killings continued at a normal pace, the riots proved to be a one-off affair that was quickly forgotten. South Central eventually cooled down; most of the rioters were Latin@s; there were almost as many white arrests as black ones (Rutten 1992).

Clinton worked in small and largely symbolic ways to "bridge the racial divide," as suggested by his sometime advisor William J. Wilson. This meant ceaseless promotion of the "one America" argument, an attempt to shift attention from race to class. Nothing epitomized this symbolic approach better than "The President's National Conversation on Race," described by radical critics as "the politics of yakkety-yak."[23]

The Clinton years reiterated the Carter presidency racially, and bridged between the Reagan and Obama years in terms of neoliberalism. To be sure, Clinton deserves some credit. Despite the Democrats' maneuvering and rebranding, and notwithstanding ferocious right-wing hostility to Clinton, the 1990s were a decade of relative racial peace and prosperity. It helped that this was a period of spirited economic growth, driven by the rise of Silicon Valley, the internet revolution, and transformations wrought by these "postindustrial" technological events in both the U.S. and world economies.[24] During the 1990s, the black and Latin@ shares of the national income distribution rose slightly; black and Latin@ unemployment rates were cut in half: The black rate fell from 14.2 percent in 1992 to 7.3 percent in 2000; Latin@ unemployment dropped from 11.8 percent in 1991 to 5.0 percent in 2000 (U.S. Department of Labor 1995, 2001). The poverty rate also fell dramatically (U.S. Census Bureau 2001, 18).

Some of Clinton's economic policies were attempts to accommodate the neoliberal agenda initially proposed under Reagan. At times his maneuvers were creative and even relatively egalitarian. For example, he significantly increased support for the working poor through the Earned Income Tax Credit (EITC), and made additional federal commitments to low-income housing, nutrition, health, and education. The EITC was an effort to support the working poor, and particularly those with children, through the tax system rather than welfare. Tax credits (or "refunds") were indexed to inflation, and could exceed the amount of taxes owed by as much as $5,800/family (in US$ 2012). This was a back-door approach to income subsidization, billed as a "market incentive" for the working poor. It did not at all help the millions of unemployed, who, of course, did not pay income taxes and could thus receive no tax credit, but it definitely helped the working poor.[25] EITC has operated steadily since its enactment in 1993; in 2012 the program distributed the whopping sum of $62 billion (U.S. Department of the Treasury 2013).

In other initiatives, Clinton's accommodations were more problematic. His global trade initiatives, which included support for the World Trade Organization and The North American Free Trade Agreement (NAFTA), both carried over from the Bush I period, would have regressive race (and class, and environmental) consequences in the United States. NAFTA undercut wages in both the United States and Mexico, spurring a corporate agribusiness invasion south of the border. Companies like Cargill and ConAgra took control of corn production, driving millions of Mexican@s out of their traditional *ejidos* (communal agricultural systems) and into the *maquilas* (corporate sweatshops) on the U.S. border. These policies also vastly ramped up migration to the United States.[26]

After the Republican victories in the 1994 elections and their promulgation of a fully neoliberal economic program (the "Contract with America"), Clinton was reduced to strategies of compromise; he made numerous concessions, not only in the area of welfare, which probably had the most visible and direct negative impact on people of color, but also in tax policy, domestic spending, and deregulation of corporations, especially in the financial arena (Meeropol 1998).

"George Bush doesn't care about black people," Kanye West famously said (West 2005).[27] Bush II had acquired a centrist reputation as Governor of Texas (Latin@-friendly, for instance). But as president he steered consistently to the right, and implemented a hardcore neoliberal agenda that outdid Reagan on several fronts. His failed attempt to privatize Social Security was of a piece with other privatization initiatives in education (No Child Left Behind) and health (Medicare drug expenditures). There is a pattern here: dismantlement of the welfare state. Bush argued that Social Security discriminates against blacks because they have a lower life expectancy (Kranish 2005); if their Social Security accounts could just be transformed into privately owned individual retirement accounts (IRAs), they could get at their money faster (presumably before they died young). Beyond that callousness, the privatization initiative represented a potentially endless windfall for Wall Street, a paradigmatic effort privately to appropriate public resources. The scheme died ignominiously.

Bush had been "born again" after a somewhat dissolute youth. His personal redemption narrative resonated with a populist and religious base that was heavily Southern Baptist. He was a creature of big oil and the Christian right. His electoral larceny was blessed by the Supreme Court in *Bush v. Gore* (2000), an anti-democratic decision foully grounded in civil rights law. In addition, without major racist chicanery in the 2000 Florida election, the presidential vote would not have even been close.[28] He was a "racial realist," ideologically speaking. Clarence Lusane describes this position as follows:

> In the post-civil rights movement era, racial realism appears to be not only logical but also progressive and modern. Legal segregation is over. High-profile minorities exist in every field and occupation. Public discourse on race is intolerant of racist slurs and insults. Indeed, the only reason race remains an issue is due to the continual harping by civil rights leaders who use the issue to justify their existence. The racial realists argue that as far as public policy is concerned, there is no need for any new legislation....
>
> (2006, 60)

Racial "realism," part of the developing "colorblind" racial project, could also trace its lineage back to neoconservatism. It still had traction with some high-profile minorities, the same ones Bush knew and appointed (Lusane 2006; Hattam and Lowndes 2013). It appealed to black conservatives as well.[29] As a religiously conversant Southern Baptist, Bush not only cemented the loyalty of millions of evangelical white Protestants, but some black and brown folk too. Sometimes he seemed to be speaking especially to the faithful. His use of the phrase "wonder-working power," for instance, referred to a hymn about salvation through Jesus: "There's power, power, wonder-working power in the blood of the Lamb." Carter and Clinton might have referred to their Baptist roots, but never preached the gospel from the bully pulpit.

Bush followed Clinton's lead in shunning the 2001 UN World Conference against Racism (WCAR), which occurred days before the 9/11/2001 attacks and thus was almost wiped out of history, especially U.S. history. Both men were scared off by the idea of confronting the very long history of U.S. complicity with racism and imperialism in a contemporary global forum. Afraid they would be asked for apologies and reparations for slavery, forced to admit their complicity with South African apartheid (the CIA had fingered then-underground Nelson Mandela for arrest in 1962 (Johnston 1990)),[30] or challenged about their ongoing support for Israeli policies, both U.S. presidents boycotted the conference in Durban.[31]

Bush carried out a series of actions that can best be described as ideological anti-anti-racism. One example among many was the purging and reconstitution of the U.S. Civil Rights Commission. Prompted by Abigail Thernstrom as well as other right-wing critics, he dismissed anti-racist scholar and activist Mary Frances Berry from her Chairship of the Commission—she had occupied that post since her appointment by Bush's father in 1992—elevating Thernstrom herself to Vice-Chair. Also dismissed was Cruz Reynoso, previously the first Chican@ Justice of the California Supreme Court. Bush's Justice Department, led first by John Ashcroft and then by the toxic Alberto Gonzalez, featured as its Assistant Attorney General for Civil Rights one Bradley Schlozman.[32] This new right warrior intervened in the *Gratz* (2003) and *Grutter* (2003) cases with *amicus curiae* briefs opposing affirmative action admissions policies at the University of Michigan.

Of all the problematic activities regarding race that Bush II undertook, the most notorious, and the most archetypal, was undoubtedly his blundering reaction to the inundation and destruction of the City of New Orleans by Hurricane Katrina in August–September 2005. The administration's preparation and response were lacking and at times oblivious, but its worst sins were not the errors of noncommission during and immediately after the storm, but rather its support for the urban reconfiguration (or should we say "urban renewal"), gentrification, and permanent reduction of the city's black population in the longer-run aftermath of the storm.

In what would prove to be a template for neoliberal programs of urban privatization and "structural adjustment" that would later be applied to ghettos and barrios across the country (Detroit, Philadelphia, Chicago, Milwaukee, and elsewhere), black New Orleans was stripped, not only of housing—poor black residents who had lost their homes were driven permanently from the city[33]—but also of its public schools, public hospitals, and public services. This was accomplished not by the federal government alone, but by a strategic alliance of business-oriented officials and agencies at all levels of government, working closely with large financial and real estate interests (Woods 2005; Lipsitz 2006; Marable and Clarke, eds. 2007; Klein 2008; Luft 2008; Bond-Graham, 2010).

No discussion of the Bush II years and race can dispense with the subject of Islamophobia. In the aftermath of the 9/11 attacks, this somewhat ill-defined set of beliefs and attitudes—racist, religiously chauvinistic, xenophobic, and with a long history in the United States—acquired a high degree of popular currency. Although Bush himself took pains to repeat the mantra "Islam means peace" several times, his administration defined itself by means of the "war on terror," both globally and domestically. The invasion of Iraq in March 2003 was opposed by millions of protestors, in a brief recapitulation of the anti-Vietnam War protests a generation before. But to no avail. U.S. war policy targeted Muslims, Arabs, and South Asians both around the world and domestically. In Iraq, Afghanistan, and elsewhere the administration reprised the worst offenses of imperial rule, embracing torture, kidnapping, assassination, and a range of other extrajudicial and unconstitutional practices (Jaffer and Singh 2009; Cole 2009.) In the United States, Middle Eastern Americans and South Asians (MEASAs), who were generally U.S. citizens and documented immigrants, were swept up in an extensive program of quasi-racial profiling (Love 2011).

Inclined to despotism both abroad and at home, the Bush forces mainly harmed black communities through neglect: Bush's dereliction of duty during and after the Katrina disaster of 2005 was the clearest instance of this. His abandonment of New Orleans's black population was part of a larger renunciation of interest in the well-being of the black community that involved local, state, and federal officials of all stripes, including some Democrats.

Bush's economic mismanagement and corruption led to the catastrophic economic meltdown of 2008, but to be fair, much of the groundwork for that crisis had been laid under Clinton. The subprime mortgage crisis that exploded under Bush II constituted the largest regressive racial redistribution of resources to have occurred in U.S. history. It impoverished black and brown families at unprecedented rates (as well as many white families). As a result, over a couple of years the already huge gap between black and white wealth *more than doubled*, as did the gap between whites and Latin@s. Millions of black and brown families were cast out of the "coping stratum," lower-middle-class status to which they had obtained limited access during the Clinton years (Reid and Laderman 2009; Rugh and Massey 2010; Hill 2011; Taylor et al. 2012).

A proper analysis of the racial dimensions of the subprime mortgage collapse in 2008 would exceed the scope of this book. Still, it is important to note that the "subprime" mortgage instrument links neoliberalism and race quite closely. During the 1990s and 2000s, under both Clinton and Bush II, extensive marketing campaigns targeted lower-income, and especially black and brown families, to consider home purchase. These programs were combined public and private ventures, pushed by both administrations, and facilitated by the parastatal home lending guarantor agencies Fannie Mae and Freddy Mac (Morgenstern and Rosner 2011). In addition, these measures were extensively lobbied for by the biggest banks: Citi, Goldman Sachs, and Wells Fargo among others.

"Steering" campaigns proliferated in retail home lending to lure borrowers of color to take out subprime and Alt-A mortgages—which were loan "products" of an "assigned risk" type, aimed at less credit-worthy borrowers. In numerous cases, however, the families pushed into the assigned risk pool had credit scores in the "prime" range, that is, equivalent to other, largely white, preferred borrowers. This steering occurred because fees and commissions earned by loan officers in the subprime range were higher than those earned through making prime mortgage loans. As in so many other patterns of racial discrimination, the visuality of black or brown racial identity, its corporeal, phenomic presence and immediacy, combined with greater vulnerability—perhaps economic, perhaps political, perhaps fear of profiling—facilitated unequal and damaging treatment at the hands of power-holders who were usually white. Consider "vote caging," or gerrymandering in segregated neighborhoods, or "stop and frisk " policing, as other examples of these same practices. Black or brown identity often offers the most convenient way to select subjects for the "racial tax" that is discrimination. Where does the Wells Fargo or Bank of America "greeter" send you when you enter a retail bank branch to inquire about a home mortgage?

At the Wall St. level, subprime loans were justified as "opportunity finance," a kind of affirmative action lending policy. Karen Ho (2009) quotes "an African American male managing director" at a major Wall St. investment firm:

> You may not have the best credit, but because Wall Street is out there creating markets for aggressive markets [sic], and you will pay a relatively higher rate, but it won't be as high of a rate if you—well, frankly, you would not have gotten a loan from the banks, so it is hard to even compare it to that. So the capital markets have made [borrowing money] much more efficient, so you just have to pay the cost of capital, which is exactly the way it should be.... Nobody should be denied credit within reasonable means....

"Of course," Ho adds, "as the devastation of the subprime crisis continues to unfold, Wall Street's experiment with broader access and 'opportunity finance' has shown itself to be more akin to the creation of a niche market for the purposes of exploiting the poor, creating a bubble real-estate market, and mortgaging the future" (Ho 2009, 299–300).[34] As Ho's final remark suggests, racial discrimination in the subprime mortgage crisis nearly pulled the Wall Street temple down on everybody, not just in downtown Manhattan but across the globe. Neoliberalism is premised on racism in many different ways.

Obama and Colorblindness

Is he a mere token, a shill for Wall Street? Or is he Neo, "the one"? If neither alternative is plausible, then we are in the realm of everyday 21st-century U.S. politics. Yet Barack Obama has transformed the U.S. presidency in ways we cannot yet fully appreciate. Obama is not simply the first nonwhite (that we know of) to occupy the office. He is the first to have lived in the global South, the first to be a direct descendent of colonized people, the first to have a genuine movement background. Consider: How many community meetings, how many movement events did Obama attend before entering electoral politics (Lizza 2007)?

None of that has meant that, two-thirds of the way through his entire time in office, Obama has acted in an appreciably different way from, say, Bill Clinton acted. Both men started their terms with congressional majorities, which they both lost after only two years. Of course, Clinton was hurt by scandal, but in Obama's case he IS the scandal: a black man in the White House. But what you are ain't what counts. It's what you do that counts.

Obama is certainly no more powerful than any of his predecessors; he is constrained as they were by the U.S. system of rule. Of course, he is more hemmed in than his predecessors by the U.S. racial regime, by structural racism. Indeed he confronts racism as no other president has ever done. No other president has experienced racism directly:

> Moreover, while my own upbringing hardly typifies the African American experience—and although, largely through luck and circumstance, I now occupy a position that insulates me from most of the bumps and bruises that the average black man must endure—I can recite the usual litany of petty slights that during my forty-five years have been directed my way: security guards tailing me as I shop in department stores, white couples who toss me their car keys as I stand outside a restaurant waiting for the valet, police cars pulling me over for no apparent reason. I know what it's like to have people tell me I can't do something because of my color, and I know the bitter swill of swallowed back anger. I know as well that Michelle and I must be continually vigilant against some of the debilitating story lines that our daughters may absorb—from TV and music and friends and the streets—about who the world thinks they are, and what the world imagines they should be.
>
> (Obama 2008b, 233)

No other president has ever felt the need to be racially vigilant in the way Obama has.

On the other hand, he has a "kill list." All presidents kill people, but Obama is the first to take charge systematically and publically of these egregious and unconstitutional uses of exceptional powers. In this he echoes Carl Schmitt, the Nazi political theorist, whose famous dictum is "Sovereign is he who decides on the exception" (2004 [1922]; see also Agamben 2005; Butler 2006). The drones, the surveillance, and the moralistic lectures about parenting and hip-hop culture that Obama likes to deliver only to blacks, all contradict the anti-racist legacy of the civil rights movement that arguably put him in office.

Obama himself largely deploys colorblind racial ideology, although he occasionally critiques it as well. Beneath this ostensibly postracial view the palpable and quite ubiquitous system of racial distinction and inequality remains entrenched, as Gramsci might say. Though modernized and "moderated," structural racism has been fortified, not undermined, by civil rights reform; Obama is not challenging it, at least not directly. Obama has not interceded for blacks against their greatest cumulative loss of wealth in U.S. history, the Great Recession of 2008. He has not explicitly criticized the glaring racial bias in the U.S. prison system. He has not intervened in conflicts over workers' rights—particularly in the public sector where many blacks and other people of color are concentrated. When massive demonstrations took place against public sector union-busting in Wisconsin in February and March of 2011, Obama was conspicuously silent.

In many ways Obama is reiterating the center-left neoliberalism first developed by Bill Clinton. David Theo Goldberg (2008, 42–44) has written of a "racial neo-liberalism" that is linked to political theories of absolutism, state sovereignty, and "exceptional" states (drawing on classical sources and once again echoing Schmitt). This modern state governs a *civil* society. It has an *outside* that is not civil. Its outside consists of slums, occupied territories, prisons, and the underground underworlds where fugitives, undocumented, poor, and homeless people live (Mbembe 2001; Davis 2006; Goffman 2009; Park 2013). "Those people" are dangerous, criminal, less "civilized," less deserving. Goldberg's "threat of race" centers on this frontier between these two social spaces, let us call them. They can neither be entirely joined nor separated. The border between them must be strenuously policed, an effort that requires electrified fences, Hellfire missiles, and extraordinary rendition. As Goldberg suggests, this is the form racism takes today: supervision and control of the racial "threat" in defense of an ever-more confined and restricted zone of prosperity: the ostensibly "civil" society of neoliberalism.

In its abandonment of the social, in its repudiation of the welfare state, in its passionate embrace of market rationality, neoliberalism gives its adherents permission to ignore the others, the darker nations, the poors, of the United States and the entire planet. Though harnessed to greed, neoliberalism is also about exercising unfettered power, both throughout the economy, the marketplace; and through the state. Workers, women, people of color, LGBT people too, are disposable in this world: They are somewhere on the spectrum that runs from human beings to "bare life."

Could Obama have changed that? Has he signed onto it? Could he have assisted many of those poors, at least many in the United States, through public employment programs perhaps? Such initiatives, descending from the New Deal, focused on impoverished people who today tend disproportionately to be people of color, were proposed by Obama's left-wing supporters, notably Van Jones. In 2009 Jones suggested that public employment be aimed at "green" jobs: everything from building solar energy farms on federal land to weatherstripping doors and windows in the ghetto.[35] Could Obama have subsidized the mortgages of low-income people—again, disproportionately black and brown, and many victimized by corrupt real-estate and financial practices in the run-up to the 2008 crash—the way he subsidized banks, insurance companies, Big Pharma, the auto industry, and out-on-a-limb hedge funds?

Parallel to those questions: Could Obama have disciplined the market, the way he has disciplined South Waziristan and the Occupy movement? (Well, maybe not by attacking Greenwich, Connecticut, or East Hampton with predator drones, but how about bringing criminal indictments against the Wall St. fraudsters?) In his first term he was assiduous in bailing out Wall Street, the "too big to fail" banks, big auto, and numerous other besieged fortresses of capital. His Affordable Care Act, claimed as his greatest accomplishment, is also a huge giveaway to the insurance companies and Big Pharma.

Obama's subsidization policies (and those of Ben Bernanke at the Federal Reserve Board) did not extend to Main Street. They did not lead to Martin Luther King, Jr. Boulevard. Small gestures were made to the foreclosable and underwater homeowner; (very) small mercies were directed at the millions of overburdened student debtors. Reorienting his policy choices in this direction would have been politically difficult and risky, but it would have undone some of the neoliberal moorings that tied this president not only to his predecessors, but also to the oligarchic and anti-democratic power elites (or if you prefer, "ruling class") that runs the country.

This is the dilemma of the Obama administration, made more severe, or more poignant, by the tremendous burdens, obligations (and yes, some thrills too) of being a black president. The Obama administration wants a strong state: It is at war, both overtly and covertly. The president has a "kill list."

Like a Roman emperor, President Obama is constantly putting down rebellion. Of course, all U.S. presidents have done this, always. The state demands loyalty; secrecy is extensive, and those who reveal state secrets are harshly punished. Meanwhile surveillance is effectively total. Center-left neoliberalism under Obama combines the politics of "permanent war" with those of modest redistribution: notably in respect to employment, wages, and tax policy. Obama inherited from Bush II not only the Great Recession of 2008, but also the permanent war state, the great Moloch with its limitless appetite for prisoners, its obsessive quest to discipline, punish, and surveil its citizens. Under Obama there have been reductions in the permanent war—the 2011 exit from Iraq; the promised 2014 near-exit from Afghanistan—but the use of unmanned drones firing Hellfire Missiles hardly qualifies as a policy of peace. Below a certain socioeconomic status level the United States is a police state, and Obama does not seem willing, or perhaps is unable, to do much about it.

Some have suggested that Obama is so constrained by the oligarchy, so hemmed in by the FIRE sector (Finance, Insurance, and Real Estate, to which we might add Big Pharma and Big Oil) that he is so beholden to the oligarchy's ownership of the U.S. political process (especially after the *Citizens United* case (2010), that he has to rely on a "long game" (Sullivan 2012; Lewis 2012). On this account, only a political strategy premised on demographic shifts and their impact on voting can avail the democratic and egalitarian needs of the majority of the (soon to be majority non-white) American people.

The idea here is that the state can play a guiding role in fostering "smart growth" and ameliorating inequality, mediating between the corporate overlords and the growing numbers of excluded masses: increasingly people of color, increasingly working-class or poor, increasingly female. On the anti-racist left, we often see, and complain about, Obama's deflection of race, his refusal to engage with race issues unless there is a huge outcry: "If I had a son, he would look a lot like Trayvon" (Thompson and Wilson 2012). "Another way of saying that is Trayvon Martin could have been me, thirty-five years ago" (Obama, July 19, 2013).[36] But from Obama's point of view, he is "normalizing race," leading the United States, and socializing the nervous/racist white masses, to the "majority-minority" demographic that is coming their way.

Obama's approach to immigration is a good example of his centrism; he has run the most comprehensive deportation regime of any administration in history, but at the same time supports immigration reform and a "path to citizenship." Thus Obama both immunizes himself from nativist attacks of the Republican right wing, and distinguishes himself (and the Democrats) from their opponents' virulent and racist anti-immigrant politics. For the small price of supporting similar reforms to those Bush II sought and was denied in 2007, Obama locks up three-quarters of the Latin@vote.

At best Obama's civil rights policy (civil rights not civil liberties) has been an incremental reversal of Bush II's. Although Obama has an earlier history of anti-racial profiling activity,[37] he has not developed any serious anti-poverty or criminal justice reform policies. As we write, ex-felon disenfranchisement deprives 5.3m Americans, disproportionately black and brown, almost all poor people, and, of course, mostly men, of the right to vote (Manza and Uggen 2006; Chung 2013), but this is an area that is politically risky to enter, especially for a neoliberal regime, however "moderate." Contrast this with immigration reform, which is supported by at least some major corporate interests, as well as by a majority of voters and most people of color.

As a black politician, Obama heads the modern-day version of an "entrist" cohort of officials of color, both elected and appointed, who are working within the state at various levels: electoral, administrative, national or local. On January 17, 2009, just before his first inauguration, the Obama campaign launched Organizing for America (OFA), a mass lobbying group, similar to MoveOn.org. Officially separate from the Democratic Party, OFA overlapped with the Obama campaign and, by 2013, had absorbed much of its campaign technology as well: its lists, the profound attention/research/surveillance it directs towards its base of millions of users/voters.

Notably, OFA does not directly mobilize low-income voters; it does not cross the digital divide, which is both a class divide and a race divide. Obama relies on his political positions, and on the truculence and racism of his opposition, to attract the support of lower-income voters of color, to increase their voting rates. Why do they come out for him when he delivers so little? Because he is black and because he is way better than the alternative. And many of them, as we have argued here, do not and cannot act politically; they have been demobilized by the system of "crime and punishment"; their racial identity places them outside civil society, half a century after the enactment of civil rights reforms, long after "the Great Transformation" promised an inclusive and egalitarian society, and once again failed to realize that promise.

Where's the (Tea) Party?

Neoliberal policies shrink the public sphere, and seek to privatize state resources, often precipitating state fiscal crisis in support of these ends. Tax revolt is a crucial component of right-wing populism that can link Wall St. and Main St. Who benefits from such initiatives? Neoliberalism increasingly pits public space and the civic commons against private space and privatized services. The suburbs are under pressure too, but their schools have not been repossessed as yet.[38] And the rich, the 1 percent, can staff their gated economic enclaves with undocumented immigrant gardeners and private security patrols. They can send their children to private schools. As the public sphere is devalued, democracy is weakened. Neoliberalism decrees school closures and the privatization of education at every level. It demands layoffs and assaults unions. It attacks workers in the public sector and forces government to reduce social services such as public health and transportation. At its worst it drives the public sector into insolvency. The City of Detroit declared bankruptcy on July 18, 2013; other cities such as Stockton, California, have done so as well.

These trends generate a massive, disenfranchised, urban, largely black and brown (yes there are some whites too) U.S. subaltern stratum, not only an underclass *á la* William Julius Wilson, but also a racially distinct melange: *the others.* Not just the subordinate, inegalitarian dimension of this group's collective identity carries weight here (the "sub" of subaltern); but also the "alterity" of the term. The growing subaltern have the potential for disruption, both political and in everyday life. They also hover on the margins of "bare life," experiencing the police state everyday: profiled, surveilled, "stopped and frisked." This growing stratum of U.S. society, "working poor," "on the run," fugitives and "clandestinos," prisoners and ex-felons (Newman 2000; Dow 2005; Goffman 2009; Park 2013), are aliens in the United States, whether they are citizens or not. Neoliberalism can render you homeless, useless, mentally or physically ill, a stranger in your own country.

A new trend on the right is a divided Republican Party. The GOP is in danger of incurring a cavernous split between the demographic imperative to move toward the political center and the demands of its narrowing base in the red states. Its strongest support is regionally confined: to the South, the intermountain West, and a few other pockets like Kansas. It is white, older, increasingly male, paranoid, and racist. Funded by a substantial sector of financial capital and in a major way by Big Oil, the Republican Party pledges its allegiance to neoliberal economics and to reactionary politics every chance it gets. The 1 percent (both Republican and Democrat) can still effectively buy elections and indeed governments: locally, state-wide, and regionally, not only in Dixie, but all through the country: Wisconsin, Pennsylvania, Michigan ... But Republican long-run prospects are shrinking in many of those politically contested states. Although the right-wing seems unlikely to organize a democratic (small d) voting majority, it has been more successful in organizing an obstructionist anti-democratic minority, based on gerrymandering at the state level, and of course on big money.

The Republican right wing may yet succeed in running out the clock on Obama's second term. It possesses many political and economic resources: the U.S. Supreme Court above all, but also the control of state legislatures, governors' mansions, and the House of Representatives. In the era of *Citizens United*, its oligarchs are able to buy legislators (and elections) extensively; we are living in a new gilded age. The right wing's power at the state level is also propped up by extensive gerrymandering. On top of all that, Republicans actively seek to prevent political action by various constituencies of color, youth, and low-income people (notably by restricting voting).[39] Their assaults on the franchise are conspicuously racialized: vote-caging, restricting voting hours, requiring photo IDs, prohibiting students from voting in their university/college area of residence (Piven et al. 2009). Yet it is difficult to see how a policy of obstructionism can indefinitely delay immigration reform, a position that has already consolidated the expanding Latin@ vote in the Democratic column. It is also unclear how the right wing's assault on abortion rights can help it with the women's vote, which is also trending Democratic.

The emergence in 2009 of the various political organizations and fractions that collectively became known as the *Tea Party* took political analysts by surprise. It was widely assumed that the outcome of the 2008 Presidential contest—Barack Obama's victory *and* John McCain's defeat—signaled that conservatism was in retreat and had perhaps run its course after decades of popular political support. What was clearly unanticipated was the scope of the grassroots mobilization that moved American conservatism further to the right and, as Lawrence Rosenthal and Christine Trost argue, "resurrected themes that mainstream conservatism had rejected as too radical forty years earlier" (Rosenthal and Trost 2012, 3). Tea Party activists advance a fundamentalist reading of the U.S. Constitution to argue for "states' rights" in opposition to what is perceived to be an increasingly bloated and illegitimate federal government under the sway of liberal ideology. At its extreme, such a perspective informs and undergirds strategic doctrines such as nullification, the effort by states to overturn laws. The Tea Party is a right-wing populist movement that couples its incoherent reading of the Constitution with the neoliberal ideology of free-market absolutism.

Avoiding or taking what can be considered a libertarian view on social issues (notably same-sex marriage),[40] Tea Party activists want to maintain a sustained focus on fiscal policy and the oppressiveness of "big government." As Tea Party-backed U.S. Senator Rand Paul has stated, "The Tea Party doesn't see politics in black and white, but black and red" (quoted in Lowndes 2012, 159).

Given this perspective, in what ways can the Tea Party movement be read and understood as a racial project? First, Tea Party activists and supporters were mobilized not only by the financial collapse of 2008 and the federal response to it, but equally by the election of Obama. The outrage expressed over bank bailouts and massive loans to automakers, entities supposedly "too big to fail," was matched by fears of the "other" who came to occupy the Oval Office. Five of the six national Tea Party organizations have "birthers," those who assert that Obama is not a natural born U.S. citizen and therefore cannot legally be president, in their leadership ranks (Lowndes 2012, 157). Obama's universally recognized and self-affirmed American blackness overlaps with his "foreignness"—his Kenyan father, his Indonesian stepfather, his childhood in Jakarta and even Honolulu. He enacts the unconscious racist nightmares of much of the American right (and a few in the American left as well). It is small wonder that as late as April 2011, 45 percent of Tea Party members still believed that Obama was not born in the United States (cited in Rosenthal and Trost 2012, 9). Tea Party supporters suggest that Obama does not share the values that most Americans live by and that he does not understand the problems of people like themselves (Zernike and Thee-Brenan 2010). Tea Party supporters were more likely (25 percent vs. 11 percent of all survey respondents) to think that the Obama administration "favors blacks over whites," and over half of supporters (52 percent compared to 28 percent of all survey respondents) believed that in recent years "too much has been made of the problems facing black people."[41]

The core constituency of the Tea Party consists of older, middle-class whites who fear the demographic change around them and the loss of rights, privileges, and resources that such change forebodes:

> Tea Partiers see themselves as the "real Americans" who have worked hard all their lives and earned everything they have. They view liberals, unions, and often minorities, as forces trying to take away what they possess and redistribute it to the "undeserving", the poor who haven't worked hard.
>
> (Rosenthal 2013)

While the Tea Party movement has attempted to distance itself from overt expressions of racism, the racial attitudes of many Tea Party supporters are disturbing. Tea Party supporters believe blacks and Latin@s to be less intelligent, less hardworking, and less trustworthy than whites (Parker 2009). In a notorious incident on March 19, 2009, black Congressional Representatives André Caron, Emanuel Cleaver, and John Lewis were subject to racial epithets and spat upon by Tea Partiers protesting the passage of federal healthcare reform. In July 2010, the NAACP publicly condemned "rampant racism" in the Tea Party movement, and subsequently issued a report, *Tea Party Nationalism*, that dismissed the "non-racial" claims of the movement and surveyed the links between Tea Party organizations and explicitly white supremacist groups:

> The result of this study contravenes many of the Tea Parties' self-invented myths, particularly their supposedly sole concentration on budget deficits, taxes and the power of the federal government. Instead, this report found Tea Party ranks to be permeated with concerns about race and national identity and other so-called social issues. In these ranks, an abiding obsession with Barack Obama's birth certificate is often a stand-in for the belief that the first black president of the United States is not a "real American."
>
> (Burghart and Zeskin 2010)

The Tea Party movement resembles the new right movement of the 1970s and 1980s (Perlstein 2013). Both are hostile to a perceived liberal cultural elite that has imposed its will on the majority of Americans and has rallied the support of the poor, welfare recipients, people of color, and other "marginal" groups to redistribute the hard-earned resources of the "producer" class. Both right-wing movements have relied on "coded" racial language and politics. The Tea Party, however, operates under conditions of colorblind hegemony, so its activists try to avoid making reference to race.[42] Many recent studies point out that Tea Partiers are explicitly and often self-consciously aware of being white in an increasingly racially diverse country. They frequently label welfare recipients and "illegal immigrants" as intruders and parasites (Democracy Corps 2013).

What has shifted since the earlier years of the racial reaction (discussed in Chapter 7) is a more sustained focus on the state itself. As Joseph Lowndes notes,

> In the populist imagination of the modern right forged in the 1960s and 1970s, hardworking white Americans were threatened by blacks below and their liberal elite allies above. The current absence of a black freedom movement, along with the election of a black president, has shifted white populist anger almost entirely upward toward the state itself.
>
> (2012, 152–153)

Lawrence Rosenthal argues,

> The election of a black president and the assumption of power by the liberal Democratic Party have fundamentally transformed the vise-like effect of such classical populist formulations as producerism. Now, both the liberal elite and their client base are on top. The experience is less one of being squeezed from top and bottom, but rather one of being flattened from above.
>
> (Rosenthal 2013, 5)

The Tea Party's anti-statist politics is indeed a racial project. It appeals to whites who benefited from the New Deal and who consider themselves the "real Americans," who see their social status as threatened by the "undeserving poor," and who worry about the "stranger (of color) at the door." Most of these themes are generally not publicly articulated, but now and then, such sentiments seep out. In June 2012, a board member of the Ozark Tea Party made a speech at their annual rally with the following joke:

> A black kid asks his mom, "Mama, what's a democracy?"
>
> "Well, son, that be when white folks work every day so us po' folks can get all our benefits."
>
> "But mama, don't the white folk get mad about that?"
>
> "They sho do, son. They sho do. And that's called racism."[43]

The *demographic shift* of the U.S. population to a "majority-minority" pattern is a politically unprecedented situation. Reforms in 1965 and 1986 removed some of the overtly racist components of the immigration laws[44] that had shaped U.S. policy since the 1920s, and thereby set off enormous shifts in the racial composition of the U.S. population. The emerging "majority-minority" demographic will mean that no single racially defined group, including those considered white, will be a majority in the country. Although we are still a few decades away from the emergence of that pattern nationally, major regions and cities are already majority-minority: California became a M-M state in 2000; New Mexico attained M-M status in 2002; Texas became M-M in 2005; and Hawaii and the District of Columbia have long been M-M (U.S. Bureau of the Census 2007). Arizona, Florida, New York, Nevada, New Jersey, and Maryland are projected to lose their white majorities around 2025. The three largest cities—New York, Los Angeles, and Chicago—are now M-M. Across the entire country, whites are poised to become one racially defined minority group among others, probably at some point in the middle of this century.[45]

Immigration dynamics are shaping both the divisions in the Republican Party and the deeper demographic shifts we have mentioned. Demography is not destiny, but anti-immigrant hostility—inevitably racist—is one of the most venerable traditions in U.S. politics (Ngai 2005; Chavez 2013 [2008]; Schrag 2010). Nativism today confronts obstacles that did not exist in the past. In contrast to the sweeping anti-immigrant upsurges of yore (Higham 2002 [1955]), today a significant immigrant rights movement exists in the United States; this is unprecedented in U.S. history. Before the rise of the modern civil rights movement, exhortations on behalf of "Anglo-conformity" (Gordon 1964) were taken quite seriously. Virulent nativist assaults such as the anti-Irish movements of the 1840s (the American Native party or "Know-Nothings"), the 1870s and 1890s assaults on west coast Asian communities (Saxton 1971; Pfaelzer 2008), and the 1930s mass deportations of Mexican@s from Southern California (Balderrama and Rodríguez 2006 [1995]) would prove considerably harder to stage today. The outcome of present-day immigration struggles is dependent on a lot of political contention at the local, national, and global levels, but pressures for inclusion unquestionably have greater resonance today than ever before.[46]

Immigration dynamics have not only reshaped racial demography and race politics in the past half-century; they have reshaped American society (de Genova, ed. 2006). This is evident in the deep transformations of the roles of Asians and Latin@s. Many Asian immigrants arrived after 1965, but poor and unskilled Asians were discouraged from coming after 1990. Today a bifurcated Asian American class pattern exists, largely structured by immigration policies. In much of Asian America today, immigrants and their descendants constitute a professional class, while significant working-class and impoverished sectors remain. Asian migration patterns have been tied since 1900 to American imperial practices on the Pacific Rim and beyond. Even liberal whites underestimated how race-neutral immigration rules, coupled with state practices in Asia to expand educational opportunities, resulted in one of the most significant migrations of skilled people from one region to another in world history.

The racialization of Latin@s has also shifted dramatically. Policies of immigration control and repression (policing, deportation, and incarceration) have divided and eroded public culture, notably in the Southwest but nationally as well. The policing and militarization of the border, the extension of immigration surveillance and repression into the interior (Coleman 2007), combined with the continuing recruitment of immigrant labor at all strata of the workforce, have steadily transformed U.S. society. The U.S.–Mexico border was until recently a low-waged, free labor market, with minimal state regulation. It is now a 2000 mile-long crime scene, where trafficking and vigilantism operate symbiotically with official nativism.[47]

Meanwhile not just the Obama presidency, but a host of recent developments have demonstrated the growing isolation and marginalization of the Republican Party. It has become the white people's party, driven in large measure by racial, religious, and gender/sexuality-based resentment.[48] As the Republican Party locks in its white identity, and as the demographic increase of the U.S. population of color continues, it is hard to avoid the impression that after what seemed like an endless reactionary march, the U.S. electoral system will have to move again toward the left. In the short term, though, there are undoubtedly still political gains to be made through immigrant-bashing, law-and-order fearmongering, use of racial "code words," and above all, appeals to be colorblind.

Notes

1. On the Powell memo, see Phillips-Fein 2010, 150–165; Harvey 2004, 43–44. Out of Powell's memo came these right-wing think tanks: Cato, Heritage, and the American Enterprise Institute, as well as numerous others. Some of these organizations had been around for years already, but had not seen themselves as particularly activist. Others were founded in response to business class demands (Stefancic and Delgado 1996; Woodward 2008). Powell was appointed to the Supreme Court by Nixon in 1973, two years after circulating the memo. Though he was a genteel segregationist for most of his life, by the 1970s he had become a racial centrist, whose position in the 1978 *Bakke* case shaped affirmative action policy for more than 20 years.
2. Reagan's victory was also helped by the debacle of the Iranian hostage crisis and Carter's failed rescue attempt, known as Operation Eagle Claw.
3. While Reagan's rise predated Prop. 13, the measure's popular base in California was congruent with his base as governor. Though Reagan never pledged not to raise taxes—and in fact did so several times as president—he remained an icon of anti-welfare statism.
4. In channeling resentment against the poor and especially against people of color, authoritarian populist ideology often neglects those *rentiers* entirely; in contemporary Republican Party parlance (and sometimes in Democratic Party discourse as well) they become the "job-creators," for example. It was not always thus. The Jeffersonian tradition was hostile to banks; agrarians from Andrew Jackson to William Jennings Bryan have shared these views. In the 1870s, 1890s, and 1930s substantial class resentments against the "trusts" and banks sometimes outweighed anti-black and anti-immigrant currents, though this was not

the usual pattern. See Steinbeck 1939, Chapter 22; Kazin 1995; Saxton 2003 [1990]. In the wake of the Great Recession of 2008, hostility to banks and the "too big to fail" formula echoed the producerist sentiments of earlier times. The "we are the 99%" formula of the Occupy movement has its origins in this Jeffersonian hostility to banks and *rentier* interests. (Sanders 2008; Graeber 2012.)

5. The continuities are unmistakable between this rap of a quarter-century ago and the right-wing rhetoric of today. Consider Republican presidential candidate Mitt Romney's famous remarks that were leaked to the press during the 2012 campaign:

   > Romney: There are 47 percent of the people who will vote for the president no matter what. All right, there are 47 percent who are with him, who are dependent upon government, who believe that they are victims, who believe that government has a responsibility to care for them, who believe that they are entitled to health care, to food, to housing, to you name it. That that's an entitlement. And the government should give it to them. And they will vote for this president no matter what. And I mean, the president starts off with 48, 49, 48—he starts off with a huge number. These are people who pay no income tax. Forty-seven percent of Americans pay no income tax. So our message of low taxes doesn't connect. And he'll be out there talking about tax cuts for the rich. I mean that's what they sell every four years. And so my job is not to worry about those people—I'll never convince them that they should take personal responsibility and care for their lives. What I have to do is convince the 5 to 10 percent in the center that are independents that are thoughtful, that look at voting one way or the other depending upon in some cases emotion, whether they like the guy or not, what it looks like. I mean, when you ask those people … we do all these polls—I find it amazing—we poll all these people, see where you stand on the polls, but 45 percent of the people will go with a Republican, and 48 or 4 … [Recording stops.] (Mother Jones Newsteam 2012)

6. The United States had been actively involved in organizing the Chilean coup of September 11, 1973. As Secretary of State Henry Kissinger said at the time, "I don't see why we need to stand by and watch a country go communist due to the irresponsibility of its people. The issues are much too important for the Chilean voters to be left to decide for themselves" (Hersh 1983, 265; see also Marchetti and Marks 1974; Klein 2008).
7. The beat goes on today: as we write these words, surveillance and punishment are more with us than ever. The undeclared war in Vietnam has been recapitulated in the U.S. occupations of Iraq and Afghanistan, and in the undeclared "war on terror." Numerous U.S. government agencies have targeted Americans of Middle Eastern and South Asian (MEASA) descent for roundups and harassment. Such policies, repressive and Islamophobic, have distinctive racist overtones; they mirror broadly observable prejudices in U.S. civil society. The U.S. government, it has recently been revealed, is monitoring *all* telephone, email, and web traffic worldwide. These warrantless searches were instituted under Bush II and ramped up under Obama. J. Edgar Hoover and his boys had nothing on these guys.
8. Of course, the term had been in circulation since Justice Harlan's (mendacious) claim in his *Plessy* dissent that "Our Constitution is color-blind, and neither knows nor tolerates classes among citizens" (Gotanda 1996).

9. In "massive resistance" we can see an early glimmer of neoliberalism's overlap with white supremacy, in the confluence between privatization and the "right" to discriminate.
10. Lee Atwater (1951–1991) was Bush I's campaign manager and subsequently Chairman of the Republican National Committee. He was also a high-up official in the Reagan campaign and mentor to Bush II guru Karl Rove. Atwater also had a side career as a rhythm and blues guitar player, releasing an album with—wait for this—Isaac Hayes, Chuck Jackson, B.B. King, Sam Moore, Billy Preston, Arletta Nightingale, Carla Thomas, and others. These stars contributed to different tracks on the record (Lee Atwater and the Red Hot and Blue Band 2001). On his deathbed at the age of 40, Atwater "apologized" (whatever that means) to the candidates he had race-baited: Michael Dukakis, Harvey Gantt, and Tom Turnipseed. Atwater reset the standard for race-baiting in "post-civil rights" era electoral politics.
11. Carbado and Harris note the persistent conflation between "is" claims and "should" claims in respect to racism, the "tendency both in law and public discourse to treat normative claims about race as empirical ones. Put another way, the dominant analytical framework treats 'should' or 'ought' as 'is' or 'does'" (2008, 28). In other words, the normative idea (itself quite problematic) that race "should" not play a role in, say, college admissions decisions often slips easily into the claim that it can be disregarded in admissions procedures. Many other examples can be cited.
12. In his opinion in the *Bakke* case (1978), Justice Blackmun attempted to tackle this issue. He asked whether it was possible to overcome racial discrimination by simply ignoring race, and answered that question fairly resoundingly in the negative: "I suspect that it would be impossible to arrange an affirmative-action program in a racially neutral way and have it successful. To ask that this be so is to demand the impossible. In order to get beyond racism, we must first take account of race. There is no other way. And in order to treat some persons equally, we must treat them differently. We cannot—we dare not—let the Equal Protection Clause perpetuate racial supremacy" (U.S. Supreme Court 1978).
13. Various full employment schemes were mooted under the Great Society's influence, for example the Humphrey-Hawkins Act. Probably the most serious proposal—A. Philip Randolph and Bayard Rustin's "Freedom Budget"—had its origins in the civil rights movement (Le Blanc and Yates 2013; Rustin 2003 [1965], 197–201).
14. "Long Road Out of Eden" is the title of an Eagles track and eponymous album (Eagles 2007).
15. In 1976 Carter had received a majority of evangelical votes over Ford. In the mid-1970s the Christian right was still in its formative stages, and the Southern Baptist Convention was being drawn into politics by right-wing religious movements and televangelists; these were reacting to the Warren Court's ban on prayer in the public schools and to the new reality of *Roe v. Wade.* Mobilized by the Christian Coalition and their local preacher, they went for Carter, the first of their kind ever to capture the White House, but their hearts were on the right, to which they would return with Reagan and where they would remain. Carter was an evangelical Southern Baptist, but not a fundamentalist. A modern liberal and technocrat, his religious views had been influenced by Reinhold Niebuhr. He was a lay preacher and taught Sunday school in the rural community where his family were planters.
16. Reagan was strategic enough, however, to make symbolic concessions on racial issues. He signed a bill to establish a Martin Luther King, Jr. commemorative national holiday (he had opposed this at first), and agreed after prolonged delays to the Civil Liberties Act of

1988, which granted reparations and redress to the Japanese American community for their barbarous treatment during World War II.

17. Before becoming president, Reagan had opposed both the 1964 Civil Rights Act and the 1965 Voting Rights Act. As president, he strongly supported the apartheid government in South Africa. His Justice Department urged over 50 states, counties, and cities to modify their affirmative action plans "voluntarily," removing numerical goals and quotas. It was hinted that failure to comply "voluntarily" might result in court action. Reagan also pioneered efforts to eliminate government record-keeping on race. In March 1985, the Office of Management and Budget ordered the Department of Housing and Urban Development and the Veterans Administration to stop tracking the racial and ethnic characteristics of Americans who received benefits from these two agencies. These policies were recommended by the Heritage Foundation, a leading right-wing think tank, in its "Agenda 83" report (Holwill, ed. 1983).
18. In the 1992 presidential campaign—with Los Angeles burning in the background—Bill Clinton seized upon some anti-white remarks by hip-hop activist and author Sister Souljah to repudiate "black racism," and not coincidentally to challenge Jesse Jackson, then the nation's leading black politician. Clinton's comments were presented in a speech before Jackson's organization, the National Rainbow Coalition. The net effect of the incident was to reassure centrist white voters that Clinton could "stand up" to the black and left base of the Democratic Party.
19. Lani Guinier, the first black woman ever to receive tenure at Harvard Law School, had been a classmate of Bill and Hillary Clinton at Yale Law School in the 1970s. An authority on voting rights, Guinier was nominated in April 1993 for the position of Assistant Attorney General for Civil Rights, the administration's highest civil rights-oriented position. The nomination came under severe attack from the new right, notably in respect to the issue of affirmative action (Guinier was labeled as a "quota queen," a notably racist and sexist phrase), but also because she had written extensively about racial gerrymandering. Clinton failed to defend his nominee, who was also abandoned by such liberal Democrats as Edward Kennedy. After a prolonged period of savaging of Guinier's distinguished record, her nomination was withdrawn in June 1993. See Guinier 1995.
20. In 1966 Frances Fox Piven and Richard A. Cloward published an article in *The Nation* titled "The Weight of the Poor: A Strategy to End Poverty" (Piven and Cloward 2010 [1966]). Their proposal was to organize as many poor people as possible to apply for AFDC, since many more qualified than were enrolled and receiving cash payments. This intervention—a potentially effective strategy for distributing large quantities of money to the poor, helped spark the National Welfare Rights movement and drew howls of anger from right-wing groups.
21. A veteran of SNCC, the Mississippi Freedom Summer Campaign of 1964, and MLK Jr's Poor People's March on Washington of 1968, Marian Wright Edelman was the first black woman admitted to the practice of law in the State of Mississippi. She founded the Children's Defense Fund in 1973; Hillary Clinton was an active ally and board member of the CDF. Edelman fiercely criticized the new PWORA/TANF program as far more punitive and onerous, and denounced her former allies for punishing poor children as an electoral strategy. Her husband Peter Edelman resigned from his position as an Assistant Secretary in the Department of Health and Human Services in protest of Clinton's welfare policy (Edelman 1997). Clinton later abandoned Peter Edelman *again* after his proposed

appointment to the United States Court of Appeals for the District of Columbia Circuit, the second-most important court in the country, ran into opposition in the Senate.

22. Reagan's "New Federalism" was announced in his 1982 State of the Union address (Reagan 1982).
23. The official title of the effort, launched late in Clinton's second term on June 14, 1997, was "One America in the 21st Century: The President's Initiative on Race." The deprecatory remarks may be found in Reed 1997b; Steinberg 2007.
24. The rise of Silicon Valley was related to the new social movements of the 1960s, and thus to the black movement, in ways that are not generally recognized. See Markoff 2005.
25. Since earned-income credits vary with the number of children per family, reproducing as a tax expenditure what used to be a direct outlay. Tax policy is family policy! Tax policy is racial policy!
26. We do not have space here to address NAFTA and the WTO adequately. These policies should be seen as reiterations of long-established patterns of mass low-waged labor recruitment and imperial economic management on a global scale. Those patterns, in turn, are deeply structured by racial dominance and subjection. On NAFTA see Hing 2010.
27. Bush later said in his memoir *Decision Points* that being called a racist was the thing that hurt him most in his entire presidency.
28. For example, the use of "vote-caging" in the Florida registration process. See Piven et al. 2009.
29. Some key racial realists were Abigail Thernstrom, Shelby Steele, John McWhorter, and Tamar Jacoby, intellectuals on the political right. There were centrist and even left-wing racial realists too, sometimes people who abhorred Bush II on other grounds, but bought into one or another version of colorblindness (Kahlenberg 1997).
30. The WCAR had positive effects elsewhere, notably in Brazil. See Htun 2004.
31. One of the present authors was a participant at Durban and took part in the some of the preparations for the WCAR as well. Yes, there were expressions of anti-Semitism at the Conference, as well as critical responses to it. There were also numerous critiques of governments around the world, including South Africa itself, for various racist practices. In a highly charged setting, this was inevitable, and not an acceptable reason for boycotting a meeting of this importance.
32. Schlozman was a right-wing lawyer who had dedicated his work to voter suppression, among a range of other anti-anti-racist activities. From within the department, he led an effort to politically influence the selection and retention of U.S. attorneys around the county. He also pursued the anti-poverty organization ACORN on trumped-up voting fraud allegations and succeeded in destroying it. Schlozman was reprimanded after a Congressional investigation found he had reorganized the staff of his division along ideological grounds. See U.S. Department of Justice 2008.
33. Public housing that had survived the storm and was fit for reoccupation—solid brick apartment buildings that had mostly been built under the New Deal in the 1930s and were now nearly 100 percent black-occupied—were demolished on the order of the Federal Housing Administration.
34. Ho has a lot to say about racism and sexism in those Wall St. highrises too. For example, she points to the pressures women analysts feel not to wear comfortable shoes or sneakers on their way to work, changing to dressier shoes in the office; to do so would indicate that

they are commuting, rather than living close by the financial district, and hence that they are of lower status. Black analysts feel pressure not to associate with each other at work, even if they are friends: "Like one of the guys from finance, he just happened to be a friend, but anytime that we are in wordprocessing at the same time and people see us, they are like 'What's going on with you two?'" (Ho 2009, 117, 119). For similar stories about high-end law firms, see Carbado and Gulati 2013.

35. Jones was a movement activist and intellectual briefly employed as the White House Council on Environmental Quality's Special Advisor for Green Jobs. A policy wonk with a Yale law degree, he was also the founder of two movement organizations: the Ella Baker Center for Human Rights, and Green for All. He was booted fairly rapidly when his left-wing past became embarrassing to Obama. See Jones 2008, 2012.
36. In what became a national scandal, Trayvon Martin, a 17-year-old black youth walking in a largely white Florida neighborhood, was shot and killed by a "neighborhood watch" vigilante in 2011.
37. In 2000 Obama, then an Illinois state senator, sponsored and enacted Senate Bill 1324, a bill that required police to gather and report data about the race and ethnicity of all motorists stopped for moving violations. Although this measure only dealt with profiling in a partial way—only law enforcement profiling, only drivers, only data collection—it nevertheless did acknowledge the injustice of the practice.
38. Some suburban and exurban areas, like the Inland Empire of Southern California, experienced substantial economic downturns in the post 2008 crash. Along with urban neighborhoods, they often face virtual extortion by large retail employers—especially WalMart—that seek to replace outsourced industrial employment with low-income, no-benefit (and obviously non-union) jobs. For detailed analysis of the neighborhood cleavages this can involve, see Dawson 2011, 92–135.
39. In *Shelby County v. Holder* (2013), the Supreme Court struck down Section 4 of the Voting Rights Act, which had required voting districts with a history of racial discrimination to obtain permission from the Justice Department before implementing shifts in electoral practices and voting requirements. The removal of this part of the law, a key 1965 achievement of the civil rights movement, was followed virtually instantaneously by the imposition of restrictive voting procedures, not only in the South but in such places as Pennsylvania and Michigan, where Republicans control both the legislature and the governorship.
40. Democracy Corps (co-founded by James Carville and Stan Greenberg) found that when asked about gay marriage, Tea Party Republicans were apt to say "who cares" or "it's not the government's business" (Democracy Corps 2013).
41. New York Times/CBS News Poll: National Survey of Tea Party Supporters, April 5–10; http://s3.amazonaws.com/nytdocs/docs/312/312.pdf
42. Inevitably, racist attitudes and actions pop up from within the Tea Party ranks:

    > In quick succession in one week's time, a protestor waves a sign "bye bye black sheep" and a small chorus chimes in and puts it to the popular song ditty of "Bye, Bye, Blackbird" in front of Desert Vista High School in Phoenix where President Obama spoke about housing finance reform. Hundreds of attendees at a Missouri state fair roared with laughter and applause at a rodeo clown's mocking Obama. In Orlando, a knot of protestors waved racially insulting signs including "Kenyan Go Home" at Obama's motorcade. (Hutchinson 2013)

43. Tea Party leaders in Arkansas later distanced themselves from the remarks when a newspaper contacted them for comment, and the broad member in question subsequently said she would stop using what she said was an "ice-breaker" joke in her speech (Celock 2012).
44. Although not free of conflict—sometimes of the black vs. brown variety, the civil rights connection to immigrant rights remains strong—most notably embodied in the legacy of the Immigration and Nationality Act of 1965, which was a civil rights bill in its own right and a priority of the Kennedys.
45. Population projections are notoriously iffy. In 2004 the U.S. Bureau estimated that in 2050 the proportion of the U.S. population designated as "Whites, non-Hispanic" would represent 50.1 percent of the total U.S. population (U.S. Bureau of the Census 2004).
46. Immigration reform has huge consequences for voting patterns, especially over the medium and long term; this has been clear in respect to Latin@ voting patterns since 1994, when Latin@ voters in California, who had been seen as a swing constituency, were pushed into the Democratic Party column as a result of California Governor Pete Wilson's promotion of Proposition 187 (Ono and Sloop 2002; Jacobson 2008; Wroe 2008; HoSang 2010). Of course, catastrophic events on the order of the 9/11 tragedy are always possible—such tragedies remain susceptible to racialization and nativism. In the past, the United States has often recurred to "domestic foreign policy" in response to political threats. In other words, the country has tended to address major social conflicts (and sometimes international ones) by recourse to racist domestic practices. This is exemplified by the internment of Japanese Americans during World War II, the Palmer raids on Eastern and Southern Europeans in the 1920s, and the enormous waves of Islamophobia that followed the 9/11 attack.
47. Thanks to John S.W. Park for assistance on these points.
48. In U.S. history, there has generally been one political party that took charge of racial rule. This has been especially true vis-à-vis black/white demarcations, for example the organization by the Democratic Party of white supremacist rule in the Jim Crow era. But rapid swings are possible. After the critical election of 1932, U.S. blacks (those who could vote) shifted their loyalties away from the "party of Lincoln" *en masse* (Weiss 1983; Katznelson 2005). This occurred even though Roosevelt's New Deal coalition effectively delegated control of the South to the plantocratic/agrarian/racist/"Dixiecrat" wing of his party. After the civil rights reforms of the mid-1960s, large numbers of white voters, particularly those based in the South, similarly embraced the Republicans.

Conclusion: The Contrarieties of Race

The destiny of the colored American ... is the destiny of America.

—Frederick Douglass[1]

Introduction

A great human sacrifice created the United States and all the Americas: the twin genocides of conquest and slavery. Although an immense effort has been made to repair the damage that sacrifice caused, the destruction can never really be undone. Much of the work of repair has been carried out by the victims themselves and their successors, who have tried to make a life on the gravesite of their ancestors, and have sought to make "the destiny of America" finally theirs. That has not happened yet. Some of the work of restoration has also been done by the descendants of the original criminals, and by people who arrived at the crime scene later: white anti-racists and more recent immigrants. These people also suffered in the shadows of the foundational genocides and tried to come to terms with the "rituals of blood" (Patterson 1999) that descended from it.

Our aim in this book has been to provide a *theoretically informed examination of the United States as a racially organized social and political system.* Race itself has proven to be a very contradictory notion. The idea of race barely existed before the Enlightenment and the onset of modernity; indeed it has had a rather rocky relationship with the rationalism and scientism in which the Enlightenment was grounded. Race is certainly a modern concept: It is linked to the conquest of the Americas, the rise of capitalism, the circumnavigation of the globe, the Atlantic slave trade, and the rise of European and then United States domination of the Middle East, Indian Ocean, and Pacific rim as well.[2] Yet the race-concept also preserves premodern and irrational characteristics, most notably its "ocular" elements: "You can't judge a book by its cover," goes the saying, but reference to the human body is an inescapable element of the race-concept.

We regard race as a *master category* of oppression and resistance in the United States. This does not mean that race somehow created class or sex/gender conflict, or that it was more central than the other major social cleavages of the analytic framework of intersectionality. Rather, it means that in the United States race has served as a *template* for both difference and inequality. The establishment and reproduction of race has established supposedly fundamental distinctions among human beings ("othering"), ranking and hierarchizing them for purposes of domination and exploitation. The importance of the phenomic dimensions of race—its corporeality, its ocularity—cannot be overstated. From the beginning of the conquest and settlement of the Western hemisphere, the necessity of distinguishing between settlers and natives, between free and slave, has profoundly shaped racial cleavages and conflicts, establishing the concept and categories of race as terms of oppression and resistance.

Today, the race-concept is frequently rejected as little more than an illusion. In contemporary popular discourse it is often claimed that "there is only one race—the human race." Yet even as it is dismissed, race is also taken for granted. Though at times denied ethical legitimacy and scientific recognition, racial identity continues to constitute a fundamental aspect of human identity. How one sees oneself and how one is seen by others are both profoundly, and often contradictorily, shaped by notions of race.

Throughout this book, we have sought to understand the shifting political meaning of race. We have endeavored to explain the racial contradictions, both embedded and emergent, that are operating in the United States. We have argued that race and racism remain unstable, contested, and ubiquitous, at both the experiential or "micro-" level and the structural or "macro-" level of U.S. society.

In this concluding chapter, we address the main points of our account of racial formation in the United States. We concentrate on core theoretical and political themes, and do not attempt to systematize the arguments of the whole book. The following section, *Race as a Master Category: The Political Technology of Rule and Resistance*, frames some of the key issues: the long-term presence of race on North American shores; its relationship to oppression and resistance; and its sociohistorical attachment to the human body. Next, we turn to *Paradigms of Race in the United States*, where we note the inveterate reductionism of the main theoretical approaches to race and racism, the ethnicity-, class-, and nation-based paradigms. Then, in *The Trajectory of Racial Politics*, we focus on the post-World War II period, considering the brief rise and prolonged decline of the black movement (and its allied new social movements), as well as their accomplishments and disappointments in the struggle for radical democracy and meaningful political-economic equality. Next, we turn our attention to the present, considering first *Colorblindness as a Hegemonic Racial Project*, and then *Race-Consciousness as a Racial Project.* We conclude the chapter with a section on *Racial Rearticulation: Can It Happen Again?* There the question is future directions, both theoretical and political.

Race as a Master Category: The Political Technology of Rule and Resistance

From the very inception of the American nation, race has provided a *template* for other sociopolitical cleavages and conflicts. Concepts of race have profoundly informed and legitimated domination and inequality. They have also shaped resistance, insurgency, and radical democratic struggles.

Because race is located on the body, it has proved a convenient means of rule, a political technology through which power can be both exercised and naturalized. As a means by which power can be "made flesh," race has gained an enormous hold on North American political culture. Racialization began very early in the United States and never went away, though processes of racial formation have varied greatly across both time and space.

Conquest and settlement had its own racial logic vis-à-vis indigenous people. Settlers did practice slavery, but their main goal in North America was acquisition of land, territorial (dis)possession. Settler colonialism was largely oblivious to indigenous peoples' identities and cultures; the Indians' particularities were of interest to the Europeans and their descendants only to the extent that they proved useful for purposes of subjugation and rule. The racialization of the Indians began very early, producing not only genocidal but also deracinating effects.

Slavery rapidly acquired a racial logic as the European settlement of North America colonies developed a tremendous need for mass labor. There was never any hesitation about coercing labor: Native Americans and Europeans (mainly Irish) were enslaved first, the latter in very large numbers. But these "local" solutions didn't work: Indians were vulnerable to diseases and prone to escape; indenture was a still a contract, not full-scale chattelization of the other. Nor was the available labor supply adequate in size. The turn to African slavery was ready to hand: The Portuguese and Spanish empires had already adopted it, and British ships were already engaged in supplying slaves to Brazil and the Caribbean.

Racialization involved the promotion of certain corporeal characteristics such as skin color and hair texture to a greater degree of importance than other presumably "normal" human variations, such as, say, physical height or eye color (Newman 1977). These phenomic traits, initially associated with African bodies or with indigenous bodies in the Americas, were soon elevated to the status of a "fundamental" (and later biological) difference. The attachment of this process of "othering" to immediately visible corporeal characteristics facilitated the recognition, surveillance, and coercion of these people, these "others." This phenomic differentiation helped render certain human bodies exploitable and submissible. It not only distinguished Native Americans and Africans from Europeans by immediately observable, "ocular" means; it also occupied the souls and minds that inhabited these bodies, stripping away not only people's origins, traditions, and histories, but also their individuality and differences. In response to these outrages and assaults, resistance developed from individual to collective forms, "groupness" or "fusion" grew, and soon enough also took on a racial framework, if only to face the white oppressors.[3]

The corporeality and ocularity of race—its visibility in the immediate present, in real time, allowed for its politicization as the fundamental cleavage in U.S. society. This is not to say that race either created, prefigured, displaced, or trumped other categories of social/biological "difference." Rather, other forms of stratification and difference that existed alongside or even prior to processes of racialization—religious, tribal, economic, geographical—found new expression and were given new meaning in a system increasingly dominated by the logic of race.

The intersection of race and *gender* gains particular importance because sex/ gender also is a corporeal phenomenon. The chattelization of the body has been a common experience for both people of color and women. In many ways racial difference and sex/gender-based difference resemble each other because they are both grounded in the body. Millions of people, after all, are *both* people of color and women. Gender differentiation resembles racial differentiation in numerous discomfiting ways. Sexual relations, sexual coercion, can both uphold and breach racial norms: On the one hand, it can demonstrate male power. Consider the prerogatives of the property-holders of human chattel (they were all male): their tendency to normalize rape and concubinage for instance. On the other hand, the race–sex/gender intersection can also reveal commonality and shared humanity, breaking apart supposedly impregnable racial boundaries, and creating racially "hybrid" identities via miscegenation (Hodes 1999). Therefore anything from assault and immiseration to transcendence and resistance could and did occur on this liminal frontier. In turn, racialization problematizes gender boundaries: Consider the plantation "mistress" and her conflicting roles; the racist defeminization implicit in the "mammy" role, the racist hypersexualization implicit in the "Sapphire" role (West 2012).[4]

What about *class* and the racial body? David Roediger (2007 [1991]) has revolutionized our understanding of these intersections in many ways. His work on U.S. class formation as a process of conflictual racial socialization follows Du Bois in emphasizing the links between racism and the submission of white workers to capitalist control. Roediger also stresses issues of masculinity, desire, and shame in this disciplining process. White degradation requires (much) greater black degradation. Still, in the view of Roediger, and in those of such other scholars as Hahn (2003) or Painter (2010), blacks observe and comprehend racism (and whiteness) with far more dignity and political depth than white culture could ever manage, whether through its rude art of minstrelsy or its other attempted exorcisms of the ongoing "fact of blackness."

Corporeality is the "fact of blackness," and in numerous ways, of "brownness," "redness," "yellowness," and indeed "whiteness" as well. The phenomic distinguishes race from ethnicity (culture) and nation (peoplehood), as well as from class. This "phenomenology" of race was an early form of the "social construction of race." It was driven not by any consolidated view on who black people were or who Native Americans were (those views developed later), or even who Europeans were. Instead, immediate and practical political needs shaped race: to assert control, to police the empire, to take possession of land and to extract labor. Religion provided whatever poor theory was available to explain these initial practices.

Only after conquest was assured and slave-trading was an established transnational business, in the 17th and 18th centuries, did "enlightened" debates take place among whites as to the nature and humanity of the native and the African. Kant and

Hegel, Locke and Hume, Voltaire and Jefferson (see Count, ed. 1950; Eze, ed. 1997; Bernasconi and Lott, eds. 2000), all the great thinkers in fact, made preposterous claims about race.[5] It was only after the founding genocides were established historical facts—the mines of Potosí, the liquidation of the Arawak, the Angolan "way of death" (Miller 1996 [1988])—that rationalization became necessary: "Sure there were terrible brutalities, but these backward peoples had to be dragged kicking and screaming into the modern world," and so on. Even Marx, who denounced "the turning of Africa into a warren for the commercial hunting of black skins," was susceptible to this sort of thinking.

In the United States the theoretical framework for deciphering the social construction of race began in earnest with Du Bois.[6] It derived in part from pragmatism, both for "the Doctor" and for the Chicago School of Sociology, where Du Bois's insights were re-invented by white people. Social constructionists at Chicago rejected much of the biologistic approach to race. They saw it, as Du Bois had seen it as well, as the product of a crude Darwinism that had developed out of the 19th-century efforts to rationalize the brutalities of primitive accumulation, slavery, and empire. With evolutionary accounts and eugenics, scientific means of ideologizing race largely supplanted religious ones.

Even with social constructionism, in the hands of Robert E. Park (the "race relations cycle"), of Gunnar Myrdal, of post-World War II ethnicity theorists (Glazer and Moynihan), or indeed in our own racial formation theory in this book, we social scientists continue to reiterate that early ocular view of race. It must be remembered that the visibility of race was used as a tool to consolidate domination, to seize land, and to recruit and extract mass labor. All this is still going on today. The racism of the past is still active in the present.

To what extent is this racial body, this phenomic raciality, enmeshed in politics, even in today's supposedly colorblind age? To look at the nightly news in 2014 America is to answer that question clearly: the highlighting of black and brown crime; as well as racial profiling, the murders of blacks and Latin@s by whites and especially by the police, continue at a steady pace, as if civil rights had never happened.[7] If profiling were not "ocular," it would not exist. Corporeality continues to determine popular understandings of race and thus to shape both white supremacy and colorblind hegemony in the United States today.

Paradigms of Race in the United States

Theory is driven by demand; by the necessity to explain, account for, and manage (as well as to resist) socio-historical changes. At the close of World War II, Ashley Montagu and others associated with the United Nations labeled race "man's most dangerous myth" (Montagu 1945) in direct response to the horrors of Nazi race science. The civil rights upsurge in the postwar period generated the need for new racial theory to address issues of inequality, marginalization, and disenfranchisement. The three paradigms we have discussed—ethnicity (culture)-based, class (inequality)-based, and nation (peoplehood)-based—all emerged from this historical crucible.

The post-World War II black movement represented the second great upsurge in U.S. racial history. The first such upsurge, of course, was the Civil War and Reconstruction. Both in the mid-19th century and in the mid-20th, these movements were connected to larger, global, insurgencies: abolitionism and anti-imperialism in particular. Triggered by the vast mobilizations and demographic shifts during World War II and its aftermath, the Civil Rights movement in the United States was a "case," maybe the largest case, of the racial upsurge that took place around the world in the mid-20th century (Winant 2001).

Ethnicity theory was originally driven by the need to explain (and control) massive European immigration to the United States around the turn of the 20th century. It was revived in the post-World War II period in response to the civil rights upsurge. It was the only accommodation-oriented racial paradigm that was available. Greatly facilitated by the Myrdal study (1944), ethnicity theory was resuscitated to inform and support liberal race politics and civil rights reforms. The assimilationist and cultural pluralist tendencies in ethnicity theory were originally accounts of the great European migrations of the late 19th and early 20th centuries—stories of slow, gradual integration of non-Protestant, not quite white people, into the American mainstream (Jacobson 1999).

Ethnicity theory's encounter with blackness from the late 1940s through the 1960s was naive and meliorist. It assumed that people of color could access the same mobility, and be granted the same opportunities, that European, non-WASP immigrants like Jews and Italians had acquired, especially after World War I, and that the Irish had gradually achieved in the decades after the Civil War.

The ethnicity paradigm was conceived in reference to an unprecedented and perhaps unique historical period of immigration and assimilation. Although it is still popularly regarded as a general theory of group incorporation, ethnicity theory might more appropriately be seen as specific to one particular historical conjuncture: one limited period of U.S. immigration and settlement *that might never be repeated.*[8] Fabricating such a grand theory based on limited case studies in specific historical circumstances is, of course, problematic. Ethnicity theory neglected normative whiteness; it largely failed to notice the corporeal significance of race. In linking post-World War II black "progress" to that of earlier European immigrant groups, ethnicity theory denied the emancipatory and democratic dimensions of the black struggle. It also gestured toward the neoconservative orientation its chief analysts would later pursue.

Class-based theory—Mainstream economics, liberal sociology, and Marxism were also challenged by the civil rights upsurge. Most centrally, they had to take sides: for or against the welfare state? *On the pro side* were those who favored extending the New Deal to include blacks and the "other others" who had been excluded in the 1930s. This was something the government itself embraced, in the form of the Great Society.

Beyond that lay Marxism, and many class theorists identified as such—as social democrats on one end of the left spectrum and Marxist-Leninists on the other. While left variants of the class paradigm of race educated and mobilized many people, they could never attain a foothold in the racial state. With the benefit of hindsight we can see that the social democrats who advised the Democratic Party to adopt redistributive policies were bound to be disappointed. Obama, we read, has banned the term "redistribution" from the White House (Harwood 2013). Clinton too danced to the tune of Wall Street. Even his advisor William J. Wilson's (2012 [1987]) sage counsel about lessening racial inequality by adopting a policy of redistribution along class lines was largely disregarded by his patron. Abjuring across-the-board redistribution policies has been the price that neoliberal economic hegemony exacted from Democratic administrations.

The Democrats were only able—perhaps only allowed—to make small, badly needed, minimally effective, redistributive reforms, such as the Earned Income Tax Credit under Clinton and the Obamacare health "reforms"—the Affordable Care Act.[9] Both the Wilson and the Massey/Denton stratification analyses effectively pointed to the intractability of racial inequality in the absence of much more radical transformations than the United States has seen since Civil War and Reconstruction days. These and other class theorists of race produced useful policy analysis. They chronicled the evacuation of jobs (Wilson 1997) and the persistence and indeed deepening of segregation (Massey and Denton 1993). Beyond the ghetto, Douglas Massey's (2008) work on immigration suggested the emergence of a more complex pattern of stratification, with limited mobility for some Latinos but not for all.

Marxist-Leninist approaches to race were demolished by the global collapse of their ideology. While some vestiges of social democracy survived the dissolution of the Soviet Union and the adoption of the Deng Xiaoping version of neoliberalism in China, not many race theories from the M-L trend endured. Even in 1980, when Brezhnev still ruled the USSR and Mao's body was barely cool in its Tiananmen mausoleum, the impossibility of communism in the United States was plain to see.

On the con side it was the right-wing class theorists of race who opposed the welfare state. The rise and consolidation of neoliberalism, beginning with the Reagan administration and continuing today, represented a profound victory for them, a deep defeat for people of color, and a stark rejection of the democratic and egalitarian gains achieved by the movement and its allies. Neoliberalism incorporated colorblind racial ideology, indeed depended upon it and saw it elevated to hegemonic status, beginning in the Reagan years and especially after Obama was elected.

Nation-based theories of race, along with class theories, played an important role in challenging the dominant ethnicity paradigm during the later stages of the black movement's rising phase (roughly 1966 to 1970) and as the declining phase of the trajectory set in during the early 1970s. This was the black power era. Malcolm lay dead, but his influence loomed large. The Black Panther Party had some tremendous achievements—notably in "politicizing the social," but also in community service (Nelson 2013). The diverse nationalist currents of this brief period—black,

Latino, Asian, and Native American—were all limited by the problematic of racial "lumping," the downside, so to speak, of the "peoplehood" framework. Within each racially-derived notion of "the nation"—the black nation, Aztlán and panethnic concepts of *La Raza*, indigeneity, and Asian American panethnicity as well—there were enormous divisions, class-based, ideological, and ethnic. Collectivity proved ephemeral, and thus the concept of peoplehood faltered as well.

Beyond this, nation-based activists and intellectuals were unable to delineate a successful strategy to oppose racial reaction. Although the sense of peoplehood that lies at the core of nationalism could not be consolidated theoretically or practically, it did survive as an informal cultural framework. Especially in the black community, where it had a centuries-long history, nationalism was quite resilient (Walters 1997; Dawson 2003). Amplifying and diffusing the already present race-consciousness that existed within and among communities of color, the nation-based paradigm continued to operate as a theoretically rich framework for cultural and political activism. Although constantly susceptible to the pitfalls of authoritarianism (Gilroy 2000) and to decay into apolitical symbolism, today the nation-based paradigm has shed many of its earlier separatist and merely gestural dimensions. Perhaps what Huey P. Newton once called "intercommunalism" is the direction in which 21st century U.S. racial nationalism is heading. Reductionist as it may be, to the extent that this paradigm has been able to uphold the banner of race consciousness through the dark night of colorblind racial hegemony, it offers clues and lessons for the U.S. racial future.

* * *

The three paradigms of race that developed during the postwar period were all limited by their partiality. They all relied on one central category—culture, inequality, or peoplehood—in their interpretations of racial dynamics in the United States. None of the paradigms had a clear conception of race itself. All reduced race to a manifestation of another, supposedly more fundamental, sociopolitical cleavages or differences.

This reductionism systematically neglected the uniqueness of race: its corporeal manifestations, its ubiquity, its permanent instability. Since racialization began in the early days of conquest and slavery, race has infused all identities in North America: we emphasize its scope and sweep. Racial identification, racial interpellation, has always involved "lumping," both by the state and in everyday society.

Just as some people (mainly property-holding white men) have benefited through the authoritarian and dehumanizing characteristics of racial difference, others (mainly working people of color) have continually resisted those dynamics. Practices of resistance have sought to reinvent racial identities and to overturn racial institutions: hence the permanent instability we stress throughout this book. Because the racial paradigms of ethnicity, class, and nation were all based on the reduction of race to a manifestation of some other, supposedly more fundamental and "objective" human or social characteristic, none of the paradigms could visualize race as a unique type of social identity and social structure, corporeal, central to modernity itself, varying across time and space, operating at both the individual and collective levels of U.S. (and world) society. Consequently, the race-concept remained something of a theoretical cypher, a congeries of distinct and unreconciled elements: Politics, ethics, culture, collectivity, history, geography, science, and religion all partook of race, and all jostled for influence over its meaning.

Still, despite their limitations the three paradigms each contributed something important to the mix of racial theory; they each furnished some of the key dimensions of the synthetic account of racial formation theory that we have presented here.

Trajectories of Racial Politics

Derrick Bell insightfully described and lamented the "permanence of racism" (1992). We acknowledge that racism is a constitutive dimension of U.S. society, but we also argue that racism has limits, that it is widely contested, and that it is both politically organized and politically resisted. So how should we understand racial *change?* We answer this question by focusing on the trajectory of U.S. racial politics in the post-World War II period.

From the standpoint of the black movement and its allies, this trajectory can be envisioned as a rising and then falling arc. The movement achieved substantial democratic reforms only to see these gains substantially, if not completely, contained starting in the 1970s. Containment involved greater inclusion in the U.S. racial system, but did not eliminate the inveterate white supremacy whose origins lay in the colonial and slavery era. From the standpoint of the U.S. racial regime, the trajectory proceeded conversely: A long-standing pattern of stability and social control was disrupted and transformed by the black movement's radical political challenge. This destabilizing threat was subsequently contained, in part by repression, but mainly by incorporation. What was crucial to the recalibration of the U.S. racial system was the political and ideological rearticulation of the movement's vision of race and democracy.

It was an enormous achievement to put an end to official Jim Crow—the legally sanctioned and popularly supported (by most whites at least) racial despotism that had governed the United States for almost a century. The enactment of civil rights laws in the mid-1960s marked a real if partial democratization, an accommodation of the demands of a mass movement too wide and too deep to be resisted any longer. The post-World War II shift or racial "break" (Winant 2001) involved more than legislated and judicial reforms. Political incorporation was required as well as large-scale cultural reorientation. Both the mass movement and the elite supporters of civil rights also saw the reforms as essential elements of U.S. foreign policy, key ideological and political responses to the Cold War and the anti-imperial upsurge sweeping the "darker nations" of the planet (Prashad 2007; Dudziak 2011).

Civil rights reforms happened, though movement demands were often compromised and attenuated in the process of translating them into law. As Bell noted, major reforms could only be enacted in a "moderate" fashion, and only if their key provisions were acceptable to whites and compatible with the supposed values of U.S. politics and culture: the American "civil religion" of individualism, equality, competition, opportunity, and the accessibility of "the American dream" to all who strove for it. For movement activists and intellectuals, acceptance of the reform agenda meant forgoing a more radical vision of social transformation in exchange for short-term gains, or facing marginalization or repression if they would not.

The radical vision that was largely abandoned was the "dream," Dr. King's dream, in which racial justice (not color blindness) played the central part. King's vision in "Beyond Vietnam: A Time to Break Silence," his April 4, 1967 speech at New York's Riverside Church, also definitively linked the civil rights movement with anti-imperialism around the world (King 2002a). To be "free at last" meant something deeper than the gaining of partial access to key social and political institutions. It meant more than limited reforms and palliation of the worst excesses of white supremacy. It meant a *substantive reorganization of the U.S. social system.* It meant political implementation of egalitarian economic and democratizing political measures. Above all it meant redistribution of resources along social democratic lines and the extension of full citizenship to people of color. This radical alternative was also intimately linked to *global* questions: notably the end of U.S. war-making in the global South, particularly in Vietnam.

To achieve such a radical democratic program was beyond the reach of the 1960s black movements and its allies. The black movement in particular was facing repression, was internally divided along many axes, and lacked sufficient "mainstream" (that is white) support.

It was especially in reference to issues of redistribution that the "moderate" custodians of racial reform drew their boundary line, both in practical terms and in theoretical ones. To undo official, explicit, legalized racial inequality was permissible; to create racial equality through positive state action was not. Economic and political elites were threatened by the prospect of redistribution. Demands for substantive redress for the unjustified expropriation and restriction of black economic and political resources, both historically and in the present, were both economic and political anathema to the ruling class. Redistribution of resources to people of color meant not only social democracy but *radical* democracy, the political inclusion of millions whose marginalized status had guaranteed not only white supremacy but also elite rule for centuries. The potentially permanent linkage between the "third world" abroad and the "third world within" was also particularly frightening to the established powers (Kelley 1996; von Eschen 2006).

To contain such a radical vision, moderate civil rights reform became part of the political mainstream, which moved from domination to hegemony. The key component of modern political rule, of hegemony as theorized by Gramsci most profoundly, is the capacity to *incorporate opposition.* By selectively adopting the movement's demands, by developing a comprehensive program of limited reform that hewed to a centrist political logic and reinforced key dimensions of U.S. nationalist ideology, political elites were able to define a new racial "common sense." This new racial ideology celebrated (and inflated) the significance of the concessions won. It divided the movement between more moderate and more radical tendencies. It permitted the reassertion of a certain broad-based racial stability, and defused a great deal of political opposition.

The partial reconfiguration of the U.S. racial system both made real concessions and left major issues unsettled and unaddressed. The fundamental problems of racial injustice and inequality, and of white supremacy more generally, remained: moderated perhaps, but hardly resolved. As the trajectory of post-World War II racial politics swung into its declining phase in about 1970, after the supposed triumph of the "civil rights revolution," the U.S. state, the nation's cultural apparatuses, and the people themselves had to manage and reconcile the contradictory conditions that anti-racist movements and civil rights reforms had created. This was, and remains, a tough assignment.

Sure, reforms happened. But race also retained its significance as a definitive dimension of the U.S. social structure. In other words, race continued to define North American identities and institutions. The "post-civil rights" era tugging and hauling, the escalating contestation over the meaning of race, resulted in ever more disrupted and contradictory notions of racial identity. The significance of race ("declining" or increasing?), the interpretation of racial equality (colorblind or race-conscious?), the institutionalization of racial justice (reverse discrimination or affirmative action?), and the very categories—black, white, Latin@/Hispanic, Asian American, and Native American, that were employed to classify racial groups—all these were called into question after the civil rights "victories" of the mid-1960s.

The declining phase of the political trajectory of race has now lasted more than four decades, despite the 2008 election of Barack Obama and his reelection in 2012. Yes, Obama has proved disappointing in many respects, but the expectations attending his ascent were outlandish across the entire political spectrum.

Over the post-World War II decades, the *rearticulation* of racial ideology has been central both to the rise and the containment of the black movement and its allied movements. Rearticulation was a key weapon in the movement's rise: It provided a vital moral component of the movement's claim to represent the true American ideals; it played a crucial role in the movement's development of nonviolent strategy and tactics. It enabled the movement's "inside/outside" political strategy.

But the racial reaction also learned how to use strategies of rearticulation to defuse the radical democratic and egalitarian thrust of the movement. Rearticulation proved far more effective than repression in containing the radical thrust of the black movement, and of its allied movements as well. A clear sequence of ideological tropes deepened and extended "post-civil rights" era rearticulations of racism: first code words, then reverse racism, and finally colorblindness.

At each stage of its development, the racial reaction carried out what we might call cumulative "latent functions" (Merton 1968). Code words channeled white shame, fear, and rage; reverse racism deracialized discrimination, effectively absolving whites; and colorblindness reasserted American nationalism and the "unity" of "the American people" across the supposedly disappearing boundaries of race.

Based on this evolving racial "common sense," the racial reaction was able to build a mass base, largely but not entirely composed of working- and middle-class whites who were threatened by racial equality and racial democracy. These whites (or their parents and grandparents) had benefited from the welfare state under the New Deal, which was predominantly a whites-only affair, and was quite anti-immigrant as well. When the New Deal restrictions on social investment in communities of color were lifted in the mid-1960s, many whites got off the freedom train.

The new right worked assiduously to fan white racial fears (code words), and to stigmatize such state-based reform policies as affirmative action, fair housing, and desegregation, as discriminatory toward whites (reverse racism). It revived nativism. Joined by right-wing populist anti-tax groups and armed with the age-old ideology of producerism, reverse racism activists reframed their defense of white privileges as a political and legal offense. Although they claimed to be fighting discrimination of all types, their real problem was civil rights reforms such as affirmative action, fair housing, voting rights, and immigration.[10] Ultimately, after years of Supreme Court hedging and trending toward the right, it became clear that the Court viewed racial discrimination as something that happened principally to white people.

But the containment of civil rights was not the end of the racial reaction's project to reverse the gains of the movement. The objective had always been larger than that. It was to dismantle the welfare state, to limit taxation and other forms of regulation of capital, and to ensure the docility and desperation of the "others": the poor, the workers, who were increasingly people of color but also white people, and even the middle classes. This was the neoliberal agenda. It was nationalist and "authoritarian populist."[11]

Neoliberalism both overlapped with and required colorblindness. It required a racial ideology that repudiated the civil rights agenda of state-enforced equality and state-based extension of democratic rights, without regressing to explicit white supremacy or reverting to explicit policies of Jim Crow segregation. Repelling, repressing, and rearticulating the black movement's (and allied movements') agendas would not be enough for this purpose. In order to achieve hegemony for the neoliberal project of reinforced social inequality in a U.S. rid of its welfare state, with all the redistributive dimensions of social rights finally repudiated, it would be necessary not only to oppose demands for racial justice and racial democracy; it would be necessary to take race off the table.

Colorblindness as a Hegemonic Racial Project

Today, in the 21st century, the concept of "colorblindness" is hegemonic in the United States. It has become the racial common sense and *desideratum* of our time. This does not mean that it is free of contradictions, however.

Those advocating a colorblind view of race assert that the goals of the civil rights movement have been substantially achieved, that overt forms of racial discrimination are a thing of the past, and that the United States is in the midst of a successful transition to a "post-racial" society. From a colorblind standpoint, any hints of race consciousness are tainted by racism. Thus it is suggested that the most effective anti-racist gesture, policy, or practice is simply to ignore race (Skrentny 1996; Connerly 2007). Critics of colorblindness, in contrast, point to the pervasive presence of race and racism—white supremacy—throughout the U.S. social structure. They emphasize the enduring significance of race and the persistence of racism, arguing that it continues to generate inequality across the entire society, most notably in such areas as education, employment, criminal "justice," health, and housing, but elsewhere as well. In order to address the persistence of racial inequalities, they argue that race-conscious policies and practices are necessary, specifically to target and address the sources and causes of racial disparities (Brown et al. 2003; Feagin 2006; Kennedy 2013).

Both positions lay claim to the legacy of the black movement of the 1950s and 1960s. Indeed, colorblindness itself both reflects and subverts that legacy. Early on, colorblindness provided the general framework for anti-racist movement goals, a moment most familiar from the famous sentence in Dr. King's August 28, 1963, speech: "I have a dream that my four children will one day live in a nation where they will be judged not by the color of their skin but by the content of their character" (King 2002b)[12] But colorblindness represented something very different in the last years of Jim Crow segregation than it did in the early 21st century. In August 1963 as the marchers converged on the Lincoln Memorial and Dr. King's and other civil rights leaders' voices rang out across the capital, overt racism, the U.S. version of *apartheid*, was still the law of the land. Desperate public officials and private citizens, many of them avowed white supremacists, were determined to preserve it at all costs from the growing consensus that sought change.

And things did change. An overtly racist ideology, buttressed by "scientific" claims, was widely disavowed. The Civil Rights Act of 1964 and the Voting Rights Act of 1965 led to the subsequent demise of state and local Jim Crow laws. Anti-miscegenation laws were deemed unconstitutional by the U.S. Supreme Court in 1967. Colorblindness, therefore, cannot simply be seen as a deceptive political hoax or naive matter of wishful thinking. It is a result, however intended or unintended, of the partial dismantlement of the U.S. *apartheid* system in the 1960s. Only by challenging that system, and by creating new, more egalitarian racial dynamics, was it even possible to advance the colorblind position.

"Partial dismantlement." Consider the contrast between the 1960s and today. Half a century later, racism is mostly tacit. Although profiling is ubiquitous and discriminatory practices are often thinly veiled at best, explicitly racial laws are frowned upon. Although race is supposedly a suspect category, courts wink at implicitly discriminatory measures and indeed preoccupy themselves with supposed discrimination against whites. The reforms of the civil rights era seem increasingly ineffective against an ongoing structural racism that sees, hears, and undoes no evil. To ignore ongoing racial inequality, racial violence, racial disenfranchisement, racial profiling, quasi-official resegregation of schools and neighborhoods, and anti-immigrant racism—it's a long list—under the banner of colorblindness is to indulge in a thought process composed in substantial parts of malice, disingenuousness, and wishful thinking.

Can we really embrace a colorblind approach to race in the face of recurrent nativism with its "show me your papers" laws and extensive network of harassment, imprisonment, and deportation? Can we ignore the existence of a prison system whose highly disproportionate confinement of black and brown people is a national scandal? Mass incarceration has become a racialized system of social control and super-exploitation with blacks and Latinos making up more than 60 percent of the current prison population (Mauer 2006 [1999]; Alexander 2012). Health disparities by race remain clearly evident with regards to access to healthcare, disease prevention, and life expectancy (Smedley, Stith, and Nelson 2003; Ansell 2011). Can we agree with the colorblind approach to race when, as Gary Orfield and Erica Frankenberg (2013), Jonathan Kozol (2012 [1991]), and many others have documented, school segregation has not only persisted but been both exacerbated and normalized in the United States? Can we accept claims that racism is "a thing of the past" when median white net worth is now *twenty times* greater than median black net worth, having *more than doubled* since the onset of the great recession of 2008 (Kochhar et al. 2011; see also Oliver and Shapiro 2006)? Regressive redistribution almost as abysmal has plagued Latin@s over the same period. How can such a rapid shift for the worse, how can a leap in economic inequality of such dramatic scope, be blamed on anything other than the victimization of black and brown people who aspired to middle-class status? How can it be reconciled with the concept of colorblindness?[13] How can we take seriously professions of belief in colorblind attitudes, when they are rife with irrationalities and contradictions (Brown et al. 2003; Carbado and Harris 2008; Bonilla-Silva 2009; Wise 2010)? From the cradle to the grave, race continues to shape and define our prospects, opportunities, life chances, and dreams.

Even more ominous is the realization that even past gains can be rolled back. In June 2013, the U.S. Supreme Court substantially weakened the Voting Rights Act, thereby allowing nine states to change their election laws without advance federal approval (Liptak 2013). This decision allows states, counties, and municipalities to enact or move forward with voter identification laws that have the effect of disenfranchising groups of color. Was our confidence in Jim Crow's passing premature, as Derrick Bell argued?

The litany of racial inequalities goes on (and on), but the appeal of colorblind ideology cannot be easily dismissed. It promotes a compelling common sense, a general "rule of thumb," to guide and inform both institutional and individual practices. It provides a facile means for individuals to denounce racist beliefs and actions of a certain type—those that are explicit, overt, unconscionable, and morally unacceptable.

Colorblindness allows people (mainly whites, but not only whites) to indulge in a kind of anti-racism "lite." While explicit forms of racial animus (such as hate speech) are widely condemned, policies and practices that continue to produce racially disparate outcomes are accepted and even encouraged under the guise of moving us "beyond" race and towards a truly colorblind society.

Not surprisingly, attitudes vary by race regarding the persistence of racial inequality and whether the state needs to proactively do something about racial discrimination. In July 2013, Gallup pollsters asked respondents, "Do you think new civil rights laws are needed to reduce discrimination against blacks?" While only 17 percent of whites replied "yes," 53 percent of blacks and 46 percent of Latinos replied in the affirmative (Gallup 2013). We may all want to get to the post-racial promised land, but group differences abound with respect to how far along the road we are and what are the best means by which to get there.

Despite the withering criticism directed at the concept of colorblindness, we will not succeed in overthrowing colorblindness if we see it as erroneous, deceptive, or merely a hoax. *Colorblindness is also aspirational.* Indeed it is precisely because the old U.S. apartheid system was formally dismantled, and because the new racial dynamic that was substituted for it was more open and fluid, that it became possible to advance the colorblind position. That it has attained hegemonic status as the racial "common sense" of the present has been the outcome of a prolonged period of rearticulation by the political right—a sustained attempt to contain the radical democratic potentialities of what we call the Great Transformation.

As a racial project, indeed as a bid for racial hegemony in the United States today, colorblindness is a rude beast: ineffective, uneven, ungainly, deceptive, contradictory. But since hegemony itself is about the selective and strategic incorporation of opposition, it comes as no surprise that there are contradictions in the very logic of colorblind ideology. In the long run, colorblind racial ideology is only credible and can only "work" to the extent that it reflects the successes of the "post-civil rights" era in ameliorating racial injustice and inequality. A purely fabricated, mythical colorblindness could hardly be sustained intellectually, politically, or even socially in the interactions of everyday life. The effectiveness of colorblind ideology depends on its verisimilitude, on the credibility of its claim that U.S. racial conditions have improved—that we now have less discrimination, less racial violence, less racial repression and, correspondingly, more tolerance, more equality, and more inclusion.

Concepts of race, racial categories, and racial meanings continue to haunt and circulate in all social domains. Both in everyday life and in the political sphere, race organizes U.S. society. In civil society, people continually use race: We rely on perceived racial categories in social interaction, in the presentation of self, and to "navigate" in varied social settings. Consider such matters as getting a job, shopping in a department store, attending university, or dating. In political life too *the state needs race to rule.* Racial profiling and mass (racial) incarceration, for example, have become constitutive of the policies and practices of social control. Patterns of immigration and developing trends in U.S. racial demography have created and revived a whole series of political opportunities. Ongoing nativist appeals exploit white anxieties about the nation's future and fears of the "other" in our midst. Immigrant rights advocates rally an electorate increasingly composed of people of color on behalf of redistributive economic policies and the extension of democratic rights. Overall, however, structural racism still steers the ship of state. Disinvestment in education generates a "school to prison pipeline" (Knefel 2013). Persistent poverty and unemployment, engineered under neoliberalism by the failure to carry out needed social investment, produces increased demand for social control and repression. In the United States, all of this is immediately understood in racial terms.

Race-Consciousness as a Racial Project

Critics of colorblind ideology have argued that race-conscious policies and practices are necessary to address the persistent and entrenched forms of racial inequality in the United States. What does it mean to "notice" race?

Just as colorblind racial ideology occludes recognition of race beneath the veneer of a supposedly already-accomplished universality, race-consciousness works to highlight racial differences and particularities. This may take various forms, both democratic and despotic, both emancipatory and reactionary. Generally speaking, race-consciousness involves *noticing* the social fact of race, the presence of racial identity/difference, racial inequality, and racial hierarchy. Across a broad political spectrum ranging from left to right, from social practices of inclusion to those of exclusion, conflicting racial projects make use of these concepts, practices, and structures for a wide range of purposes. How is racial identity (signification) linked to racial inequality and hierarchy (domination and subordination)? How are new racial projects generated?

At one extreme, there is an aggressive white supremacist movement, organized to a significant extent, and with many sympathizers as well. This movement is generally far right; it has a substantial Internet presence on various racist and fascist sites. There is a substantial neo-Confederate political current in the United States that bridges between the far right and new right (Murphy 2001; Sack 2001; MacLean 2009). Although we have mentioned these political currents from time to time, and have noted their anti-democratic, counter-egalitarian, and biologistically racist proclivities, we have not devoted extensive attention to them in this book.

The new right largely avoids, or seeks to suppress, its connections with the white supremacist race-consciousness of the far right. For the most part, the new right has embraced colorblind racial ideology, melding it as far as possible with neoliberalism. To be sure there are endless occasions when the race-consciousness that colorblindness seeks to suppress busts out into the open: in arguments for "the right to discriminate" for example, or in producerism (recall Mitt Romney's "47%" analysis of electoral politics, delivered in Boca Raton, Florida, in 2012). Our key point here is that colorblindness is yoked to neoliberal assaults on the welfare state and to exclusionary, anti-democratic (small "d") politics.

On the left, there is an egalitarian, radical democratic, anti-racist current. Composed of numerous organizations concerned not only with countering explicitly racist actions, policies, and discourse, but also with improving and strengthening the status and living conditions of people of color, various movement groups and their supporters are active across the entire range of social and political conflicts. Indeed they often address issues that are not explicitly framed in racial terms: rape crisis centers, battered women's shelters, tenants' rights groups, access to quality education, immigrants rights....

For the racial justice movement, noticing race and achieving race consciousness is a very different matter than it is in the white supremacist or new right areas of the political spectrum; in no sense is this movement the "equal and opposite" of the right wing. Anti-racism affirms the goal of achieving greater social justice; this is continuous with the political logic and moral appeal that remain from the era of civil rights and black power (and, of course, from the more distant past). For all its incompleteness and disorder, the quest for radical racial democracy remains a left-wing racial project: dedicated to redistribution (an egalitarian social structure) and to the recognition of difference (racial identity) rather than its denial. This approach to race-consciousness highlights the ongoing presence and significance of racial identity, racial inequality, and racial injustice. It takes seriously the unfulfilled social justice agenda of dismantling American *apartheid* and upholds the goals of extending the reforms of the civil rights movement and challenging existing structures of racial domination. On the left, there is a general recognition—obviously incomplete and not always explicit—that racial identity is an issue of freedom and self-activity. In other words, there are or should be choices about how we racially "represent ourselves in everyday life," to speak Goffman-ese. To be able to act black or act white, to embody one's *latinidad* or not to do so, are or should be options we have, not compulsions subject to stigma, constraint, or profiling (Carbado and Gulati 2013). This race-consciousness is explicitly or implicitly *radically pragmatist*. It acknowledges the social structures and practices of race and racism: the vast fabric of inclusion and exclusion, advantage and disadvantage, and power and powerlessness that are built into a social system based on structural racism. There is an ill-defined but palpable racial solidarity here as well, something akin to the "peoplehood" concept that inspires racial nationalisms of all types.[14]

Drawing attention to race—racial identity and difference, racial inequality and oppression, racial exclusion and violence—allows us to question the inconsistencies and platitudes of colorblind racial ideology. But we recognize that race consciousness harbors certain contradictions as well. "Essentializing" race is always possible: treating it as a fundamental, transhistorical marker of difference can reduce race to a sort of uniform people are made to wear, thus reproducing—however consciously or unconsciously—the stereotyping that characterizes racism itself.[15]

We also draw attention to the risk of authoritarianism lurking behind race consciousness—observable not only in the obvious authoritarianism of white supremacy, apartheid, and colonialism, but also in movements framed in opposition to these regimes. The authoritarian trap has plagued many resistance and oppositional movements. Democratic commitments in Marxist movements, for example, have given way to Stalinism and other forms of repression; anticolonial movements have spawned dictatorships; religious movements against persecution have persecuted their own dissenters; feminism has been split, sometimes in highly antagonistic ways, between "difference" and "inequality" factions, with some groups denouncing others quite vitriolically. Race consciousness, though an obviously indispensable rejoinder to the shallowness of colorblindness, cannot deny the inherent fluidity and sociohistorical situatedness of racial identity and racial difference, without risking a collapse into a authoritarianism of its own (Gilroy 2000, 1999).

Not only amongst the talking heads on TV or in the far-fetched racial jurisprudence that dominates the present period, but also in everyday life today, we are often exposed to the putative common sense of "post-civil rights" era colorblindness. Many of our students tell us that they "don't see race," that "a person is just a person" to them, and that they seek "to treat everyone as an individual." Mostly, of course, it is white students who say this, but by no means do these expressions come only from the lips of whites.

For a long time we argued with such claims: "You don't see race? Have you had your eyes checked lately?" (On this point, see Obasogie 2013.) But in recent years we have come to see that response as counterproductive, tending to validate the self-righteousness that frames colorblindness—whether willfully or naively. We are now taking a new approach in our efforts to counter the "anti-racism lite" that such positions entail. Rather than arguing directly against colorblindness, we want to recognize the unresolved dimensions, the contradictions that necessarily follow from the civil rights movement's (and its allies') combined accomplishments: their incomplete but real successes, their tentative visions of a solidaristic and "beloved" community, as well as their mistakes and limits, their necessary compromises, and their repression at the hands of a state and society built on racial despotism. Most of all, we want to recognize and rework the racial reaction's post-1980s rearticulation of anti-racism into colorblindness. It was this long-acting racial project that most effectively contained the radical democratic aspirations of the black movement and its allies.

Racial Rearticulation: Can It Happen Again?

If the "post-civil rights" years are characterized by anything, it is the experience of tension between colorblindness and race consciousness. Rather than denying that race matters, rather than arguing that nothing has changed, we should go deeper into the *contrarieties of race*.

Although drawing attention to race—racial identity and difference, racial inequality and oppression, racial exclusion and violence—allows us to question the depth and seriousness of colorblind racial ideology, we also want to recognize that race-consciousness exhibits contradictions as well. It is easy to mischaracterize race or misinterpret the significance of racial identity. Just when does race matter, anyway? Always, sometimes? If the answer is "sometimes," what about those situations when race "doesn't matter"? Are there conditions under which we should *not* notice race? Is not racial identity often ambiguous and contradictory? How should we interpret transracial solidarity and alliance? How should we interpret transracial identity, or transracial friendship, or indeed love across the color-line? These old themes no doubt retain something of their transgressive and unsettling character, but they are also increasingly normal, regular, and unremarkable (Daniel 2001; Parker and Song, eds. 2001). Can trust and solidarity exist across racial lines? Is it possible either in individual or collective social practice, to "get beyond" race? If so, how definitive is racial identity? If not, what are the implications for multiculturalism, democracy, humanism?

Race, we argue, has served as a fundamental organizing principle of injustice in the United States—one that has influenced the definition of rights and privileges, the distribution of resources, and the ideologies and practices of subordination and oppression. Racial domination has defined processes of "otherness" and marginalization; over the years it has "made up people" in ways that have indelibly shaped other dimensions of inequality and difference in the United States. Even under colorblind hegemony, race still operates as a master category: It is something that *must* be denied, or else the whole ideology of "American exceptionalism," "the American assumption" (Du Bois's term for "the American dream"), "government of the people, by the people, for the people," and indeed "the American people" itself, falls into tatters.

We have described racial formation as a process of continuing encounters between despotic and democratic racial projects. As hegemonic racial ideology, colorblindness has to be enforced, not only in state policies and court decisions, but in popular culture and everyday life as well. This means that colorblind racial ideology and the social fact of race consciousness have a deep and queasy relationship with one another (Carbado and Harris 2008). Sure, to challenge colorblindness you must be race-conscious. But to police the ideological boundaries of colorblindness you must *also* be race-conscious.

Although the state needs race to rule, it is also confronted by anti-racist opposition and constrained by its own commitment to the achievement of racial hegemony through the "colorblindness" construct. In general, it cannot explicitly name, utilize, or exploit the race concept; instead it is forced to exercise racial rule covertly. The effects of the Great Transformation still resonate. This is a contradictory and conflictual situation, in which the racial regime simultaneously *disavows* its raciality and *deploys* it as broadly and deeply as ever. The crisis of hegemonic colorblindness generates the continuing instability of race in the United States today. Colorblindness underwrites neoliberal policies of superexploitation, anti-welfare statism, and "accumulation by dispossession." Here we see the limits of President Obama's post-racial appeals, and the enormous difficulties involved in stemming, much less cleaning up, the ongoing accumulation of racial "waste."[16] These contradictions extend to everyday life, where, on the one hand, we are supposed to be "postracial" and colorblind, and, on the other hand, we remain as race-conscious as ever!

Given the instability and processual quality of racial formation—Gramsci's "formation and overcoming of unstable equilibria"—the hegemony of colorblind racial ideology seems particularly vulnerable and transitory. Changing domestic demographics, patterns of migration, the organization of repression, the politics of poverty, and propaganda initiatives (aka "the news")—to pick just some obvious terrains—are all bubbling cauldrons of racial conflict. It is not likely that race consciousness is going to subside over time, especially in a social environment trending steadily towards deepening inequality in many social domains, and moving inexorably towards a "majority-minority" demographic.

Colorblindness is a highly contradictory phenomenon. In the past, it was a call for racial equality and inclusion. Today, it is largely an ideological framework for the effacement of race consciousness. But it can also be a vehicle for *deepening and variegating race consciousness*, especially if we can rearticulate the concept to mean something like "race-conscious when you need to be, when democracy and justice demand you to be." A new and better understanding of race would recognize that the race concept's meaning is being made and remade from moment to moment. This understanding points to a *radical racial pragmatism.*

Throughout this book, we have emphasized the concept of *rearticulation.* This idea refers to the *ideological appropriation of elements of an opposing position.* It is thus a central part of hegemony, which proceeds by "incorporating opposition." After the 1960s, the racial reaction appropriated the ideal of colorblindness—which had been a radical, movement ideal—thereby turning it into a cheap simulacrum of the movement's ideal, a parody of the "dream," something that ratified instead of challenged the racial status quo. *Was that then the end of the story?* Was that the only time that such a bold political move could be pulled off? Or can that appropriation, that theft of a democratic ideal, be *re*-appropriated, *rearticulated once again*, such that a new paradigm of race based *both* on difference and solidarity, *both* on particularity and equality, might emerge? We would certainly not want to call such an ideal "colorblind," but we would expect it to include the possibility of overcoming racial difference, at least in part, through a creative type of consciousness and action, a radical racial pragmatism. An emphasis on "self-reflective action," to invoke a term from John Dewey (1939), is at the heart of the new racial politics needed in the 21st century.

The desire remains strong—not only in our hearts but in those of many others—for a more emancipatory concept of race and a more fulfilling, less conflicted, race consciousness. What would that look like? To be very specific, *what do you want your race consciousness to be?*[17]

If colorblind hegemony falters, if the "common sense" appeal of colorblindness cannot be consolidated, if the emperor of colorblindness is revealed to be wearing no clothes, then what comes next? From a colorblind perspective, one has not to "notice" race, not to see it. Or one wouldn't be "blind" to it, right? But what happens to race-consciousness under conditions of colorblind hegemony? Quite clearly, awareness of raciality does not dry up like a raisin in the sun. Just as colorblind racial ideology serves as a means to occlude recognition of race beneath the veneer of a supposedly already-accomplished universality, race-consciousness works to highlight racial differences and particularities. It can be linked to despotic or democratic ends, framed in defense of coercion, privilege, and undeserved advantage, or alternatively deployed in support of inclusion, human rights, and social justice.

Parallel to the question, what do you want your race consciousness to be? is another question: *What would a racial justice-oriented social policy look like to you?* What types of policies and practices—at the level of the state, civil society, and major institutions—would help us achieve a more comprehensive, deeper, and lasting racial democracy in the United States? We offer our own answers to these questions in the final section of this chapter.

* * *

Since racism is so large, combating it must also be a large-scale practice. The reparations idea provides a valuable guidepost here (Munford 1996; Henry 2007). Reparation means repair, making whole, making good what was evil. As a sociopolitical project, reparations can be seen to extend from the large to the small, from the institutional to the personal (Yamamoto 1999).

Redistribution fits as well, but here we must be careful: The politics of income and wealth distribution are "double-entry" bookkeeping items. Not only the allocation of resources is involved, but also the derivation of revenues. If reparations were to be paid for the crime against humanity that was African slavery, it would be important to look at both the inflow and the outflow sides of the process. On the outflow side, reparations should take the form of social investment (think of a "Marshall Plan for the Cities" or something similar). Payments to individuals or families would be problematic. Slavery's historical outcome in structural racism is the main evil we want to annul. On the inflow side, there is a danger that reparations would be paid out of general revenues, unduly assessing present-day working people for the crimes of past colonialists, slavocrats, and robber barons, perpetuating rather than attenuating racial conflicts, and allowing new variants of the colorblind argument to loom up in the future. An alternative revenue-oriented strategy would raise the money by means of a wealth tax, thus recognizing how many present-day capital hoards had their origins in slavery. Insurance companies indemnified slaveowners if their slaves escaped or shipbound Africans revolted, for example (Ogletree 2003).[18]

Beyond reparations, anti-racist practice can be understood macro-politically in terms of *social citizenship* and micro-politically in terms of *acculturation and socialization.*

The concept of *social citizenship* was proposed by T.H. Marshall (1950) as an obligation of the post-World War II welfare state, the proximate stage in the achievement of popular sovereignty. Rights, Marshall argued, had been acquired by the populace in historical stages: first economic, then political. The time had now come for the achievement of *social rights.* He meant that it was now possible and indeed necessary to consolidate and deepen the welfare state: not only through strengthening the social "safety net" but through inclusion, through the institution of far-reaching social democracy. Marshall's framework was post-World War II Britain, and perhaps the industrial democracies of Europe and the United States. It was offered when the British flag still flew over Lagos and Singapore, and when Jim Crow still flourished; it was proposed when postmodern criticism of the limits of "rights talk" (in critical race theory, for example) had not yet been made. His idea of social rights did not encompass the diasporic and globalized issues of inequality and injustice that anti-racists face today. Yet we can make use of the concept of social rights to think anew about political inclusion, social provision, even world citizenship.

By *acculturation and socialization* we mean the reawakening of the 1960s concept that "the personal is political" as a key principle of anti-racist personal practice. No one—no matter what their racial identity is—can be free of racism in their heads or hearts; it is too deeply ingrained in the U.S. social structure. Structural racism determines that a comprehensive system of advantages and disadvantages—economic, political, cultural, and psychological—suffuses U.S. society. Yet a great deal of thought and action has been devoted to the problem of fostering anti-racist practice at the individual and experiential level. Developing these skills, fostering the interruption and interrogation of racism, and extending the reach of anti-racism in workplace, politics, family, school, cultural life, and indeed every interaction, is an important dimension of the practice we want to support.

While we have offered some tentative and sketchy answers to these questions, on a deeper level such serious issues can only be addressed adequately through the creative thought and political action of many people. Those are the masses, the multitude, whose "freedom dreams" (Kelley 2003) can transfigure and rearticulate the unstable and conflicted racial system yet again. Racial formation theory was developed to help explain the post-World War II challenge to the U.S. system of racial oppression: its rise and fall, its successes and failures. Surely, those movement-based challenges were not the last we shall ever know. If our approach has any value, it lies in the suggestion that racial politics is a *creative practice*, both individual and collective. Our actions and ideas—both individual and collective—should be seen as projects that have the potential to undo racial injustice and generate broader racial equality, creating greater freedom in every way. Racial formation theory should help us think about race and racism as *continuing encounters between despotism and democracy*, in which individuals and groups, confronted by state power and entrenched privilege but not entirely limited by those obstacles, make choices and locate themselves over and over in the constant racial reconstruction of everyday life.

Notes

1. Douglass 2000 (1862), 485.
2. Winant (2001) offers a theoretically oriented historical sociology of the rise of the race-concept and the racialization of the planet in the modern epoch. For additional literature see Count 1950; Hannaford 1996; Davis 1999 [1975]; Fredrickson 1997; Bernasconi and Lott, eds. 2000. Obviously, any brief list will only scratch the surface of this vast topic.
3. The historical accounts provided by Thornton (1998), Lovejoy and Trotman (2003), Mullin (1995), and others suggest that African ethnicities may have been intermediate forms of slaves' collective mobilization. Thornton argues, for example, that numerous slave revolts were betrayed as a result of inter-ethnic rivalries. These authors also discuss how in the U.S. context slave owners, and the market in human chattel all on its own, worked to break up ethnic ties on individual plantations and in particular localities. Klein and Luna (2009) discuss some of these patterns in Brazil.
4. There are masculine tropes here as well: the "Sportin' Life" character in *Porgy and Bess* (Du Bose Heyward and George and Ira Gershwin, 1935); convict leasing and indeed incarceration itself as instances of race/class/gender intersectionality. The racist male tropes that have been applied to President Obama on innumerable web sites and political publications have their origins in 19th-century minstrelsy and 20th-century film culture (Bogle 2001; Robinson 2007; Lowndes 2013).
5. We 20th and 21st-century writers can only imagine the ridicule to which our great efforts at racial theorizing will be subjected in later periods. We can only welcome our critics, present and future....
6. Of course, "the Doctor" had important precursors: Frederick Douglass, George Washington Williams, and others, but none achieved his comprehensive level.
7. "[W]'ve been here before," writes Robin D.G. Kelley,

    > We were here with Latasha Harlins and Rodney King, with Eleanor Bumpurs and Michael Stewart. We were here with Anthony Baez, Michael Wayne Clark, Julio Nuñez, Maria Rivas, Mohammed Assassa. We were here with Amadou Diallo, the Central Park Five, Oscar Grant, Stanley "Rock" Scott, Donnell "Bo" Lucas, Tommy Yates. We were here with Angel Castro, Jr. Bilal Ashraf, Anthony Starks, Johnny Gammage, Malice Green, Darlene Tiller, Alvin Barroso, Marcillus Miller, Brenda Forester. We've been here before with Eliberto Saldana, Elzie Coleman, Tracy Mayberry, De Andre Harrison, Sonji Taylor, Baraka Hall, Sean Bell, Tyisha Miller, Devon Nelson, LaTanya Haggerty, Prince Jamel Galvin, Robin Taneisha Williams, Melvin Cox, Rudolph Bell, Sheron Jackson. And Jordan Davis, killed in Jacksonville, Florida, not long after Trayvon Martin. His murderer, Michael Dunn, emptied his gun into the parked SUV where Davis and three friends sat because they refused to turn down their music. (Kelley 2013)

8. The dynamics of immigration have shifted dramatically between the turn of the 20th century and the present. The U.S. now relates to the global South and global East through a policy of "accumulation by dispossession" (Harvey 2005). Immigrants are a lot darker than they were a century ago. Displaced and impoverished workers and peasants from Latin America and the Caribbean, as well as from the Pacific Rim, continue to immigrate, their human flow modulated but hardly contained by boom and bust, "bubble" and recession.

And the United States has also become more racially predatory domestically, practicing a similar policy of "accumulation by dispossession" at home as well. Consider post-Katrina New Orleans or the subprime housing crisis—to pick just two prominent examples. So is the United States less able to integrate immigrants than it was in previous historical periods? Where will the country find an "engine of mobility" to parallel that of the late 19th and early 20th centuries, the epoch of mass labor recruitment to the industrial economy? In short, the country's economic capacity to absorb enormous numbers of immigrants, low-wage workers and their families, and a new globally based (and very female) servant class (see Glenn 2002), without generating the sort of established subaltern groups we associate with the terms race and racism, seems to us more limited than was the "whitening" of Europeans a century earlier, this argument's key precedent. On this matter, see Perlmann 2005.

9. "Reforms" in quotation marks here because the ACA was (a) modeled on a Heritage Foundation proposal later enacted by a Republican governor, Mitt Romney, then of Massachusetts; and (b) won support from the FIRE sector (the industries of Finance, Insurance, and Real Estate) by promising to deliver *c*.50m new customers to private insurance companies on a silver platter. Owning a health insurance policy was made mandatory, a tax according to the Supreme Court. The small alternative, the "public option," was dumped. In fairness Obama did succeed at raising taxes slightly on the rich when the Bush II tax cuts expired. The cost of that was being forced to accept the "sequester," Congress's withholding of funding for already enacted social programs (as well as military spending). The 2013 cost of the sequester was $85.4b (Congressional Budget Office 2011). All hail progressive and redistributive reform!
10. The Supreme Court legal doctrine of "invidious intent" helped the racial reaction tremendously, because anti-racism policies and programs logically framed their objectives in racial terms. By contrast advocates for the racial *status quo* could argue in "colorblind" terms.
11. On this concept, see the debate between Bob Jessop, Stuart Hall, et al. in *New Left Review* (Jessop et al. 1984; Hall 1985).
12. Noting the distortions and perversions perpetrated—largely by the right wing—on Dr. King's "I Have a Dream" speech, Michael Eric Dyson once proposed a ten-year moratorium on referring to it (Dyson 2001). That moratorium has now expired. The speech belongs to the tradition that Bercovitch (1978) called the "American Jeremiad."
13. The calamitous 2008 recession impacted groups of color far more than it did whites. From 2005 to 2009, median net worth fell by 66 percent among Latino households, 54 percent among Asian households, and 53 percent among black households compared with a decrease of just 16 percent among white households (Kochhar et al. 2011, 14). The entire subprime mortgage crisis was a racial crisis, with disproportionate numbers of black and Latino borrowers facing foreclosures and losing their homes. Long excluded from equal access to mortgage credit, people of color were first "steered" into unsustainable loans, and then dispossessed of their meager equities through foreclosures, "short sales," and often fraudulent banking practices.
14. Of course, white supremacism and authoritarian racism generate solidarity too. As Herbert Blumer pointed out, "race prejudice" against another group is often the most effective and rapid means of establishing solidarity and "group position," both for the individual within her/his "own" group, and for the group itself to fortify its adhesive capacity (Blumer 1958).

15. Some scholars have warned about the scholarly reification of race, suggesting that race should not be treated as something "real"—as a legitimate social category in its own right, untethered from the mooring of racial oppression. This is visible in writings about the subject, sometimes large books, that insist on placing quotation marks around the term "race" (Darder and Torres 2004). While we have learned from many of these works, we stress that the instability of the race-concept does not imply the non-existence of race.
16. On racism as "waste," see Feagin, Vera, and Batur 2001. These authors draw the concept from Bataille 1988–1991.
17. Some of the following text appeared in earlier form in Omi and Winant 2012.
18. British slaveowners were compensated for their "losses" in 1833 when Parliament abolished slavery, and North American slavocrats regained their autarchic local autonomy in the "Compromise" of 1877, which Du Bois (2007 [1935]) called a counterrevolution. No former slaves were ever compensated for their losses of family members, property, or pay, much less their kidnapping, confinement, and torture at the hands of their "masters."

Works Cited

Abram, Morris. "What Constitutes a Civil Right?" *The New York Times Magazine*, June 10, 1984.

Abu-Jamal, Mumia. *We Want Freedom: A Life in the Black Panther Party*. Boston: South End Press, 2008.

Acuña, Rodolfo. *Occupied America: A History of Chicanos*, 7th ed. Boston: Longman/Pearson 2011 (1972).

Adams, Julia. *The Familial State: Ruling Families and Merchant Capitalism in Early Modern Europe*. Ithaca: Cornell University Press, 2005.

Agamben, Giorgio. *State of Exception*, trans. Kevin Attell. Chicago: University Of Chicago Press, 2005.

Ahmad, Muhammad, Ernie Allen, and John H. Bracey, ed. *The Black Power Movement. Part 3, Papers of the Revolutionary Action Movement, 1962–1996 (microform)*. A guide to primary sources on the RAM is available at Lexis-Nexis; http://www.lexisnexis.com/documents/academic/upa_cis/16313_blackpowermovempt3.pdf.

Alcoff, Linda Martín. "In Arizona, Censoring Questions About Race." *The New York Times*. April 1, 2012; http://www.opinionator.blogs.nytimes.com/2012/04/01/in-arizona-censoring-questions-about-race/.

Alexander, Michelle. *The New Jim Crow*, rev. ed. New York: The New Press, 2012.

Allen, Danielle S. *Talking to Strangers: Anxieties of Citizenship since* Brown v. Board of Education. Chicago: University of Chicago Press, 2004.

Allen, Robert L. *Reluctant Reformers: Racism and Social Reform Movements in the United States*. New York: Doubleday, 1974.

Allen, Robert L. *Black Awakening in Capitalist America: An Analytic History*. Lawrenceville, NJ: Africa World Press, 1990 [1970].

Allen, Robert L. "Reassessing the Internal (Neo) Colonialism Theory." *The Black Scholar*, Vol. 35, no. 1 (Spring 2005).

Allen, Theodore W. *The Invention of the White Race*, 2 vols. New York: Verso 2012 (1994; 1997).

Allitt, Patrick. *Religion in America Since 1945: A History*. New York: Columbia University Press, 2005.

Allport, Gordon W. *The Nature of Prejudice*. Reading, MA: Addison-Wesley, 1979 (1954).

Almaguer, Tomás. *Racial Fault Lines: The Historical Origins of White Supremacy in California*. Berkeley: University of California Press, 2008 (1994).

Althusser, Louis. "Ideology and Ideological State Apparatuses (Notes towards an Investigation)." In *Lenin and Philosophy and Other Essays*, trans. Ben Brewster. New York: Monthly Review Press 2001 (1971).

Amadae, S.M. *Rationalizing Capitalist Democracy: The Cold War Origins of Rational Choice Liberalism*. Chicago: University of Chicago Press, 2003.

American Sociological Association. *The Importance of Collecting Data and Doing Social Scientific Research on Race.* Washington, D.C.: American Sociological Association, 2003.

Anderson, Benedict. *Imagined Communities: Reflections on the Origin and Spread of Nationalism*, 3rd ed. New York: Verso, 2006.

Anderson, Elijah, ed. *Against the Wall: Poor, Young, Black, and Male.* Philadelphia: University of Pennsylvania Press, 2009.

Anderson, Jervis. *Bayard Rustin: Troubles I've Seen*, 2nd ed. Berkeley: University of California Press, 1998.

Ansell, David A. *County: Life, Death and Politics at Chicago's Public Hospital.* Chicago: Academy Chicago Publishers, 2011.

Appiah, Kwame Anthony. *In My Father's House: Africa in the Philosophy of Culture.* New York: Oxford, 1992.

Aptheker, Herbert. *American Negro Slave Revolts.* New York: International Publishers, 1983 (1963).

Aronowitz, Stanley. *False Promises: The Shaping of American Working Class Consciousness.* Durham: Duke University Press, 1991 (1973).

artasiamerica; http://www.artspiral.org (digital archive) (n.d.).

Asante, Molefi Kete. *The Afrocentric Idea*, 2nd ed. Philadelphia: Temple University Press, 1998.

Atwater, Lee and the Red Hot and Blue Band, "Red Hot and Blue," Curb Records, ASIN: B000000CSI; audio CD, 2001.

Bachrach, Peter, and Morton Baratz. *Power and Poverty.* New York: Oxford University Press, 1970.

Baker, Lee D. *From Savage to Negro: Anthropology and the Construction of Race, 1896–1954.* Berkeley: University of California Press 1998.

Balderrama, Francisco E., and Raymond Rodríguez. *Decade of Betrayal: Mexican Repatriation in the 1930s.* Albuquerque: University of New Mexico Press, 2006 (1995).

Balibar, Étienne, and Immanuel Wallerstein. *Race, Nation, Class: Ambiguous Identities*, 2nd ed. New York: Verso, 2011.

Banton, Michael. "Ethnic Groups and the Theory of Rational Choice." In *Sociological Theories: Race and Colonialism.* Paris: UNESCO, 1980.

Banton, Michael. "Max Weber on 'Ethnic Communities': A Critique." *Nations and Nationalism*, Vol. 13, no. 1 (2007).

Bardacke, Frank. *Trampling Out the Vintage: Cesar Chavez and the Two Souls of the United Farm Workers.* New York: Verso, 2012.

Barrera, Mario. *Race and Class in the Southwest: A Theory of Racial Inequality.* Notre Dame: University of Notre Dame Press, 2002 (1979).

Barrera, Mario, Carloz Muñoz, and Gil Ornelas. "The Barrio as Internal Colony." In Harlan Hahn, ed., *People and Politics in Urban Society.* Beverly Hills, CA: Sage, 1972.

Barth, Frederik, ed. *Ethnic Groups and Boundaries: The Social Organization of Culture Difference.* Long Grove, IL: Waveland Press, 1998 (1969).

Bataille, Georges. *The Accursed Share: An Essay on General Economy*, trans. Robert Hurley. New York: Zone Books, 1988–1991.

Baxandall, Rosalyn, and Linda Gordon, eds. *Dear Sisters: Dispatches from the Women's Liberation Movement.* New York: Basic, 2000.

Beatty, Jack. *Age of Betrayal: The Triumph of Money in America, 1865–1900.* New York: Knopf, 2007.

Beauvoir, Simone de. *The Second Sex*, trans. H.M. Parshley. New York: Vintage, 1989.

Becker, Gary S. *The Economics of Discrimination.* Chicago: University of Chicago Press, 1971 (1957).

Beckert, Sven. "Propertied of Different Kind: Bourgeoisie and Lower Middle Class in the Nineteenth-Century United States." In, Burton J. Bledstein and Robert D. Johnston, eds., *The Middling Sorts: Explorations in the History of the American Middle Class.* New York: Routledge, 2001.

Bederman, Gail. *Manliness and Civilization: A Cultural History of Gender and Race in the United States, 1880–1917.* Chicago: University of Chicago Press, 1996.

Belfrage, Sally. *Freedom Summer.* Charlottesville: University Press of Virginia, 1965.

Bell, Derrick. *Faces at the Bottom of the Well: The Permanence of Racism.* New York: Basic Books, 1992.

Bellah, Robert N. "Civil Religion in America." *Daedalus*, Vol. 134, no. 4 (Fall 2005).

Benston, Kimberly W. *Baraka: The Renegade and the Mask.* New Haven: Yale University Press, 1976.

Bercovitch, Sacvan. *The American Jeremiad.* Madison: University of Wisconsin Press, 1978.

Berger, Suzanne. *Peasants Against Politics: Rural Organization in Brittany, 1907–1967.* Cambridge, MA: Harvard University Press, 1972.

Berlet, Chip, and Matthew N. Lyons. *Right-Wing Populism in America: Too Close for Comfort.* New York: Guilford Press, 2000.

Bernasconi, Robert, and Tommy Lee Lott, eds. *The Idea of Race.* Cambridge, MA: Hackett, 2000.

Beverley, John. *Subalternity and Representation: Arguments in Cultural Theory.* Durham: Duke University Press, 1999.

Biddiss, M.D. *Father of Racist Ideology: The Social and Political Thought of Count Gobineau.* London: Weidenfeld and Nicholson, 1970.

Billig, Michael. *Banal Nationalism.* Newbury Park: Sage, 1995.

Bittker, Boris. *The Case for Black Reparations.* Boston: Beacon 2003 (1973).

Black, Edwin. *War Against the Weak: Eugenics and America's Campaign to Create a Master Race*, 2nd ed. New York: Four Walls Eight Windows, 2012.

Blackburn, Robin. *The Making of New World Slavery: From the Baroque to the Modern, 1492–1800.* New York: Verso, 1997.

Blackmon, Douglas. *Slavery by Another Name: The Re-Enslavement of Black Americans from the Civil War to World War II.* New York: Anchor 2009.

Blalock, Hubert M. *Toward a Theory of Minority-Group Relations.* New York: Wiley, 1967.

Blauner, Robert. *Racial Oppression in America.* New York: Harper and Row, 2001 (1972).

Blauner, Robert. *Still the Big News: Racial Oppression in America.* Philadelphia: Temple University Press, 2011.

Blight, David W. *Beyond the Battlefield: Race, Memory and the American Civil War.* Amherst: University of Massachusetts Press, 2002.

Block, Fred L., Richard A. Cloward, Barbara Ehrenreich, and Frances Fox Piven. *The Mean Season: The Attack on the Welfare State.* New York: Pantheon, 1987.

Block, Fred L., and Margaret Somers. "In the Shadow of Speenhamland: Social Theory and the Old Poor Law." *Politics and Society*, Vol. 31, no. 2 (June 2003).

Blumer, Herbert. "Race Prejudice as a Sense of Group Position." *Pacific Sociological Review*, Vol. 1, no. 1 (Spring 1958).

Boas, Franz. "The Instability of Human Types." Papers on Interracial Problems Communicated to the First Universal Races Congress Held at the University of London, July 26–29, 1911, ed. Gustav Spiller. Boston: Ginn and Co., 1912a.

Boas, Franz. *Changes in Bodily Forms of Descendants of Immigrants.* New York: Columbia University Press, 1912b.

Boas, Franz. *Anthropology and Modern Life.* New York: Norton, 1962.

Boas, Franz. *Race and Democratic Society.* New York: Biblo and Tannen, 1969 (1945).

Bobbitt, Phillip. *The Shield of Achilles: War, Peace, and the Course Of History.* New York: Knopf, 2002.

Bobo, Lawrence. "Racial Attitudes and Relations at the Close of the Twentieth Century." In Neil J. Smelser, William Julius Wilson, and Faith Mitchell, eds., *America Becoming: Racial Trends and Their Consequences, Vol. 1.* Washington, D.C.: National Academies Press, 2001.

Bobo, Lawrence. "President Obama: Monumental Success or Secret Setback?" TheRoot.com, July 17, 2008; http://www.theroot.com/id/47320.

Bobo, Lawrence D., and Michael C. Dawson. "A Change Has Come: Race, Politics, and the Path to the Obama Presidency." *Du Bois Review: Social Science Research on Race*, Vol. 6, no.1 (2009).

Bobo, Lawrence D., Melvin L. Oliver, James H. Johnson, Jr., and Abel Valenzuela, Jr., eds. *Prismatic Metropolis: Inequality in Los Angeles.* New York: Russell Sage Foundation, 2002.

Boggs, James. *Racism and Class Struggle.* New York: Monthly Review Press, 1970.

Boggs, James, and Grace Lee Boggs. "The City Is the Black Man's Land." *Monthly Review*, Vol. 18, no. 2 (June 1966).

Bogle, Donald. *Toms, Coons, Mulattoes, Mammies, and Bucks: An Interpretive History of Blacks in American Films*, 4th ed. New York: Bloomsbury, 2001.

Bolton, Kenneth, and Joe R. Feagin. *Black in Blue: African-American Police Officers and Racism.* New York: Routledge, 2004.

Bonacich, Edna. "A Theory of Ethnic Antagonism: The Split Labor Market," *American Sociological Review*, 37 (1972).

Bond, Patrick, ed. *Fanon's Warning: A Civil Society Reader on the New Partnership for Africa's Development.* Lawrenceville, NJ: Africa World Press, 2002.

Bond, Patrick. " African Resistance to Global Finance, Free Trade, and Global Profit-Taking." In Richard Vestra, ed. *Confronting Global Neoliberalism: Third World Resistance and Development Strategies.* Atlanta: Clarity Press, 2010.

Bond-Graham, Darwin C. *Bounce Back: Social Movements and Self-activity Through the Katrina Catastrophe.* Unpublished Ph.D Dissertation, University of California, Santa Barbara, 2010.

Bonilla-Silva, Eduardo "Rethinking Racism: Toward a Structural Interpretation." *American Sociological Review*, Vol. 62, no. 3 (June 1997).

Bonilla-Silva, Eduardo. *Racism Without Racists: Color-Blind Racism and the Persistence of Racial Inequality in America*, 3rd ed. Latham, MD: Rowman & Littlefield, 2009.

Borstelmann, Thomas. *The Cold War and the Color Line: American Race Relations in the Global Arena.* Cambridge, MA: Harvard University Press, 2003.

Boston, Thomas. *Race, Class, and Conservatism.* London: Allen and Unwin, 1998.

Bracey, John H., Jr., August Meier, and Elliot Rudwick, eds. *Black Nationalism in America.* Indianapolis: Bobbs-Merrill, 1970.

Brady, John. *Bad Boy: The Life and Politics of Lee Atwater.* New York: Addison-Wesley, 1997.

Branch, Taylor. *Parting The Waters: America in the King Years 1954–63.* New York: Simon and Schuster, 1988.

Branch, Taylor. *Pillar of Fire: America in the King Years 1963–65.* New York: Simon and Schuster, 1998.

Breines, Winifred. *The Trouble Between Us: An Uneasy History of White and Black Women in the Feminist Movement.* New York: Oxford University Press, 2007.

Briones, Matthew M. *Jim and Jap Crow: A Cultural History of 1940s Interracial America.* Princeton: Princeton University Press, 2013.

Brodkin, Karen. *How Jews Became White Folks and What That Says About Race in American.* New Brunswick, NJ: Rutgers University Press, 1998.

Brown, Kathleen M. "Beyond the Great Debates: Gender and Race in Early America. *Reviews in American History*, Vol. 26, no. 1 (1998).

Brown, Michael K. *Race, Money, and the American Welfare State.* Ithaca: Cornell University Press, 1999.

Brown, Michael K., Martin Carnoy, Elliott Currie, Troy Duster, David B. Oppenheimer, Marjorie M. Shultz, and David Wellman. *White-Washing Race: The Myth of the Color-Blind Society.* Berkeley and Los Angeles: University of California Press, 2003.

Brown, Scot. *Fighting for Us: Maulana Karenga, the US Organization, and Black Cultural Nationalism.* New York: New York University Press, 2003.

Brubaker, Rogers. *Citizenship and Nationhood in France and Germany.* Cambridge, MA: Harvard University Press, 1992.

Brubaker, Rogers, Mara Loveman, and Peter Stamatov. "Ethnicity as Cognition." *Theory and Society*, Vol. 33 (2004).

Bulmer, Martin. *The Chicago School of Sociology: Institutionalization, Diversity, and the Rise of Sociological Research.* Chicago: University of Chicago Press, 1986.

Burawoy, Michael. "Race, Class, and Colonialism," *Social and Economic Studies*, Vol. 24, no. 4 (December, 1974).

Burghart, Devin, and Leonard Zeskind. *Tea Party Nationalism.* Institute for Research & Education on Human Rights (IREHR), October 19, 2010; http://www.irehr.org/issue-areas/tea-party-nationalism.

Burnham, Walter Dean. "Post-Conservative America." *Socialist Review*, 72 (November–December 1983).

Business Week. "The 1970s: A Second Look" (Editorial, Sept. 14, 1974).

Butler, Judith. *Bodies That Matter: On the Discursive Limits of "Sex."* New York: Routledge, 1993.

Butler, Judith. *The Psychic Life of Power: Theories in Subjection.* Stanford: Stanford University Press, 1997a.

Butler, Judith. "Further Reflections on Conversations of Our Time." *Diacritics*, Vol. 27, no. 1 (Spring 1997b).

Butler, Judith. *Gender Trouble: Feminism and the Subversion of Identity.* New York: Routledge, 2006 (1990).

Butler, Judith. *Precarious Life: The Powers of Mourning and Violence*, 2nd ed. New York: Verso, 2006.

Button, James W. *Black Violence.* Princeton: Princeton University Press, 1978.

Calderón, José. "'Hispanic' and 'Latino': The Viability of Categories for Panethnic Unity." *Latin American Perspectives*, Vol. 19, no. 4 (Autumn 1992).

California Supreme Court. *People v. Hall* 4 Cal. 399 (1854).

Calloway, Colin G., ed. *The World Turned Upside Down: Indian Voices from Early America.* New York: Bedford/St. Martins Press, 1994.

Carbado, Devon W. "Racial Naturalization." *American Quarterly*, Vol. 57, no. 3 (September 2005).

Carbado, Devon W., and Cheryl I. Harris, "The New Racial Preferences." 96 *California Law Review*, Vol. 1139 (October 2008).

Carbado, Devon, and Mitu Gulati. *Acting White? Rethinking Race in Post-Racial America.* New York: Oxford University Press, 2013.

Carmines, Edward G., and James A. Stimson. *Issue Evolution: Race and the Transformation of American Politics.* Princeton: Princeton University Press, 1989.

Carson, Clayborne. *In Struggle: SNCC and the Black Awakening of the 1960s.* Cambridge, MA: Harvard University Press, 1995 (1981).

Caslin, Sinead. "Going Native." The Imperial Archive, http://www.qub.ac.uk/schools/SchoolofEnglish/imperial/key-concepts/Going-native.htm; accessed Sept. 6, 2008.

Celock, John. "Inge Marler, Arkansas Tea Party Leader, Makes Racist Joke At Event." *The Huffington Post*, June 14, 2012; http://www.huffingtonpost.com/2012/06/14/inge-marler-tea-party-arkansas-leader-racist-joke_n_1597334.html

Center for Constitutional Rights, August 12, 2013. *"Floyd, et al. v. City of New York, et al."*; http://www.ccrjustice.org/floyd.

Chabot, Sean. *Transnational Roots of the Civil Rights Movement: African American Explorations of the Gandhian Repertoire.* Lanham, MD: Lexington Books, 2011.

Chase, Allen. *The Legacy of Malthus*, 2nd ed. New York: Knopf, 1980.

Chatterjee, Partha. *Empire and Nation: Selected Essays 1985–2005.* New York: Columbia University Press, 2010.

Chávez, Ernesto. "Birth of a New Symbol: The Brown Berets' Gendered Chicano National Imaginary." In Joe Austin and Michael Willard, eds. *Generations of Youth: Youth Cultures and History in Twentieth Century America.* New York: NYU Press, 1998.

Chavez, Leo R. *The Latino Threat: Constructing Immigrants, Citizens, and the Nation.* Stanford: Stanford University Press, 2013 (2008).

Childs, John Brown. "Afro-American Intellectuals and the People's Culture," *Theory and Society*, Vol. 13 (1984).

Chung, Jean. "Felony Disenfranchisement: A Primer." Washington D.C.: The Sentencing Project, June 2013.

Churchill, Ward, and Jim Vander Wall. *Agents of Repression: The FBI's Secret Wars Against The Black Panther Party and The American Indian Movement*, 2nd. ed. Boston: South End Press, 2001 (1988).

Citrin, Jack, ed. *Proposition 13 at 30.* Berkeley: Berkeley Public Policy Press, 2009.

Clark, Kenneth. *Dark Ghetto*. New York: Harper and Row, 1965.

Clarke, John Henrik, ed. *Marcus Garvey and the Vision of Africa*. Baltimore: Black Classic Press, 2011 (1974).

Clinton, George. "Paint the White House Black." On *Hey Man, Smell My Finger*. Paisley Park Records: B000008EDO, 1993.

Cloward, Richard and Frances Fox Piven. "The Weight of the Poor: A Strategy to End Poverty." *The Nation*, May 2, 1966; http://www.thenation.com/article/weight-poor-strategy-end-poverty.

Cockburn, Alexander. "How Many Democrats Voted for Taft-Hartley?" *Counterpunch*, September 6, 2004; https://www.counterpunch.org/2004/09/06/how-many-democrats-voted-for-taft-hartley/.

Cohen, Thomas. *The Fire of Tongues: Antonio Vieira and the Missionary Church in Brazil and Portugal*. Stanford: Stanford University Press, 1998.

Cohn, D'Vera. "Census Bureau Considers Changing Its Race/Hispanic Questions." Pew Research Center; http://www.pewsocialtrends.org/2012/08/07/census-bureau-considers-changing-its-racehispanic-questions/.

Cole, David. *The Torture Memos: Rationalizing the Unthinkable*. New York: The New Press, 2009.

Coleman, Matthew. "A Geopolitics of Engagement: Neoliberalism, the War on Terrorism, and the Reconfiguration of Immigration Enforcement." *Geopolitics*, Vol. 12, no. 4 (2007).

Coles, Robert. *The South Goes North*, Vol. 3 of *Children of Crisis*. Boston: Little, Brown, 1971.

Collins, Patricia Hill. *Black Feminist Thought: Knowledge, Consciousness, and the Politics of Empowerment*. New York: Routledge, 2008 (1999).

Collins, Patricia Hill, and John Solomos. "Introduction: Situating Race and Ethnic Studies." In idem, eds. *Sage Handbook of Race and Ethnic Studies*. Thousand Oaks, CA: Sage Publications, 2010.

Comaroff, Jean, and John L. Comaroff. *Of Revelation and Revolution: Christianity, Colonialism, and Consciousness in South Africa*, 2 vols. Chicago: University of Chicago Press, 1991 and 1997.

Condé, Maryse. *I, Tituba, Black Witch of Salem*. New York: Ballantine, 1994.

Congressional Budget Office. "Estimated Impact of Automatic Budget Enforcement Procedures Specified in the Budget Control Act," September 12, 2011; http://www.cbo.gov/publication/42754.

Conley, Dalton. *Being Black, Living in the Red: Race, Wealth, and Social Policy in America*, 2nd ed. Berkeley: University of California Press, 2009.

Connerly, Ward. "Let's Strive for the 'Colorblind' Ideal." *San Francisco Chronicle*, September 19, 2003.

Connerly, Ward. *Creating Equal: My Fight Against Race Preferences*, 2nd ed. New York: Encounter Books/Perseus, 2007.

Cooper, Anna Julia. *The Voice of Anna Julia Cooper: Including A Voice From the South and Other Important Essays, Papers, and Letters*, ed. Charles Lemert. Lanham MD: Rowman & Littlefield, 1998.

Cooper, Frederick, and Ann Laura Stoler, eds. *Tensions of Empire: Colonial Cultures in a Bourgeois World*. Berkeley: University of California Press, 1997.

Coser, Lewis A. *The Functions of Social Conflict*. New York: Free Press, 1956.

Cotler, Julio. "The Mechanics of Internal Domination and Social Change in Peru." In Irving L. Horowitz, ed. *Masses in Latin America.* New York: Oxford University Press, 1970.

Count, Earl W., ed. *This Is Race: An Anthology Selected from the International Literature on the Races of Man.* New York: Henry Schuman, 1950.

Cowie, Jefferson. *Stayin' Alive: The 1970s and the Last Days of the Working Class.* New York, New Press, 2010.

Crawford, Alan. *Thunder on the Right: The "New Right" and the Politics of Resentment.* New York: Pantheon Books, 1980.

Crenshaw, Kimberlé W. "Demarginalizing the Intersection of Race and Sex: A Black Feminist Critique of Antidiscrimination Doctrine, Feminist Theory and Antiracist Politics." *University of Chicago Legal Forum*, 1989.

Crenshaw, Kimberlé W. "Mapping the Margins: Intersectionality, Identity Politics, and Violence Against Women of Color." *Stanford Law Review*, Vol. 43, no. 6 (July 1991).

Crenshaw, Kimberlé, Neil Gotanda, Gary Peller, and Kendall Thomas, eds. *Critical Race Theory: The Key Writings That Formed the Movement.* New York: The New Press, 1996.

Cross, Theodore. *Black Capitalism: Strategy for Business in the Ghetto.* New York: Simon and Schuster, 1974.

Cruse, Harold. "Revolutionary Nationalism and the Afro-American," *Studies on the Left*, Vol. 2, no. 3 (1962).

Cruse, Harold. *The Crisis of the Negro Intellectual.* New York: William Morrow, 1967.

Cruse, Harold. *Rebellion or Revolution?* New York: William Morrow, 1968.

Cullotta, Karen Ann. "New Owners to Reopen Window Plant, Site of a Sit-In in Chicago." *The New York Times*, Feb. 26, 2009.

Curry, Constance. *Deep in Our Hearts: Nine White Women in the Freedom Movement.* Athens: University of Georgia Press, 2000.

Dahl, Robert A. *Pluralist Democracy in the United States: Conflict and Consent.* Chicago: Rand McNally, 1967.

Daniel, G. Reginald. *More Than Black? Multiracial Identity and the New Racial Order.* Philadelphia: Temple University Press, 2001.

Darder, Antonia, and Rodolfo D. Torres. *After Race: Racism After Multiculturalism.* New York: New York University Press, 2004.

Davenport, Charles B. *Heredity in Relation to Eugenics.* New York: Arno Press, 1972 (1911).

Davis, Angela Y. *Abolition Democracy: Beyond Empire, Prisons, and Torture.* New York: Seven Stories Press, 2005.

Davis, Angela Y. *Women, Race and Class.* New York: Vintage, 2011 (1983).

Davis, David Brion. *The Problem of Slavery in The Age of Revolution, 1770–1823.* New York: Oxford University Press, 1999 (1975).

Davis, Mike. *Planet of Slums.* New York: Verso, 2006.

Dawley, Alan. *Class and Community: The Industrial Revolution in Lynn.* Cambridge, MA: Harvard University Press, 2000 (1975).

Dawson, Michael C. *Black Visions: The Roots of Contemporary African-American Political Ideologies.* Chicago: University of Chicago Press, 2003.

Dawson, Michael. *Not In Our Lifetimes: The Future of Black Politics.* Chicago: University of Chicago Press, 2011.

Deegan, Mary Jo. *Race, Hull-House, and the University of Chicago: A New Conscience Against Ancient Evils.* Westport, CT: Praeger, 2002.

De Genova, Nicholas. "The Legal Production of Mexican/Migrant 'Illegality.'" *Latino Studies*, Vol. 2, no. 2 (July 2004).

De Genova, Nicholas, ed. *Racial Transformations: Latinos and Asians Remaking the United States.* Durham: Duke University Press, 2006.

Delaney, Martin R. *Principia of Ethnology: The Origin of Races and Color, with an Archaeological Compendium of Ethiopian and Egyptian Civilization.* Whitefish, MT: Kessinger Publishing, 2009 (1879).

D'Emilio, John. *Lost Prophet: The Life and Times of Bayard Rustin.* Chicago: University of Chicago Press, 2004.

Democracy Corps. Inside the GOP: Report on Focus Groups with Evangelical, Tea Party, and Moderate Republicans. October 3, 2013; http://www.democracycorps.com/Republican-Party-Project/inside-the-gop-report-on-focus-groups-with-evangelical-tea-party-and-moderate-republicans/.

Denby, Charles, pseudonym Matthew Ward. *Indignant Heart: A Black Worker's Journal.* Detroit: Wayne State University Press, 1989 (1952).

Denver Art Museum. *Painting a New World: Mexican Art and Life, 1521–1821*, abridged ed. Denver/Austin: Denver Art Museum/University of Texas Press, 2004.

Dewey, John. *How We Think.* New York: Heath, 1933.

Dewey, John. *Intelligence in the Modern World; John Dewey's Philosophy*, Joseph Ratner, ed. New York: Modern Library, 1939.

Dewey, John. *Reconstruction in Philosophy.* Boston: Beacon, 1948 (1919).

Dewey, John. *Individualism Old and New.* Carbondale: Southern Illinois University Press, 1984 (1930).

Dickerson, Debra J. "Colorblind: Barack Obama Would Be the Great Black Hope in the Next Presidential Race—If He Were Actually Black." *Salon*, January 22, 2007; http://www.salon.com/2007/01/22/obama_161/.

Diop, Cheikh Anta. *African Origins of Civilization—Myth or Reality.* Chicago: Lawrence Hill, 1989.

Diop, Cheikh Anta. *Civilization or Barbarism—An Authentic Anthropology.* Chicago: Lawrence Hill, 1991.

Dollard, John. *Caste and Class in a Southern Town.* New York: Harper and Row, 1937.

Donner, Frank J. *Protectors of Privilege: Red Squads and Police Repression in Urban America.* Berkeley: University of California Press, 1990.

Douglass, Frederick. "The Meaning of the Fourth of July to the Negro." Speech delivered at Corinthian Hall, Rochester, NY, July 5, 1852. In Philip Foner and Yuval Taylor, eds. *Frederick Douglass: Selected Speeches and Writings.* Chicago: Chicago Review Press, 2000.

Douglass, Frederick. "The Future of the Negro People of the Slave States." Speech delivered at the Emancipation League, Tremont Temple, Boston, February 5, 1862. In Philip Foner and Yuval Taylor, eds. *Frederick Douglass: Selected Speeches and Writings.* Chicago: Chicago Review Press, 2000.

Dow, Mark. *American Gulag: Inside U.S. Immigration Prisons.* Berkeley: University of California Press, 2005.

Drinnon, Richard. *Facing West: The Metaphysics of Indian-Hating and Empire-Building.* Norman: University of Oklahoma Press, 1997.

D'Souza, Dinesh. *Obama's America: Unmaking the American Dream.* Washington, D.C.: Regnery 2012.

Du Bois, W.E.B. "Whither Now and Why." *The Education of Black People: Ten Critiques 1906–1960*, Herbert Aptheker, ed. Amherst: University of Massachusetts Press, 1973 (1960).

Du Bois, W.E.B. "The African Roots of the War." In David Levering Lewis, ed. *W.E.B. Du Bois: A Reader.* New York: Henry Holt, 1995 (1915).

Du Bois, W.E.B. *The Philadelphia Negro: A Social Study.* Philadelphia: University of Pennsylvania Press, 1998 (1899).

Du Bois, W.E.B. *The Souls of Black Folk.* Norton Critical Edition, edited by Henry Louis Gates, Jr. and Terri Hume Oliver. New York: Norton, 1999 (1903).

Du Bois, W.E.B. *Black Reconstruction in America: An Essay toward a History of the Part which Black Folk Played in the Attempt to Reconstruct Democracy in America, 1860–1880.* New York: Oxford University Press, 2007 (1935).

Dudziak, Mary L. *Cold War Civil Rights: Race and the Image of American Democracy*, 2nd ed. Princeton: Princeton University Press, 2011.

Duneier, Mitchell. *Sidewalk.* New York: Knopf, 2000.

Durkheim, Emile. *The Rules of Sociological Method: And Selected Texts on Sociology and its Method*, ed. Steven Lukes. New York: Free Press, 2014.

Dyson, Michael Eric. *I May Not Get There with You: The True Martin Luther King, Jr.* New York: Free Press, 2001.

Eagles. *Long Road Out of Eden.* Lost Highway/Polydor, 2007.

Eberhardt, Jennifer, and Susan Fiske, eds. *Confronting Racism: The Problem and the Response.* New York: Russell Sage Foundation, 1998.

Echols, Alice. *Daring To Be Bad: Radical Feminism in America 1967–1975.* Minneapolis: Univesrity of Minnesota Press, 1989.

Edelman, Marian Wright. *Kids and Guns: A National Disgrace.* Washington, D.C.: Educational Fund To End Handgun Violence, 1993.

Edelman, Marian Wright. *The State of America's Children.* Boston: Beacon, 2000.

Edelman, Peter. "The Worst Thing Bill Clinton Has Done." *The Atlantic*, Vol. 279, no. 3 (March 1997).

Edgar, David. "Reagan's Hidden Agenda: Racism and the New Right," *Race and Class*, Vol. 22, no. 3 (Winter 1981).

Edin, Kathryn, and Laura Lein. *Making Ends Meet: How Single Mothers Survive Welfare and Low-Wage Work.* New York: Russell Sage, 1997.

Edsall, Thomas Byrne with Mary Edsall, *Chain Reaction: The Impact of Race, Rights, and Taxes on American Politics*, rev. ed. New York: Norton, 1992.

Eisenhower, John S.D. *Intervention! The United States and the Mexican Revolution, 1913–1917.* New York: Norton, 1995.

Ellison, Ralph. "*An American Dilemma:* A Review" *Shadow and Act.* New York: Random House, 1964.

Ellison, Ralph. "*The Little Man at Chehaw Station.*" *Going to the Territory.* New York: Vintage, 1995 (1986).

El Plan de Santa Barbara (April 1969); http://www.ucsblhp.blogspot.com/2012/04/el-plan-de-santa-barbara.html.

Epstein, Steven. "Gay Politics, Ethnic Identity: The Limits of Social Constructionism." *Socialist Review*, 17 (1987).

Erick-Wanzer, Darrel, ed. *The Young Lords: A Reader.* New York: New York University Press, 2010.

Espiritu, Yen Le. *Asian American Panethnicity: Bridging Institutions and Identities.* Philadelphia: Temple University Press, 1993.

Essien-Udom, E.U. *Black Nationalism: A Search for Identity in America.* Chicago: University of Chicago Press, 1962.

Evans, Rowland, and Robert Novak, "Ed Davis, Toned-Down Favorite," *Washington Post*, February 3, 1978.

Evans, Sara M. *Personal Politics: The Roots of Women's Liberation in the Civil Rights Movement and the New Left.* New York: Knopf, 1979.

Eze, Emmanuel Chukwudi, ed. *Race and the Enlightenment: A Reader.* Malden, MA: Wiley-Blackwell, 1997.

Fang, Lee. *The Machine: A Field Guide to the Resurgent Right.* New York: New Press, 2013.

Fanon, Franz. *Black Skin, White Masks: The Experiences of a Black Man in a White World*, trans. Charles Lam Markmann. New York: Grove Press, 1967.

Faust, Drew Gilpin. *This Republic of Suffering: Death and the American Civil War.* New York: Vintage, 2009.

Feagin, Joe, and Chris Elias. "Rethinking Racial Formation Theory: A Systemic Racism Critique." *Ethnic and Racial Studies*, Vol. 36, no. 6 (2013).

Feagin, Joe R. *Systemic Racism: A Theory of Oppression.* New York: Routledge, 2006.

Feagin, Joe R., and Harlan Hahn, *Ghetto Revolts: The Politics of Violence in America's Cities.* New York: Macmillan, 1973.

Feagin, Joe R., Hernán Vera, and Pinar Batur. *White Racism: The Basics*, 2nd ed. New York: Routledge, 2001.

Federici, Silvia. *Caliban and the Witch: Women, the Body, and Primitive Accumulation.* New York: Autonomedia, 2004.

Fischer, Claude S., Michael Hout, Martin Sanchez Jankowski, Samuel R. Lucas, Ann Swidler, and Kim Voss. *Inequality by Design: Cracking the Bell Curve Myth.* Princeton: Princeton University Press, 1996.

Flores, Guillermo. "Internal Colonialism and Racial Minorities in the US: An Overview." In Frank Bonilla and Robert Girling, eds. *Structures of Dependency.* Stanford: Stanford University Press, 1973.

Foley, Neil. *The White Scourge: Mexicans, Blacks, and Poor Whites in Texas Cotton Culture.* Berkeley: University of California Press, 1999.

Foucault, Michel. *The History of Sexuality, Vol.1: The Will to Knowledge*, trans. Robert Hurley. New York: Vintage, 1990 (1978).

Foucault, Michel. "Governmentality." In Graham Burchell, Colin Gordon, and Peter Miller, eds. *The Foucault Effect: Studies in Governmentality.* Chicago: University of Chicago Press, 1991.

Foucault, Michel. *Ethics: Subjectivity and Truth*, Paul Rabinow, ed. New York: New Press, 1997.

Fox, Jonathan, and Gaspar Rivera-Salgado, eds. *Indigenous Mexican Migrants in the United States.* Boulder: Lynne Rienner, 2004.

Fox, Stephen R. *The Guardian of Boston: William Monroe Trotter.* New York: Scribners, 1971.

Frank, Thomas. *What's the Matter with Kansas? How Conservatives Won the Heart of America*, 2nd ed. New York: Holt 2005.

Frankenberg, Erica, and Gary Orfield, eds. *The Resegregation of Suburban Schools: A Hidden Crisis in American Education.* Cambridge, MA: Harvard Education Publishing Group, 2012.

Franklin, John Hope. *George Washington Williams: A Biography.* Durham, NC: Duke University Press, 1998 (1985).

Franklin, Raymond. *Shadows of Race and Class.* Minneapolis: University of Minnesota Press, 1991.

Fraser, Steve, ed. *The Bell Curve Wars: Race, Intelligence, and the Future of America.* New York: Basic, 1995.

Fraser, Steve. "The Hollowing Out of America." *The Nation*, Dec 3, 2012; http://www.thenation.com/article/171563/hollowing-out-america#axzz2ccxV3aFR.

Frazier, E. Franklin. "Myrdal's *An American Dilemma*" (review). *American Journal of Sociology*, Vol. 50 (1945).

Frazier, E. Franklin. *Black Bourgeoisie.* New York: Free Press, 1957a.

Frazier, E. Franklin. *The Negro in the United States*, rev. ed. New York: Macmillan, 1957b.

Fredrickson, George M. "African Americans and African Africans." *New York Review of Books*, Vol. 38, no. 15 (September 26, 1991).

Fredrickson, George M. *Black Liberation: A Comparative History of Black Ideologies in the United States and South Africa.* New York: Oxford University Press, 1995.

Fredrickson, George M. *The Comparative Imagination: On the History of Racism, Nationalism, and Social Movements.* Berkeley: University of California Press, 1997.

Fredrickson, George M. *Racism: A Short History.* Princeton: Princeton University Press, 2002.

Friedman, Milton. *Capitalism and Freedom.* Chicago: University of Chicago Press, 2002 (1962).

Fujino, Diane. *Samurai among Panthers: Richard Aoki on Race, Resistance, and a Paradoxical Life.* Minneapolis: University of Minnesota, 2012.

Gallagher, Charles A. "Color-blind Privilege: The Social and Political Functions of Erasing the Color Line in Post Race America." *Race, Gender and Class*, Vol. 10, no. 4 (2003).

Gallup. "Four Key Findings on Race Relations." July 29, 2013. http://www.gallup.com/video/163712/four-key-findings-race-relations.aspx?ref=image.

Garrow, David. *Protest at Selma: Martin Luther King Jr. and the Voting Rights Act of 1965.* New Haven: Yale University Press, 1978.

Garrow, David, ed. *Birmingham, Alabama, 1956–1963: The Black Struggle for Civil Rights.* New York: Carlson Publishing, 1989.

Gates, Henry Louis, Jr., ed. *The Classic Slave Narratives.* New York: Penguin 2002.

Geary, Patrick J. *The Myth of Nations: The Medieval Origins of Europe.* Princeton: Princeton University Press, 2002.

Genovese, Eugene. *Roll, Jordan, Roll: The World the Slaves Made.* New York: Pantheon, 1974.

Georgakas, Dan, and Marvin Surkin. *Detroit: I Do Mind Dying: A Study in Urban Revolution*, 3rd ed. Chicago: Haymarket, 2012 (1975).

Geronimo. *Geronimo: My Life*, as related to S.M. Barrett. New York: Dover 2005 (1905).

Gerth, Hans, and C. Wright Mills, eds. *From Max Weber: Essays in Sociology.* New York: Oxford University Press, 1958.

Geschwender, James A. *Class, Race, and Worker Insurgency: The League of Revolutionary Black Workers.* New York: Cambridge University Press, 1977.

Giddings, Franklin Henry. *Civilization and Society: An Account of the Development and Behavior of Human Society*, Howard W. Odum, ed. New York: Henry Holt, 1932.

Gilmore, Glenda Elizabeth. *Gender and Jim Crow: Women and the Politics of White Supremacy in North Carolina, 1896–1920.* Chapel Hill: University of North Carolina Press, 1996.

Gilroy, Paul. "The End of Anti-Racism." In Martin Bulmer and John Solomos, eds. *Racism.* New York: Oxford University Press, 1999.

Gilroy, Paul. *Against Race: Imagining Political Culture beyond the Color Line.* Cambridge, MA: Harvard University Press, 2000.

Glaude, Eddie S., Jr. *Exodus!: Religion, Race, and Nation in Early Nineteenth-Century Black America.* Chicago: University of Chicago Press, 2000.

Glaude, Eddie S., Jr., ed. *Is it Nation Time? Contemporary Essays on Black Power and Black Nationalism.* Chicago: University of Chicago Press, 2002.

Glazer, Nathan. "Blacks and Ethnic Groups: The Difference and the Political Difference It Makes," in idem, *Ethnic Dilemmas, 1964–1982.* Cambridge, MA: Harvard University Press, 1983.

Glazer, Nathan. *Affirmative Discrimination: Ethnic Inequality and Public Policy.* Cambridge, MA: Harvard University Press, 1987 (1975).

Glazer, Nathan, *We Are All Multiculturalists Now.* Cambridge, MA: Harvard University Press, 1997.

Glazer, Nathan, and Daniel P. Moynihan, *Beyond the Melting Pot: The Negroes, Puerto Ricans, Jews, Italians, and Irish of New York City*, 2nd ed. Cambridge, MA: MIT Press, 1970 (1963).

Glazer, Nathan, and Daniel P. Moynihan, "Introduction," in idem, eds., *Ethnicity: Theory and Experience.* Cambridge, MA: Harvard University Press, 1975.

Glenn, Evelyn Nakano. *Unequal Freedom: How Race and Gender Shaped American Citizenship and Labor.* Cambridge, MA: Harvard University Press, 2002.

Glover, Karen S. *Racial Profiling: Research, Racism, and Resistance.* Lanham, MD: Rowman and Littlefield, 2009.

Gobineau, Arthur. *The Inequality of Human Races*, trans. Adrian Collins. New York: Howard Fertig, 1999 (1853–1855).

Goff, Phillip Atiba, Jennifer L. Eberhardt, Melissa J. Williams, and Matthew Christian Jackson. "Not Yet Human: Implicit Knowledge, Historical Dehumanization, and Contemporary Consequences." *Journal of Personality and Social Psychology*, Vol. 94, no. 2 (February 2008).

Goffman, Alice. "On the Run: Wanted Men in a Philadelphia Ghetto." *American Sociological Review*, Vol. 74, no. 3 (June 2009).

Goldberg, David Theo. "Hate, or Power?" In idem. *Racial Subjects: Writing on Race in America.* Routledge, 1997.

Goldberg, David Theo. *The Threat of Race: Reflections on Racial Neoliberalism.* Malden, MA: Wiley-Blackwell, 2008.

Goldberg, David, and Trevor Griffey, eds. *Black Power at Work: Community Control, Affirmative Action, and the Construction Industry.* Ithaca: ILR Press, 2010.

Goldfield, Michael. *The Color of Politics: Race and the Mainsprings of American Politics.* New York: New Press, 1997.

Goldman, Emma. "The Traffic in Women." In idem. *Anarchism and Other Essays*, 2nd ed. New York: Mother Earth Publishing Association, 1911; http://www.marxists.org/reference/archive/goldman/works/1910/traffic-women.htm.

Goluboff, Risa L. *The Lost Promise of Civil Rights.* Cambridge, MA: Harvard University Press, 2007.

Gomez, Laura E. *Manifest Destinies: The Making of the Mexican American Race.* New York: New York University Press, 2008.

Gómez-Quiñones, Juan. *Sembradores, Ricardo Flores Magón y el Partido Liberal Mexicano: A Eulogy and Critique.* Los Angeles: Aztlán Publications, 1973.

Gonzalez, Juan. *Harvest of Empire: A History of Latinos in America*, 2nd ed. New York: Penguin 2011 (2001).

Gooding-Williams, Robert, ed. *Reading Rodney King/Reading Urban Uprising.* New York: Routledge, 1993.

Goodwin, Jeff, James M. Jasper, and Francesca Polletta, eds. *Passionate Politics: Emotions and Social Movements.* Chicago: University of Chicago Press, 2001.

Gordon, Linda. *The Great Arizona Orphan Abduction.* Cambridge, MA: Harvard University Press, 2001.

Gordon, Linda, and Allen Hunter. "Sex, Family, and the New Right: Anti-Feminism as a Political Force." In Dawn Keetley and John Pettegrew, *Public Women, Public Words: A Documentary History of American Feminism*, Vol. 3. Lanham, MD: Rowman & Littlefield, 2005.

Gordon, Milton. *Assimilation in American Life: The Role of Race, Religion, and National Origins.* New York: Oxford University Press, 1964.

Gossett, Thomas F. *Race: The History of an Idea in America*, 2nd ed. New York: Oxford University Press, 1997 (1965).

Gould, Stephen Jay. *The Mismeasure of Man.* New York: Norton, 1981.

Graeber, David. *Debt: The First 5,000 Years.* New York: Melville House, 2012.

Graham, Hugh Davis. "Richard Nixon and Civil Rights: Explaining an Enigma." *Presidential Studies Quarterly;* The Nixon Presidency, Vol. 26, no. 1 (Winter 1996).

Gramsci, Antonio. *Selections from the Prison Notebooks*, eds. and trans. Quintin Hoare and Geoffrey Nowell Smith. New York: International Publishers, 1971.

Grant, Madison. *The Passing of the Great Race, Or, the Racial Basis of European History.* New York: Scribners, 1916.

Graves, Joseph L. Jr. *The Emperor's New Clothes: Biological Theories of Race at the Millennium.* Piscataway, NJ: Rutgers University Press, 2001.

Greenberg, Stanley B. *Race and State in Capitalist Development.* New Haven: Yale University Press, 1980.

Greene, Daniel. *The Jewish Origins of Cultural Pluralism: The Menorah Association and American Diversity.* Bloomington: Indiana University Press, 2011.

Greenhouse, Steven. "Cleaning Companies in Accord with Striking Houston Janitors," *The New York Times*, November 21, 2006.

Greenwald, Anthony G., Colin Tucker Smith, N. Sriram, Yoav Bar-Anan, and Brian A. Nosek. "Implicit Race Attitudes Predicted Vote in the 2008 U.S. Presidential Election." *Analyses of Social Issues and Public Policy*, Vol. 9, no. 1 (2009).

Greenwald, Anthony G., Mark A. Oakes, and Hunter G. Hoffman. "Targets of Discrimination: Effects of Race on Responses to Weapons Holders." *Journal of Experimental Social Psychology*, Vol. 39 (2003).

Gregory, Steven. *Black Corona: Race and the Politics of Place in an Urban Community.* Princeton: Princeton University Press, 1998.

Griffin, Farah Jasmine. *"Who Set You Flowin'?" The African-American Migration Narrative.* New York: Oxford University Press, 1996.

Guglielmo, Thomas A. *White on Arrival: Italians, Race, Color, and Power in Chicago, 1890–1945.* New York: Oxford University Press, 2004.

Gugliotta, Guy. "New Estimate Raises Civil War Death Toll." *The New York Times*, April 2, 2012.

Guha, Ranajit, and Gayatri Chakravoty Spivak, eds. *Selected Subaltern Studies*, 2nd ed. New York: Oxford University Press, 1988.

Guigni, M.G. "Was It Worth the Effort? The Outcomes and Consequences of Social Movements." *Annual Review of Sociology*, Vol. 24, 1988.

Guinier, Lani. *The Tyranny of the Majority: Fundamental Fairness in Representative Democracy.* New York: Free Press, 1995.

Gutiérrez, Ramón A. *When Jesus Came the Corn Mothers Went Away: Marriage, Sexuality and Power in New Mexico, 1500–1846.* Stanford: Stanford University Press, 1991.

Gutman, Herbert C. *The Black Family in Slavery and Freedom, 1750–1925.* New York: Vintage, 1976.

Guy-Sheftall, Beverly. "Black Feminist Studies: The Case of Anna Julia Cooper." *African American Review*, Vol. 43, no. 1 (Spring 2009).

Gwaltney, John Langston. *Drylongso: A Self-Portrait of Black America.* New York: Vintage, 1980.

Haas, Jeffrey. *The Assassination of Fred Hampton: How the FBI and the Chicago Police Murdered a Black Panther.* Chicago: Chicago review Press, 2011.

Hacking, Ian. *The Social Construction of What?* Cambridge, MA: Harvard University Press, 1999.

Hacking, Ian. "Making Up People." *London Review of Books*, Vol. 28, no. 16 (August 17, 2006).

Hahn, Steven. *A Nation under Our Feet: Black Political Struggles in the Rural South from Slavery to the Great Migration Reform.* Cambridge, MA: Harvard University Press, 2003.

Haley, Alex. *Roots.* New York: Doubleday, 1976.

Hall, Stuart. "Race, Articulation, and Societies Structured in Dominance." In Marion O'Callaghan, ed. *Sociological Theories: Race and Colonialism.* Paris: UNESCO, 1980.

Hall, Stuart. "Authoritarian Populism: A Reply to Jessop et al." *New Left Review*, Vol. 1, no. 151 (May–June 1985).

Hanchard, Michael. *Party Politics: Horizons in Black Political Thought.* New York: Oxford, 2006.

Hancock, Ange-Marie. *The Politics of Disgust: The Public Identity of the Welfare Queen.* New York: New York University Press, 2004.

Handlin, Oscar. *The Uprooted: The Epic Story of the Great Migrations That Made the American People.* Philadelphia: University of Pennsylvania Press, 2002 (1951).

Hanisch, Carol. "The Personal is Political" 1969; http://www.carolhanisch.org/CHwritings/PIP.html.

Hanke, Lewis. *All Mankind is One: A Study of the Disputation Between Bartolomé de Las Casas and Juan Ginés de Sepélveda in 1550 on the Intellectual and Religious Capacity of the American Indian.* Normal: Northern Illinois University Press, 1974.

Hannaford, Ivan. *Race: The History of an Idea in the West.* Washington, D.C.: Woodrow Wilson Center Press/Baltimore: Johns Hopkins University Press, 1996.

Haraway, Donna J. *Primate Visions: Gender, Race, and Nature in the World of Modern Science.* New York: Routledge 1990.

Harding, Vincent. "Religion and Resistance Among Antebellum Negroes, 1800–1860." In August Meier and Eliott Rudwick, eds. *The Making of Black America*, 2 vols. New York: Atheneum, 1969.

Harmon, Amy. "In DNA Era, New Worries About Prejudice." *The New York Times*, November 11, 2007.

Harris, Cheryl I. "Whiteness as Property" 106 *Harvard Law Review.* 1709–1795 (1993).

Harris, Leslie M. "The New York City Draft Riots of 1863." In idem. *In the Shadow of Slavery: African Americans in New York City, 1626–1863.* Chicago: University of Chicago Press, 2003.

Harris-Perry, Melissa. *Sister Citizen: Shame, Stereotypes, and Black Women in America.* New Haven: Yale University Press, 2011.

Harvey, David. "The New Imperialism: Accumulation by Dispossession." *Socialist Register* 2004.

Harwood, John. "Don't Dare Call the Health Law 'Redistribution.'" *The New York Times*, November 23, 2013.

Hattam, Victoria and Joseph Lowndes. "Birmingham to Baghdad: The Micro Politics of Regime Change." In Gerald Berk, Dennis C. Galvan, and Victoria Hattam, eds. *Political Creativity: Reconfiguring Institutional Order and Change.* Philadelphia: University of Pennsylvania Press, 2013.

Hayek, Friedrich A. *The Road to Serfdom.* New York: Routledge 2001 (1944).

Haynes, Stephen R. *Noah's Curse: The Biblical Justification of American Slavery.* New York: Oxford University Press, 2002.

Hechter, Michael. *Internal Colonialism: The Celtic Fringe in British National Development.* New Brunswick: Transaction, 1998 (1975).

Heilbroner, Robert L. *The Worldly Philosophers: The Lives, Times and Ideas of The Great Economic Thinkers.* New York: Touchstone/Simon and Schuster, 2000 (1953).

Hellerstein, Judith, and David Neumark. "Workplace Segregation in the United States: Race, Ethnicity, and Skill." NBER Working Paper No. 11599. Cambridge MA: National Bureau of Economic Research, Sept. 2005.

Henry, Charles P. *Long Overdue: The Politics of Racial Reparations.* New York: New York University Press, 2007.

Herbert, Bob. "Impossible, Ridiculous, Repugnant." *The New York Times*, October 6, 2005.

Herrnstein, Richard J., and Charles Murray. *The Bell Curve: Intelligence and Class Structure in American Life.* New York: Free Press, 1994.

Hersh, Seymour M. *The Price of Power: Kissinger in the Nixon White House.* New York: Summit Books, 1983.

Higham, John. *Strangers in the Land: Patterns of American Nativism, 1860–1925.* New Brunswick, NJ: Rutgers University Press, 2002 (1955).

Hill, Anita. *Reimagining Equality: Stories of Gender, Race and Finding Home.* Boston: Beacon, 2011.

Hill, Gladwin. "Nixon Denounces Press as Biased." *The New York Times*, Nov. 8, 1962.

Hill, Laura Warren, and Julia Rabig, eds. *The Business of Black Power: Community Development, Capitalism, and Corporate Responsibility in Postwar America.* Rochester, NY: University of Rochester Press, 2012.

Hill, Robert A., and Barbara Bair, eds. *Marcus Garvey Life and Lessons: A Centennial Companion to the Marcus Garvey and Universal Negro Improvement Association Papers.* Berkeley: University of California Press, 1988.

Hilliard, David, with Lewis Cole. *This Side of Glory: The Autobiography of David Hilliard and the Story of the Black Panther Party.* Boston: Little Brown, 1993.

Hing, Bill Ong. *Ethical Borders: NAFTA, Globalization, and Mexican Migration.* Philadelphia: Temple University Press, 2010.

Hirabayashi, Lane Ryo. *Politics of Fieldwork: Research in an American Concentration Camp.* Tucson: University of Arizona Press, 1999.

Hirschfeld, Magnus. *Racism*, trans. Eden and Cedar Paul. London: Victor Gollancz, 1973 (1938).

Hirschman, Albert O. *Exit, Voice, and Loyalty: Responses to Decline in Firms, Organizations, and States.* Cambridge, MA: Harvard University Press, 1971.

Ho, Karen. *Liquidated: An Ethnography of Wall St.* Durham: Duke University Press, 2009.

Hobsbawm, Eric J., and Terence O. Ranger, eds. *The Invention of Tradition.* New York: Cambridge University Press, 1983.

Hochschild, Adam. *King Leopold's Ghost: A Story of Greed, Terror, and Heroism in Colonial Africa.* Boston: Houghton Mifflin 1998.

Hodes, Martha. *White Women, Black Men: Illicit Sex in the Nineteenth-Century South.* New Haven: Yale University Press, 1997.

Hodes, Martha. *Sex, Love, Race: Crossing Boundaries in North American History.* New York: New York University Press, 1999.

Hofstadter, Richard. *The Age of Reform: From Bryan to FDR*, 2nd ed. New York: Alfred A. Knopf, 1965.

Holwill, Richard N., ed. "Agenda 83: Mandate for Leadership." Washington, D.C.: Heritage Foundation, 1983.

Horne, Gerald. *Black and Red: W.E.B. Du Bois and the Afro-American Response to the Cold War, 1944–1963.* Albany: State University of New York Press, 1986.

HoSang, Daniel Martinez. *Racial Propositions: Ballot Initiatives and the Making of Postwar California.* Berkeley: University of California Press, 2010.

Htun, Mala. "From 'Racial Democracy' to Affirmative Action: Changing State Policy on Race in Brazil." *Latin American Research Review*, Vol. 39, no. 1 (2004).

Huang, Yunte. *Transpacific Imaginations: History, Literature, Counterpoetics.* Cambridge, MA: Harvard University Press, 2008.

Huntington, Samuel P. *Who Are We?: The Challenges to America's National Identity.* New York: Simon and Schuster, 2005.

Hurston, Zora Neale. *The Sanctified Church.* Berkeley: Turtle Island, 1984 (1929).

Hutchinson, Earl Ofari. "Method to Racist Madness in Fresh Racial Attacks on President Obama." *The Huffington Post*, August 13, 2013.

Iceland, John, and Daniel H. Weinberg, with Erika Steinmetz. "Racial and Ethnic Residential Segregation in the United States: 1980–2000." US Bureau of the Census Special Report. Washington D.C.: Government Printing Office, August 2002.

Ignatiev, Noel. *How the Irish Became White.* New York: Routledge, 1995.

Indians.com. "DNA Tests Being Used to Bolster Indian Heritage Claims"; http://www.indianz.com/News/2005/010071.asp.

Irons, Jenny. *Reconstituting Whiteness: The Mississippi State Sovereignty Commission.* Nashville: Vanderbilt University Press, 2010.

Jackson, Walter. *Gunnar Myrdal and America's Conscience.* Chapel Hill: University of North Carolina Press, 1990.

Jacobson, Matthew Frye. *Whiteness of a Different Color: European Immigrants and the Alchemy of Race.* Cambridge, MA: Harvard University Press, 1999.

Jacobson, Robin. *The New Nativism: Proposition 187 and the Debate over Immigration.* Minneapolis: University of Minnesota Press, 2008.

Jaffer, Jameel, and Amrit Singh. *Administration of Torture: A Documentary Record from Washington to Abu Ghraib and Beyond.* New York: Columbia University Press, 2009.

James, C.L.R., Grace Lee, Martin Glaberman, and Cornelius Castoriadis. *Facing Reality.* Chicago: Charles H. Kerr, 2006 (1958).

James, Winston. *Holding Aloft the Banner of Ethiopia: Caribbean Radicalism in Early Twentieth Century America*, 2nd ed. New York: Verso, 1999.

Jefferson, Thomas. *Thomas Jefferson: Writings — Autobiography / Notes on the State of Virginia Public and Private Papers / Addresses / Letters.* Merrill D. Peterson, ed. New York: Library of America 1984 (1785).

Jefferson, Thomas."On the Constitutionality of a National Bank"; http://www.yale.edu/lawweb/avalon/amerdoc/bank-tj.htm.

Jeffries, Michael P. *Paint the White House Black: Barack Obama and the Meaning of Race in America.* Stanford: Stanford University Press, 2013.

Jessop, Bob. *State Theory.* Malden, MA: Polity, 1990.

Jessop, Bob, Kevin Bonnett, Simon Bromley and Tom Ling. "Authoritarian Populism, Two Nations, and Thatcherism." *New Left Review*, Vol. 1, no. 147 (September–October 1984).

Joas, Hans. *The Creativity of Action*, 2nd ed., trans. Jeremy Gaines and Paul Keast. Chicago: University of Chicago Press, 1996.

Johnson, Charles S. *Shadow of the Plantation.* Chicago: University of Chicago Press, 1996 (1934).

Johnson, Walter. *Soul by Soul: Life Inside the Antebellum Slave Market.* Cambridge, MA: Harvard University Press, 2001.

Johnson, Walter. *River of Dark Dreams: Slavery and Empire in the Cotton Kingdom.* Cambridge, MA: Harvard University Press, 2013.

Johnston, David. "C.I.A. Tie Reported In Mandela Arrest." *The New York Times*, June 10, 1990; http://www.nytimes.com/1990/06/10/world/cia-tie-reported-in-mandela-arrest.html.

Jones, Jessica. "Cherokee By Blood and the Freedmen Debate: The Conflict of Minority Group Rights in a Liberal State," 22 *National Black Law Journal*, 1 (2009).

Jones, Van. *The Green Collar Economy: How One Solution Can Fix Our Two Biggest Problems.* New York: Harper, 2008.

Jones, Van. *Rebuild the Dream.* New York: Nation Books, 2012.

Jones-Correa, Michael, and David L. Leal. "Becoming 'Hispanic': Secondary Panethnic Identification among Latin American-Origin Populations in the United States." *Hispanic Journal of Behavioral Sciences*, Vol. 18, no. 2 (May 1996).

Jordan, Don, and Michael Walsh. *White Cargo: The Forgotten History of Britain's White Slaves in America.* New York: New York University Press, 2008.

Jordan, Winthrop D. *White Over Black: American Attitudes toward the Negro, 1550–1812.* Chapel Hill: University of North Carolina Press, 1977 (1968).

Jordan, Winthrop D. *White Over Black: American Attitudes Toward the Negro, 1550–1812*, 2nd ed. Chapel Hill: University of North Carolina Press, 2012 (1968).

Joseph, Peniel E., ed. *The Black Power Movement: Rethinking the Civil Rights-Black Power Era.* New York: Routledge, 2006.

Jun, Helen Heran. *Race For Citizenship: Black Orientalism and Asian Uplift from Pre-Emancipation to Neoliberal America.* New York: New York University Press, 2011.

Jung, Moon-Kie. "The Racial Unconscious of Assimilation Theory." *Du Bois Review: Social Science Research on Race*, Vol. 6, no. 2 (2009).

Kaczorowski, Robert J. "To Begin the Nation Anew: Congress, Citizenship, and Civil Rights after the Civil War." *American Historical Review*, Vol. 92, no. 1 (February 1987).

Kahlenberg, Richard D. *The Remedy: Class, Race, and Affirmative Action.* New York: Basic, 1997.

Kahn, Jonathan. *Race in a Bottle: The Story of BiDil and Racialized Medicine in a Post-Genomic Age.* New York: Columbia University Press, 2012.

Kairys, David. "Race Trilogy." 67 *Temple Law Review* 1994.

Kallen, Horace. "Democracy versus the Melting-Pot: A Study of American Nationality: Part I and Part II." *The Nation*, Feb. 18, 1915, Feb. 25, 1915.

Kallen, Horace. *Culture and Democracy in America.* New York: Boni and Liveright, 1924.

Kang, Jerry, Judge Mark Bennett, Devon Carbado, Pam Casey, Nilanjana Dasgupta, David Faigman, Rachel Godsil, Anthony G. Greenwald, Justin Levinson, and Jennifer Mnookin. "Implicit Bias in the Courtroom." 59 *UCLA Law Review* 1124 (2012).

Kantorowicz, Ernst H. *The King's Two Bodies: A Study in Medieval Political Theology.* Princeton: Princeton University Press, 1957.

Kaplan, Amy. *The Anarchy of Empire in the Making of U.S. Culture.* Cambridge, MA: Harvard University Press, 2005.

Kaplan, Karen. "Ancestry in a Drop of Blood," *Los Angeles Times*, August 30, 2005.

Kasinitz, Philip. *Caribbean New York: Black Immigrants and the Politics of Race.* New York: Cornell University Press, 1992.

Katz, Judith H. *White Awareness: Handbook for Anti-Racism Training*, 2nd ed. Norman: University of Oklahoma Press, 2003.

Katz, Michael B., and Thomas J. Sugrue. *W.E.B. Du Bois, Race, and the City: The Philadelphia Negro and Its Legacy.* Philadelphia: University of Pennsylvania Press, 1998.

Katznelson, Ira. *When Affirmative Action Was White: An Untold History of Racial Inequality in Twentieth-Century America.* New York: Norton, 2005.

Katzelson, Ira. *Fear Itself: The New Deal and the Origins of Our Time.* New York: Liveright/Norton, 2013.

Katzew, Ilona. *Casta Painting: Images of Race in Eighteenth-Century Mexico.* New Haven: Yale University Press, 2005.

Kazin, Michael. *The Populist Persuasion: An American History*. New York: Basic, 1995.

Keen, Mike Forest. *Stalking the Sociological Imagination: J. Edgar Hoover's FBI Surveillance of American Sociology.* Westport, CT: Greenwood Press, 1999.

Kelley, Robin D.G. *Race Rebels: Culture, Politics, and the Black Working Class.* New York: Free Press, 1996.

Kelley, Robin D.G. *Freedom Dreams: The Black Radical Imagination.* Boston: Beacon, 2003.

Kelley, Robin D.G. "The U.S. v. Trayvon Martin: How the System Worked." *CounterPunch*, July 15, 2013; http://www.counterpunch.org/2013/07/15/the-us-v-trayvon-martin/.

Kelley, Robin D.G., and Elizabeth Esch. "Black Like Mao: Red China and Black Revolution." In Fred Ho and Bill Mullen, eds. *Afro Asia: Revolutionary Political and Cultural Connections between African Americans and Asian Americans.* Durham: Duke University Press, 2008 (1999).

Kevles, Daniel J. *In the Name of Eugenics: Genetics and the Uses of Human Heredity*, 2nd ed. Cambridge, MA: Harvard University Press, 1998.

Kennedy, Randall. *For Discrimination: Race, Affirmative Action, and the Law.* New York: Pantheon, 2013.

Killens, John Oliver. *And Then We Heard the Thunder.* Washington, D.C.: Howard University Press, 1983 (1963).

Killian, Lewis M. *The Impossible Revolution Phase 2: Black Power and the American Dream*, 2nd ed. New York: Random House, 1975.

Kilson, Martin, and Clement Cottingham, "Thinking About Race Relations: How Far Are We Still From Integration?" *Dissent*, Fall, 1991.

Kim, Nadia Y. *Imperial Citizens: Koreans and Race from Seoul to L.A.* Stanford: Stanford University Press, 2008.

King, Martin Luther, Jr. "The Sit-In Movement." Martin Luther King, Jr. Research and Education Institute, Stanford University; http://www.mlk-kpp01.stanford.edu/index.php/kingpapers/article/chapter_14_the_sit_in_movement/. n.d.

King, Martin Luther, Jr. *Why We Can't Wait.* New York: Signet, 1964.

King, Martin Luther, Jr. *The Autobiography of Martin Luther King, Jr.*, ed. Clayborne Carson. New York: Grand Central Publishing, 2001.

King, Martin Luther, Jr. "Beyond Vietnam: A Time to Break Silence." In Clayborne Carson and Kris Shepard, eds. *A Call to Conscience: The Landmark Speeches of Dr. Martin Luther King, Jr.* New York: Grand Central Books, 2002a.

King, Martin Luther, Jr. "I have a Dream." In Clayborne Carson and Kris Shepard, eds. *A Call to Conscience: The Landmark Speeches of Dr. Martin Luther King, Jr.* New York: Grand Central Books, 2002b.

Klare, Karl. "The Horizons of Transformative Labour and Employment Law." In Joanne Conaghan, Richard Michael Fischl, and Karl Klare, eds. *Labour Law in an Era of Globalization: Transformative Practices and Possibilities.* New York: Oxford University Press, 2004.

Klare, Karl E. "Judicial Deradicalization of the Wagner Act and the Origins of Modern Legal Consciousness, 1937–1941." 62 *Minnesota Law Review* 265 (1977–1978).

Klein, Herbert S., and Francisco Vidal Luna. *Slavery in Brazil.* New York: Cambridge University Press, 2009.

Klein, Naomi. *The Shock Doctrine: The Rise of Disaster Capitalism.* New York: Picador, 2008.

Klinkner, Philip A., and Rogers Smith. *The Unsteady March: The Rise and Decline of Racial Equality in America.* Chicago: University of Chicago Press, 2002.

Kluger, Richard. *Simple Justice: The History of Brown v. Board of Education and Black America's Struggle for Equality.* New York: Vintage, 2004 (1976).

Knefel, Molly. "The School-to-Prison Pipeline: A Nationwide Problem for Equal Rights." *Rolling Stone*, November 7, 2013; http://www.rollingstone.com/music/news/the-school-to-prison-pipeline-a-nationwide-problem-for-equal-rights-20131107#ixzz2oFoOdTK3.

Knowles, Louis L., and Kenneth Prewitt, eds. *Institutional Racism in America.* Englewood Cliffs, NJ: Prentice-Hall, 1969.

Kochhar, Rakesh, Richard Fry, Paul Taylor, Gabriel Velasco, and Seth Motel. "Twenty-to-One: Wealth Gaps Rise to Record Highs Between Whites, Blacks and Hispanics." *Social and Demographic Trends Report*, Pew Research Center, July 26, 2011; http://www.pewsocialtrends.org/2011/07/26/wealth-gaps-rise-to-record-highs-between-whites-blacks-hispanics/.

Koerner, Brendan I. "Blood Feud." *Wired*, Vol. 13, no. 9 (September 2005).

Kondo, Dorinne. *About Face: Performing Race in Fashion and Theater.* New York: Routledge, 1997.

Kornweibel, Theodore, Jr. *Seeing Red: Federal Campaigns Against Black Militancy, 1919–1925.* Bloomington: Indiana University Press, 1998.

Kozol, Jonathan. *Savage Inequalities: Children in America's Schools.* New York: Broadway Books, 2012 (1991).

Kramer, Paul. *The Blood of Government: Race, Empire, the United States, and the Philippines.* Chapel Hill: University of North Carolina Press, 2006.

Kranish, Michael. "Bush Argues His Social Security Plan Aids Blacks," *Boston Globe*, January 30, 2005; http://www.boston.com/news/specials/social_security/bush_argues_his_social_security_plan_aids_blacks/?page=full.

Kristol, Irving. "The Negro of Today is Like the Immigrant of Yesterday." *The New York Times Magazine*, September 11, 1966.

Krugman, Paul. "Partying Like It's 1929." *The New York Times*, March 21, 2008.

Kryder, Daniel. *Divided Arsenal: Race and the American State During World War II.* New York: Cambridge University Press, 2001.

Kuhn, Thomas S. *The Structure of Scientific Revolutions*, 2nd ed. Chicago: The University of Chicago Press, 1970.

Laclau, Ernesto. *Politics and Ideology in Marxist Theory: Capitalism, Fascism, Populism.* London: Verso, 1978.

Laclau, Ernesto, and Chantal Mouffe, "Recasting Marxism: Hegemony and New Political Movements." *Socialist Review*, 66 Vol. 12, no. 6 (November–December 1982).

Laclau, Ernesto and Chantal Mouffe. *Hegemony and Socialist Strategy: Towards a Radical Democratic Politics*, 2nd ed. London and New York: Verso, 2001 (1985).

Ladner, Joyce A., ed. *The Death of White Sociology.* New York: Random House, 1973.

Lai, Him Mark, Genny Lim, and Judy Yung. *Island: Poetry and History of Chinese Immigrants on Angel Island 1910–1940*, 2nd ed. Seattle: University of Washington Press, 1991.

Lamis, Alexander P. *The Two Party South*, 2nd ed. New York: Oxford University Press, 1990.

Laraña, Enrique, Hank Johnston, and Joseph R. Gusfield, eds. *New Social Movements: From Ideology to Identity*, 2nd ed. Philadelphia: Temple University Press, 1994.

Lassiter, Matthew D. *The Silent Majority.* Princeton: Princeton University Press, 2007.

Lasswell, Harold D. *Politics: Who Gets What, When, How.* New York: Peter Smith Publishers, 1950 (1936).

Latty, Yvonne, and Ron Tarver. *We Were There: Voices of African American Veterans, from World War II to the War in Iraq*, 2nd ed. New York: Amistad/HarperCollins, 2005.

Lawson, Bill E., and Donald F. Koch, eds. *Pragmatism and the Problem of Race.* Bloomington, IN: Indiana University Press, 2004.

Le Blanc, Paul and Michael D. Yates. *A Freedom Budget for All Americans: Recapturing the Promise of the Civil Rights Movement in the Struggle for Economic Justice Today.* New York: Monthly Review Press, 2013.

Lee, Chana Kai. *For Freedom's Sake: The Life of Fannie Lou Hamer.* Urbana: University of Illinois Press, 2000.

Lee, Sandra Soo-Jin. "Racializing Drug Design: Implications of Pharmacogenomics for Health Disparities," *American Journal of Public Health*, Vol. 95, no. 12 (2005).

Lemann, Nicholas. *The Big Test: The Secret History of the American Meritocracy.* New York: Farrar, Straus, and Giroux, 2000.

Lenin, V.I. *Questions of National Policy and Proletarian Internationalism.* Moscow: Progress Publishers, 1970 (1915).

Lerner, Gerda. *The Creation of Patriarchy.* New York: Oxford University Press, 1987.

Lester, Julius. *Look Out Whitey! Black Power's Gon' Get Your Mama!* New York: Dial, 1968a.

Lester, Julius. *To Be a Slave.* New York: Dial, 1968b.

Lévi-Strauss, Claude. *The Savage Mind*, trans. John and Doreen Weightman. Chicago: University of Chicago Press, 1966.

Lewis, David Levering. *W.E.B. Du Bois, 1868–1919: Biography of a Race.* New York: Holt, 1993.

Lewis, Michael. "Obama's Way." *Vanity Fair*, October 2012; http://www.vanityfair.com/politics/2012/10/michael-lewis-profile-barack-obama.

Lewis, W. Arthur. "Economic Development with Unlimited Supplies of Labor." *Manchester School of Economic and Social Studies*, Vol. 22 (1954).

Lieberman, Robert C. *Shifting the Color Line: Race and the American Welfare State.* Cambridge, MA: Harvard University Press, 1998.

Lind, Michael. *The Next American Nation: The New Nationalism and the Fourth American Revolution.* New York: Free Press, 1995.

Lipset, Seymour M. "What's Wrong with Sociology?" *Social Problems*, Vol. 9, no. 2 (June 1994).

Lipset, Seymour Martin. *The First New Nation: The United States in Historical and Comparative Perspective.* New York: Transaction, 2003 (1963).

Lipsitz, George. *The Possessive Investment in Whiteness: How White People Profit from Identity Politics.* Philadelphia: Temple University Press, 1998.

Lipsitz, George. "Abolition Democracy and Global Justice." *Comparative American Studies*, Vol. 2, no. 3 (August 2004).

Lipsitz, George. "Learning from New Orleans: The Social Warrant of Hostile Privatism and Competitive Consumer Citizenship." *Cultural Anthropology*, Vol. 21, no. 3 (Aug. 2006).

Lipsitz, George. *Footsteps in the Dark: The Hidden Histories of Popular Music.* Minneapolis: University of Minnesota Press, 2007.

Liptak, Adam. "Justices Void Oversight of States, Issue at Heart of Voting Rights Act." *The New York Times*, June 26, 2013, A1.

Lizza, Ryan. "The Agitator: Barack Obama's Unlikely Political Education." *The New Republic*, March 19, 2007.

Lo, Clarence. *Small Property Versus Big Government: Social Origins of the Property Tax Revolt*, 2nd ed. Berkeley: University of California Press, 1995.

Locke, Alain Leroy. *Race Contacts and Interracial Relations: Lectures on the Theory and Practice of Race*, Jeffrey C. Stewart, ed. Washington, D.C.: Howard University Press, 1992 (1915).

Locke, Alain, ed. *The New Negro: Voices of the Harlem Renaissance.* New York: Simon and Schuster, 1997 (1925).

Loewen, James W. *Sundown Towns: A Hidden Dimension of American Racism.* New York: New Press, 2005.

Lopez, Ian F. Haney. *Racism on Trial: The Chicano Fight for Justice.* Cambridge, MA: Harvard University Press, 2003.

Los Angeles County Museum of Art. "ASCO: Elite of the Obscure, A Retrospective, 1972–1987" (museum exhibit, 2011); http://www.lacma.org/art/exhibition/asco.

Love, Erik. *Confronting Islamophobia: Civil Rights Advocacy in the United States.* Unpublished Ph.D. dissertation, University of California, Santa Barbara, 2011.

Lovejoy, Paul E. and Nicholas Rogers, eds. *Unfree Labour in the Development of the Atlantic World.* Ilford, Essex: Frank Cass, 1994.

Lovejoy, Paul E., and David Vincent Trotman. *Trans-Atlantic Dimensions of Ethnicity in the African Diaspora*. New York: Continuum, 2003.

Lowi, Theodore J. *The End of Liberalism: Ideology, Policy, and the Crisis of Public Authority.* New York: Norton, 1969.

Lowndes, Joseph. "The Past and Future of Race in the Tea Party Movement." In Lawrence Rosenthal and Christine Trost, eds. *Steep: The Precipitous Rise of the Tea Party.* Berkeley: The University of California Press, 2012.

Lowndes, Joseph. "Barack Obama's Body: The Presidency, the Body Politic, and the Contest over American National Identity." *Polity*, Vol. 45, no. 4 (Oct. 2013).

Lowy, Michael. "Marxists and the National Question." *New Left Review*, 96 (March–April 1976).

Luft, Rachel E. "Looking for Common Ground: Relief Work in Post-Katrina New Orleans as an American Parable of Race and Gender Violence." *NWSA Journal*, Vol. 20, no. 3 (Fall 2008).

Lukes, Steven. *Power: A Radical View.* New York: Macmillan, 2005 (1974).

Lusane, Clarence. *Colin Powell and Condoleezza Rice: Foreign Policy, Race, and the New American Century.* Westport, CT: Praeger, 2006.

Lusane, Clarence. *The Black History of the White House.* San Francisco: City Lights, 2011.

Luxemburg, Rosa. *The Accumulation of Capital.* New York: Routledge 1973 (1913).

Luxemburg, Rosa. *The National Question: Selected Writings by Rosa Luxemburg*, ed. Horace B. Davis, Monthly Review Press, 1976 (1909).

Lyman, Stanford M. *The Black American in Sociological Thought: A Failure of Perspective.* New York, Putnam, 1972.

Lyman, Stanford M. *Militarism, Imperialism, and Racial Accommodation: An Analysis and Interpretation of the Early Writings of Robert E. Park.* Fayetteville: University of Arkansas Press, 1992.

MacIver, Robert M., ed. *Discrimination and National Welfare.* New York: Harper, 1949.

MacLean, Nancy. "Neo-Confederacy versus the New Deal: The Regional Utopia of the Modern American Right." In Matthew Lassiter and Joseph Crespino, eds. *The Myth of Southern Exceptionalism.* New York: Oxford University Press, 2009.

Malcolm X. "The Ballot or the Bullet." Speech delivered April 12, 1964, at Cory Methodist Church in Cleveland, OH; http://www.malcolmxfiles.blogspot.com/p/ballot-or-bullet-april-12–1963.html.

Malcolm X. *Malcolm X Speaks*, ed. George Breitman. New York: Grove Weidenfeld, 1990 (1965).

Manasse, Ernst Moritz. "Max Weber on Race," *Social Research*, Vol. 14, no. 2 (June 1947).

Mann, James. *Rise of the Vulcans: The History of Bush's War Cabinet.* New York: Penguin, 2004.

Manza, Jeff, and Christopher Uggen. *Locked Out: Felon Disenfranchisement and American Democracy.* New York: Oxford University Press, 2006.

Marable, Manning. "Black Nationalism in the 1970s: Through the Prism of Race and Class," *Socialist Review*, 50–51 (March–June 1980).

Marable, Manning. *W. E. B. Du Bois: Black Radical Democrat.* Boston: Twayne, 1986.

Marable, Manning. *Malcolm X: A Life of Reinvention.* New York: Penguin, 2011.

Marable, Manning, and Kristen Clarke, eds. *Seeking Higher Ground: The Hurricane Katrina Crisis, Race, and Public Policy Reader.* New York: Palgrave/MacMillan, 2007.

Marchetti, Victor, and John D. Marks. *The CIA and the Cult of Intelligence.* New York: Knopf, 1974.

Markoff, John. *What the Dormouse Said: How the Sixties Counterculture Shaped the Personal Computer Industry.* New York: Viking, 2005.

Marks, Carole. *Farewell—We're Good and Gone: The Great Black Migration.* Bloomington: Indiana University Press, 1989.

Marsh, Jason, Rodolfo Mendoza-Denton, and Jeremy A. Smith, eds. *Are We Born Racist? New Insights from Neuroscience and Positive Psychology.* Boston: Beacon, 2010.

Marshall, T.H. *Citizenship and Social Class: And Other Essays.* London: Pluto Press, 1987 (1950).

Martha and the Vandellas. "Nowhere to Run." 7-inch single, Gordy Records G7039, 1965.

Martí, José. *Our America (Nuestra América): Writings on Latin America and the Struggle for Cuban Independence*, trans. Elinor Randall, Juan de Onis, and Roslyn Held. New York: Monthly Review Press, 1977 (1899).

Martinez, Elizabeth Sunderland, ed. *Letters from Mississippi: Reports from Civil Rights Volunteers and Freedom School Poetry of the 1964 Freedom Summer.* Brookline, MA: Zephyr Press, 2007 (1965).

Martinot, Steve. *The Rule of Racialization: Class, Identity, Governance.* Philadelphia: Temple University Press, 2002.

Marx, Karl. *Capital*, Vol 1. New York: International Publishers, 1967.

Marx, Karl and Frederick Engels. *Manifesto of the Communist Party*. Beijing: Foreign Language Press, 1968 (1848).

Marx, Karl, and Frederick Engels. *On Colonialism: Articles from the New York Tribune and Other Writings*. New York: International Publishers, 1972a.

Marx, Karl, and Frederick Engels. *Ireland and the Irish Question: A Collection of Writings*. New York: International Publishers, 1972b.

Massey, Douglas S. *Categorically Unequal: The American Stratification System*. New York: Russell Sage, 2007.

Massey, Douglas S., ed. *New Faces in New Places: The Changing Geography of American Immigration*. New York: Russell Sage Foundation, 2008.

Massey, Douglas S. and Nancy A. Denton. *American Apartheid: Segregation and the Making of the Underclass*. Cambridge, MA: Harvard University Press, 1993.

Massey, Douglas S., Rafael Alarcon, Jorge Durand, and Humberto González. *Return to Aztlán: The Social Process of International Migration from Western Mexico*. Berkeley: University of California Press, 1987.

Massey, Douglas. S. Jonathan Rothwell, and Thurston Domina. "The Changing Bases of Segregation in the United States." *The Annals of the American Academy of Political and Social Science*, Vol. 626, no. 1 (November 2009).

Matthews, Chris, MSNBC News, January 27, 2010; http://www.youtube.com/watch?v=15tVXQEcZlo.

Mauer, Marc. *Race to Incarcerate*, 2nd ed. New York: The New Press, 2006 (1999).

Mayer, Henry. *All on Fire: William Lloyd Garrison and the Abolition of Slavery*. New York: St. Martin's Press, 1998.

Mbembe, Achille. *On the Postcolony*. Berkeley: University of California Press, 2001.

McAdam, Douglas. *Political Process and the Development of Black Insurgency*. Chicago: University of Chicago Press, 1984.

McAdam, Douglas. *Freedom Summer*. New York: Oxford University Press, 1988.

McCarthy, Thomas A. *Race, Empire, and the Idea of Human Development*. New York: Cambridge University Press, 2009.

McClintock, Anne. *Imperial Leather: Race, Gender, and Sexuality in the Colonial Contest*. New York: Routledge, 1995.

McKernan, Signe-Mary, Caroline Ratcliffe, Margaret Simms, and Sisi Zhang. "Do Racial Disparities in Private Transfers Help Explain the Racial Wealth Gap? New Evidence from Longitudinal Data." White Paper, The Urban Institute, Washington, D.C., August 2011.

McLennan, Rebecca. *The Crisis of Imprisonment: Protest, Politics, and the Making of the American Penal State, 1776–1941*. New York: Cambridge University Press, 2008.

McWhorter, Diane. *Carry Me Home: Birmingham, Alabama, the Climactic Battle of the Civil Rights Revolution*. New York: Simon and Schuster, 2001.

Mead, Lawrence M. *The New Politics of Poverty: The Nonworking Poor in America*. New York: Basic Books, 1993.

MECHA, "El Plan de Santa Barbara: A Chicano Plan for Higher Education; Analyses and Positions by the Chicano Coordinating Council on Higher Education." Oakland: La Causa Publications, 1969; http://www.nationalmecha.org/documents/EPSB.pdf.

Meeropol, Michael. *Surrender: How the Clinton Administration Completed the Reagan Revolution*. Ann Arbor: University of Michigan Press, 1998.

Melucci, Alberto. *Nomads of the Present: Social Movements and Individual Needs in Contemporary Society.* Philadelphia: Temple University Press, 1989.

Merton, Robert K. "Manifest and Latent Functions." In *Social Theory and Social Structure*, 3rd ed. New York: Free Press, 1968.

Métraux, Alfred. "United Nations Economic and Security Council, Statement by Experts on Problems of Race." *American Anthropologist*, New Series, Vol. 53, no. 1 (Jan.–Mar. 1951).

Meyer, Gerald. "The Cultural Pluralist Response to Americanization: Horace Kallen, Randolph Bourne, Louis Adamic, and Leonard Covello." *Socialism and Democracy Online* 56, Vol. 25, no. 2; http://www.sdonline.org/; viewed 4/28/2012.

Mignolo, Walter. *Local Histories/Global Designs: Coloniality, Subaltern Knowledges, and Border Thinking.* Princeton: Princeton University Press, 2000.

Mignolo, Walter. *The Darker Side of Western Modernity: Global Futures, Decolonial Options.* Durham: Duke University Press, 2011.

Miles, Robert. *Racism.* New York: Routledge, 1989.

Miller, Joseph C. *Way of Death: Merchant Capitalism and the Angolan Slave Trade, 1730–1830.* Madison: University of Wisconsin Press, 1996 (1988).

Miller, Kelly. "A Review of Hoffman's 'Race Traits and Tendencies of the American Negro.'" Washington D.C.: The American Negro Academy, Occasional Papers, No. 1 (1897). (Available in Library of Congress, American Memory Series, African American Pamphlet Collection); http://www.gutenberg.org/files/31279/31279-h/31279-h.htm.

Miller, Kelly. *Race Adjustment; Essays on the Negro in America.* Miami: Mnemosyne Publishers, 1969 (1908).

Miller, Perry. *Errand into the Wilderness.* New York: Harper and Row, 1956.

Mills, Charles W. *The Racial Contract.* Ithaca: Cornell University Press, 1999.

Mills, Charles W. *The Sociological Imagination.* New York: Oxford University Press, 2000 (1959).

Mills, Charles W. "Racial Liberalism." *PMLA*, Vol. 123, no. 5 (Oct. 2008).

Montagu, M.F. Ashley. *Man's Most Dangerous Myth: The Fallacy of Race*, 2nd ed. New York: Columbia University Press, 1945.

Montalvo, Frank F., and G. Edward Codina. "Skin Color and Latinos in the United States." *Ethnicities*, Vol. 1, no. 3 (2001).

Montgomery, David. *The Fall of the House of Labor.* New York: Cambridge University Press, 1987.

Moore, Carlos. "Marxism: A Prolet-Aryan Outlook." *Berkeley Journal of Sociology*, Vol. 14 (1974–1975).

Moore, Joan W. *Mexican Americans.* Englewood Cliffs, NJ: Prentice-Hall, 1970.

Moore, Richard B. "The Critics and Opponents of Marcus Garvey" In John Henrik Clarke, ed. *Marcus Garvey and the Vision of Africa.* Baltimore: Black Classic Press, 2011 (1974).

Morgan, Edmund S. *American Slavery, American Freedom: The Ordeal of Colonial Virginia.* New York: Norton 2003 (1975).

Morgenstern Gretchen, and Joshua Rosner. *Reckless Endangerment: How Outsized Ambition, Greed, and Corruption Led to Economic Armageddon.* New York: Times Books, 2011.

Morris, Aldon D. *Origins of the Civil Rights Movement.* New York: Free Press, 1984.

Morris, Aldon, and Carol Mueller, eds. *Frontiers in Social Movement Theory.* New Haven: Yale University Press, 1992.

Morrison, Toni. *Playing in the Dark: Whiteness and the Literary Imagination.* New York: Vintage, 1993.

Moses, Wilson Jeremiah. *The Golden Age of Black Nationalism, 1850–1925.* New York: Oxford University Press, 1988 (1978).

Moses, Wilson Jeremiah. *Afrotopia: The Roots of African American Popular History.* New York: Cambridge University Press, 1998.

Mosse, George L. *Toward the Final Solution: A History of European Racism.* Madison: University of Wisconsin Press, 1985.

Mosse, George. *Nationalism and Sexuality: Respectability and Abnormal Sexuality in Modern Europe.* New York: Howard Fertig, 1997 (1981).

Mother Jones Newsteam, "Full Transcript of the Mitt Romney Secret Video," September 19, 2012; http://www.motherjones.com/politics/2012/09/full-transcript-mitt-romney-secret-video.

Mouffe, Chantal. "Working-Class Hegemony and the Struggle for Socialism," *Studies in Political Economy*, Vol. 12 (Fall 1983).

Moyers, Bill. "Two Versions of John Lewis' Speech," *Moyers and Company*, July 24, 2013; http://www.billmoyers.com/content/two-versions-of-john-lewis-speech/.

Mullin, Michael. *Africa in America: Slave Acculturation and Resistance in the American South and the British Caribbean, 1736–1831.* Urbana: University of Illinois Press, 1995.

Mullings, Leith. *New Social Movements in the African Diaspora: Challenging Global Apartheid.* Houndmills, Basingstoke (UK): Palgrave/MacMillan, 2009.

Mulroy, Kevin. *The Seminole Freedmen: A History.* Norman: University of Oklahoma Press, 2007.

Munford, Clarence J. *Race and Reparations: A Black Perspective for the Twenty-First Century.* Trenton, NJ: Africa World Press, 1996.

Murphy, Paul V. *The Rebuke of History: The Southern Agrarians and American Conservative Thought.* Chapel Hill: University of North Carolina Press, 2001.

Murray, Charles. *Losing Ground: American Social Policy, 1950–1980.* New York: Harper, 1996 (1984).

Myrdal, Gunnar. *An American Dilemma: The Negro Problem and Modern Democracy*, 20th anniversary ed. New York: Harper and Row, 1962 (1944).

Myrdal, Gunnar. *Economic Theory and Under-developed Regions.* London: Duckworth, 1963.

Nabokov, Peter. *Tijerina and the Courthouse Raid.* Albuquerque: University of New Mexico Press, 1969.

Naison, Mark. *Communists in Harlem During the Depression.* Urbana: University of Illinois Press, 1983.

Nappy Roots. "Sick and Tired." In idem. *Wooden Leather.* Atlantic Records, 2003.

Nash, Gary. "The Hidden History of Mestizo America." *Journal of American History*, Vol. 82 no. 3 (Dec. 1995).

Navarro, Armando. *La Raza Unida Party: A Chicano Challenge to the US Two Party Dictatorship.* Philadelphia: Temple University Press, 2000.

Nelson, Alondra. *Body and Soul: The Black Panther Party and the Fight against Medical Discrimination.* Minneapolis: University of Minnesota Press, 2013.

Nest, Michael. *Coltan.* Malden, MA: Polity, 2011.

Newman, Katherine S. *No Shame in My Game: The Working Poor in the Inner City.* New York: Vintage, 2000.

Newman, Randy. "Short People." On idem, *Little Criminals.* Los Angeles: Warner Brothers, 1977.

Ngai, Mae. *Impossible Subjects: Illegal Aliens and the Making of Modern America.* Princeton: Princeton University Press, 2005.

Nolan, Kathleen. *Police in the Hallways: Discipline in an Urban High School.* Minneapolis: University of Minnesota Press, 2011.

Noiriel, Gérard. *The French Melting Pot: Immigration, Citizenship, and National Identity.* Minneapolis: University of Minnesota Press, 1996.

Obama, Barack. "A More Perfect Union." Speech at the National Constitution Center, Philadelphia, March 18, 2008. *The New York Times*, March 18, 2008a; http://www.nytimes.com/2008/03/18/us/politics/18text-obama.html?pagewanted=all.

Obama, Barack. *The Audacity of Hope: Thoughts on Reclaiming the American Dream*, 2nd ed. New York: Vintage, 2008b.

Obama, Barack. "Remarks by the President on Trayvon Martin"; http://www.whitehouse.gov/the-press-office/2013/07/19/remarks-president-trayvon-martin.

Obasogie, Osagie. "The Return of Biological Race? Regulating Innovations in Race and Genetics through Administrative Agency Race Impact Assessments." *Southern California Interdisciplinary Law Journal*, Vol. 22, no. 1 (Fall 2013).

Obasogie, Osagie K. *Blinded by Sight: Seeing Race Through the Eyes of the Blind.* Stanford: Stanford University Press, 2013.

O'Connor, Alice, Chris Tilly, and Lawrence Bobo, eds. *Urban Inequality: Evidence From Four Cities.* New York: Russell Sage Foundation, 2001.

October League. *The Struggle for Black Liberation and Socialist Revolution.* Chicago: October League, 1976.

Ogbar, Jeffrey O.G. "The Formation of Asian-American (sic) Nationalism in the Age of Black Power, 1966–1975." *Souls*, Vol. 3, no. 3 (Summer 2001).

Ogletree, Charles J. "Reparations for the Children of Slaves: Litigating the Issues," 2 *University of Memphis Law Review* 33 (2003).

Okamoto, Dina G. "Institutional Panethnicity: Boundary Formation in Asian-American (sic) Organizing." *Social Forces*, Vol. 85, no. 1 (September 2006).

Okihiro, Gary Y. *Margins and Mainstreams: Asians in American History and Culture.* Seattle London: University of Washington Press, 1994.

Oliver, Melvin L. and Thomas M. Shapiro, *Black Wealth, White Wealth: A New Perspective on Racial Inequality*, 2nd ed. New York: Routledge, 2006.

Oliver, Melvin L., and Tom M. Shapiro. "Sub-Prime as a Black Catastrophe: First Came Racial Redlining. Then Came Racial Targeting of Toxic and Predatory Loans. Both Spelled Economic Disaster for African Americans." *The American Prospect*, October 2008.

Omi, Michael, and Howard Winant. "Racial Formation Rules: Continuity, Instability, and Change." In Daniel HoSang, Oneka LaBennett, and Laura Pulido, eds. *Racial Formation in the 21st Century.* Berkeley: University of California Press, 2012.

Omi, Michael, and Howard Winant. "Resistance is Futile? A Response to Feagin and Elias." *Ethnic and Racial Studies*, Vol. 36, no. 6 (2013).

Ondaatje, Michael L. *Black Conservative Intellectuals in Modern America.* Philadelphia: University of Pennsylvania Press, 2009.

Ono, Kent A., and John M. Sloop. *Shifting Borders: Rhetoric, Immigration, and Californa's Proposition 187.* Philadelphia: Temple University Press, 2002.

Opoku-Agyemang, Naana Jane, Paul E. Lovejoy, and David D. Trotman, eds. *Africa and Trans-Atlantic Memories: Literary and Aesthetic Manifestations of Diaspora and History.* Trenton, NJ: Africa World Press, 2008.

Oppenheimer, Martin. "The Sub-Proletariat: Dark Skins and Dirty Work." *Critical Sociology*, Vol. 4, no. 2 (January 1974).

Orfield, Gary and Erica Frankenberg. *Educational Delusions? Why Choice Can Deepen Inequality and How to Make Schools Fair.* Berkeley: University of California Press, 2013.

Painter, Nell Irvin. *The History of White People*. New York: Norton, 2010.

Park, John S.W. *Illegal Migrations and the Huckleberry Finn Problem.* Philadelphia: Temple University Press, 2013.

Park, Robert E. "Our Racial Frontier on the Pacific." *Race and Culture*, Vol. 1 of *The Collected Papers of Robert E. Park*, Everett Hughes et al., eds. Glencoe, IL: Free Press, 1926 (1950).

Park, Robert E. *Race and Culture*, Vol. 1 of *The Collected Papers of Robert E. Park*, Everett Hughes et al., eds. Glencoe, IL: Free Press, 1950.

Parker, Christopher. *Fighting for Democracy: Black Veterans and the Struggle against White Supremacy in the Postwar South.* Princeton: Princeton University Press, 2009.

Parker, Christopher S. and Matt A. Barreto. *Change They Can't Believe In: The Tea Party and Reactionary Politics in America.* Princeton: Princeton University Press, 2013.

Parker, David, and Miri Song, eds. *Rethinking* "Mixed Race." London: Pluto, 2001.

Parsons, Talcott, and Edward Shils, eds. *Toward a General Theory of Action: Theoretical Foundations for the Social Sciences.* New Brunswick: Transaction Press, 2001 (1951).

Parsons, Talcott, and Kenneth B. Clark, eds. *The Negro American.* Boston: Beacon, 1967.

Passel, Jeffrey S. *Changing Numbers, Changing Needs: American Indian Demography and Public Health.* Washington, D.C.: National Academies Press, 1996.

Pateman, Carole. *The Sexual Contract.* Stanford: Stanford University Press, 1988.

Patterson, Orlando. *Rituals Of Blood: The Consequences of Slavery in Two American Centuries.* New York: Basic, 1999.

Payne, Charles M. *I've Got the Light of Freedom: The Organizing Tradition and the Mississippi Freedom Struggle.* Berkeley: University of California Press, 2007 (1995).

Peele, Gillian. *Revival and Reaction: The Right in Contemporary America.* New York: Oxford University Press, 1984.

Peery, Nelson. *The Negro National Colonial Question.* Chicago: Workers Press, 1975.

Peña, Manuel H. *The Texas-Mexican Conjunto: History of a Working-Class Music.* Austin: University of Texas Press, 1985.

Pepper, William F. *An Act of State: The Execution of Martin Luther King.* New York: Verso, 2008.

Perlmann, Joel. *Italians Then, Mexicans Now: Immigrant Origins and Second-Generation Progress, 1890 to 2000.* New York: Russell Sage, 2005.

Perlstein, Rick. *Nixonland: The Rise of a President and the Fracturing of America.* New York: Scribner, 2008.

Perlstein, Rick. *Before the Storm: Barry Goldwater and the Unmaking of the American Consensus.* New York: Nation Books, 2009 (2001).

Perlstein, Rick. "Exclusive: Lee Atwater's Infamous 1981 Interview on the Southern Strategy." *The Nation*, November 13, 2012; http://www.thenation.com/article/170841/exclusive-lee-atwaters-infamous-1981-interview-southern-strategy.

Perlstein, Rick. "The Grand Old Tea Party: Why Today's Wacko Birds are Just like Yesterday's wingnuts." *The Nation*, November 25, 2013; http://www.thenation.com/article/177018/grand-old-tea-party?page=full.

Perry, Jeffrey B. *Hubert Harrison: The Voice of Harlem Radicalism, Vol. 1, 1883–1918.* New York: Columbia University Press, 2008.

Persons, Stow. *Ethnic Studies at Chicago, 1905–1945.* Urbana: University of Illinois Press, 1987.

Peterson, William. "Concepts of Ethnicity." In idem, M. Novak, and P. Gleason, *Concepts of Ethnicity: Selections from the Harvard Encyclopedia of American Ethnic Groups.* Cambridge, MA: Harvard University Press, 1982.

Pettigrew, Thomas F. "The Changing—Not Declining—Significance of Race." *Contemporary Sociology*, Vol. 9, no. 1 (January 1980).

Pfaelzer, Jean. *Driven Out: The Forgotten War against Chinese Americans.* Berkeley: University of California Press, 2008.

Phillips, Kevin P. *The Emerging Republican Majority.* New York: Anchor, 1970.

Phillips, Kevin. *American Dynasty: Aristocracy, Fortune, and the Politics of Deceit in the House of Bush.* New York: Penguin, 2004.

Phillips, Kevin. *American Theocracy: The Peril and Politics of Radical Religion, Oil, and Borrowed Money in the 21st Century.* New York: Penguin, 2007.

Phillips-Fein, Kim. *Invisible Hands: The Businessmen's Crusade Against the New Deal.* New York: Norton, 2010.

Pillai, K.G. Jan. "Shrinking Domain of Individious Intent." 9 *William and Mary Bill of Rights Journal* 525 (2001); http://www.scholarship.law.wm.edu/wmborj/vol9/iss3/2.

Pitt, Leonard. *Decline of the Californios: A Social History of the Spanish-Speaking Californias, 1846–1890.* Berkeley: University of California Press, 1999 (1966).

Piven, Frances Fox, and Richard A. Cloward. *Poor People's Movements: Why They Succeed, How They Fail.* New York: Vintage, 1978.

Piven, Frances Fox, and Richard A. Cloward. *Regulating the Poor: The Functions of Public Welfare.* New York: Vintage, 1993 (1971).

Piven, Frances Fox, and Richard A. Cloward. "The Weight of the Poor: A Strategy to End Poverty." *The Nation*, March 8, 2010 (May 2, 1966).

Piven, Frances Fox, Lorraine C. Minnite, Margaret Groarke and Adam S. Cohen. *Keeping Down the Black Vote: Race and the Demobilization of American Voters.* New York: The New Press, 2009.

Platt, Anthony M. *E. Franklin Frazier Reconsidered.* New Brunswick, NJ: Rutgers University Press, 1991.

Pogrund, Benjamin. *Sobukwe and Apartheid.* New Brunswick: Rutgers University Press, 1991.

Polanyi, Karl. *The Great Transformation: The Political and Economic Origins of Our Time*, 2nd ed. Boston: Beacon, 2001 (1944).

Polletta, Francesca, and Jasper, James M. "Collective Identity and Social Movements." *Annual Review of Sociology*, 2001.

Porter, Eric. *The Problem of the Future World: W.E.B. Du Bois and the Race Concept at Midcentury.* Durham: Duke University Press, 2010.

powell, john a. *Racing to Justice: Transforming Our Conceptions of Self and Other to Build a More Inclusive Society.* Bloomington: Indiana University Press, 2012.

powell, john a., and Stephen Menendian. "Constructing the Other: Understanding Structural Marginalization." Unpublished manuscript on file with authors.

Powell, Lewis F. "Attack on the American Free Enterprise System." Confidential memo to the US Chamber of Commerce, 1971; http://www.law.wlu.edu/deptimages/Powell%20 Archives/PowellMemorandumPrinted.pdf.

Powers, Thomas. *The Killing of Crazy Horse.* New York: Vintage, 2011.

Prashad, Vijay. *Everybody Was Kung Fu Fighting: Afro-Asian Connections and the Myth of Cultural Purity.* Boston: Beacon, 2002.

Prashad, Vijay. *The Darker Nations: A People's History of the Third World.* New York: The New Press, 2007.

Prashad, Vijay. "Waiting for the Black Gandhi: Satyagraha and Black Internationalism." In Michael O. West, William G. Martin, and Fanon Che Wilkins, eds. *From Tousaint to Tupac: The Black International Since the Age of Revolution.* Chapel Hill: University of North Carolina Press, 2009.

Prewitt, Kenneth. *What is Your Race? The Census and Our Flawed Efforts to Classify Americans by Race.* Princeton: Princeton University Press, 2013.

Price, David H. *Threatening Anthropology: McCarthyism and the FBI's Surveillance of Activist Anthropologists.* Durham: Duke University Press, 2004.

Prins, Harald E.L. "Toward a World without Evil: Alfred Métraux as UNESCO Anthropologist (1946–1962)." UNESCO Symposium 2007; http://www.portal.unesco.org/en/ev.php-URL_ID=30431&URL_DO=DO_TOPIC&URL_SECTION=201.html.

Pulido, Laura. *Black, Brown, Yellow, and Left: Radical Activism in Los Angeles.* Berkeley: University of California Press, 2006.

Quadagno, Jill. *The Color of Welfare: How Racism Undermined the War on Poverty.* New York: Oxford University Press, 1994.

Quan, Natalie. "Black and White or Red All Over? The Impropriety of Using Crime Scene DNA to Construct Racial Profiles of Suspects." 84 *Southern California Law Review* 1403 (September 2011).

Quijano, Anibal. "Coloniality of Power, Eurocentrism, and Latin America." *Nepantla: Views from South*, Vol. 1, no. 3 (2000).

Radhakrishnan, R. "Nationalism, Gender, and the Narrative of Identity." In Andrew Parker, Mary Russo, Doris Sommer, and Patricia Yaeger, eds. *Nationalisms and Sexualities.* New York: Routledge, 1992.

Radical America, "Racism and Busing in Boston: Editorial Statement," Vol. 8, no. 6 (November–December 1974).

Radical America, "Racism and Busing in Boston: Comments and Criticism," Vol. 9, no. 3 (May–June 1975).

Rage Against the Machine. "Mic Check." *The Battle of Los Angeles.* Epic Records.

Rainwater, Lee, and William Yancey, eds. *The Moynihan Report and the Politics of Controversy.* Cambridge, MA: MIT Press, 1967.

Ransby, Barbara. *Ella Baker and the Black Freedom Movement: A Radical Democratic Vision*, 2nd ed. Chapel Hill: University of North Carolina Press, 2005.

Rawick, George P. *From Sundown to Sunup: The Making of the Black Community.* Westport, CT: Greenwood, 1972.

Reagan, Ronald. "Address Before a Joint Session of the Congress Reporting on the State of the Union," January 26, 1982; http://www.presidency.ucsb.edu/ws/?pid=42687.

Reed, Adolph, Jr. *W.E.B. Du Bois and American Political Thought: Fabianism and the Color Line.* New York: Oxford University Press, 1997a.

Reed, Adolph L., Jr. "Yackety-Yak about Race." *The Progressive*, Dec 1, 1997b.

Reed, Adolph L., Jr. "Black Particularity Reconsidered." In Eddie S. Glaude, Jr., ed. *Is It Nation Time?: Contemporary Essays on Black Power and Black Nationalism.* Chicago: University of Chicago Press, 2002.

Reich, Michael. *Racial Inequality: A Political-Economic Analysis.* Princeton: Princeton University Press, 1981.

Reid, Carolina, and Elizabeth Laderman. "The Untold Costs of Subprime Lending: Examining the Links among Higher-Priced Lending, Foreclosures and Race in California," Working Paper, Institute for Assets and Social Policy, Brandeis University, April 15, 2009.

Reid, Ira De A. *Postwar Problems of Migration.* New York: Milbank Memorial Fund, 1947.

Revolutionary Union, *Red Papers 5: National Liberation and Proletarian Revolution in the US.* Chicago: Revolutionary Union, n.d.

Richter, Daniel K. *Facing East from Indian Country: A Native History of Early America.* Cambridge: Harvard University Press, 2003.

Ricourt, Milagros, and Ruby Danta. *Hispanas de Queens: Latino Panethnicity in a New York City Neighborhood.* Ithaca: Cornell University Press, 2002.

Rieder, Jonathan. *Canarsie: The Jews and Italians of Brooklyn against Liberalism.* Cambridge, MA: Harvard University Press, 1985.

Riggs, Marlon. *Color Adjustment.* San Francisco: California Newsreel, 1992.

Roberts, Ronald Suresh. *Clarence Thomas and the Tough Love Crowd: Counterfeit Heroes and Unhappy Truths.* New York: New York University Press, 1996.

Robinson, Cedric J. *Black Marxism: The Making of the Black Radical Tradition.* Chapel Hill: University of North Carolina Press, 2000 (1983).

Robinson, Cedric. *Forgeries of Memory and Meaning: Blacks and the Regimes of Race in American Theater and Film before World War II.* Chapel Hill: University of North Carolina Press, 2007.

Robles, Kathleen L. and Richard Griswold del Castillo. "The History of Chicano Park"; http://www.chicanoparksandiego.com.

Rodríguez, Clara E. *Changing Race: Latinos, the Census, and the History of Ethnicity in the United States.* New York: New York University Press, 2000.

Roediger, David. *Working Toward Whiteness: How America's Immigrants Became White; The Strange Journey from Ellis Island to the Suburbs.* New York: Basic, 2005.

Roediger, David R. *The Wages of Whiteness: Race and the Making of the American Working Class*, 2nd ed. New York: Verso, 2007 (1991).

Roediger, David R. *How Race Survived U.S. History: From Settlement and Slavery to the Obama Phenomenon.* New York: Verso, 2008.

Roediger, David R., and Elizabeth D. Esch. *The Production of Difference: Race and the Management of Labor in US History.* New York: Oxford University Press, 2012.

Roemer, John. *Equality of Opportunity.* Cambridge, MA: Harvard University Press, 2000.

Rogers, Christy. "Subprime Loans, Foreclosure, and the Credit Crisis: What Happened and Why?" Kirwan Institute for the Study of Race and Ethnicity, The Ohio State University, December 2008; http://www.kirwaninstitute.osu.edu/reports/2008/11_2008_SubprimeForeclosureRacePrimer.pdf.

Rogin, Michael. *Two Declarations of Independence: The Racialized Foundations of American National Culture.* Berlin: Free University Press, 1996.

Rogin, Michael Paul. *Fathers and Children: Andrew Jackson and the Subjugation of the American Indian.* New Brunswick: Transaction, 1991.

Romo, David Dorado. *Ringside Seat to a Revolution: An Underground Cultural History of El Paso and Juárez, 1893–1923.* El Paso: Cinco Puntos Press, 2005.

Rose, Arnold. *The Power Structure: Political Process in American Society.* New York: Oxford University Press, 1967.

Rosenfeld, Seth. *Subversives: The FBI's War on Student Radicals, and Reagan's Rise to Power.* New York: Picador, 2013.

Rosengarten, Theodore. *All God's Dangers: The Life of Nate Shaw.* Chicago: University of Chicago Press, 2000 (1974).

Rosenthal, Lawrence. *The Tea Party, the Government Shutdown, and Obamacare.* Policy Brief for The Foundation for Law, Justice and Society, 2013.

Rosenthal, Lawrence, and Christine Trost. *Steep: The Precipitous Rise of the Tea Party.* Berkeley: University of California Press, 2012.

Ross, Edward A. *The Old World in the New: The Significance of Past and Present Immigration to the American People.* New York: Century, 1914.

Roth, Wendy D. *Race Migrations: Latinos and the Cultural Transformation of Race.* Stanford: Stanford University Press, 2012.

Rubin, Gayle. "The Traffic in Women: Notes on the 'Political Economy' of Sex." In Rayna Reiter, ed. *Toward an Anthropology of Women.* New York: Monthly Review Press, 1975.

Rucker, Walter C., Jr. and James N. Upton, eds. *Encyclopedia of American Race Riots*, 2 vols. Westport, CT: Greenwood, 2006.

Rugh, Jacob S., and Douglas S. Massey. "Racial Segregation and the American Foreclosure Crisis." *American Sociological Review*, Vol. 75, no. 5 (October 2010).

Rusher, William. *The Making of a New Majority Party.* Ottawa, IL: Greenhill Publications, 1975.

Rustin, Bayard. "From Protest to Politics: The Future of the Civil Rights Movement." *Commentary*, Feb., 1964.

Rustin, Bayard. "The Lessons of the Long Hot Summer," *Commentary*, Oct., 1967.

Rustin, Bayard. "Some Lessons from Watts." In D.W. Carbado and D. Weise, eds. *Time on Two Crosses; The Collected Writings of Bayard Rustin.* San Francisco: Cleis Press, 2003 (1965).

Rustin, Bayard. *Time on Two Crosses: The Collected Writings of Bayard Rustin*, Devon W. Carbado and Donald Weise, eds. Berkeley: Cleis, 2003.

Rutten, Tim. "A New Kind of Riot." *The New York Review of Books*, June 11, 1992.

Ryan, Joseph W. *Samuel Stouffer and the GI Survey: Sociologists and Soldiers During the Second World War.* Knoxville: University of Tennessee Press, 2013.

Sack, Kevin. "Member's Racist Ties Split Confederate Legacy Group." *The New York Times*, December 8, 2001.

Said, Edward W. *Culture and Imperialism.* New York: Alfred A. Knopf, 1993.

Sale, Kirkpatrick. *SDS.* New York, Random House, 1973.

Sanders, Bernie (Senator, VT). "Billions for Bailouts! Who Pays?" *The Huffington Post*, September 19, 2008; http://www.huffingtonpost.com/rep-bernie-sanders/billions-for-bailouts-who_b_127882.html.

Samson, Frank L. "Multiple Group Threat and Malleable White Attitudes Towards Academic Merit." *Du Bois Review: Social Science Research on Race*, Vol. 10, no. 1 (March 2013).

Sartre, Jean-Paul. *Critique of Dialectical Reason*, Vol. 1, rev. ed., Jonathan Ree, trans. Alan Sheridan-Smith. London: Verso, 2004.

Satter, Beryl. *Family Properties; How the Struggle over Race and Real Estate Transformed Chicago and Urban America.* New York: Picador/Holt, 2009.

Saxton, Alexander. *The Indispensable Enemy: Labor and the Anti-Chinese Movement in California.* Berkeley: University of California Press, 1971.

Saxton, Alexander. *The Indispensable Enemy: Labor and the Anti-Chinese Movement in California.* Berkeley: University of California Press, 1975.

Saxton, Alexander. *The Rise and Fall of the White Republic: Class Politics and Mass Culture in Nineteenth Century America.* New York: Verso, 2003 (1990).

Scheff, Thomas J., and Suzanne M. Retzinger. *Emotions and Violence: Shame and Rage in Destructive Conflicts.* Lexington, MA: Lexington Books, 1991.

Schiebinger, Londa. *Nature's Body: Gender in the Making of Modern Science*, 2nd ed. New Brunswick, NJ: Rutgers University Press, 2004.

Schmidt, Ingo. "Rosa Luxemburg's 'Accumulation of Capital': New Perspectives on Capitalist Development and US Hegemony." *Socialist Studies/Études Socialistes*, Vol. 6, no. 2 (Fall 2010).

Schmitt, Carl. *Political Theology: Four Chapters on the Concept of Sovereignty*, trans. G.D. Schwab. Chicago: University of Chicago Press, 2004 (1922).

Schrag, Peter. *Not Fit for Our Society: Immigration and Nativism in America.* Berkeley: University of California Press, 2010.

Schwendinger, Herman, and Julia R. Schwendinger. *The Sociologists of the Chair: A Radical Analysis of the Formative Years of North American Sociology, 1883–1922.* New York: Basic, 1974.

Scott, James C. *Domination and the Arts of Resistance: Hidden Transcripts.* New Haven: Yale University Press, 1990.

Scott, James C. *Seeing Like a State: How Certain Schemes to Improve the Human Condition Have Failed.* New Haven: Yale University Press, 1998.

Scott, Joan W. "Deconstructing Equality Versus Difference." *Feminist Studies*, Vol. 14 (1988).

Segev, Tom. *1967: Israel, the War, and the Year that Transformed the Middle East.* New York: Metropolitan Books, 2007.

Shelby, Tommie. *We Who Are Dark: The Philosophical Foundations of Black Solidarity.* Cambridge, MA: Harvard University Press, 2007.

Shockley, John. *Chicano Revolt in a Texas Town.* Notre Dame: University of Notre Dame Press, 1974.

Silk, Leonard, and David Vogel. *Ethics and Profits: The Crisis of Confidence in American Business.* New York: Simon and Schuster, 1976.

Silverstein, Paul A. *Algeria in France: Transpolitics, Race, and Nation.* Bloomington: Indiana University Press, 2004.

Simpson, Christopher, ed. *Universities and Empire: Money and Politics in the Social Sciences During the Cold War.* New York: New Press, 1999.

Singh, Nikhil Pal. *Black is a Country: Race and the Unfinished Struggle for Democracy.* Cambridge: Harvard University Press, 2004.

Sitkoff, Harvard. *A New Deal for Blacks: The Emergence of Civil Rights as a National Issue.* New York: Hill and Wang, 1978.

Sitkoff, Harvard. *The Struggle for Black Equality.* New York: Hill and Wang, 1981.

Skrentny, John David. *The Ironies of Affirmative Action: Politics, Culture, and Justice in America.* Chicago: University of Chicago Press, 1996.

Slate, Nico. *Black Power Beyond Borders: The Global Dimensions of the Black Power Movement.* New York: Palgrave Macmillan, 2012.

Slaughter, Sheila. "The Danger Zone: Academic Freedom and Civil Liberties." *Annals of the American Academy of Political and Social Science*, Vol. 448 (March 1980).

Smedley, Brian D., Adrienne Y. Stith, and Alan R. Nelson, eds. *Unequal Treatment: Confronting Racial and Ethnic Disparities in Health Care.* Washington, D.C.: National Academy Press, 2003.

Smethurst, James Edward. *The Black Arts Movement: Literary Nationalism in the 1960s and 1970s.* Chapel Hill: University of North Carolina Press, 2005.

Smith, Rogers. *Stories of Peoplehood: The Politics and Morals of Political Membership.* New York: Cambridge University Press, 2003.

Snipp, C. Matthew. *American Indians: The First of This Land.* New York: Russell Sage Foundation, 1989.

Soss, Joe, Richard C. Fording, and Sanford F. Schram. *Disciplining the Poor: Neoliberal Paternalism and the Persistent Power of Race.* Chicago: University of Chicago Press, 2011.

Southern, David W. *Gunnar Myrdal and Black-White Relations: The Use and Abuse of An American Dilemma.* Baton Rouge: Louisiana State University Press, 1987.

Sowell, Thomas. *Race and Culture: A World View.* New York: Basic, 1995.

Spiro, Jonathan P. *Defending the Master Race: Conservation, Eugenics, and the Legacy of Madison Grant.* Burlington: University of Vermont Press, 2009.

Squires, Gregory D., and Derek S. Hyra. "Foreclosures—Yesterday, Today, and Tomorrow." *City and Community*, Vol. 9, no. 1 (March 2010).

Stack, Carol B. *All Our Kin: Strategies for Survival in a Black Community.* New York: Harper and Row, 1974.

Stalin, Joseph. *Marxism and the National-Colonial Question.* San Francisco: Proletarian Publishers, 1975 (1908).

Stanfield, John H. "The 'Negro Problem' Within and Beyond the Institutional Nexus of Pre-World War I Sociology." *Phylon*, Vol. 43, no. 3 (1982).

Stanfield, John H. *Philanthropy and Jim Crow in American Social Science.* Westport, CT: Greenwood Press, 1985.

Stannard, David E. *American Holocaust: Columbus and the Conquest of the New World.* New York: Oxford University Press, 1992.

Starobin, Robert S. *Industrial Slavery in the Old South.* New York: Oxford University Press, 1970.

Stavans, Ilan. *José Vasconcelos: The Prophet of Race.* New Brunswick, NJ: Rutgers University Press, 2011.

Steele, Claude M. *Whistling Vivaldi: And Other Clues to How Stereotypes Affect Us.* New York: Norton 2010.

Steensland, Brian. *The Failed Welfare Revolution: America's Struggle Over Guaranteed Income Policy.* Princeton: Princeton University Press, 2007.

Stefancic, Jean, and Richard Delgado. *No Mercy: How Conservative Think Tanks and Foundations Changed America's Social Agenda.* Philadelphia: Temple University Press, 1996.

Stein, Judith. *Pivotal Decade: How the United States Traded Factories for Finance in the 1970s.* New Haven: Yale University Press, 2010.

Steinbeck, John. *The Grapes of Wrath.* New York: Penguin, 1939.

Steinberg, Stephen. *Turning Back: The Retreat from Racial Justice in American Thought and Policy*, 2nd ed. Boston: Beacon, 2001.

Steinberg, Stephen. *Race Relations: A Critique.* Stanford: Stanford University Press 2007.

Stepan, Nancy Leys, and Sander L. Gilman. "Appropriating the Idioms of Science: The Rejection of Scientific Racism." In Sandra Harding, ed. *The "Racial" Economy of Science: Toward a Democratic Future.* Bloomington: Indiana University Press, 1993.

Stiglitz, Joseph E. "Foreword." In Karl Polanyi, *The Great Transformation.* Boston: Beacon, 2001 (1944).

Stoddard, Theodore Lothrop. *The Rising Tide of Color Against White World-Supremacy.* New York: Scribners, 1920.

Stoler, Ann Laura. *Race and the Education of Desire: Foucault's History of Sexuality and the Colonial Order of Things.* Durham: Duke University Press, 1995.

Stoler, Ann Laura. "Tense and Tender Ties: The Politics of Comparison in North American History and (Post) Colonial Studies." *The Journal of American History*, Vol. 88, no. 3 (Dec. 2001).

Stoler, Ann Laura. *Carnal Knowledge and Imperial Power: Race and the Intimate in Colonial Rule.* Berkeley: University of California Press, 2002.

Stoler, Ann Laura, ed. *Haunted by Empire: Geographies of Intimacy in North American History.* Durham: Duke University Press, 2006.

Stouffer, Samuel Andrew et al. *The American Soldier*, 2 vols. Vol. 1: *Adjustment during Army Life*; Vol. 2: *Combat and its Aftermath.* Princeton: Princeton University Press, 1949–1950.

Sugrue, Thomas J. *The Origins of the Urban Crisis: Race and Inequality in Postwar Detroit.* Princeton: Princeton University Press, 1996.

Sugrue, Thomas J. *Not Even Past: Barack Obama and the Burden of Race.* Princeton: Princeton University Press, 2010.

Sullivan, Andrew. "Obama Still Isn't President in the South." *The Sunday Times* (London), Aug. 9, 2009.

Sullivan, Andrew. "How Obama's Long Game Will Outsmart His Critics." *Newsweek/The Daily Beast*, Jan 16, 2012; http://www.thedailybeast.com/newsweek/2012/01/15/andrew-sullivan-how-obama-s-long-game-will-outsmart-his-critics.html.

Swain, Carol M. *The New White Nationalism in America: Its Challenge to Integration.* New York: Cambridge University Press, 2002.

Szwed, John F. *Space is the Place: The Lives and Times of Sun Ra.* Cambridge, MA: Da Capo Press, 1998.

Tallbear, Kimberly. "DNA, Blood, and Racializing the Tribe," *Wicazo Sa Review*, Vol. 18, no. 1 (2003).

Taueber, Kent, and Alma Taueber. "The Negro as an Immigrant Group: Recent Trends in Racial and Ethnic Segregation in Chicago." *American Journal of Sociology*, Vol. 69, no. 4 (1964).

Tapscott, Horace. *Songs of the Unsung: The Musical and Social Journey of Horace Tapscott.* Steven L. Isoardi, ed. Durham: Duke University Press, 2001.

Taguieff, Pierre-André. "The New Cultural Racism in France." In Martin Bulmer and John Solomos, eds. *Racism.* New York: Oxford University Press, 1999.

Taguieff, Pierre-André. *The Force of Prejudice: On Racism and Its Doubles*, trans. Hassan Melehy. Minneapolis: University of Minnesota Press, 2001.

Taylor, Paul, Mark Hugo Lopez, Jessica Martínez, and Gabriel Velasco. "When Labels Don't Fit: Hispanics and Their Views of Identity." Pew Research Hispanic Trends Project, April 4, 2012; http://www.pewhispanic.org/files/2012/04/PHC-Hispanic-Identity.pdf.

Taylor, Ula Yvette. *The Veiled Garvey: The Life and Times of Amy Jacques Garvey.* Chapel Hill: University of North Caroloina Press, 2001.

Telles, Edward E., and Vilma Ortiz. *Generations of Exclusion: Mexican Americans, Assimilation, and Race.* New York: Russell Sage Foundation, 2009.

Thernstrom, Stephan, and Abigail Thernstrom. *America in Black and White: One Nation, Indivisible.* New York: Simon and Schuster, 1999.

Thomas, Clarence. Concurring in *Adarand Constructors, Inc. v. Peña*, 515 U.S. 200 (1995).

Thomas, Dorothy Swaine, and Richard S. Nishimoto. *The Spoilage.* Berkeley: University of California Press, 1946.

Thomas, Dorothy Swaine, Charles Kikuchi, and James Sakoda. *The Salvage.* Berkeley: University of California Press, 1952.

Thomas, James M. "The Racial Formation of Medieval Jews: A Challenge to the Field." *Ethnic and Racial Studies*, Vol. 33, no. 10 (November 2010).

Thomas, William Isaac, and Dorothy Swaine Thomas. *The Child in America: Behavior Problems and Programs.* New York: Knopf, 1928.

Thomas, William I., and Florian Znaniecki. *The Polish Peasant in Europe and America*, 5 vols. Abridged ed., ed. Eli Zaretsky. Urbana: University of Illinois Press, 1984. Original editions: Chicago: University of Chicago Press, 1918 (Vols. 1–2); Boston: Richard G. Badger, 1918–1920 (Vols. 3–5);

Thompson, Krissah. "Cornel West's Criticism of Obama Sparks Debate among African Americans." *The Washington Post*, May 18, 2011; http://www.articles.washingtonpost.com/2011–05–18/politics/35232208_1_obama-and-race-obama-aides-barack-obama.

Thompson, Robert Farris. *Flash of the Spirit: African and Afro-American Art and Philosophy.* New York: Random House, 1983.

Thompson, Krissah, and Scott Wilson. "Obama on Trayvon Martin: 'If I had a son, he'd look like Trayvon'." *Washington Post*, March 23, 2012.

Thornton, John. *Africa and Africans in the Making of the Atlantic World, 1400–1800*, 2nd ed. New York: Cambridge: University Press, 1998.

Thornton, John K. *A Cultural History of the Atlantic World, 1250–1820.* New York: Cambridge University Press, 2012.

Thornton, Russell. *American Indian Holocaust and Survival: A Population History Since 1492.* Oklahoma City: University of Oklahoma Press, 1987.

Tijerina, Reies Lopez. *Mi Lucha Por La Tierra.* Mexico, DF: Fondo de Cultura Económica, 1978.

Todorov, Tsvetan. *The Conquest of America: The Question of the Other*, trans. Richard Howard. New York: Harper and Row, 1984.

Todorov, Tsvetan. *On Human Diversity: Nationalism, Racism, and Exoticism in French Thought*, trans. Catherine Porter. Cambridge, MA: Harvard University Press, 1993.

Tolnay, Stewart. "The Great Migration and Changes in the Northern Black Family, 1940 to 1990." *Social Forces*, Vol. 75, no. 4 (June 1997).

Torgovnick, Marianna. *Gone Primitive: Savage Intellects, Modern Lives.* Chicago: University of Chicago Press, 1991.

Tucker, William H. *The Funding of Scientific Racism: Wickliffe Draper and the Pioneer Fund.* Urbana: University of Illinois Press, 2007.

Ture, Kwame (Stokely Carmichael) and Charles V. Hamilton, *Black Power: The Politics of Liberation.* New York: Vintage 1992 (1967).

Tyson, Timothy B. *Radio Free Dixie: Robert F. Williams and the Roots of Black Power.* Chapel Hill: University of North Carolina Press, 1999.

UNESCO. "Statement on Race." Issued July 18, 1950; revised June 8, 1951 as "Statement on the Nature of Race and Race Differences"; both available at: http://www.unesdoc.unesco.org/images/0012/001229/122962eo.pdf.

U.S. Bureau of the Census. *1790 Census of Population and Housing.* Published 1791; http://www.census.gov/prod/www/abs/decennial/1790.html.

U.S. Bureau of the Census (2001). Current Population Reports, Appendix. Time Series Poverty Estimates, Table A-1, "Poverty Status of People by Family Relationship, Race, and Hispanic Origin: 1959 to 2000." In "Poverty in the United States: 2000"; http://www.census.gov/prod/2001pubs/p60–214.pdf.

U.S. Bureau of the Census, Population Division, Population Projections Branch. "Projected Population of the United States, by Race and Hispanic Origin: 2000 to 2050," Table 1A, March 18, 2004; http://www.census.gov/ipc/www/usinterimproj/.

U.S. Bureau of the Census, "State and County QuickFacts," January 12, 2007; http://www.quickfacts.census.gov/qfd/states/15000.html.

U.S. Bureau of the Census, National Population Projections, http://www.census.gov/population/www/projections/, release date Aug.14, 2008.

U.S. Bureau of the Census, "Historical Poverty Tables—People, Table 6," September 12, 2012; http://www.census.gov/hhes/www/poverty/data/historical/people.html.

U.S. Department of Justice, 2008. Office of the Inspector General and Office of Professional Responsibility, "An Investigation of Allegations of Politicized Hiring and Other Improper Personnel Actions in the Civil Rights Division," US DOJ Special Report, July 2, 2008 (released publicly January 13, 2009); http://www.justice.gov/oig/special/s0901/final.pdf.

U.S. Department of Labor. Bureau of Labor Statistics (2001). "Employment Situation: December 2000"; http://www.bls.gov/news.release/history/empsit_01052001.txt.

U.S. Department of Labor. Bureau of Labor Statistics (1995). "Over 137 Million Persons Worked in 1994, 2.1 Million More Than in 1993"; http://www.bls.gov/news.release/history/work_121395.txt.

U.S. Department of the Treasury, Internal Revenue Service, "Statistics for Tax Returns with EITC," updated May 10, 2013; http://www.eitc.irs.gov/central/eitcstats/.

U.S. District Court, Southern District, CA. *Gonzalo Mendez et al v. Westminister sic School Dist. of Orange County*, 64 F.Supp. 544 (S.D. Cal. 1946); affirmed 161 F.2d 774 (9th Cir. 1947) (en banc).

U.S. Office of Management and Budget. Directive No. 15: "Race and Ethnic Standards for Federal Statistics And Administrative Reporting "Standards for the Classification of Federal Data on Race and Ethnicity." Adopted May 12, 1977. In Appendix, *Federal Register*, June 9, 1994; http://www.whitehouse.gov/omb/fedreg_notice_15.

U.S. Supreme Court. *Belk v. Charlotte-Mecklenburg Bd. of Education*, 269 F.3d 305 (4th Cir. 2001).

U.S. Supreme Court. *Bush v. Gore*, 531 U.S. 98 (2000).

U.S. Supreme Court. *Citizens United v. Federal Election Commission*, 558 U.S. 310 (2010).

U.S. Supreme Court. *Gratz v. Bollinger*, 539 U.S. 244 (2003).

U.S. Supreme Court. *Griggs v. Duke Power Co.*, 401 U.S. 424 (1971a).

U.S. Supreme Court. *Grutter v. Bollinger*, 539 U.S. 306 (2003).

U.S. Supreme Court. *Lochner v. New York*, 198 U.S. 45 (1905).

U.S. Supreme Court. *Loving v. Virginia*, 388 U.S. 1 (1967)

U.S. Supreme Court. *Regents of the University of California v. Allan Bakke*, 438 U.S. 265 (1978).

U.S. Supreme Court. *Roe v. Wade*, 410 U.S. 113 (1973).

U.S. Supreme Court. *Santa Clara County v. Southern Pacific Railroad Company*. 118 U.S. 394 (1886).

U.S. Supreme Court. *Shelby County v. Holder*, 570 U.S. ____ (2013). Note: As of this writing this case has not yet been assigned a page number in Vol. 570 of the U.S. Supreme Court cases. It does have a docket number (12–96). The case was decided on June 25, 2013.

U.S. Supreme Court. *Swann et al. v. Charlotte-Mecklenburg Board of Education et al.* 402 U.S. 1 (1971b).

U.S. Supreme Court. *Washington v. Davis*, 426 U.S. 229 (1976).

Van Deburg, William L. *New Day in Babylon: The Black Power Movement and American Culture, 1965–1975.* Chicago: University of Chicago Press, 1992.

Van Deburg, William. *Modern Black Nationalism: From Marcus Garvey to Louis Farrakhan.* New York: New York University Press, 1996.

van den Berghe, Pierre L., *Race and Racism: A Comparative Perspective.* New York: Wiley, 1967.

Vargas, Zaragoza. *Labor Rights are Civil Rights: Mexican American Workers in Twentieth-Century America.* Princeton: Princeton University Press, 2007.

Vasconcelos, José. *La Raza Cósmica/The Cosmic Race*, bilingual edition. Los Angeles: Dept. of Chicano Studies, California State University, Los Angeles, 1979.

Viguerie, Richard. *The New Right: We're Ready to Lead.* Falls Church, VA: The Viguerie Company, 1981.

Visweswaran, Kamala. *Un/common Cultures: Racism and the Rearticulation of Cultural Difference*. Durham: Duke University Press, 2010.

Vitalis, Robert. "The Noble American Science of Imperial Relations and its Laws of Race Development." *Comparative Studies in Society and History*, Vol. 52, no. 4 (2010).

von Eschen, Penny M. *Race against Empire: Black Americans and Anticolonialism, 1937–1957.* Ithaca: Cornell University Press, 1997.

von Eschen, Penny M. *Satchmo Blows Up the World: Jazz Ambassadors Play the Cold War.* Cambridge, MA: Harvard University Press, 2006.

Wacquant, Loïc. *Punishing the Poor: The Neoliberal Government of Social Insecurity.* Durham: Duke University Press, 2009.

Wade, Nicholas. "Race is Seen as Real Guide to Track Roots of Disease." *The New York Times*, July 30, 2002.

Wade, Nicholas. "Unusual Use of DNA Aided in Serial Killer Search," *The New York Times*, June 3, 2003.

Wallerstein, Immanuel M. *The Modern World-System.* 3 volumes. New York and San Diego: Academic Press, 1974, 1980, 1989.

Walters, Ronald W. *Pan Africanism in the African Diaspora: An Analysis of Modern Afrocentric Political Movements.* Detroit: Wayne State University Press, 1997.

Walters, Ronald W. *White Nationalism, Black Interests: Conservative Public Policy and the Black Community.* Detroit: Wayne State University Press, 2003.

Ward, Geoff. "Race and the Justice Workforce: A System Perspective." In R. Peterson, L. Krivo, and J. Hagan, eds. *The Many Colors of Crime: Inequalities of Race, Ethnicity and Crime in America.* New York: New York University Press, 2006.

Ware, Vron. *Beyond the Pale: White Women, Racism, and History.* New York: Verso, 1992.

Warner, William Lloyd, and Leo Strole. *The Social Systems of American Ethnic Groups.* New Brunswick, NJ: Transaction, 1976 (1947).

Washington, Booker T. "Atlanta Exposition Address" (1895). In Finkelman, Paul, ed. *Milestone Documents in African American History.* Pasadena: Salem Press, 2010.

Waters, Mary C. *Ethnic Options: Choosing Identities in America.* Berkeley: University of California Press, 1990.

Waters, Mary C. *Black Identities: West Indian Immigrant Dreams and American Realities.* Cambridge, MA: Harvard University Press, 2000.

Watson, Bruce. *Freedom Summer: The Savage Season of 1964 That Made Mississippi Burn and Made America a Democracy.* New York: Penguin, 2010.

Watts, Jerry Gafio. *Amiri Baraka: The Politics and Art of a Black Intellectual.* New York: New York University Press, 2001.

Weaver, Vesla M., and Amy E. Lerman. "Political Consequences of the Carceral State." *American Political Science Review*, Vol. 104, no. 4 (2010).

Weber, Max. *From Max Weber: Essays in Sociology*, eds. and trans. Hans H. Gerth and C. Wright Mills. New York: Oxford University Press, 1958.

Weber, Max. *Weber: Political Writings*, eds. and trans. Peter Lassman and Ronald Speirs. New York: Cambridge University Press, 1994.

Weber, Max. *The Russian Revolutions*, eds. and trans. Gordon C. Wells and Peter Baehr. Ithaca: Cornell University Press, 1996.

Weber, Max. "Politics as a Vocation." In H.H. Gerth and C. Wright Mills, eds. *From Max Weber: Essays in Sociology.* New York: Oxford, 2008.

Weglyn, Michi. *Years Of Infamy: The Untold Story Of America's Concentration Camps.* Seattle: University of Washington Press, 1996 (1976).

Weiner, Tim, *Enemies: A History of the FBI.* New York: Random House, 2012.

Weiss, Nancy J. *Farewell to the Party of Lincoln: Black Politics in the Age of FDR.* Princeton: Princeton University Press, 1983.

Weitz, Eric D. *A Century of Genocide: Utopias of Race and Nation.* Princeton: Princeton University Press, 2003.

West, Carolyn M. "Mammy, Jezebel, Sapphire, and Their Homegirls: Developing an 'Oppositional Gaze' Toward the Images of Black Women." In Joan C. Chrisler, Carla Golden, and Patricia D. Rozee eds., *Lectures on the Psychology of Women*, 2nd ed. New York: McGraw Hill, 2012.

West, Cornel. *Prophesy Deliverance! Toward A Revolutionary Afro-American Christianity.* Philadelphia: Westminster, 1982.

West, Kanye, interviewed by Matt Lauer, at the Concert for Hurricane Relief, September 2, 2005; http://www.youtube.com/watch?v=IqgcdnLHwzE.

Wheeler, Mary E., and Susan T. Fiske. "Controlling Racial Prejudice: Social-Cognitive Goals Affect Amygdala and Stereotype Activation." *Psychological Sciences*, Vol. 16, no. 1 (2005).

White, Richard. *The Middle Ground: Indians, Empires, and Republics in the Great Lakes Region, 1650–1815*, 20th anniversity ed. New York: Cambridge University Press, 2010.

Wieviorka, Michel. *The Arena of Racism.* Thousand Oaks, CA: Sage, 1995.

Wildman, Stephanie M., with Margalynne Armstrong, Adrienne D. Davis, and Trina Grillo. *Privilege Revealed: How Invisible Preference Undermines America.* New York: New York University Press, 1996.

Wilentz, Sean. *Chants Democratic: New York City and the Rise of the American Working Class, 1788–1850.* New York: Oxford, 2004 (1984).

Willhelm, Sidney M. *Who Needs the Negro?* Cambridge: Schenkman, 1970.

Williams, Linda F. *The Constraint of Race: Legacies of White Skin Privilege in America.* University Park: Pennsylvania State University Press, 2003.

Williams, Vernon J., Jr. *Rethinking Race: Franz Boas and His Contemporaries.* Lexington: University of Kentucky Press, 1996.

Williams, Walter E. *The State Against Blacks.* New York: McGraw-Hill, 1982.

Williams, Yohuru R. "American Exported Black Nationalism: The Student Nonviolent Coordinating Committee, the Black Panther Party, and the Worldwide Freedom Struggle, 1967–1972." *Negro History Bulletin*, Vol. 60, no. 3 (July–September 1997).

Williamson, Joel. *A Rage for Order: Black-White Relations in the South Since Emancipation.* New York: Oxford University Press, 1986.

Williamson, Joel. *New People: Miscegenation and Mulattoes in the United States.* Baton Rouge: Louisiana State University Press, 1995.

Wilson, James Q., and Richard J. Herrnstein. *Crime and Human Nature: The Definitive Study of the Causes of Crime.* New York: Simon and Schuster, 1985.

Wilson, William J. *Power, Racism, and Privilege.* New York: Free Press, 1973.

Wilson, William J. *When Work Disappears: The World of the New Urban Poor.* New York: Vintage, 1997.

Wilson, William J. *More Than Just Race: Being Black and Poor in the Inner City.* New York: Norton, 2009a.

Wilson, William J. *The Declining Significance of Race: Blacks and Changing American Institutions*, 2nd ed. Chicago: University of Chicago Press, 2012 (1978).

Wilson, William Julius. "The Black Community in the 1980s: Questions of Race, Class, and Public Policy," *The Annals of the American Academy of Social and Political Science*, Vol. 454 (March, 1981).

Wilson, William Julius. "Foreword: The Moynihan Report and Research on the Black Community." *The Annals of The American Academy of Political and Social Science*, January 2009b.

Wilson, William Julius. *The Truly Disadvantaged: The Inner City, the Underclass, and Public Policy.* Chicago: University of Chicago Press, 2012 (1987).

Wimsatt, William Upski. "Wigger: Confessions of a White Wannabe." *Chicago Reader*, July 7, 1994; http://www.chicagoreader.com/chicago/wigger/Content?oid=884951.

Winant, Howard. "It Was Just a Bad Dream ... Everything's Fine Now, Dear ... You Can Go Back to Sleep ...." *Contemporary Sociology*, Vol. 27, no. 6 (Nov. 1998).

Winant, Howard. *The World is a Ghetto: Race and Democracy Since World War II.* New York: Basic, 2001.

Winant, Howard. "Teaching Race and Racism in the 21st Century: Thematic Considerations." In Manning Marable, ed. *The New Black Renaissance: The Souls Anthology of Critical African American Studies.* Boulder: Paradigm, 2006.

Winant, Howard. "The Dark Side of the Force: One Hundred Years of the Sociology of Race." In Craig Calhoun, ed. *Sociology in America: A History.* Chicago: University of Chicago Press, 2007.

Winant, Howard. "A Dream Deferred: Toward the US Racial Future." In David Grusky and Tamar Kricheli-Katz, eds. *The New Gilded Age: The Critical Inequality Debates of Our Time.* Stanford, Stanford University Press, 2012.

Wise, Tim J. *Colorblind: The Rise of Post-Racial Politics and the Retreat from Racial Equity.* San Francisco, CA: City Lights Books, 2010.

Woldoff, Rachel, and Seth Ovadia. "Not Getting Their Money's Worth: African-American Disadvantages in Converting Income, Wealth, and Education into Residential Quality," *Urban Affairs Review*, Vol. 45 no. 1 (Sept. 2009).

Wolfenstein, Eugene Victor. "Race, Racism, and Racial Liberation." *Western Political Quarterly*, Vol. 30, no. 2 (June 1977).

Wolpe, Harold. "The Theory of Internal Colonialism: The South African Case." In Ivar Oxaal, Tony Barnett, and David Booth, eds. *Beyond the Sociology of Development: Economy and Society in Latin America and Africa.* London: Routledge, 1975.

Wolpe, Harold. *Race, Class, and the Apartheid State.* Paris: UNESCO, 1988.

Woodard, Komozi. *A Nation within a Nation: Amiri Baraka (LeRoi Jones) and Black Power Politics.* Chapel Hill: University of North Carolina Press, 1999.

Woods, Clyde. "Do You Know What it Means to Miss New Orleans? Katrina, Trap Economics, and the Rebirth of the Blues." *American Quarterly*, Vol. 57, no. 4, (Dec. 2005).

Woodward, Bob. *The War Within: A Secret White House History 2006–2008.* New York: Simon and Schuster, 2008.

Woodward, C. Vann. "Dangerous Liaisons," review of Martha Hodes, *White Women, Black Men: Illicit Sex in the Nineteenth-Century South. New York Review of Books*, Vol. 45, no. 3 (Feb. 19, 1998).

Woodward, C. Vann. *The Strange Career of Jim Crow.* New York: Oxford University Press, 2002 (1955).

Wright, Richard. *Black Power; A Record of Reactions in a Land of Pathos.* New York, Harper and Row, 1954.

Wroe, Andrew. *The Republican Party and Immigration Politics: From Proposition 187 to George W. Bush.* New York: Palgrave MacMillan, 2008.

Wuthnow, Robert. *Red State Religion: Faith and Politics in America's Heartland.* Princeton: Princeton University Press, 2011.

Yamamoto, Eric. *Interracial Justice: Conflict and Reconciliation in Post-Civil Rights America.* New York: New York University Press, 1999.

Zelinsky, W. *Nation Into State: The Shifting Symbolic Foundations of American Nationalism.* Chapel Hill: University of North Carolina Press, 1988.

Zernike, Kate, and Megan Thee-Brenan. "Poll Finds Tea Party Backers Wealthier and More Educated." *The New York Times*, April 15, 2010, A1.

Zimring, Franklin, Gordon Hawkins, and Sam Kamin. *Punishment and Democracy: Three Strikes and You're Out in California.* New York: Oxford, 2003.

Zlolniski, Christian. *Janitors, Street Vendors, and Activists: The Lives of Mexican Immigrants in Silicon Valley.* Berkeley: University of California Press, 2006.

Zolberg, Aristide R. *A Nation by Design: Immigration Policy in the Fashioning of America.* Cambridge, MA: Harvard University Press, 2008.

Index